PEGASUS ENCYCLOPEDIA

365 INVENTIONS AND INVENTORS

www.pegasusforkids.com

© **B. Jain Publishers (P) Ltd.** All rights reserved. No part of this book may be reproduced, stored in a retrieval system or transmitted, in any form or by any means, mechanical, photocopying, recording or otherwise, without any prior written permission of the publisher.

Published by Kuldeep Jain for B. JAIN PUBLISHERS (P) Ltd., D-157, Sector 63, Noida - 201307, U.P

Printed in India

CONTENTS

1. Assembly Line - Eli Olds — 9
2. Ac Motor - Nikola Tesla — 9
3. Adhesive Plastic Covered Bandage - Paul Carl Beiersdorf — 10
4. Aeroplane - Karl Jatho — 10
5. Aerosol Spray Can - Erik Rotheim — 11
6. Air Conditioning - Willis Carrier — 11
7. Airbag - Allen Breed — 12
8. Airplane - Orville & Wilbur Wright — 12
9. Airship - Henri Giffard — 13
10. Albert Einstein — 13
11. Alessandro Volta — 14
12. Alexander Fleming — 14
13. Alexander Graham Bell — 15
14. Alfred Noble — 16
15. Ambulance - Knights of St. John — 16
16. Anders Celcius — 17
17. Answering Machine - Valdemar Poulsen — 17
18. Archimedes — 18
19. Aristotle — 18
20. Artificial Heart - Willem Kolff — 19
21. Artificial Limbs - Ambrose Paré — 20
22. Aspirin - Felix Hoffmann — 20
23. ATM - John Shepherd-Barron — 21
24. Atomic Bomb - J. Robert Oppenheimer — 21
25. Audio Tape - Fritz Pfleumer — 22
26. Automobile (internal combustion) - Karl Benz — 22
27. Bacteria - Anton Van Leeuwenhoek — 23
28. Ballpoint Pen - Ladislao & Georg Biro — 23
29. Band-Aid - Earl Dickson — 24
30. Barcode - Joseph Woodland & Bernard Silver — 24
31. Barbie - Ruth Handler — 25
32. Barometre (mercury) - Blaise Pascal — 26
33. Barometre (aneroid) - Lucien Vidie — 26
34. Basic (co-inventor) - John Georgr Kemeny — 27
35. Battery - Alessandro Volta — 27
36. Battery (dry cell) - Georges Leclanché — 28
37. Benjamin Franklin — 28
38. Bicycle - Karl Friedrich Von Drais — 29
39. Bifocal Lenses - Benjamin Franklin — 30
40. Black Box - David Warren — 30
41. Blaise Pascal — 31
42. Blood Bank - Charles Richard Drew — 31
43. Blood Transfusion - Dr Thomas Blundell — 32
44. Blowtorch - Carl Richard Nyberg — 32
45. Blue Jeans - Levi Strauss — 33
46. Braille Alphabet - Louis Braille — 33
47. Bunsen Burner - Robert Wilhelm Bunsen — 34
48. Burglar Alarm - Leon Theremin — 34
49. Calculator (pocket) - Jack Kilby — 35
50. Camera Photographic Film - George Eastman — 35
51. Car Radio - William P. Lear — 36
52. Car Windshield Wipers - Mary Anderson — 36
53. Carbonated Water - Joseph Priestley — 37
54. Carl Sagan — 37
55. Ceiling Fan - Philip Diehl — 38
56. Cellophane - Jacques E. Brandenberger — 38
57. Charles Darwin — 39
58. Charles Babbage — 39
59. Charles Goodyear — 40
60. Charles Richard Drew — 40
61. Charles Richter — 41
62. Chewing Gum - Thomas Adams — 41
63. Chloroform - Samuel Guthrie — 42
64. Chocolate Bar - Francois-Louis Cailler — 42
65. Chocolate Chip Cooies - Ruth Wakefield — 43

66. Christmas Card - Sir Henry Cole	44	
67. Clermont - Robert Fulton	45	
68. Coca Cola - Dr John Stith Pemberton	45	
69. Cocoa Powder - Coenraad Johannes Van Houten	46	
70. Coffee - Khalid	46	
71. Cold Fusion Energy (vortex technology) - Viktor Schauberger	47	
72. Colour Photography - James Clerk Maxwell & Thomas Sutton Scotland	47	
73. Compact Disc - James Russell	48	
74. Compound Mircoscope - Zacharias Janssen	48	
75. Computer - Charles Babbage	49	
76. Computer Mouse - Douglas C. Engelbart	49	
77. Contact Lens-Glass - Adolf Fick	50	
78. Cornflakes - Dr John Kellogg	50	
79. Cotton Candy - William Morrison & John C. Wharton	51	
80. Cotton Gin - Eli Whitney	51	
81. Wax Crayons - Edwin Binney & C. Harold Smith	52	
82. Credit Card - Ralph Schneider	52	
83. Crossword Puzzle - Arthur Wayne	53	
84. David Warren	53	
85. DDT - Othmar Zeilder	54	
86. Decimal Point; Logarithems - John Napier	54	
87. Diabetes Testing Kit - Helen Free	55	
88. Diesel Engine - Rudolf Diesel	55	
89. Digital Wrist Watch - Peter Petroff	56	
90. Dishwasher - Josephine Garis Cochran	56	
91. Disposable Syringe - Colin Murdoch	57	
92. Dmitri Mendeleev	57	
93. DNA Structure - James Crick, James Watson & Rosalind Franklin	58	
94. Doughnut - Hanson Crockett Gregory	58	
95. Doughlas C. Engelbart	59	
96. Drinking Straws - Marvin Stone	59	
97. Drive-in Theatre - Richard M. Hollingshed	60	
98. Dry-cleaning - Jean Baptiste Jolly	60	
99. Dynamite - Alfred Noble	61	
100. Dynamo - Werner Von Siemens	61	
101. Ear Muffs - Chester Greenwood	62	
102. Eau de Cologne - Johann Maria Farina	62	
103. Edmund Halley	63	
104. Edward Jenner	63	
105. Edwin Hubble	64	
106. Electrical Ignition System - Charles Kettering	64	
107. Electroscope - Jean Nollet	65	
108. Elevator	65	
109. Elevator Brake - Elisha Graves Otis	66	
110. Email - Ray Tomlinson	66	
111. Internal Combustion Fuel Engine - Jean-Joseph Etienne Lenois	67	
112. Enrico Fermi	67	
113. Eraser - Charles Goodyear	68	
114. Ernest Rutherford	68	
115. Erwin Schrödinger	69	
116. Escalator - Jesse W. Reno	69	
117. Eyeglasses - Salvino D' Armate	70	
118. Fan - Schuyler Wheeler	70	
119. Fasteners (clothes)	71	
120. Fax Machine - Alexander Bain	71	
121. Ferris Wheel - George Washington Gale Ferris	72	
122. Fire Extinguisher - George William Manby	73	
123. First Nuclear Power Plant - Igor Kurchatov	73	
124. First Space Station - Vladimir Chelomei	74	

25.	Flash Light - Conrad Hurbert	74	155.	Hydraulic Crane - William George Armstrong	91
26.	Floppy Disk - IBM (Alan Shugart)	75	156.	Hydraulic Press - Joseph Barmah	91
27.	Flush Toilet - John Harington	75	157.	Hydrofoil Boat - Alexander G. Bell	
28.	Flying Shuttle - John Kay	76		& Casey Baldwin	92
29.	FM Radio - Edwin Howard Armstrong	76	158.	Ice Cream - Jacob Fussell	93
30.	Fountain Pen - Lewis Edson Waterman	77	159.	Infrared Radiation - William Herschel	93
31.	Francis Crick	77	160.	Instant Photography - Edwin Herbert Land	94
32.	Frederick Banting	78	161.	Insulin - Frederick Banting & Charles Best	94
33.	Frisbee - Walter Frederick Morrison		162.	Integrated Circuit - Jack Kilby & Robert Noyce	95
	& Warren Franscioni	78	163.	Integrated Mail System -	
34.	Fuel Cells - Sir William Grove	79		Dr. V.A. Shiva Ayyadurai	95
35.	Galileo Galilei	80	164.	Internet - J.C.R. Licklider	96
36.	George De Mestral	80	165.	Iron - Henry W. Seely	96
37.	George Eastman	81	166.	Ironing Board - Sarah Boone	97
38.	George Washington Carver	81	167.	Isaac Newton	97
39.	Glider - George Cayley	82	168.	Jacuzzi - Roy Jacuzzi	98
40.	Google Web Search Engine - Sergey Brin		169.	Jagdish Chandra Bose	98
	& Larry Page	83	170.	James Watson	99
41.	Gravity - Sir Issac Newton	83	171.	James Watt	99
42.	Gregor Mendel	84	172.	Jane Goodall	100
43.	Guglilmo Marconi	84	173.	Jean Piaget	100
44.	Guitar - Antonio Torres	85	174.	Jet Engine - Henri Conada	101
45.	Gyroplane - Louis & Jacques Breguet	85	175.	Jet Engine (Turbo Jet) - Hans Von Ohain	101
46.	Gyroscope - Jean Bernard Leon Facault	86	176.	Jet Ski - Clayton Jacobsen	102
47.	Hair Dryer - Alexander F. Godefroy	86	177.	Jigsaw Puzzle - John Spilsbury	103
48.	Hand-held Metal Detector - Gerhard Fisher	87	178.	Johannes Gutenberg	103
49.	Helicopter - Igor Sikorsky	87	179.	Johannes Kepler	104
50.	Hole Punch - C.B. Brooks	88	180.	John Dalton	104
51.	Hologram - Dennis Gabor	88	181.	Jukebox - Louis Glass	105
52.	Hot Air Balloon - Joseph-Michel		182.	Kaleidoscope - Sir David Brewster	105
	& Jacques-Etienne Montgolfier	89	183.	Karl Benz	106
53.	Hovercraft - Christopher Sydney Cockerell	90	184.	Karl Landsteiner	106
54.	Hula Hoop - Richard Knerr and		185.	Kelvin Scale - Lord Kelvin	107
	Arthur "Spud" Melin	90			

186. Kevlar - Stephanie Kwolek	107	217. Metal Hull Icebreaker - Mikhail Britnev	124
187. Knapsack Parachute - Gleb Kotelnikov	108	218. Micro-processor - Gordon Moore & Robert Norton Noyce	125
188. Laser - Gordon Gould	108	
189. Laser Disc - David Paul Gregg	109	219. Microscope - Hans Janssen	125
190. Lava Lamp - Craven Walker	109	220. Microwave Oven - Percy Spencer	126
191. Lawn Mower - Edwin Beard Budding	110	221. Miner's Safety Lamp - Sir Humpfrey Davy	126
192. LA-Z-Boy Recliner - Edward Knabusch & Edwin Shoemaker	110	222. Miniature Golf - Thomas McCulloch Fairborn	127
		223. Modern Calender - Pope Gregory XIII	128
193. LED - Nick Holonyak	111	224. Modern Central Heating - Franz San Galli	128
194. Leonardo da Vinci	112	225. Modern Television - Philo T. Farnsworth	129
195. Letter Box - Philip Downing	112	226. Monopoly - Charles Darrow	129
196. Letterpress Printing - Johannes Gutenberg	113	227. Morphine - Frederick Wilhelm Adam Sertürner	130
197. Levi Strauss	113	228. Morse Code - Samuel Morse	130
198. Lie Detector - John Larson	114	229. Motion Picture Camera - William Kennedy Laurie Dickson	131
199. Light Bulb - Thomas Alva Edison	114	
200. Lighthouse	115	230. Motor - Michael Faraday	131
201. Lightening Rod - Benjamin Franklin	115	231. Motorcar - Nicolas Cugnot	132
202. Lightening Switch - Samuel Face	116	232. Motorcycle Petrol Engine - Gottleib Daimler & Wilhelm Maybach	132
203. Linoleum - Frederick Walton	116	
204. Liquid Helium - Heike Kamerlingh Onnes	117	233. Mousetrap - James Henry Atkinson	133
205. Long Distance Radio Transmission - Guglielmo Marconi	117	234. Movie Projector - Charles Francis Jenkins	133
		235. Noam Chomsky	134
206. Long Lasting Alkaline Battery - Lewis Urry	118	236. Network Computing - Robert Metcalfe	134
207. Lord Kelvin	119	237. Nicolaus Copernicus	135
208. Louis Braille	119	238. Neils Bohr	135
209. Louis Pasture	120	239. Night Vision Telescope - Dr Vladimir K. Zworykin	136
210. Magnifying Glass - Roger Bacon	120	
211. Marie Curie	121	240. Nikola Tesla	136
212. Maritime Signal Flares - Martha Coston	121	241. Nuclear Fission - Otto Hahn	137
213. Masking Tape - Richard Drew	122	242. Nuclear Reactor - Enrico Fermi	137
214. Max Planck	122	243. Nylon - Wallace Carothers	138
215. McDonalds - Ray Kroc	123	244. Odometer - Benjamin Franklin	138
216. Meccano - Frank Hornby	123	245. Ophthalmoscope - Hermann Von Helmholtz	139

246. Orville & Wilbur Wright	139	
247. Pacemaker - Wilson Greatbatch	140	
248. Paper Clip - Johann Vaaler	140	
249. Parchute - Faust Vrancic	141	
250. Parking Meter - Carlton C. Magee	142	
251. Pasteurization - Louis Pasture	142	
252. Paul Ehrlich	143	
253. Pendulum Clock - Christiaan Huygens	143	
254. Penicillin - Alexander Fleming	144	
255. Percy Spencer	144	
256. Periodic Table - Dmitri Mendeleev	145	
257. Petroleum Jelly - Robert Chesebrough	145	
258. Petroleum Refining - Edith Flanigen	146	
259. Photography - William Henry Fox Talbot	146	
260. Play-doh - Noah & Joseph Mcvicker	147	
261. Pocket Watch - Peter Henlein	147	
262. Postage Stamp - Rowland Hill	148	
263. Postage Stamp-adhesive - James Chalmers	148	
264. Postcard - John P. Charlton	149	
265. Post-it Notes - Arthur Fry	149	
266. Power Loom - Edmund Cartwright	150	
267. Power Steering Wheel - Francis W. Davis	150	
268. Pressure Cooker - Denis Papin	151	
269. Punch Card - Hermann Hollerith	151	
270. Quartz Clock - Warren Marrison	152	
271. Radio Telescope - Grote Reber	152	
272. Radium - Marie Curie	153	
273. Razor - King Camp Gillette	153	
274. Refrigerator - James Harrison & Alexander Catlin Twining	154	
275. Revolving Door - Theophilus Van Kannel	154	
276. Richter Scale - Charles Richter	155	
277. Robert Goddard	155	
278. Rocket Launch Complex - Vladimir Barmin	156	
279. Rocket Liquid Fuel (first launch) - Robert H. Goddard	156	
280. Roller Skates - James Leonard Plimpton	157	
281. Rollercoaster - L.A. Thompson	157	
282. Rotary Printing Press - William Bullock	158	
283. Rubber Vulcanization - Charles Goodyear	158	
284. Rubik's Cube - Enro Rubik	159	
285. Samuel Morse	159	
286. Sawmill - Cornelis Croneilszoon	160	
287. Scanner - Rudolf Hell	161	
288. Scrabble - Alfred Mosher Butts	161	
289. Transparent Scotch Tape - Richard Drew	162	
290. Seaplane - Glenn Curtiss	162	
291. Segway Human Transporter - Dean Kamen	163	
292. Seismograph - John Milne	163	
293. Sewing Machine - Isaac Merritt Singer	164	
294. Shampoo - Sake Dean Mahomed	164	
295. Silicone - Frederic Stanley Kipping	165	
296. Silly Putty - James Wright	165	
297. Skateboard - Bill & Mark Richards	166	
298. Sliced Bread - Otto Frederick Rohwedder	166	
299. Sliding Automatic Door - Dee Horton & Lew Hewitt	167	
300. Smallpox Vaccine - Edward Jenner	167	
301. Smoke & Heat Detector Alarm - Sidney Jacoby	168	
302. Sneakers - Bill Bowerman & Phil Knight	168	
303. Snow Blower - Arthur Sicard	169	
304. Snowmobile - Joseph-Armand Bombardier	169	
305. Soda Fountain - Samuel Fahnestock	170	
306. Sonar - Paul Langevin	170	
307. Spinning Jenny - James Hargreaves	171	

308.	Stainless Steel - Harry Brearley	171
309.	Steam Engine - James Watt	172
310.	Steamboats - John Fitch	172
311.	Stephen Hawking	173
312.	Stethoscope - René Laënnec	173
313.	Stove - Lloyd Groff Copeman	174
314.	Styrofoam - Ray McIntire	174
315.	Submarine - David Bushnell	175
316.	Subramaniyam Chandrashekhar	175
317.	Sunglasses - James Ayscough	176
318.	Suspenders - David Roth	176
319.	Swiss Army Knife - Karl Elsener	177
320.	Swivel Chair - Thomas Jefferson	177
321.	Synthetic Dye - William Perkin	178
322.	Tape Measure - Alvin L. Fellows	178
323.	Taxi Metre - Wilhelm Bruhn	179
324.	Tea Bag - Thomas Sullivan	179
325.	Teddy Bear - Morris Michtom	180
326.	Teflon - Roy Plunkett	180
327.	Telegraph - W.F. Cooke & Charles Wheatstone	181
328.	Telephone - Alexander Graham Bell	181
329.	Telephone Exchange - Tivadar Puskás	182
330.	Telescope - Hans Lippershey	182
331.	Television - John Logie Baird	183
332.	Thermometer - Anders Celcius	183
333.	Thermos Flask - James Dewar	184
334.	Thomas Alva Edison	184
335.	Time Zones - Sir Stanford Fleming	185
336.	Tractor - John Froelich	185
337.	Traffic Signal - Garnett Morgan	186
338.	Tram - Fyodor Pirotsky	187
339.	Trampoline - George Nissen	187
340.	Transistor Radio - Regency Electronics	188
341.	Tunnel Boring Machine - James Henry Greathead	188
342.	Tuxedo - Pierre Lorillard	189
343.	Typewriter - William A. Burt	189
344.	Vaccination Needle - Benjamin Rubin	190
345.	Vacuum Cleaner - Ives W. Mcgaffey	190
346.	Velcro - Georges De Mestral	191
347.	Video Games - Ralph Baer	191
348.	Video Home Security System - Marie Brown	192
349.	Vinyl - Wlado Sèmon	192
350.	Walkman - Akio Morita	193
351.	Washing Machine - Alva Fisher	193
352.	Water Screw - Archimedes	194
353.	Waterproof Raincoat - Cahrles Mackintosh	194
354.	Waterskiing - Ralph Samuelson	195
355.	Wilhelm Röntegen	195
356.	William Herschel	196
357.	Wireless Remote Control - Robert Adler	196
358.	Wireless Telgraph - Jozef Murgaš	197
359.	World Wide Web - Tim Bernes-Lee	197
360.	Wrench - Solymon Merrick	198
361.	Xerox Machine - Chester A. Carlson	198
362.	X-Rays - Wilhelm Röntegen	199
363.	Yo-Yo	199
364.	Zamboni - Frank Zamboni	200
365.	Zipper - Gideon Sundback & Whitcomb Judson	200

1. Assembly Line – Eli Olds

The invention of the assembly line is credited to Eli Olds. An assembly line is a belt where various parts of an automobile are arranged in a sequencial manner to make an end product.

Later, Henry Ford designed a moveable assembly line. Its use greatly increased the output of a factory. It was so because similar parts of automobiles were manufactured in one go and the workers only needed to assemble them saving both time and money.

2. AC Motor – Nikola Tesla

The AC motor was designed and invented by Nikola Tesla. Tesla carried detailed plans for the AC motor in his head until he actually built it. In his design, the alternating current (AC) created magnetic poles that reversed themselves without mechanical aid, as DC motors required, and caused an electronic part of the device to whirl around the motor.

Though DC current motors were considered safe they could not transmit large amounts of power. Tesla's AC motor, however, allowed the flow of energy to periodically change direction. It could thus transmit large amounts of energy. Do you know that we are supplied AC current in our homes!

3. Adhesive Plastic Covered Bandage – Paul Carl Beiersdorf

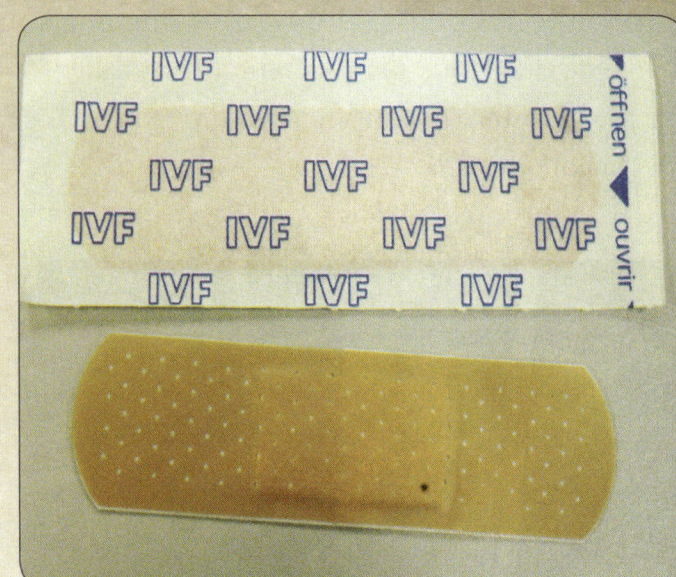

Beiersdorf AG is a German personal care company based in Hamburg. The company was founded in 1882 by pharmacist Paul Carl Beiersdorf. He is credited with inventing an adhesive plastic covered bandage and a new manufacturing process of medical plasters in 1882.

This bandage was made of latex rubber, woven fabric or plastic and was covered with an adhesive. It had an absorbant pad with an antiseptic on it to protect the wounds against bacteria, dirt and damage.

4. Aeroplane – Karl Jatho

Four months before the historic flight of the Wright Brothers in 1903, it was magistrate official Karl Jatho who had succedded to lift off in Vahrenwalder Heide, Hanover. He had designed and made *Motordrachen Nr. 2* in which he took flight. Jatho's flying machine used a single-cylinder 10 h.p. buchet engine. Also, the wings of this aircraft were flat which meant that his aircraft needed lift to take-off. The control system of this large aircraft was also not impressive.

With a number of improvements, he took further trials. In November 1903, he covered a distance of 60 meters in his flying machine. He later opened a flying school.

5. Aerosol Spray Can – Erik Rotheim

A spray can is a dispenser that holds a substance usually aerosol which is a liquid under pressure and releases it in the form of a fine spray. The concept of an aerosol spray can originated around 1790, when self-pressurized carbonated beverages were introduced in France. In November 1927, Norwegian engineer Erik Rotheim invented the first aerosol spray can and valve that could hold and dispense products and propellant systems.

The technology of the spray can was greatly improved after Rotheim's death. This technology was first used in insect sprays.

6. Air Conditioning – Willis Carrier

Air Conditioning is a system where the humidity and temperature in a room or a building are controlled. This system is used to maintain a cool atmosphere in warm conditions. William Haviland Carrier first developed this system for a Brooklyn based printing plant where fluctuations in heat and humidity caused the dimensions

of the printing paper to alter slightly. This was enough to cause a misalignment of the coloured inks. The new air conditioning machine maintained a stable environment and aligned the four-colour printing.

Did you know that he got this flash of genius while waiting for a train!

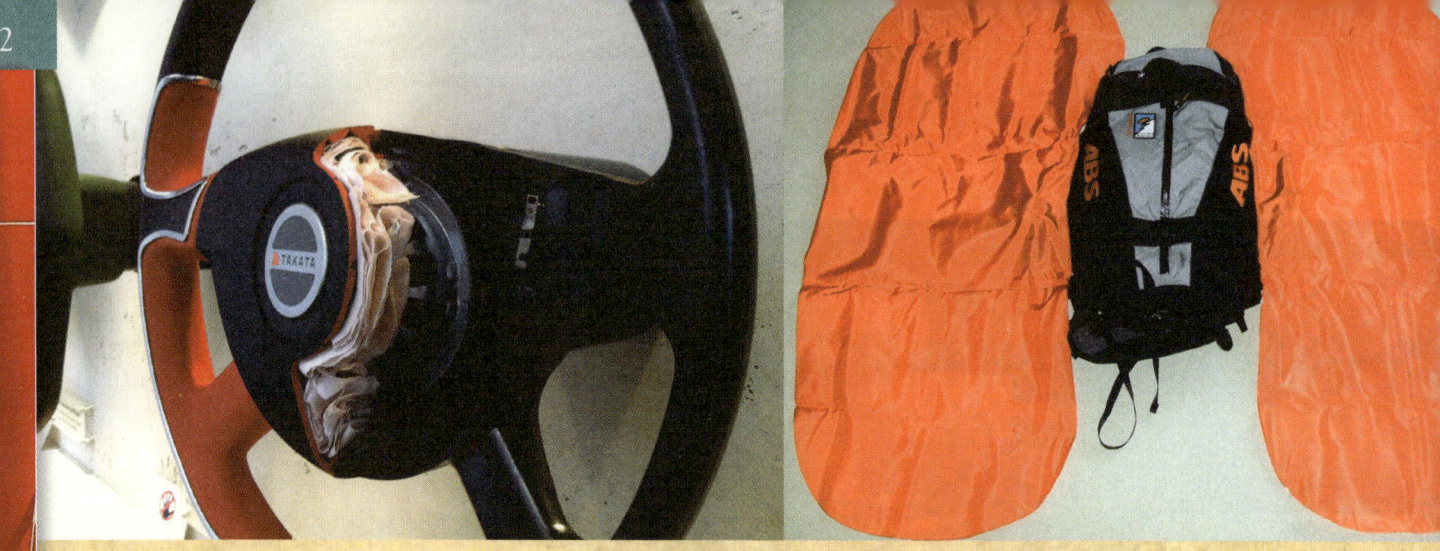

7. Airbag – Allen Breed

Airbags are a type of automobile safety restraint like seatbelts. Airbags are gas-filled cushions which are built into the steering wheel, dashboard, door, roof or seat of a car. The airbags use a crash sensor to trigger a rapid expansion to protect you from the impact of an accident. Allen Breed invented this safety system in 1968. Its purpose is to cushion occupants of a vehicle during a crash and provide protection to their bodies when they strike interior objects such as the steering wheel or a window. The airbags respond within milliseconds of a crash.

8. Airplane – Orville and Wilbur Wright

The Wright Brothers, Wilbur and Orville, successfully flew for the first time on December 17, 1903. The aircraft they had designed themselves was called *Flyer* and it first flew for 12 seconds over a distance of 120 feet. It was the first flight of an airplane.

Their interest in flight was ignited when their father gave them a small helicopter toy in their childhood. After studying aeronautical books they realized that no one has so far been able to control the aircraft while it was in the air. They began observing birds and came up with the concept of wing wraping and soon began making their own aircrafts. And it was sometime before they made history and revolutionized transportation.

9. Airship – Henri Giffard

An airship, also called a dirigible, is a self-propelled aircraft which is lighter than air and can be steered. It is usually shaped like an elongated balloon and a power screw is used to manueuver it in the air.

The first navigable full-sized airship was made by French engineer Henri Giffard in 1852. This airship had a small, steam-powered engine attached to a huge propeller. It flew for 17 miles at 5mph speed. This was the first time that mechanical power was used in flight.

10. Albert Einstein

Albert Einstein, a German born scientist, is considered among the smartest people in the world. His discoveries laid the foundations for modern physics. He is credited with formulating the *Theory of Relativity*. This theory explained how time and distance may change due to the "relative" or different speed of the object and the observer. One equation from the theory is $E=mc^2$. In this formula, "c" is the speed of light and is a constant. This formula explains how energy (E) is related to mass (m).

Albert Einstein was awarded the Nobel Prize for Physics in 1921. He also wrote many papers to explain quantum physics.

11. Alessandro Volta

Alessandro Volta, an Italian physicist, had invented the electric cell and discovered methane gas. Volta believed that in an electrically unstable state, the body gets electrically charged.

With this concept of an electrically charged body, Volta began experimenting and succeeded in creating few devices that were able to store electric charge. He proved that electric currents could be generated by appropriately connecting metals or wires. Using zinc and copper wires and saline solutions, Volta successfully construced the first electric battery. He also discovered that the inflammable gas creating bubbles in the marshes was methane.

12. Alexander Fleming

Alexander Fleming is credited with discovering penicillin, an antibody used today against most diseases. In 1928, while studying influenza, Fleming noticed that a certain mould had developed accidentally on a set of culture dishes kept in his laboratory. The mould had created a bacteria-free circle around itself. It was truly astonishing. After further experiments, he named the active substance penicillin. Later, it was with two other scientists, Howard Florey and Ernst Chain, that he developed penicillin further so that it could be produced as a drug.

13. Alexander Graham Bell

Alexander Graham Bell is most famous for inventing the telephone. He developed an early interest in the science of sound as his father and elder brothers all helped the deaf and dumb to communicate.

He too began experimenting with sound. After a lot of effort, he discovered how voice signals could be sent down a telegraph wire. Later, while further developing the telegraph, along with his assistant Thomas Watson, he invented the telephone. The first words spoken over the telephone were by Bell on March 10, 1876. He said, "Mr. Watson, come here, I want to see you".

The telephone provided a whole new approach to communication. Bell had made other inventions including a metal detector, an audiometer and a hydrofoil among others.

14. Alfred Noble

Alfred Noble was a famous scientist, inventor, businessman and founder of the Nobel Prizes. His father, an engineer, built bridges and buildings and experimented with various ways of blasting rocks.

Did you know that Noble is also credited with inventing dynamite! At that time, an Italian chemist had invented nitroglycerine, a highly explosive liquid. Alfred thought that nitroglycerine could be used to blast rocks. After many accidents, he found that when nitroglycerine was mixed with fine sand called kieselguhr, the liquid turned into a paste which could be shaped into rods. These rods were then inserted into drilled holes. Thus, dynamite was born.

15. Ambulance – Knights of St. John

During the Crusades of 11th Century, the Knights of St. John received instruction in first-aid treatment from Arab and Greek doctors. These knights were the first emergency workers, treating soldiers on both sides in a battlefield and brought the wounded to nearby tents for further treatment. These knights are credited with inventing the first ambulance service.

Later Surgeon-in-Chief of the French Grand Army, Baron Dominiquie Larrey created the first official army medical corp in 1792. Trained attendants with equipment moved out from field hospitals to give first-aid to the wounded on the battlefield and sometimes brought them to the field hospitals on stretchers.

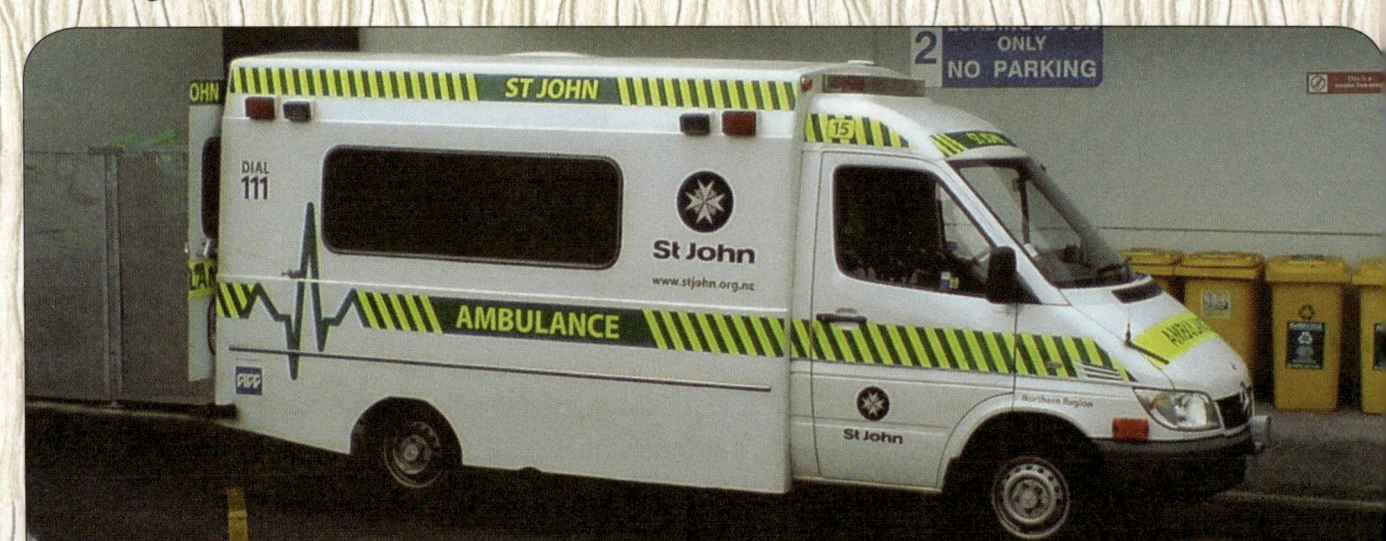

16. Anders Celsius

Anders Celsius, a Swedish astronomer, is known for inventing the Celsius temperature scale.

Celsius favoured the division of the temperature scale of a mercury thermometer at air pressure of 760mm of mercury into 100°C, where 100 was taken as the freezing point and 0 as the boiling point of water. This method was considered more precise to measure temperature. Did you know that Degree Celcius, the unit of temperature interval, is named after Andres Celcius!

Interestingly, Celsius had built the Uppsala Astronomical Observatory in 1740, the oldest astronomical observatory in Sweden!

17. Answering Machine – Valdemar Poulsen

Danish telephone engineer and inventor Valdemar Poulsen invented something called a telegraphone in 1898. This was the first practical apparatus for magnetic sound recording and its reproduction. The telegraphone was a device that could record telephone conversations. This device recorded on a wire the varying magnetic fields produced by a sound. Later, the user could play back the recorded sound on the magnetized wire to listen to the message.

The modern answering machines are based on this device.

18. Archimedes

Archimedes was a famous mathematician and inventor in ancient Greece. He is credited for discovering the relation between the surface and volume of a sphere and its circumscribing cyclinder. He is known for formulating the *Archimedes' Principle* and also for inventing a device called *Archimedes Screw* which is used to raise water.

Archimedes lived in Syracuse in Sicily. He played an important role in the defense of Syracuse against the siege laid by the Romans in 213 BCE by constructing such war machines that delayed the capture of the city.

19. Aristotle

Aristotle, ancient Greek philosopher and scientist was one of the greatest intellectual figures of Western history. His work, along with that of some other philosophers, forms the basis of Western thinking. Aristotle's intellectual range was vast, covering most of the sciences and many of the arts, including biology, botany, chemistry, ethics, history, logic, metaphysics, rhetoric, philosophy of mind, philosophy of science, physics, poetics, political theory, psychology and zoology.

20. Artificial Heart – Willem Kolff

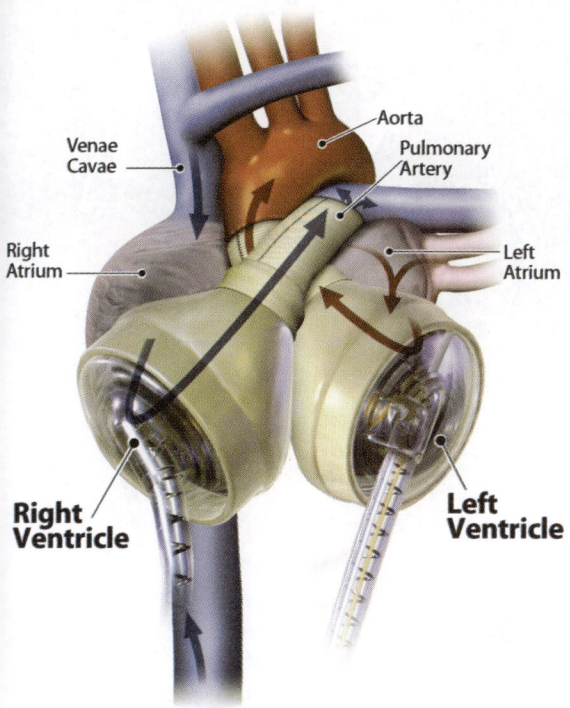

Total Artificial Heart

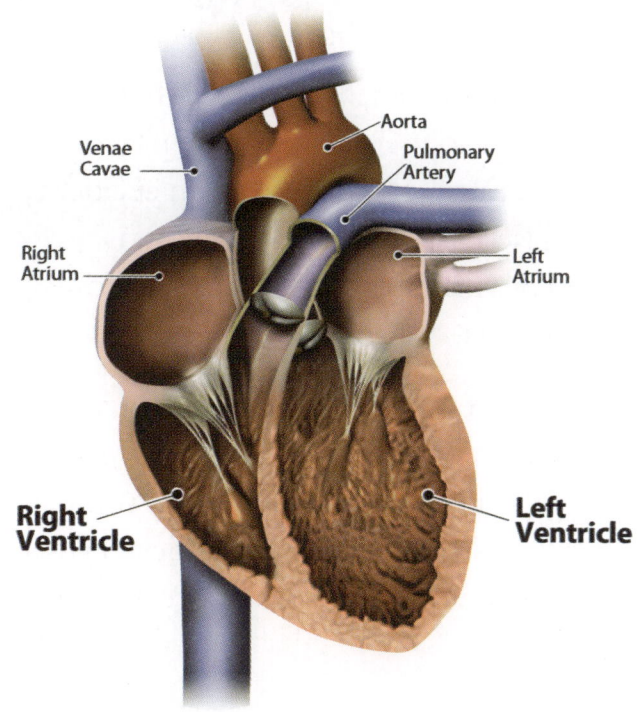

Human Heart

Willem Kolff, as a young medical assistant, became interested in the possibility of artificially simulating the function of the kidney.

After a lot of hard work, Kolff developed the first, crude artificial kidney. Working with wooden drums, cellophane tubing and laundry tubs, Kolff constructed an apparatus that drew the patient's blood, cleansed it of impurities and pumped it back into the patient. His first 15 patients lived for a few days only but Kolff was encouraged.

Later, he built one of the first heart-lung apparatuses, an artificial heart. After various improvements, the artificial heart proved to be a success. This was the birth of open heart surgery.

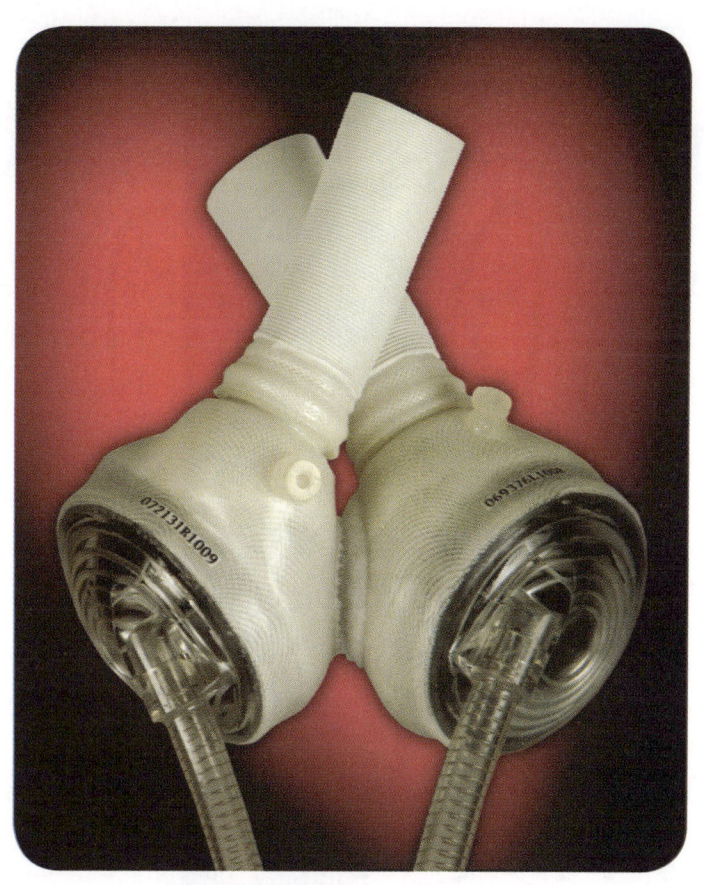

21. Artificial Limbs – Ambrose Paré

Prosthesis is an artificial decive that is used in place of a missing body part either because of a disease or an accident. Ambroise Paré, a French surgeon, is credited with inventing several surgical instruments.

Paré contributed both to the practice of surgical amputation and to the design of limb prosthesis. He also invented some ocular prosthesis – making artificial eyes from enameled gold, silver, porcelain and glass.

Among his inventions was an above-knee device that was a kneeling peg leg and foot prosthesis with a fixed position, adjustable harness and knee lock control. These fully functional limbs were precursors of modern prosthetics.

22. Aspirin – Felix Hoffmann

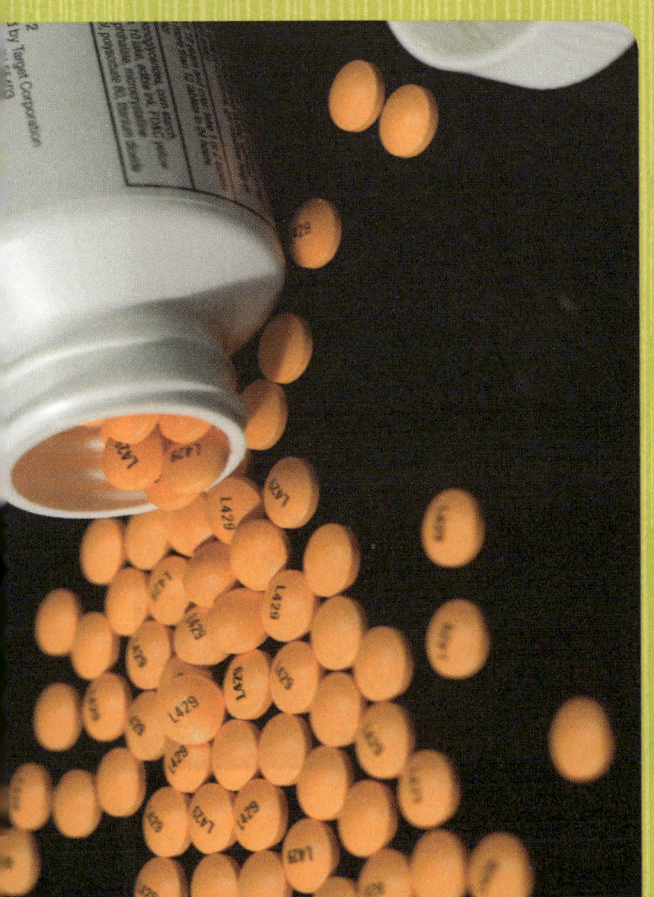

Felix Hoffmann, son of an industrialist, was interested in pharmacy. After completing his studies, he joined Farbenfabriken vorm. Friedr. Bayer & Co in 1894. Here, he worked in the chemical laboratory as a chemist.

He is credited with the invention of aspirin. This discovery was made by chance when in August 1897, he added acetylating salicylic acid with acetic acid and created acetylsalicylic acid (ASA) in a chemically pure and stable form. After further experiments, he realised that he had developed a pain-relieving, fever-lowering and anti-inflammatory substance. He called this substance aspirin.

23. ATM – John Shepherd-Barron

An ATM is a machine that allows a bank customer to withdraw, deposit and transfer funds automatically. The world's first ATM was installed in a branch of Barclays in Enfield, North London. John Shepherd-Barron, who worked for a printing firm De La Rue, had invented the ATM. In the 1960s, the ATMs were called DACS standing for De La Rue Automatic Cash System.

As plastic ATM cards did not exist back then, this machine took cheques that were marked with carbon 14, a slightly radioactive substance. The machine detected this mark and matched it against a pin number.

24. Atomic Bomb – J. Robert Oppenheimer

An atomic bomb is an extremely destructive bomb. Its power lies in the immense quantity of energy which is released at the time of impact. J. Robert Oppenheimer, a research physicist is thought to be the man behind the creation of the atomic bomb.

An atomic bomb gets its vast amounts of energy from the nuclear fission reactions. These reactions, which rapidly become chain reactions, are started when nuclei of heavy elements like Uranium and Plutonium start splitting. These reactions release huge amounts of energy almost instantly.

25. Audio Tape – Fritz Pfleumer

Fritz Pfleumer invented the magnetic tape to record sound. He developed a process for putting metal stripes on cigarette papers and said that he could coat a magnetic stripe to be used as an alternative to wire recording. In 1927, after experimenting with various materials, he used very thin paper and coated it with iron oxide powder using lacquer as glue. This was the first audio tape.

In 1930, the AEG Company in Berlin

started making audio tapes based on his idea. This tape consisted of a foil of cellulose acetate as carrier material, coated with a lacquer of iron oxide to be used as a magnetic pigment and cellulose acetate as the binder.

26. Internal Combustion Automobile – Karl Benz

In 1885, German mechanical engineer, Karl Benz designed and built the world's first practical automobile to be powered by an internal-combustion engine. An internal combustion engine is any engine that operates by burning its fuel inside the engine. These include gasoline powered engines and diesel engines. An important portion of the ICE is its ignition system which controls the time of the burning of the fuel mixture. Karl Benz is regarded as one of the inventors of the gasoline powered automobiles. He first made a gas-fueled car which was a three-wheeler followed by a four-wheeled car in 1891.

27. Bacteria – Anton Van Leeuwenhoek

Bacteria are one cell microorganisms that have no chlorophyll. These creatures can only be seen through a microscope. The father of microscopy, Anton Van Leeuwenhoek, had discovered bacteria. As an apprentice working in a store where magnifying lenses were used, he started making lenses of great curvature which magnified up to 270x diameters.

He then started making microscopes using these lenses. He first saw and described bacteria in 1674, along with yeast plants and the circulation of blood corpuscles in capillaries using his microscopes. His discovery opened up the world of microscopic life before the scientists.

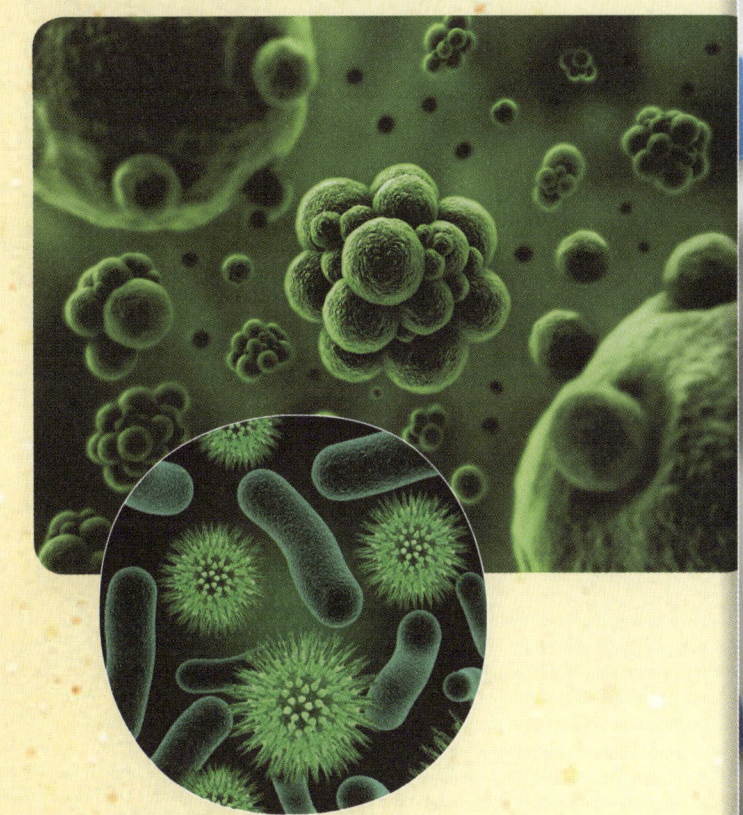

28. Ballpoint Pen – Ladislao & Georg Biro

The first ballpoint pen was invented in 1938 by Hungarian journalist Laszlo Biro. Seeing that the ink used in printing dried quickly and left the paper dry, Biro had an idea. He decided to create a pen using the same ink but he also needed a new type of pen nib. He then fitted his pen with a tiny ball bearing in its tip. As the pen moved along the paper, the ball rotated picking up ink from the ink cartridge and left it on the paper. The British Royal Air Force first used this ballpoint pen instead of the fountain pen which leaked at higher altitudes. The success of the ballpoint pen brought Biro pens into the limelight.

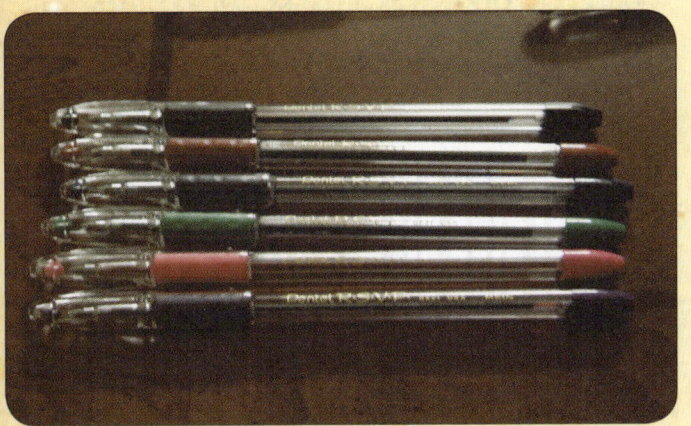

29. Band-Aid – Earl Dickson

Earle Dickson, cotton buyer for Johnson & Johnson, invented the Band-Aid in 1921. His wife Josephine Dickson was always cutting her fingers in the kitchen while making food. At that time a bandage consisted of a separate gauze and an adhesive tape that you would cut to the required size and apply yourself. But this bandage fell off easily as one worked. Then Earle decided to invent a bandage that would stay in place. He took a piece of gauze and attached it to the centre of a piece of tape and covered the product with crinoline to keep it sterile. Soon, Band-Aid started getting manufactured.

30. Barcode – Joseph Woodland & Bernard Silver

The first barcode type product was thought of and designed by inventors Joseph Woodland and Bernard Silver in October 1952. This first barcode could be described as a "bull's eye" symbol. It was made up of a series of concentric circles.

In 1948, a local food chain store owner wanted a method to automatically read product information during checkout. Bernard Silver and Norman Joseph Woodland decided to think of a solution. They, then, modified the barcode and it was in 1949 that the barcode as we know it today was made.

Did you know that the first product to have a barcode on it was a packet of Wrigley's Gum!

31. Barbie – Ruth Handler

Perhaps one of the most famous toys in the world is the Barbie doll. This famous toy was thought of and designed by Ruth Handler. She got the idea to make such a doll when she noticed her daughter and her friends using dolls to act out the future rather than the present. She then invented a grown-up, three-dimensional doll that girls could use to act out their dreams. She

named this doll after her daughter Barbara's nickname. The Barbie doll was first unveiled in the 1959 Toy Fair. The doll was an instant sensation.

The first Barbie doll was as a teenage fashion model. Today, with a large variety of Barbie dolls, she also has various career options.

32. Barometre (mercury) – Blaise Pascal

A Barometer is used to measure atmospheric pressure. Because atmospheric pressure changes with distance above or below sea level, a barometer can also measure altitude. There are two main types of barometers: mercury and aneroid. A barometer tells you when the atmospheric pressure is rising or falling. A rising pressure indicates good weather while a falling pressure indicates bad weather.

Blaise Pascal, French mathematician, physicist and religious philosopher formulated the pascal's law of pressure. The term used for the atmospheric pressure is pascal (Pa).

To formulate the law of pressure, he did experiments by making mercury barometers and measured air pressure.

33. Barometre (aneroid) – Lucien Vidie

French scientist Lucien Vidie invented the aneroid barometer in 1843. An aneroid barometer registers the change in the shape of an evacuated metal cell to measure variations on the atmospheric pressure. Aneriod means fluidless.

Lucien's barometer used a small, flexible metal box called an aneroid cell (capsule) made from an alloy of beryllium and copper. A strong spring prevented an evacuated capsule from collapsing. Small changes in external air pressure caused the cell to expand or contract. This expansion and contraction drove levers which amplified the tiny movements of the capsule displayed on the face of the aneroid barometer.

34. BASIC [co-inventor] – John George Kemeny

John George Kemeny was a computer scientist and an educator. He is however best known for co-developing the BASIC programming language in 1964 with Thomas E. Kurtz.

Kemeny and Kurtz developed the BASIC programming language in 1964. BASIC stands for *Beginners All Purpose Symbolic Instruction Code*. It was a teaching tool for the undergraduates. It is the most commonly used computer programming language and it is considered an easy step before students go on to learn other powerful computer languages. This programming language has a lot of applications and comes in various versions.

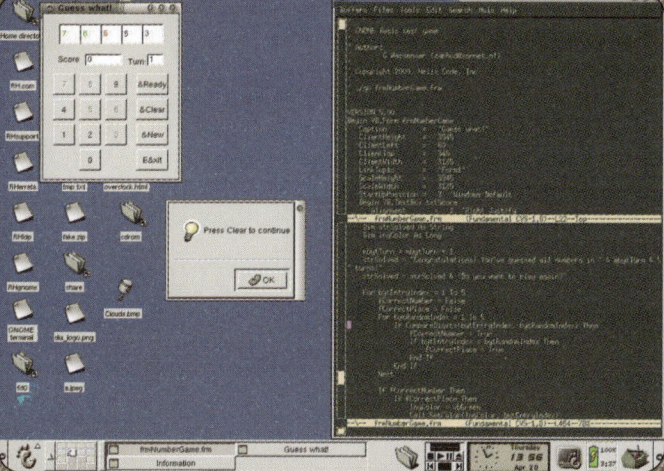

35. Battery – Alessandro Volta

In 1800, Alessandro Volta built the voltaic pile. He also discovered the first practical means of generating electricity.

A battery, which is actually an electric cell, is a device that produces electricity from a chemical reaction. In a one cell battery, you would find a negative electrode; an electrolyte, which conducts ions; a separator, also an ion conductor; and a positive electrode.

Volta constructed alternating discs of zinc and copper with pieces of cardboard soaked in brine between the metals. This was the voltaic pile, the first wet battery cell. This was the first battery that produced a reliable, steady current of electricity.

36. Battery (dry cell) – Georges Leclanché

Leclanché was a French inventor who is credited with inventing the first electrical batteries. These batteries comprised of a conducting solution (electrolyte) of ammonium chloride with a negative terminal of zinc and a positive terminal of manganese dioxide.

Leclanche assembled his original cell in a porous pot. The cathode was packed into the pot and a carbon rod was inserted into it. The zinc rod and the pot were then put inside ammonium chloride solution. The liquid acted as the electrolyte, readily seeping through the porous cup to make contact with the cathode material. This was the first dry cell battery.

37. Benjamin Franklin

Benjamin Franklin, a modern day Renaissance man excelled in many areas including science, politics, writing and inventing.

Ben was born in Boston, Massachusetts on January 17, 1706. As a 17 year old, he ran to Philadelphia and there, he began publishing a newspaper, *The Pennsylvania Gazette*. He became a popular American spokesman when his testimony in the House of Commons in England helped to get the hated Stamp Act repealed. Did you know that Franklin was one of the five people who had signed the American Declaration of Independence!

Benjamin Franklin is also credited with inventing the lightening rod, bifocal lenses, the Franklin stove, an odometer and the glass harmonica.

38. Bicycle – Karl Friedrich von Drais

German born Karl Drais invented the running machine, later known as the velocipede or the dandy horse. This invention became the basis for the two-wheeler principle behind the working of the bicycle. The velocipede, the earliest bicycle, also marked the beginning of mechanized personal transport.

This bicycle's basic design included a set of two wooden wheels, a seat and handle bars. It was the fastest means to travel with a speed of 10 miles per hour. As the bicycle had no pedals, one used their feet and pushed while the wheels rolled on the ground. Karl Drais took the first ride on his bicycle on June 12, 1817.

39. Bifocal Lenses – Benjamin Franklin

In 1784, Benjamin Franklin developed bifocal glasses. As he was getting old, he started having trouble seeing both up-close and also at a distance. Getting tired of switching between two types of glasses he kept with himself, he devised a way to have both types of lenses fitted into the same frame. He placed the distance lens at the top of the frame and the up-close lens at the bottom of the frame. In order to place the lenses thus, the lenses were cut and placed within the same single frame. They were the first of their kind glass lenses. Today, we call these glasses he had invented bifocals.

40. Black Box – David Warren

Dr David Warren is credited with inventing the Black Box flight data recorder in 1953. He thought of recording the flight crew's conversation and protect that recording when he saw a man listening to a recording using a tape recorder. The purpose of the black box was to help identify the reasons for a plane crash, by recording any clues in the flight crew's conversation. The first such boxes were painted bright red or orange to make them easier to find after a crash. The use of the black box also helped improve the flight safety standards.

Do you know that the black box is placed at the tail of the plane!

41. Blaise Pascal

Blaise Pascal, French philosopher and scientist, was one of the greatest and most influential mathematical writers of all time. He was also a religious philosopher.

He was born on June 19, 1623. He learnt Latin and Greek from his father but Pascal Sr. didn't teach him mathematics. This increased Pascal's curiosity who went on to experiment with geometrical figures and even formulated his own names for standard geometrical terms.

Pascal contributed to hydrostatics, invented the barometer and did research on the equilibrium of fluids. The *Probability Theory* is his significant contribution to mathematics.

42. Blood Bank – Charles Richard Drew

Dr Charles Richard Drew, an American medical doctor and surgeon, is credited with starting a blood bank and a system for the long-term preservation of blood plasma. He set up and operated the blood plasma bank at the Presbyterian Hospital in New York City.

He thought of a blood bank when he was asked to direct the 'Blood for Britian' program. This program was to export blood and plasma to Europe especillay Britain to save the lives of British soldiers. He then devised a method to mass produce plasma by packaging plasma in a dry form in 400 bottles. When required, distilled water was added to the plasma and it was ready to be used in three minutes.

43. Blood Transfusion – Dr Thomas Blundell

James Blundell invented blood transfusion. In 1818, he proposed that a blood transfusion would be appropriate to treat severe postpartum hemorrhage. Seeing many patients dying at childbirth, he decided to find a way to transfer blood to the patient.

Blundell experimented and observed that a quick transfusion of blood was successful. He thought of using a syringe connected to a container containing blood, infused in the patient's body. He conducted a few successful transfusions based on his observation. Do you know that blood transfusion is conducted after examining the compatibility of the patients' blood with that of the donor!

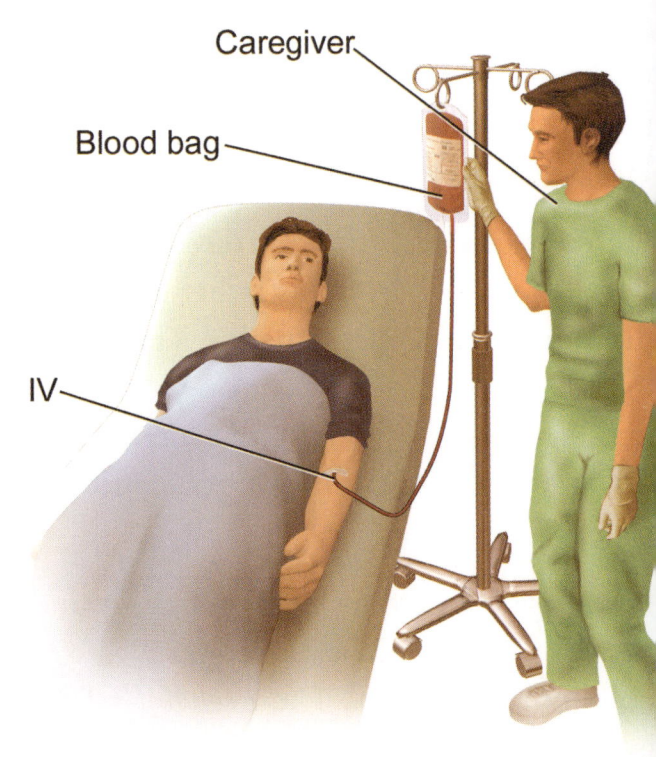

Blood Transfusion

44. Blowtorch – Carl Richard Nyberg

A blowtorch is a fuel burning tool which is used to apply directed flame and heat especially in metalworking. Carl Richard Nyberg, a Swedish inventor and industrialist, had invented the blowtorch. While working as a metal worker, Neberg developed the idea of the blowtorch to apply directed heat to a metal surface. This device varied from existing heating tools as it provided a very concentrated source of heat. To make the blowtorch safe, he included a shut off mechanism which could detect high pressure in the fuel tank to prevent an explosion.

45. Blue Jeans – Levi Strauss

In 1853, during the California gold rush everyday items were in short supply. Levi Strauss, a German immigrant, came to San Francisco with a small supply of dry goods to open a branch of his brother's New York dry goods business. One day, a miner asked him what he was selling. When Strauss told him he had rough canvas to use for tents and wagon covers, the miner said, "You should have brought pants!" adding that he couldn't find a pair of pants strong enough to last.

Then, Levi Strauss had the canvas made into waist overalls. Miners liked the pants but complained that they tended to chafe. Levi then made pants using twilled cotton cloth from France. This cloth was denim and it was the birth of jeans.

46. Braille Alphabet – Louis Braille

Braille is a system of raised dots on paper that are read by moving fingers over them by the blind. The system was invented by Louis Braille in the early 1800s.

At age three, Louis lost his sight due to an accident in his father's workshop. Later, studying at the blind school, he found the verbal knowledge imparted there inefficient. Yet he wanted to learn more.

Then in 1821, a former soldier Charles Barbier visited the blind school. He shared his invention called "night writing," a code of 12 raised dots that let soldiers share secret information without speaking. Inspired, Louis reduced Barbier's 12 dots to 6, improved the system and invented the Braille Alphabet.

47. Bunsen Burner – Robert Wilhelm Bunsen

A Bunsen burner is a flame making device that combines a flammable gas with air. It was invented by Robert Wilhelm Bunsen, German chemist and teacher in 1855 and was an improvement on previous burners.

He built the burner with his laboratory assistant, Peter Desaga. This invention improved the form of laboratory burners.

This burner produces a single open gas flame which is used for heating, sterilization and combustion. It has three main parts– a barrel, a needle valve and a metal base. It uses methane gas and burns with a pale blue flame, the primary flame and a larger colourless flame.

48. Burglar Alarm – Leon Theremin

Leon Theremin invented the burglar alarm. In 1920, while heading the experimental electronic oscillation laboratory in St. Petersburg, he became interested in the possibilities of vacuum or electron-tube technology. He first worked on a government project for an alarm that, using radio technology, went off when a person approached it.

Encouraged, he did further experiments and created the first alarm called "theremin." This alarm had an electromagnetic field which started emitting sounds when a person stepped into its field. This instrument was more sensitive than other instruments created so far. The device could detect intrusion into a building or an area or a burglary.

49. Calculator (pocket) – Jack Kilby

Since the time when people used the abacus or slide rule to perform arithmetic, scientists have been looking for easier ways to make calculations. Their task was made considerably easier when Jack Kilby invented the pocket calculator in 1970. A pocket calculator is an electronic device that can automatically do mathematical functions.

His QT-8D, an electronic calculator used integrated circuits. This early calculator could only do addition, subtraction, division and multiplication.

50. Camera Photographic Film – George Eastman

Since the 1870s, attempts had been made to make photography simpler by using a celluloid film in place of glass. The first experiments to use celluloid proved difficult. Then in 1879, an English photographer, John Carbutt, developed a sufficiently thin and transparent celluloid film. This film proved adequate for use in photography.

Then, in 1880s, George Eastman started the production of a rollfilm using a process he had devised. His first design was a roll-holder, which could be placed on the back of a camera and could carry a roll of sensitized paper capable of taking 48 photographs. As the roll-holder became popular, Eastman designed a new camera called the Kodak Camera in 1888. In 1889, the paper roll was replaced by transparent celluloid film that helped develop moving pictures.

51. Car Radio – William P. Lear

William P. Lear is credited with the invention of car radios i.e. the eight-track tape player during the 1960s used in our cars. Lear's radio had good audio quality and was easily adaptable to home and car use. His design of the radio doubled the amount of music that could be recorded on a single tape cartridge.

The eight-track was the first truly portable format for music and was a great commercial success. It represented a progressive step for audio recording and home entertainment. Motorola Company first produced a car radio based on Lear's design.

52. Car Windshield Wipers – Mary Anderson

Mary Anderson is credited with the invention of a window cleaning device in November 1903. Her invention could clean snow, rain or sleet from a windshield by using a handle inside the car. Her goal was to improve the driver's vision during stormy weather.

During a trip to New York City, she saw car drivers open their car windows, as it rained, in order to see. It was then that she thought of a solution to this problem and invented a swinging arm device which went back and forth with a rubber blade on the outside. This device was operated by the driver from within the vehicle via a lever. The windshield wipers became standard equipment in all American cars by 1916.

53. Carbonated Water – Joseph Priestley

Carbonated water, also known as club soda, soda water or fizzy water, is a kind of water into which carbon dioxide gas has been dissolved under pressure. This process known as carbonation causes the water to become bubbling. Carbonated water is the defining ingredient of carbonated soft drinks.

Joseph Priestley thought of and created the carbonated water in 1767. He first thought of making such a drink when he discovered a method of infusing water with carbon dioxide as he suspended a bowl of water above a beer vat at a local brewery. Priestley found the water thus treated had a pleasant taste and was refreshing.

54. Carl Sagan

Astronomer Carl Sagan was born on November 9, 1934, in Brooklyn, New York. He had written several books on space and a TV series called Cosmos. He won a Pulitzer Prize for his work.

He had acquired three different science degrees! Sagan was a lecturer and researcher at Harvard University until 1968. He had helped NASA with U.S. space missions to Venus, Mars and Jupiter. Particularly, his discovery of the high surface temperatures of the planet Venus is highly regarded. He had also worked on understanding the atmospheres of Venus and Jupiter and seasonal changes on Mars.

He is among the earliest scientists who had said that there might by life on other planets. He even encouraged NASA to look for life on other planets!

55. Ceiling Fan – Philip Diehl

In 1887, Philip Diehl had invented the ceiling fan. He had created the first ceiling fan by placing a fan blade on a sewing machine motor and had mounted it to the ceiling.

During the time he had created the ceiling fan, he was working with the Sewing Manufacturing Company. He later added a light fixture to the ceiling fan. In 1904, his Diehl and Co. added a split-ball joint to the ceiling fan, allowing it to be redirected. This technology led him to develop the oscillating fan three years later.

56. Cellophane – Jacques E. Brandenberger

Cellophane film was invented by Jacques E. Brandenberger in 1908. He first thought of a clear, protective, packaging layer in 1900.

Brandenberger was seated at a restaurant when a customer spilled wine onto the tablecloth. As the waiter replaced the cloth, Brandenberger thought of inventing a clear flexible film that could be applied upon the cloth, making it waterproof.

He experimented with various materials before applying liquid viscose to cloth. However, the viscose made the cloth too stiff. But he noticed that the coating peeled off in a transparent sheet. This was the beginning of the cellophane sheets which we use today in various ways.

57. Charles Darwin

Charles Darwin is among the greatest and most revolutionary scientists in history. He was a British naturalist who formulated the theory of evolution. Pre-Darwin, it was thought that all species on Earth had come individually and that none had ever changed its form. He proved that animals and plants have evolved in an orderly manner and keep on evolving even today.

In 1859, he publicized the theory of evolution in his famous book, *The Origin of Species by Natural Selection*. The book, said that all species on Earth could, in the course of time, have evolved from a common ancestry. He also said that in the struggle for life only the 'fittest' creatures survived while others failed.

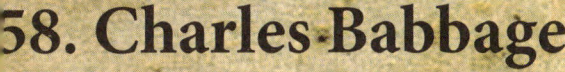

58. Charles Babbage

Charles Babbage, father of modern computer, was born in 1791 in London. He was mostly home tutored and later enrolled in Cambridge University.

The 1820s saw Babbage work on his 'Difference Engine', a machine which could perform mathematical calculations. He constructed a six-wheeled model and then planned to make a bigger, better machine - Difference Engine 2. He also worked on another invention, the more complex Analytical Engine, a revolutionary device on which his fame as a computer pioneer rests. It was intended to perform any arithmetical calculation using punched cards that would deliver the instructions as well as a memory unit to store numbers and many other fundamental components of today's computers.

59. Charles Goodyear

Born in December 1800, Charles Goodyear was the inventor of the vulcanized rubber. After receiving a public-school education, he started working with his father who was a hardware manufacturer and inventor of farm implements.

In 1830s, India-rubber industry came into being but due to poor merchandising, it declined in a few years. Also the rubber became hard as stone during winters and mushy during summer. Goodyear was however determined to make rubber a practical material to manufacture items. It was in 1844 that he was able to perfect a "vulcanized" process that prevented rubber from melting in heat.

60. Charles Richard Drew

Charles Drew, a surgeon, was the inventor of the blood bank. Though he was of African American descent, he received good education.

During his residency at Columbia University Presbyterian Hospital, Drew developed a technique for the long-term preservation of blood plasma. He found that if he separated the plasma (the liquid part of blood) from the whole blood (containing the red blood cells) and then refrigerated the two separately he could use the two for transfusion by combining them even after a week.

He also determined that each person has certain type of blood (A, B, AB or O) and therefore a person cannot receive a full blood transfusion from someone with a different blood type though everyone had the same type of plasma. Drew's discoveries has saved countless lives.

61. Charles Richter

Charles Richter is well-known for inventing the Richter scale. It is an instrument which measures the strength i.e. the amplitude of earthquakes. As a child, he developed interest in astronomy. Later, he studied physics and completed a Doctarate in theoretical physics.

While working at Caltech's Seismological Laboratory, he worked with Beno Gutenberg on a scale that interpreted seismograph readings to measure the magnitude of earthquakes. This scale was publicized in 1935. This scale which came to be known as the Richter scale recorded worldwide seismological events.

62. Chewing Gum – Thomas Adams

Chewing gum, a popular confectionery was created by Thomas Adams. He wanted to make a chewable gum but his products didn't work.

Later, at a drugstore, Adams saw a young girl chewing the spruce gum marketed by John Bacon Curtis. He recalled that Mexicans chewed chicle, a gumlike substance. Inspired Adams created the first chicle-based chewing gum in 1859. He formed the product into small balls and sold them at the local drugstore. Instantly, the gum became popular. Later, Adams, cut the gum into small strips, wrapped them in colourful paper and sold them as "Adams New York No. 1—Snapping and Stretching." He also added different flavours to his gum including sugar, mint and licorice.

63. Chloroform – Samuel Guthrie

Samuel Guthrie was an American physician from New York. He along with his other inventions, invented chloroform, an anesthesiac to bring about partial or complete loss of the sense of pain. He invented chloroform in 1831.

Chloroform was created when Samuel Guthrie distilled chloride of lime with alcohol in a copper barrel. It was then used as a mild anesthetic in amputation surgeries. It has been used on patients before surgeries ever since.

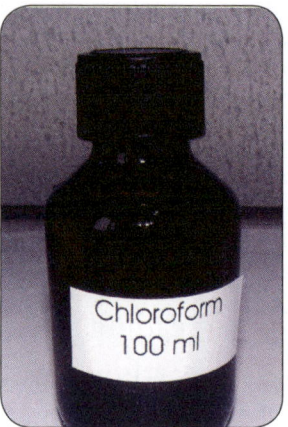
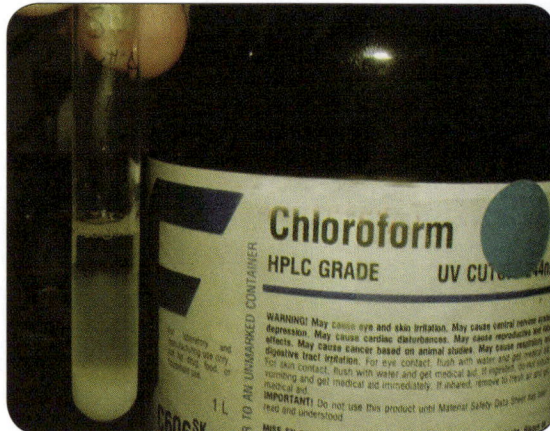

64. Chocolate Bar – Francois-Louis Cailler

The chocolate bar had been developed by Francois-Louis Cailler. He is also known as the father of the modern chocolate factory. It is believed that he learnt the art of chocolate making in Italy before setting up his chocolate business in Switzerland.

He was also the first chocolate maker to produce chocolate in individual serving blocks or chocolate bars. Before the chocolate bar was invented, customers bought as much chocolate as they wanted from a long roll of chocolate. Cailler also added various flavours to his chocolates including vanilla and spices. He was also a pioneer in selling his chocolate outside of Switzerland, another concept that had never been tried before.

65. Chocolate Chip Cookies – Ruth Wakefield

Chocolate chip cookies, a favourite treat for many people, was invented by Ruth Wakefield. She was a dietician and a food lecturer.

One day in 1930, Ruth was mixing a batch of cookies for a recipe when she ran out of baker's chocolate. So, she substituted broken pieces of Nestle's semi-sweet chocolate, expecting it to melt and absorb into the dough to create chocolate cookies. However, something unexpected happened. Instead of melting, the pieces of chocolate became part of the cookies. When she tasted, the cookies were delicious. She had thus invented the "chocolate chip cookies."

66. Christmas Card – Sir Henry Cole

Sir Henry Cole had started the custom of sending Christmas Cards. He wanted the 'Public Post Office' to reach out to people. He then had an idea of a Christmas Card. He hired London artist and his friend, John Calcott Horsley to design a Christmas card for him. It was a triptych (a card with three panels) with scenes on each of the side panels which showed the charitable essence of Christmas. Horsley made 1,000 lithographic copies of his greeting card and hand coloured each one himself.

Later, as printing methods improved, more and more Christmas cards were made. By the early 1900s, the custom of sending Christmas cards had spread all over Europe.

67. Clermont – Robert Fulton

The Clermont Steamboat was the first practical steamboat. It was pioneered by Robert Fulton in parternership with Robert Livingston. It was so because Livingstone could receive a monopoly on steam navigation on the rivers of New York State for twenty years if he had a steam-powered vessel with a travel speed of 4mph.

They built the steamboat *The Clermont* and it underwent its first voyage on August 17, 1807 from New York City. On board were a few invited guests. The Clermont made a record of travelling 150 miles in 32 hours. The return journey to New York City was covered in 30 hours. The steamboat Clermont was a success.

68. Coca Cola – Dr John Stith Pemberton

Dr John Stith Pemberton, an American pharmacist, is best known for inventing the Coca Cola. He had concocted the Coca Cola formula in a three legged brass kettle in his backyard. He added sugar, caffeine, phosphoric acid, caramel colour and a natural favouring to carbonated water to make Coca Cola. However, the ingredients of the natural flavouring were kept a secret. The name Coca Cola was suggested by Dr Pemberton's bookkeeper Frank Robinson. He also designed the logo for the drink.

The soft drink was first sold at the soda fountain in Jacob's Pharmacy in Atlanta on May 8, 1886. Did you know until 1905 the soft drink was marketed as a tonic!

69. Cocoa Powder – Coenraad Johannes van Houten

Coenraad Johannes van Houten, born in Amsterdam worked in his father's chocolate factory. He improved his father's method of pressing the fat from cocoa beans. Cocoa beans contain 54% natural fat that was taken out to make the chocolate easily digestible.

His father had invented a machine that reduced the cocoa butter content by nearly half. This created a cake which could be powdered into what is now known as cocoa powder, the base of all chocolate products. He improved this process by treating the cocoa with alkaline salts like potassium and sodium carbonates. This process removed the bitter taste of cocoa. This process is now known as "Dutching".

70. Coffee – Khalid

Coffee the most consumed drink in the world was discovered by chance by an Abyssinian goat herder named Khalid. One day, as his goats grazed, he noticed that during afternoon when he felt drowsy, his flock frolicked and skipped about after eating a certain berry. Then, either Khalid ate the berries whole or roasted or boiled them and felt instantly energetic.

Later, his wife urged him to share this miraculous discovery with the local holy man at the monastery. The chief monk, afraid, flung the berries into the fire but he and the other monks were astonished when the delicious aroma of the roasted berries filled the room. The berries were then taken out, put in water and the monks drank it. At once, they experienced the vigour as Khalid had described. Soon, the berries were exported to other places. With time, the Arabic word *qahwa* became the Turkish *kahve* then the Italian *caffé* and finally the English *coffee*.

71. Cold Fusion Energy (vortex technology) – Viktor Schauberger

Viktor Schauberger, Austrian inventor and naturalist, built a water ram pump involving a spiral flow. He is considered the father of vortex technology as his inventions and theories are based on the subtle energies of water. The theory behind cold fusion was that palladium could be fused with hydrogen at room temperature. In this manner, energy could be created without generating any radioactive waste.

While growing up near a forest, he researched on water flow and other natural phenomena. By 1929, he started making inventions based on water engineering. He even built a water turbine to produce hydroelectricity based on the vortex technology.

72. Colour Photography – James Clerk Maxwell & Thomas Sutton Scotland

Maxwell is the pioneer in the field of practical colour photography. In 1855, he proposed that if three black-and-white photographs of a scene were taken through red, green and blue filters and transparent prints of the images were projected onto a screen using three projectors equipped with similar filters, when superimposed on the screen the human eye would see a coloured photograph. He said that human eye sees colour because its inner surface is covered with millions of intermingled cone cells of three types that are sensitive to red, green and blue colours.

The first demonstration of colour photography using three photographs of a tartan ribbon was done in 1861.

73. Compact Disc – James Russell

A compact disc (CD) is a digital storage media used to store computer files, pictures and music. James Russell invented the compact disc in 1965.

Russell wanted a better music recording system that would record and replay sounds without physical contact between its parts. He thought that if the binary symbols 0 and 1 could be represented with bits of dark and light, a device could read sounds without wearing out. Also, if the binary code was kept compact even encyclopedias could be stored on a small piece of film.

Russell managed to record onto a photosensitive platter in tiny "bits" of light and dark. A laser read the binary patterns which the computer converted into an audible or visible transmission. This was the first compact disc.

74. Compound Microscope – Zacharias Janssen

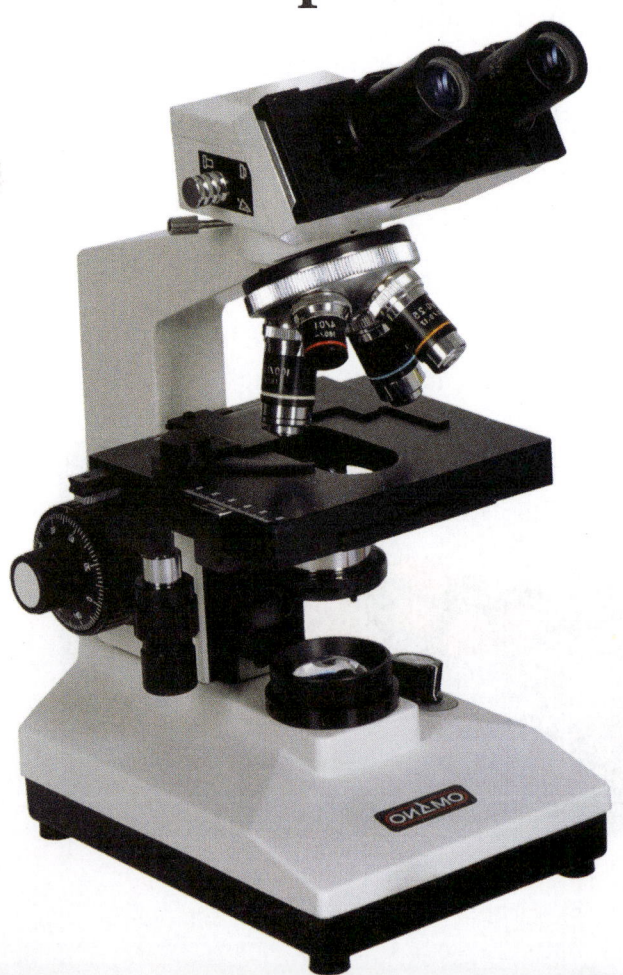

Zacharias Janssen, a Dutch spectacle-maker, is credited with inventing the first microscope. Although, he is generally believed to be the first creator of a compound microscope, there were others who too were trying to make a microscope.

Janssen's microscope consisted of three draw tubes with lenses inserted into the ends of the flanking tubes. The eyepiece lens was bi-convex and the objective lens was plano-convex, a very advanced compound design during the 1590s. Focus on this hand-held microscope was achieved by sliding the draw tube in or out while observing the sample. The Janssen microscope could magnify images up to ten times when extended to the maximum.

75. Computer – Charles Babbage

The dawn of the computer age began with the invention of the analytical engine. This mechanical 19th century computer had a processing unit that could store a number of programs. Punching cards were used to input data into Babbage's computer which would then solve the problem and provide a printed answer.

Charles Babbage developed the analytical engine after making the difference engine. However, it was the analytical engine that could solve different types of equations. His motive behind inventing these devices was a desire to create absolutely accurate mathematical tables. He initially built a six-wheeled model and demonstrated its working. It was a success and Babbage improved it further. After his death, his devices became the forerunners to modern computers.

76. Computer Mouse – Douglas C. Engelbart

Douglas C. Engelbart changed the way computers worked, from specialized machinery that only a trained scientist could use, to a user-friendly tool that almost anyone could use. He invented or contributed to several interactive, user-friendly devices including the computer mouse.

In 1964, the first prototype computer mouse was made to use with a graphical user interface (GUI), 'windows'. Engelbart made the first mouse using a wooden shell that contained a circuit board and two metal wheels in 1970. He described it as a device with a "X-Y position indicator for a display system." It was nicknamed mouse because of the tail (wire) that came out at the end of the device.

77. Contact Lens-Glass – Adolf Fick

Adolf Fick first thought of making glass contact lenses in 1888. Contact lenses are tiny removable lenses that are worn directly on the cornea of the eye. Like glasses, they improve the wearer's vision. He made lenses from heavy brown glass that were 18-21mm in diameter.

Adolf practiced as an ophthalmologist in Zurich, Switzerland. Soon, he started designing contact lenses. He used plastic casts of human eyes to make his lens moulds. He first fitted his lenses on rabbits. These lenses were large and thin and sat across the whole eye. Later, he tested his lenses on himself, before six of his patients wore them.

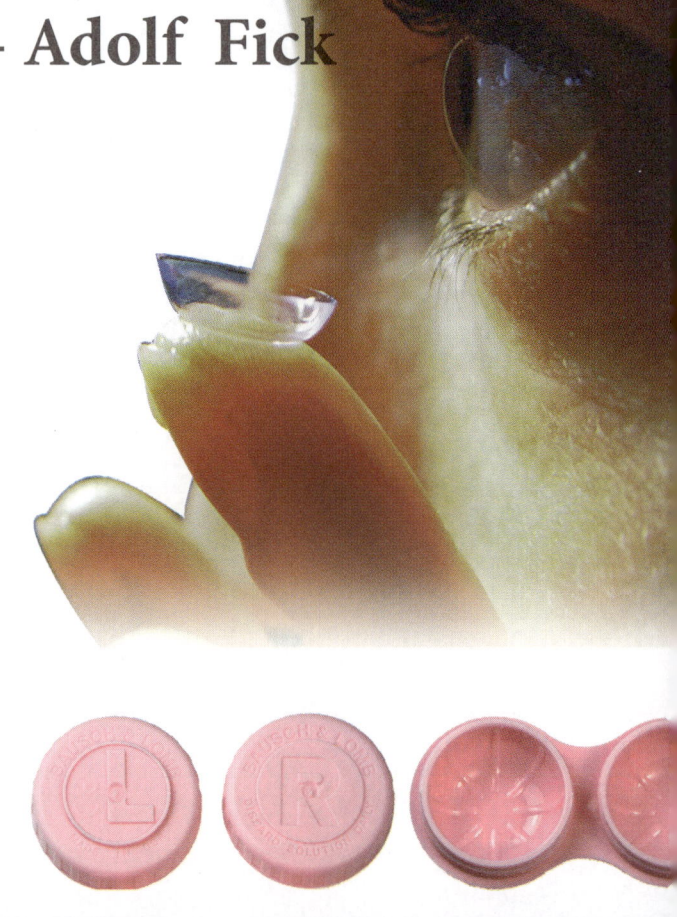

78. Cornflakes – Dr John Kellogg

John Harvey Kellogg was an American medical doctor in Battle Creek, Michigan, who ran a sanitarium focused on nutrition and exercise. He was an advocate of vegetarianism and is best known for inventing the corn flakes breakfast cereal with his brother, Will Keith Kellogg.

John Kellogg and his brother Will started the Sanitas Food Company to manufacture whole grain cereals around 1897, a time when the standard breakfast was eggs, meat, boiled grains and porridge. John and Will later argued over the recipe for the cereals as Will wanted to add sugar to the flakes. So, in 1906, Will started his own company, the Battle Creek Toasted Corn Flake Company, which eventually became the Kellogg Company.

79. Cotton Candy – William Morrison and John C. Wharton

Cotton Candy is a soft confection that looks like a fluffy mass of cotton though there is no cotton in it. It is made from finely-granulated sugar that is heated and spun into slim threads.

Cotton Candy was invented in 1897 by William Morrison and John C. Wharton, candymakers from Nashville, Tennessee. They invented a device with tiny holes in it that heated sugar in a spinning bowl. It formed a treat which they originally called "Fairy Floss." As the bowl spun around, the caramelized sugar was forced through the tiny holes, making feathery candy that melted in the mouth. They first sold cotton candy at the St. Louis World's Fair in 1904 to great profit.

80. Cotton Gin – Eli Whitney

Eli Whitney, working as a private tutor on a plantation in Georgia, learnt that Southern planters needed a way to make the growing of cotton profitable. Cotton grown by southern planters had sticky green seeds that were hard to pick out of the fluffy white cotton balls. Whitney decided to look for a solution.

In the hope of making money, Whitney experimented in a secret workshop. Within months he had created the cotton gin, a machine that quickly and easily separated the cotton fibres from their seeds. His machine used a combination of a wire screen and small wire hooks to pull the cotton through while brushes continuously removed the loose cotton lint. After the invention of the cotton gin, the yield of raw cotton doubled.

81. Wax Crayons – Edwin Binney & C. Harold Smith

Edwin Binney took over the operations of the Peeksill Chemical Co., his father's business, in 1885, a company that produced natural gas and carbon black. In 1900, along with his cousin C. Harold Smith, Edwin opened a mill in Pennsylvania to produce slate pencils for schools. Later they also produced dustless chalk made of slate waste, cement and talc. Then they saw the need for affordable wax crayons, and in 1903 Binney & Smith produced the first box of eight Crayola crayons. The crayons were of the colours black, brown, blue, red, purple, orange, yellow and green. Crayola brand crayons were the first kids crayons ever made. Today, there are over one hundred different types of crayons made by Crayola!

82. Credit Card – Ralph Schneider

As far back as the late 1800s, consumers and merchants exchanged goods through the concept of credit.

In the early 1900s, department stores started issuing their own proprietary cards. Such cards were accepted only at the business that issued the card and in limited locations. However, the scenario changed in 1949.

The story began in Diners Club when a man named Frank McNamara at the time of making a payment realized that he had forgotten his wallet. He managed to go spot free but decided to find an alternative to cash. He and his partner, Ralph Schneider, returned to Major's Cabin Grill in February 1950 and paid the bill with a small, cardboard card. Coined the Diners Club Card, it claimed to be the first credit card in widespread use. By 1951, there were 20,000 Diners Club cardholders.

83. Crossword Puzzle – Arthur Wayne

The crossword puzzle, "the most popular and widespread word game in the world," was invented by Arthur Wynne in 1913.

Wynne worked for the *New York World*.

One day, his editor asked him to invent a new game for the newspaper's Sunday "Fun" section. Wynne recalled a puzzle from his childhood called "Magic Squares," in which a given group of words had to be arranged so their letters would read the same way across and down. Wynne created a larger and more complex grid and provided clues instead of words.

Wynne's puzzle first appeared in December 21, 1913 edition of the newspaper. It was diamond-shaped, without blackened-out squares and with easy clues. The puzzle was a huge success.

84. David Warren

David Ronald de Mey Warren was born in Australia in 1925. His interest in electronics was kindled while he was still young.

Years later, as a specialist in the chemistry of aircraft fuels, he joined the Aeronautical Research Laboratories (ARL) in Melbourne. During this time, a certain passenger aircraft experienced two unexplained crashes within two years. Warren was investigating the cause behind these crashes. It then occurred to him that a small recording device installed in the cockpit could have helped determine the cause of the two crashes by allowing investigators to hear the voices of the crew and replay vital flight data.

By 1956 he had created a prototype "black box", named the "ARL Flight Memory Unit", which stored up to four hours of voice and flight-instrument data.

85. DDT – Othmar Zeidler

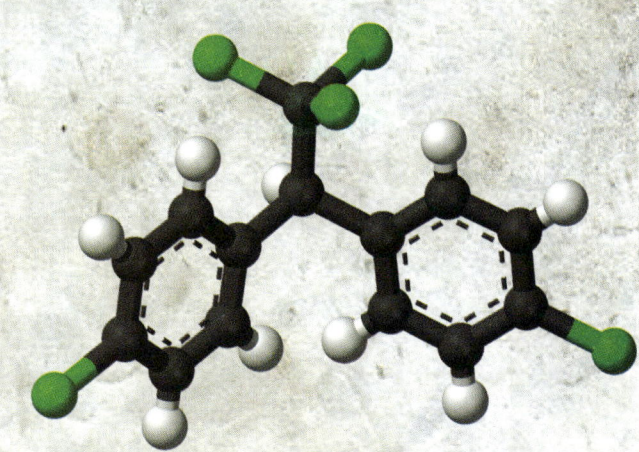

Othmar Zeidler is credited with making the insecticide Dichloro Diphenyl Trichloroethane or DDT in 1874. Othmar was a pharmacist in Vienna.

DDT is perhaps the most recognized of all insecticides because its use showed the many hazards associated with synthetic (man-made) pesticides. This colourless, odourless, insoluble toxic pesticide contains up to fourteen chemical compounds. It is known for its ability to destroy pesky insects such as flies, lice, mosquitoes, as well as agricultural pests. Although first synthesized in 1874, DDT was not used as an insecticide until 1939 when its insect-killing properties were discovered. Did you know that once in an ecosystem, DDT can pass on from crops to birds and from water to fish, eventually affecting the whole food chain!

86. Decimal Point; Logarithms – John Napier

John Napier was a Scottish mathematician and inventor. Napier is famous for the creation of logarithms and the decimal notation for fractions. His other mathematical contributions included: a mnemonic for formulas used in solving spherical triangles, two formulas known as Napier's analogies and the exponential expressions for trigonometric functions.

His technique of calculation of log got published in 1614. The logarithm technique was found to be accurate and his work was published in various languages. It helped in the trigonometric calculations in astronomy and navigation.

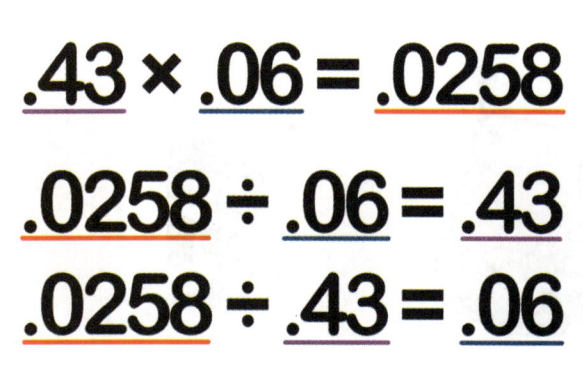

87. Diabetes Testing Kit – Helen Free

Helen M. Free and her husband, Alfred Free revolutionized diagnostic urine testing with inventing a chemically coated paper dipstick that measured a patient's blood sugar by changing colour when dipped in a urine sample.

The Frees also developed other strips for testing levels of key indicators of the disease. Once they achieved success with a number of different test strips, they turned their attention to combining several tests on a single strip. By 1981, they developed Multistix, a strip for urinalysis that had 10 different clinical tests on a single strip. Their inventions revolutionized diagnostic urine testing.

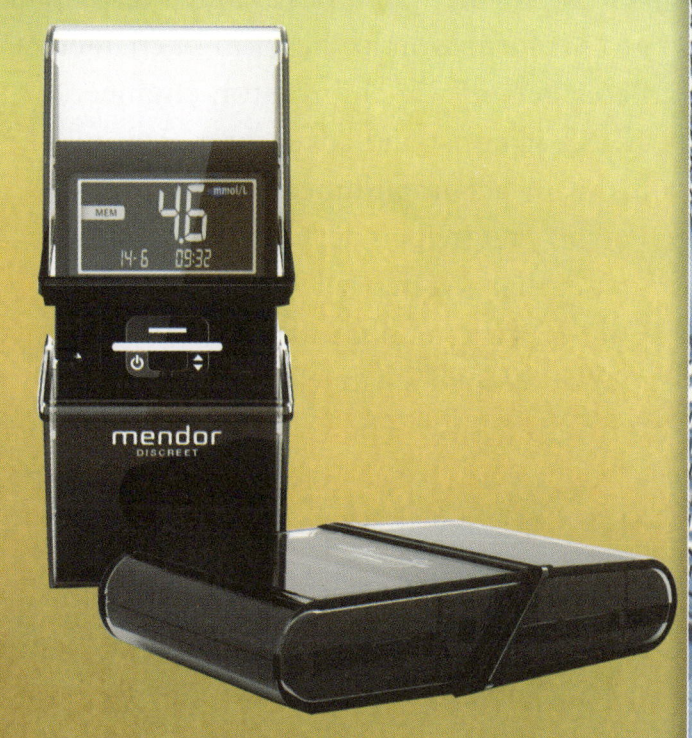

88. Diesel Engine – Rudolf Diesel

The diesel engine works by heating fuels either petroleum-based or bio-derived and causes the fuel to ignite. The diesel engine is more energy efficient, quieter and requires less maintenance. German engineer Rudolf Diesel invented the pressure-ignited heat engine, adapting the internal combustion engine so that a spark was no longer needed to ignite the fuel-air mixture.

Inspired to create a more efficient engine, he began working on his engine in 1885. He made the first working diesel engine using peanut oil as fuel on August 10, 1893. After modifying the design further, he presented a 25-horsepower, four-stroke, single cylinder compression engine in 1897.

89. Digital Wrist Watch – Peter Petroff

A digital wrist watch has a digital display. It gives information in the form of characters. Peter Petroff was an inventor, engineer, NASA scientist and adventurer. Among his many accomplishments and inventions, Petroff had helped develop the world's first digital watch. In 1968, he founded Care Electrics, a high-technology company that developed a wireless heart monitor for hospital use. The venture evolved into Electro/Data, which created the prototype of the digital watch.

Marketed by the Hamilton Watch Company as the Pulsar, the odd-looking device sold for $2,100 in 1971. Fifteen years later, digital watches became a common sight.

90. Dishwasher – Josephine Garis Cochran

Josephine Garis Cochrane, a wealthy woman, wanted a machine that could wash dishes faster than her servants, without breaking them. Unable to find one, she invented the dishwasher herself and unveiled it in World's Fair in 1893. To make the dishwasher, she first measured the dishes and then made wire compartments to fit plates, cups or saucers. The compartments were placed inside a wheel that lay flat within a copper boiler. A motor turned the wheel while hot soapy water squirted from the bottom of the boiler and rained down on the dishes.

Her dishwasher was hand-operated. Soon, it became popular and she opened her own company to manufacture them.

91. Disposable Syringe – Colin Murdoch

Colin Murdoch wanted to design a more effective vaccinator for animals and, in doing so, designed and invented the disposable syringe: a device that has saved millions of human lives.

Colin Murdoch, a trained pharmacist living in New Zealand, became a veterinarian. The idea of a disposable, pre-filled vaccination syringe came to Murdoch while he was travelling between the North and South Islands. These disposable syringes were useless after one use and needed to be thrown away. He had devised such syringes to avoid contamination through diseases from one patient to another. His invention was a great breakthrough in the field of medicine.

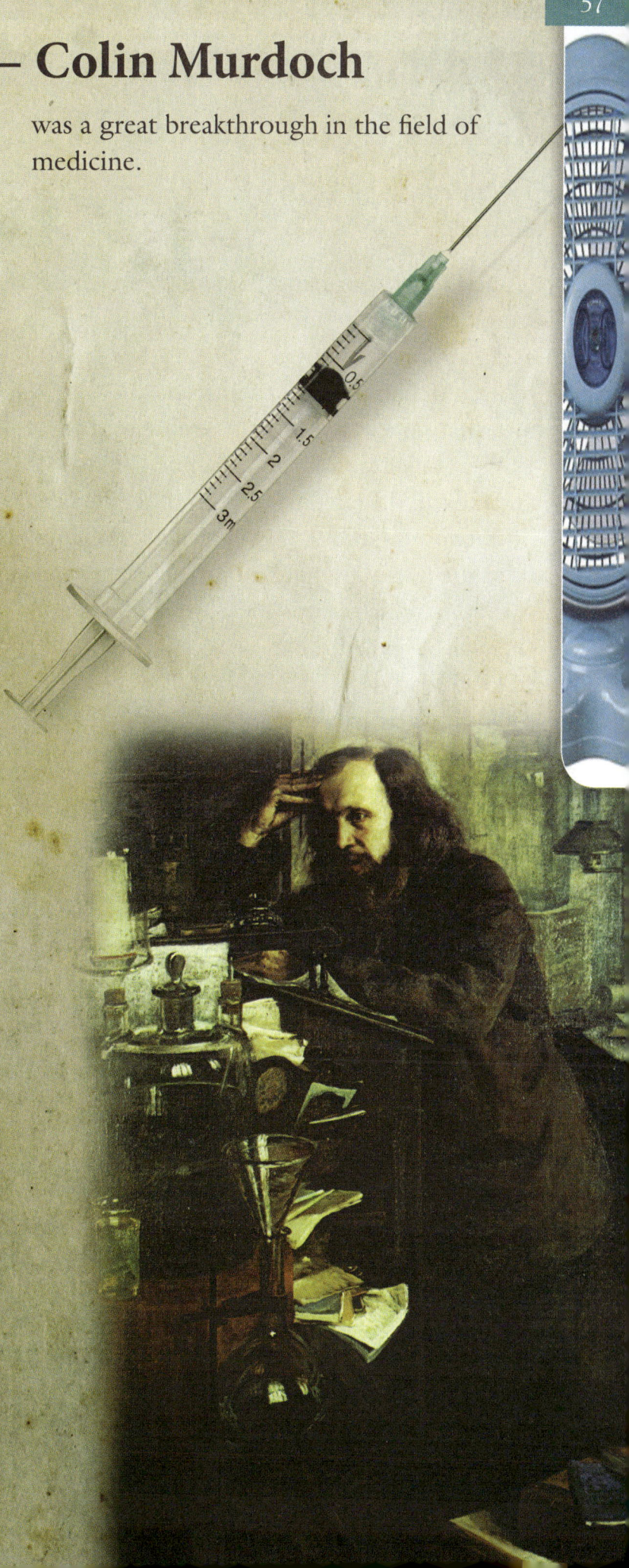

92. Dmitri Mendeleev

Dmitri Mendeleev revolutionized our understanding of the properties of atoms and created the periodic table which is on the walls of classrooms around the world.

From early in his career, Mendeleev felt that there was some type of order to the elements and he spent more than thirteen years of his life collecting data and assembling the concept, initially with the idea of resolving some of the disorder in the field for his students.

He is credited as being the creator of the first version of the periodic table of elements. He received the Noble Prize in Chemistry for his discovery of the periodic system.

93. DNA Structure – James Crick, James Watson & Rosalind Franklin

The discovery of DNA was a breakthrough in science.

Francis Crick and James Watson were studying the structure of deoxyribonucleic acid, commonly known as DNA. It is the molecule that contains the hereditary information for cells. At the same time, at King's College, London, Maurice Wilkins and Rosalind Franklin were using X-ray diffraction to study DNA. Crick and Watson used the later's findings to further their own research. In April 1953, they published their discovery of the molecular structure of DNA based on all its known features - the double helix. Their model explained how DNA replicates and how hereditary information is coded on it.

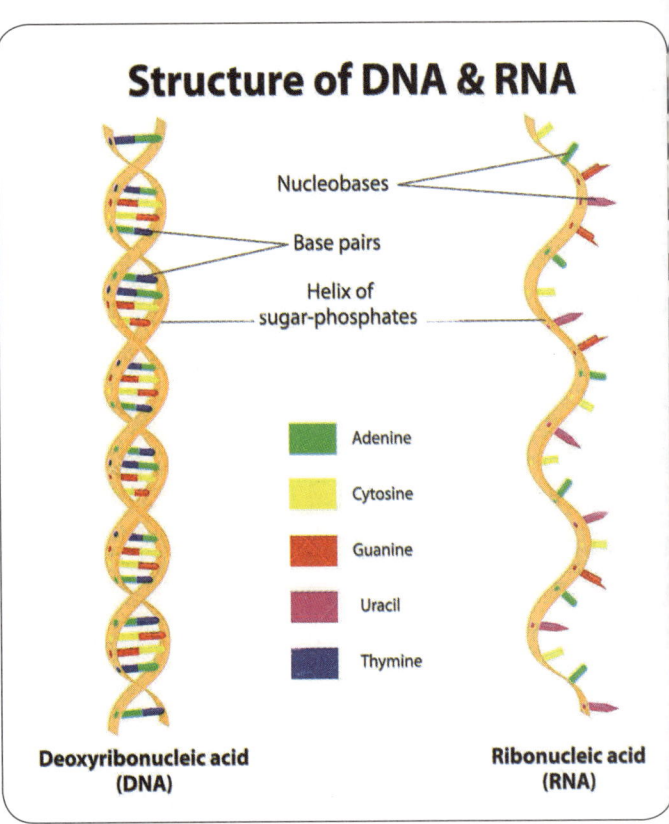

94. Doughnut – Hanson Crockett Gregory

Captain Hanson Crockett Gregory invented the donut with a hole in the middle. Before his invention doughnuts had no holes in them. Doughnuts are made of flour dough and are deep fried.

One story says that on June 22, 1847, Captain Gregory's ship was caught in a sudden storm. He placed the doughnut he was eating, as he issued instruction to the sailors, on a spoke of the steering wheel to keep his hands free. The spoke drove a hole through the raw centre of the doughnut. When he picked up the doughnut after a while, he liked the doughnut without the centre. Making a hole in the doughnut also increased the surface area exposed to the hot oil and eliminated the uncooked centre.

95. Douglas C. Engelbart

Douglas C. Engelbart was a pioneer in the design of interactive computer environments. He invented the computer mouse in 1964.

Douglas Carl Engelbart earned his Ph.D. in electrical engineering from the University of California and later began a career at the Stanford Research Institute. Around this time, he began focusing on an approach that he termed "bootstrapping," in which he asserted that computers would greatly improve the fields of engineering and science.

In 1964, Engelbart conceptualized and created the first design for the computer mouse. While Engelbart believed that the point-and-click computer device could be equipped with up to 10 buttons, the first mouse had just three.

96. Drinking Straws – Marvin Stone

In 1888, Marvin Stone thought of the spiral winding process to manufacture the first paper drinking straws. Before the invention of the straws, beverage drinkers used the natural rye grass straws.

Stone made his prototype straw by winding strips of paper around a pencil and gluing the strips together. As the paper straws became soggy as someone drank a beverage at leisure, he experimented with paraffin-coated manila paper. This experiment worked. He then set the length of the ideal straw at 8 1/2 inches with a diameter just wide enough to prevent things like lemon seeds from entering and embedding in the tube. By 1890, his factory was producing more straws than other products.

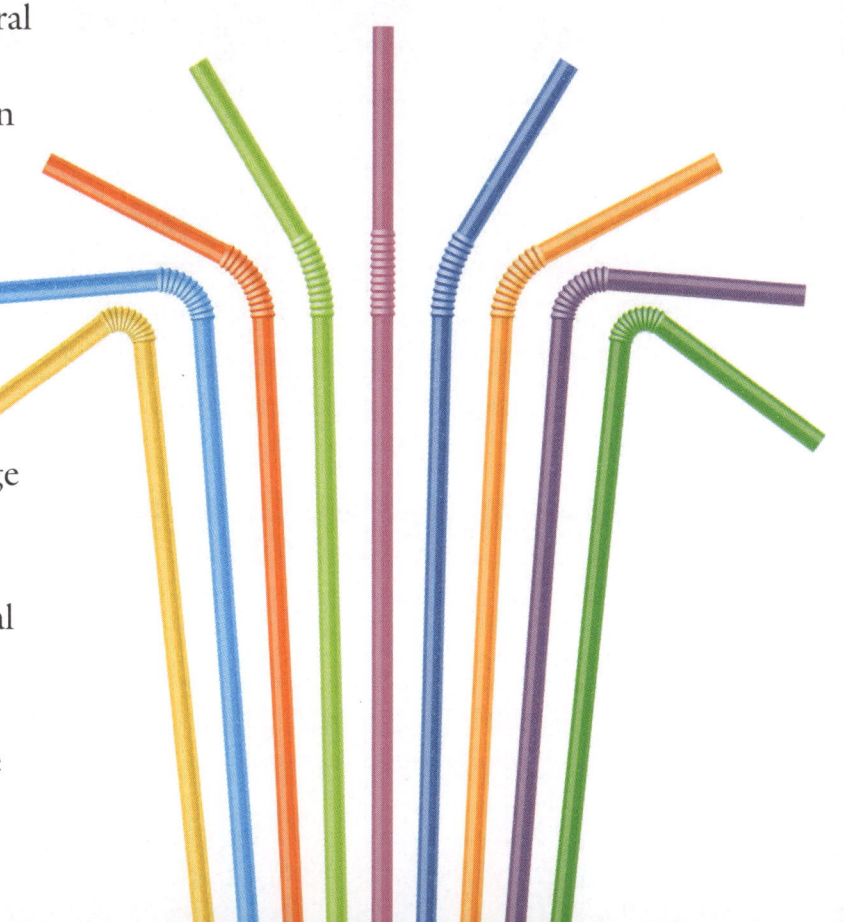

97. Drive-in Theatre – Richard M. Hollingshead

Richard Hollingshead was a young sales manager, who had a vision of an open-air movie theatre where moviegoers could watch movies from their own cars. He experimented in his own driveway where he mounted a 1928 Kodak projector on the hood of his car, projected the film onto a screen he had nailed to trees in his backyard, and used a radio placed behind the screen for sound.

He even vigorously checked the sound quality and the positioning of the cars. To adequately place the cars, he kept blocks and ramps under the front wheels of cars. Richard opened the first drive-in on June 6, 1933 at Crescent Boulevard, Camden, New Jersey.

98. Dry-cleaning – Jean Baptiste Jolly

Dry-cleaning is a form of cleaning where clothes are cleaned without the use of water. Like many inventions, dry-cleaning came about by accident. In 1855, Jean Baptiste Jolly, a French dye-works owner, noticed that his table cloth became cleaner after his maid accidentally overturned a kerosene lamp on it. Operating through his dye-works company, Jolly offered a new service and called it "dry-cleaning."

Early dry cleaners used a variety of solvents -- including gasoline and kerosene -- to clean clothes and fabrics. Nowadays, perc is used to dry clean clothes. It was not only safer and faster but did a much better job of cleaning.

99. Dynamite – Alfred Noble

Swedish industrialist, engineer and inventor, Alfred Nobel built bridges and buildings in Stockholm. His construction work inspired Nobel to research new methods of blasting rock. In 1860, he began experimenting with nitroglycerine, which is very volatile in its natural liquid state.

During his experiments, Alfred Nobel discovered that mixing nitroglycerine with silica turned the liquid into a malleable paste called dynamite. Dynamite could be easily turned into a cylinder shape, wrapped in paper and easily carried.

Dynamite is mainly used in the mining, quarrying, construction and demolition industries.

100. Dynamo – Werner Von Siemens

A dynamo is an electrical generator that produces direct current with the use of an acommutator. Dynamos were the first electrical generators capable of delivering power to industries. Dynamos were the foundation upon which many other later electric-power conversion devices were based.

Werner von Siemens, German electrical engineer, had developed the dynamo.

101. Ear Muffs – Chester Greenwood

Chester Greenwood invented ear muffs at the age of 15 years in 1873. While testing a new pair of ice skates, he grew frustrated as he tried to protect his ears from the bitter cold. After wrapping his head in a scarf, which was too bulky and itchy, he made two ear-shaped loops from wire. Then, he asked his grandmother to sew fur on them.

These were the first ear muffs and they kept the cold away from his ears. Later, he improved his ear muffs using a steel band which held them in place. His ear muffs were called Greenwood's Champion Ear Protectors. He made a fortune supplying Ear Protectors to U.S. soldiers during the World War.

102. Eau de Cologne – Johann Maria Farina

Johann Maria Farina was an Italian perfume designer and maker. Farina established the oldest perfume factory, still existing in Cologne, Germany.

He invented the subtle fragrance Eau de Cologne which became a worldwide famous fragrance especially among the royal courts. Eau de Cologne literally means 'Water of Cologne'. This fragrance was made from a mixture of citrus oils, a blend of oils of fruits and flowers, ethanol and water. Did you know that back then perfume makers named their perfumes after the towns where they had manufactured them! This was done to honour the town that they lived in or made their inventions. Interestingly, *4711 Cologne* is the most famous and till date the most popular fragrance in history.

103. Edmund Halley

Edmund Halley while studying at Oxford University, met royal astronomer John Flamsteed. Influenced by Flamsteed's project to compile a catalogue of Northern Hemisphere, Halley proposed to do the same for the Southern Hemisphere. So, he travelled to the South Atlantic island of St Helena. When he returned in 1678, he had made a record of celestial longitudes and latitudes with the correct positions of 341 stars.

In 1705, he described the parabolic orbits of 24 comets that had been observed from 1337 to 1698. He showed that the three historic comets of 1531, 1607 and 1682 were so similar in characteristics that they must have been the same comet - now known as Halley's Comet. He also accurately predicted the return of this comet in 1758.

104. Edward Jenner

Edward Anthony Jenner made a great scientific breakthrough by his discovery of the smallpox vaccine. During his training years, an interesting event occurred where Jenner overheard a girl say that she would not get smallpox because she already had cowpox.

Years later, Jenner set up his own medical practice. Then, in 1788 a wave of smallpox swept through Gloucestershire. Jenner observed that those who worked with cattle contacted cowpox but never smallpox.

In 1796, he conducted an experiment on one of his patients James Phipps, an eight year old boy. He made two cuts in James' arm and put cowpox puss into them. The boy had slight fever but he was soon healthy. A few weeks later, Jenner repeated the vaccination using smallpox puss. This time, the boy remained healthy. He did not have smallpox. This tremendous breakthough saved many lives.

105. Edwin Hubble

Edwin Hubble was an American astronomer who is known for proving the existence of galaxies other than The Milky Way.

Born in 1889 at Marshfield, Missouri, Hubble was a bright student. Years later, he joined Mount Wilson Observatory in California. There Hubble, developed an interest in "nebulae"; cloudy objects in the sky during night. He observed that these clouds of gas consisted of stars arranged in spirals. Then in 1920, he proved that the Sun was part of The Milky Way Galaxy and that the Universe was something much bigger than previously thought.

He photographed hundreds of nebulae and declared that several of these could be called galaxies. Later, he also concluded that the Andromeda Nebula was outside The Milky Way. This discovery made him world famous.

106. Electrical Ignition System – Charles Kettering

The first electrical ignition system or electric starter motor for cars was invented by GM engineers Clyde Coleman and Charles Kettering. The self starting ignition was first installed in a Cadillac on February 17, 1911. The invention of the electric starter motor eliminated the need for hand cranking.

Previously, drivers used iron hand cranks to start the internal combustion process that powered the engines in their cars. In addition to requiring great strength, the system was risky. By making cars easier and safer to operate, the self-starting engine caused a huge jump in sales, and helped foster a fast-growing automobile culture in America.

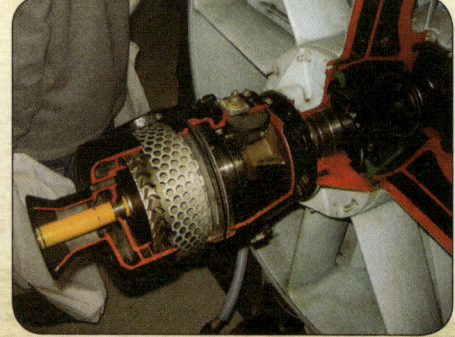

107. Electroscope – Jean Nollet

Jean Antoine Nollet was a clergyman and physicist. In 1748, Nollet invented one of the first electroscopes. It was an instrument that detected the presence of electric charge by using electrostatic attraction and repulsion. He later wrote a theory based on the continuous flow of electrical matter between charged bodies. The device detects the electrical charges in bodies by measuring the small electrical voltages and currents produced by the bodies.

It is used for detecting X-rays, cosmic rays and radioactive material. These rays pass through the air like an electric current. They either charge or discharge the electroscope.

108. Elevator

The elevator or a lift is a type of vertical transport equipment that moves people or goods between floors of a building, a vessel or any other structure. Elevators are generally powered by electric motors that either drive traction cables or counterweight systems like a hoist or pump hydraulic fluid to raise a cylindrical piston like a jack.

The first elevators were started in coal mines to transport goods and were powered by steam. It was much later that elevators were used in buildings causing a stir among the people who were fascinated by these 'ascending rooms' as they were called then by architects Burton and Hormer.

109. Elevator Brake – Elisha Graves Otis

An elevator is a platform or an enclosure shaft that transports people and goods between the floors of a building. In 1853, American inventor Elisha Otis demonstrated a freight elevator equipped with a safety device to prevent falling in case a supporting cable should break. His device had a spring mechanism to trigger teeth on the edges of the car to stop it from falling if the hoist cables fail. This increased public confidence in such devices. In 1853, Elisha established a company for manufacturing elevators. The first elevator with a brake was installed in a five-storey building owned by E.W Haughtwhat & Company of Manhattan.

110. Email – Ray Tomlinson

Computer engineer, Ray Tomlinson invented the email or the electronic mail in 1971. An email is used to send simple messages to another person across a network.

He was experimenting with SNDMSG program that was being used at ARPANET to send messages across network computers. SNDMSG was a "local" electronic message program. One could leave messages on the computer that he were using for other persons using that same computer, to read. Tomlinson modified the SNDMSG program such that the program could send electronic messages to any computer on the ARPANET network.

He chose @ symbol to tell which user was "at" what computer. @ symbol went inbetween the user's login name and the name of his/her host computer. Interestingly, the first email message was "QWERTYUIOP".

111. Internal Combustion Fuel Engine
Jean – Joseph Etienne Lenois

The internal combustion engine was invented by Jean-Joseph Etienne Lenoir. This engine provided a reliable and continuous source of power in vehicles.

The first practical internal combustion engine was heavily based on steam engines. The engine had a horizontal cylinder and a double acting, electric spark-ignition system. However, this engine was unreliable. In 1863, Lenoir improved it. His improved engine ran on petroleum and had a primitive carburetor which was attached to a three-wheeled wagon.

The improved engine was successful and today it is used widely.

112. Enrico Fermi

Enrico Fermi is widely considered as the architect of the nuclear age. He is best remembered for developing the nuclear reactor.

At the University of Rome, Fermi conducted experiments where he bombarded a variety of elements with neutrons. He then discovered that slow moving neutrons were particularly effective in producing radioactive atoms. He didn't know that he had split the atom. For his achievement, he was awarded the Nobel Prize for Physics in 1938. He continued his nuclear fission experiments at Columbia University. In 1940, Fermi and his team proved that absorption of a neutron by a uranium nucleus can cause the nucleus to split into two nearly equal parts, releasing many neutrons and huge amounts of energy. This was the first nuclear chain reaction.

113. Eraser – Charles Goodyear

The Indians of Central and South America called rubber 'Caoutchou'. The word Caoutchouc comes from "cahuchu," which meant "weeping wood." Natural rubber was harvested from the sap that oozed from the bark of a certain tree. Rubber was initially used as a pencil eraser that could "rub out" pencil marks.

Later, as rubber was used to make other products, it could not bear the harsh winters and became brittle. Then, in 1843, Charles Goodyear discovered that if sulphur was removed from rubber before heating it, it would retain its elasticity. This process was called vulcanization. This process made rubber waterproof, winter-proof and thus opened doors for an enormous market for rubber goods.

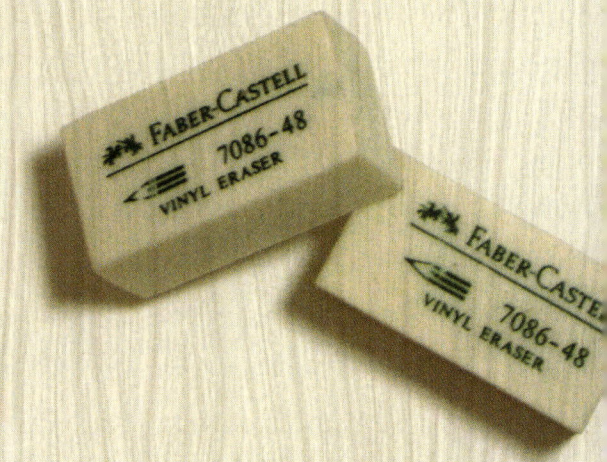

114. Ernest Rutherford

British physicist and chemist, Ernest Rutherford is known for his remarkable orbital theory of the atom in his discovery of Rutherford dispersion with his famous Gold Foil experiment. He received Nobel Prize in Chemistry in 1908 for his contribution to science.

An exceptional student, Ernest won repeated scholarships and later, became a research student at the Cavendish Laboratory. There, he discovered a detector for electromagnetic waves that had a magnetizing coil containing tiny bundles of magnetized iron wire. While experimenting, he discovered that radioactive elements, thorium and uranium, gave off two different types of rays-alpha and beta.

In 1909, he conducted an experiment which made him understand the nuclear nature of atoms. This experiment laid the foundation of Rutherford model of the atom, his greatest contribution to physics.

115. Erwin Schrödinger

Erwin Schrödinger laid the foundations of the study of wave mechanics, which are crucial to understanding the behaviour of subatomic particles and light. Born in Austria, Erwin Schrödinger was a pioneer in quantum physics and genetic theory. His greatest achievement, the Schrödinger Equation, helped to understand subatomic behaviour.

During the early 1900s, the nature and action of subatomic particles was not clearly understood. Schrödinger then began his own experiments and it was in the 1920s that he wrote his most important work. In it, he explained how different energy states of an atom's electrons could be described and even predicted via wave equations. This was his greatest contribution to quantum mechanics.

116. Escalator – Jesse W. Reno

An escalator is a conveyor type transport device. It is a moving staircase with steps that moves up or down using a conveyor belt and tracks keeping each step horizontal for the passenger. Did you know that the escalator was started as an amusement ride! In 1895, Jesse created a new novelty ride at Coney Island, a moving stairway that elevated passengers on a conveyor belt at 25 degree angle. It was displayed for two weeks when about 75,000 people took a ride on it!

After the success of his Coney Island ride, Jesse founded his own company and soon escalators were installed in a number of places.

117. Eyeglasses – Salvino D'Armate

Around 1000AD, the first vision aid was invented called a reading stone. It was a glass sphere that was laid on top of the material to be read as it magnified the letters.

Around 1284 in Italy, Salvino D'Armate is credited with inventing the first wearable eye glasses. It is believed that D'Armate had injured himself in the eye while he was experimenting with light refraction. Though his vision was reduced, he continued to experiment. It was during his experiments that he discovered how to increase the appearance of objects by viewing them through two convex glass pieces. He then went on to make eyeglasses.

118. Fan – Schuyler Wheeler

Schuyler Skaats Wheeler was an American engineer who invented the two-blade electric fan in 1882 at age 22. His two-bladed electric fan was produced by the Crocker and Curtis Electric Motor Company.

At 21, he left college to become assistant electrician of the Jablochkoff Electric Light Company and in 1882 joined the engineering staff of Thomas A. Edison.

In 1882, while working for C&C Electric Motor Company, he used one of their powerful motors to develop an electric fan. The fan had a cage to protect the blades. But all its wiring was exposed. It was the first of its kind electric fan.

119. Fasteners (clothes)

Various kinds of fasteners for clothes are used today, both for functional and decorative purposes. Button, the most common fastener, is used to secure two pieces of a fabric together.

Buttons are not only used on clothes but also on wallets and bags. As a fastener, buttons work by slipping through a fabric or thread loop or when they are slid through a buttonhole.

The first known buttons were found in the tombs of Hungarian tribes dating to late 9th century. Functional buttons with buttonholes first appeared in Germany in the 13th century. Interestingly, buttons made by artists are art objects and are known as "studio buttons". Apart from buttons, zipper, velcro, snap fasterner and hook and loop are some other kinds of cloth fastners.

120. Fax Machine – Alexander Bain

To fax or faxing is a method of encoding data, transmitting it over a telephone line or radio broadcast and receiving a hard copy of the text, line drawings or photographs at a remote location. The first fax machine was invented by Scottish mechanic and inventor Alexander Bain. He had combined parts from clock mechanisms together with telegraph machines to invent his fax machine. His fax machine transmitter scanned a flat metal surface using a stylus mounted on a pendulum. The stylus picked up images from the metal surface. Interestingly, the first fax machine simply sent 'long' and 'short' lines that could be easily interpreted by a telegraph operator.

121. Ferris Wheel – George Washington Gale Ferris

George Ferris conceived, designed and built an engineering marvel which astonished the world at its debut and became a mainstay of American recreation. He specialized in constructing steel frameworks for bridges and tunnels.

When the World's Columbian Exhibition of 1893 was being planned in Chicago, Ferris decided to build a structure that would outdo the Eiffel Tower. He then, sketched a huge, revolving "observation wheel", in detail down to the ticket price. It was sometime before his idea was approved.

Ferris' wheel was modeled on a bicycle wheel. To maintain the wheel's shape and balance, it had heavy steel beams; the "forks" in which the axle was set were two steel girder pyramids. The wheel was 264 feet high, the supporting towers were 140 feet high and the axle weighed 46 1/2 tons. The wheel carried 36 elegantly outfitted passenger cars each of which could fit 40 people sitting. The wheel was spun by either of the two 1,000 horsepower steam engines and the movement of the wheel was stopped by an oversized air brake.

At its opening on June 21, 1893, the ferris wheel became the irresistible centerpiece of the exhibition. One and a half million people took a ride on it.

122. Fire Extinguisher – George William Manby

Captain George William Manby invented the first fire extinguisher, a copper cylinder which held three gallons of water and used compressed air to release the water through a narrow tube which could be aimed towards a fire. He made the fire extinguisher in 1813 and it was originally called the 'Extincteur'. His invention became the most famous safety invention.

Sometime later, he was the also the first person to advocate a national fire brigade. George William Manby also went on to invent a few other safety devices.

123. First Nuclear Power Plant – Igor Kurchatov

Igor Vasilyevich Kurchatov was a Russian nuclear scientist who guided the development of his country's first atomic bomb and the first nuclear reactor.

After receiving his degree in Physics, he researched on various topics before focusing his attention on nuclear physics.

Then, the news of the discovery of the fission process caused great excitement in Russia. Questions about its possible application were also raised. Kurchatov conducted his own experiments and published articles on spontaneous fission, uranium-235, chain reactions and the critical mass. Then, in 1946, Kurchatov directed the construction of the first nuclear reactor in Europe.

124. First Space Station – Vladimir Chelomei

A space station is an artificial satellite placed in a fixed orbit in space for scientific research. It has human crew and it is also a place from where further space exploration ventures are undertaken and spaceships are refuelled. Vladimir N. Chelomei was the chief designer of Russia's space rocket program and he had also designed the first space station. Under Professor Chelomei's direction, researchers at the Moscow Flights Technical College developed the earth satellites *Proton* and *Polyot* and made several other advances in aviation, rocketry and space technology. The professor also directed the development of the *Salyut* type orbiting space station.

125. Flash Light – Conrad Hurbert

Conrad Hurbert did a lot of odd jobs to make a living for himself. It was so until he became aware of the tremendous profits that could be gained through the electric industry. He then opened his own company called American Electrical Novelty & Manufacturing Company. In 1897, seeing the potential of flashlights, he hired David Misell, an inventor. Together and separately, they made several flashlights.

Hubert's first flashlights were hand-made from crude paper and fiber tubes with a bulb and a rough brass reflector. In 1905, Hubert invented a flashlight with an on/off switch in the now familiar cylindrical body that contains a lamp and batteries.

126. Floppy Disk – IBM (Alan Shugart)

In 1971, IBM made the first "memory disk", as it was called then or the "floppy disk" as it is known today. The first floppy was an 8" plastic disk coated with magnetic iron oxide. Data was written to and read from the disk's surface. The floppy was called so because you could bend it. It was considered a revolutionary device at the time for its portability, as it was easy to transport data from computer to computer.

The "floppy" was invented by IBM engineers led by Alan Shugart. The first disks were designed to fill another data storage device. Overnight, additional uses for the "floppy" were thought of and it became the new file storage medium.

127. Flush Toilet – John Harington

Sir John Harington, English Elizabethan courtier, translator and author is credited with inventing the flush toilet.

It is thought that he had invented the flush toilet in 1591. He had even installed one for Queen Elizabeth but she never used it for it made a loud sound. The first flush toilet was called 'Ajax.' The forerunner to the modern flush toilet had a flush valve to let water out of the tank and a wash-down design to empty the bowl. "The Ajax" however, did not find a market in England but it was adopted in France under the name 'Angrez'.

128. Flying Shuttle – John Kay

In 1733, John Kay, son of a wool merchant, invented the flying shuttle. It was an improvement to looms that enabled weavers to weave faster. Before this invention, weavers had to pass the shuttle through the warp threads by hand. Kay's invention put the shuttle on wheels and it was controlled with a driver. The weaver operated the shuttle by pulling a cord attached to the driver. When this cord was pulled to the left, the driver caused the shuttle to shoot ("fly") through the warp in the same direction. Pulling the cord to the right sent the shuttle back.

John Kay's invention allowed the thread to be woven at a faster rate in the loom.

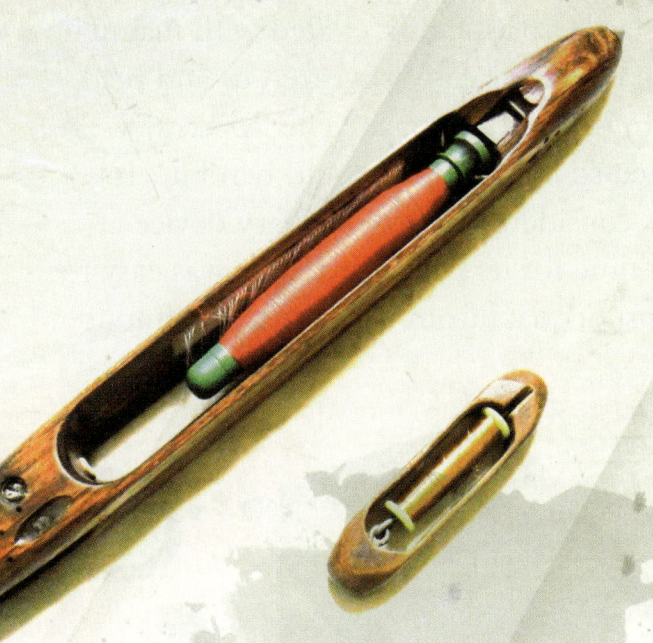

129. FM Radio – Edwin Howard Armstrong

Edwin Howard Armstrong was fascinated by Marconi's inventions as a kid and soon knew all that there was to know about wireless.

When he grew up, Armstrong began building his own homemade wireless equipment and it included a 125 foot antenna in his parent's backyard. It was much later, in 1933 that he invented the frequency-modulated or FM radio. Frequency modulation or FM improved the audio signal of radio by controlling the noise static which is caused by electrical equipment and the earth's atmosphere.

130. Fountain Pen – Lewis Edson Waterman

Lewis Edson Waterman, an insurance broker, invented the capillary feed in fountain pens. Disappointed on losing an important deal because his pen would not work, Lewis decided to invent better pens.

He began making pens in his brother's workshop using the capillary principle. This principle allowed air to induce a steady and even flow of ink. He called his fountain pens, 'the Regular', and decorated them with wood accents. He began selling his hand made fountain pens from the back of a cigar shop. He guaranteed that the pens shall work for five years. With time the orders increased and he opened a factory in Montreal in 1899, offering a variety of designs for his fountain pens.

131. Francis Crick

Francis Crick is highly regarded for his discovery of the DNA molecule structure with his colleague James D. Watson. He was a British molecular biologist, physicist and neuroscientist who jointly won a Nobel Prize in 1953 with Watson and Maurice Wilkins for their discovery.

Francis Crick was born in Northampton, England and he graduated with a degree in Physics in 1937.

Later, while pursuing his Ph.D work, he examined the physical properties of cytoplasm in the cultured fibroblast cells. After two years, he collaborated to work on protein structure. In 1951, he met James D. Watson and along with Maurice Wilkins, they tried to expose the structure of deoxyribonucleic acid (DNA). Crick and Watson then revealed the double helix structure of DNA in 1953, a tremendous breakthrough.

132. Frederick Banting

Frederick Banting is known worldwide for the discovery of the 'wonder drug' Insulin. Dr Banting had studied a wide variety of medicinal fields. He is also the youngest recipient of the Nobel Prize for Medicine and Physiology at age 32.

Frederick Banting studied medicine, a field which greatly captivated his interest. During the course of his career, Banting faced a personal loss when a close friend succumbed to diabetes. He then ardently read works that correlated diabetes with the lack of a protein hormone called insulin, secreted by the pancreatic section. Banting then along with fellow student, Dr Charles Best discovered insulin, a wonder drug.

Do you know that a crater on the moon is named 'Banting'! It is so because he had given the greatest and a priceless gift to humanity in the form of 'Insulin'.

133. Frisbee
– Walter Frederick Morrison & Warren Franscioni

The Frisbie Baking Company of Bridgeport, Connecticut made pies that were sold to many New England colleges. The students soon realized that the empty pie tins could be tossed and caught, providing endless hours of game. Many colleges claimed to have invented the Frisbee but they are merely stories. It was however in 1948 that Water Frederick Morrison and Warren Franscioni had first thought of Frisbees. They invented a plastic version of the tin Frisbee.

These plastic Frisbees had more accuracy and were light weight. Morrison called the plastic Frisbee, 'Pluto Platter'.

134. Fuel Cells – Sir William Grove

Sir William Robert Grove was a judge and a scientist. He put forth the general theory of conservation of energy. He is however renowned for pioneering the fuel cell technology.

In 1839, Grove developed a novel form of the electric cell. He made this cell using zinc and platinum electrodes which he exposed to two acids and separated them by a porous ceramic pot. Then in 1842, he developed the first fuel cell which he called the gas voltaic battery. This cell produced electrical energy by combining hydrogen and oxygen.

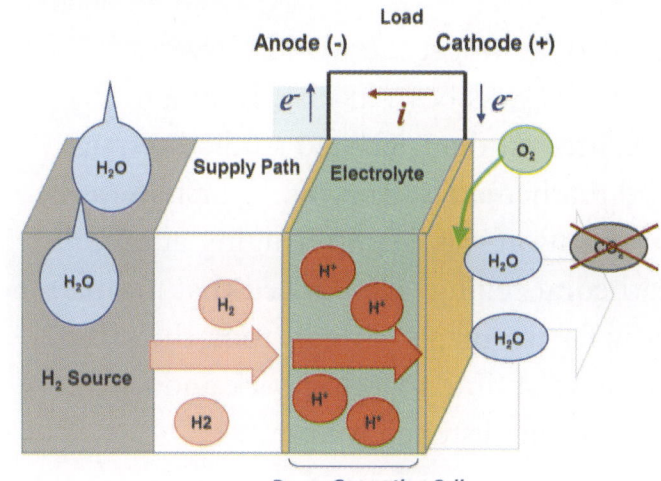

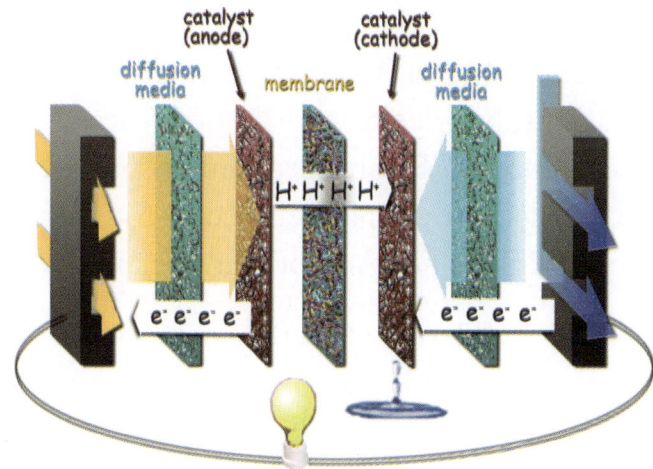

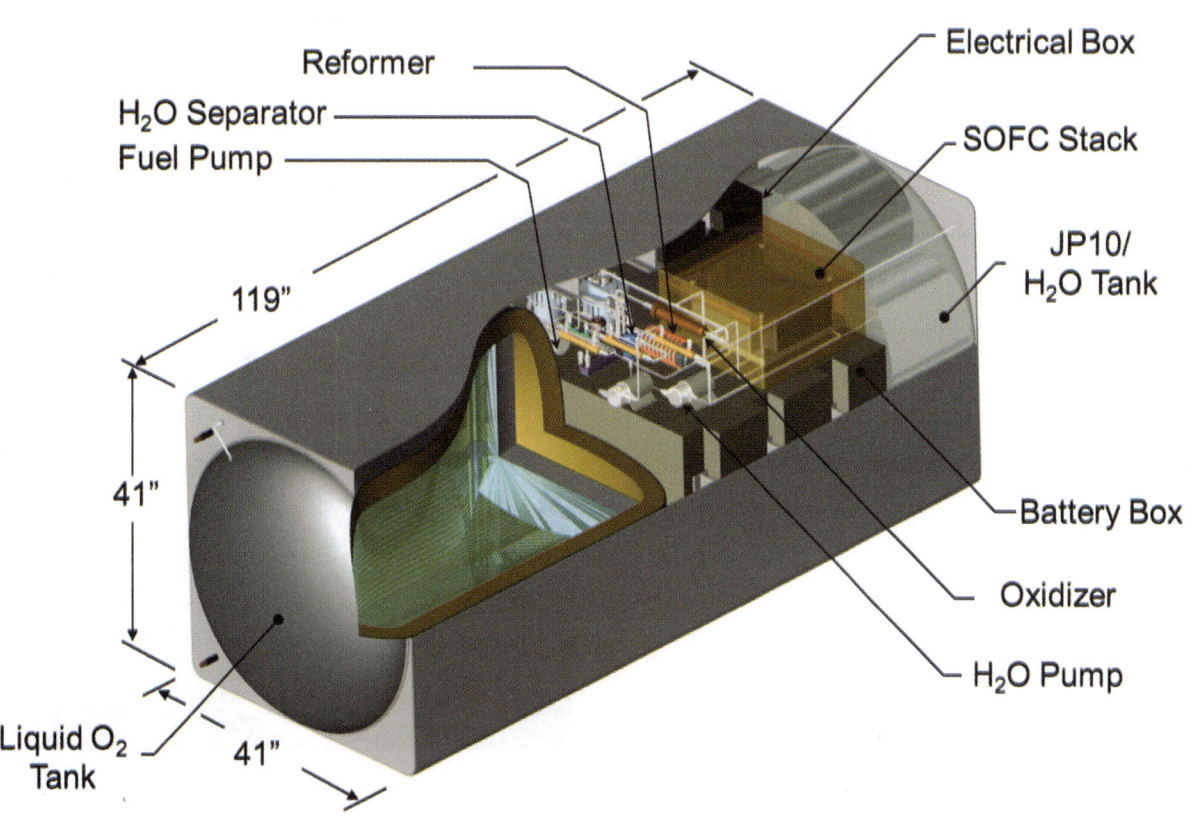

135. Galileo Galilei

Galileo, amongst the world's greatest scientists, was born in Pisa, Italy. An excellent student, Galileo studied physics and mathematics. Among his first scientific observation was a lamp hanging at a cathedral ceiling. He noticed that no matter how far the map swung, it took the same amount of time to swing back and forth. But no one listened to him.

In 1585, Galileo started teaching and experimented with pendulums, levers, balls and other objects. Using mathematical equations, he tried to explain how these objects moved. But his experiments were disregarded for people believed in the ideas of old thinkers like Aristotle unquestingly.

In 1592, Galileo studied the works of Copernicus who had said that the Sun

was the centre of the universe. This view clashed with the opinion that Earth was the centre of the universe. Galileo then built a telescope and observed the skies. As Galileo studied the planets and the Sun, he became convinced that the Earth orbited the Sun and that Copernicus was right. In 1632, for his ideas, he was put under house arrest at his home in Tuscany. Until his last, Galileo made discoveries and wrote them much to the anger of the church.

136. George De Mestral

George de Mestral is credited with the invention of the Velcro loop and fasteners. Velcro is an effective way to fasten fabrics and other materials. De Mestral was born in a small village near Lausanne, Switzerland. As a teenager, he did many odd jobs to pay his fees and graduated as an electrical engineer.

One day, De Mestral observed the manner in which burr's barbed hooks clung to his clothing. An idea suddenly came to him. Based on the logistics of barbed hooks, he invented a material that would attach hundreds of tiny hooks to cloth tape. He thus invented a material called Velcro that could be attached to clothings and much more. Velcro comes from the French words velour (velvet) and crochet (hooks).

Velcro today is used as an effective tool to fasten clothing, office equipment and many other objects.

137. George Eastman

George Eastman, the man behind Kodak, was born in Waterville New York into a poor family. At school, he used his creativity to keep himself from getting bored. When 20, he started working as a Junior Bookkeeper at Rochester Savings Bank.

After a while, on a vacation, he thought of making a small camera to replace the large and bulky cameras. After a few years, in 1880, Eastman quit his job to start experimenting with chemicals to create a "dry plate" to make photography easier. He finally made a dry plate and in 1884, he also made a transparent and flexible rollfilm for his camera. This film was cut into strips and put in a roll.

He then thought of making a smaller camera for his new "paper film". He then made a box sized camera in 1888. This camera was called KODAK! The age of photography was born.

138. George Washington Carver

George was born in 1864 on a small farm in Missouri. He was raised by his employers as their own son. He initially wanted to be an artist. But he combined his love for science, art and plants and studied botany. Later, George began to teach as a professor at Iowa State. In 1896, at the request of Booker T. Washington, he moved to an all black college in Tuskegee, Alabama and there headed the agriculture department.

While there, Carver taught his students to use crop rotataion. Carver's research into crop rotation helped the southern farmers to become more successful. He also invented products that could be made from crops like soybean, peanuts and sweet potato. All his efforts thus went into making the southern states agriculturally rich.

139. Glider – George Cayley

Sir George Cayley is an important person in the history of aeronautics. He designed many types of gliders. His built his first aerial device in 1796, a model helicopter with contra-rotating propellers. In 1804, Cayley designed and built a model monoplane glider which looked similar to the modern gliders. This glider had an adjustable cruciform tail, a kite-shaped wing mounted at a high angle of incidence and a moveable weight to alter the centre of gravity. It was probably the first gliding machine to make significant flights. He next designed an improved glider with repositioned wings to give it more stability while in flight.

Interestingly, in 1849, Cayley made a large gliding machine similar to his 1799 glider model. He tested the glider with a ten year boy aboard. The gliding machine carried the boy aloft for a short flight. This manned flight greatly boasted research in the field of aeronautics.

140. Google Web Search Engine – Sergey Brin & Larry Page

A search engine is a program that searches the Internet and finds webpages for the user based on the keywords that the user has submitted. Google, the most used search engine was invented by Larry Page and Sergey Brin. They invented the search engine in their dormitory room on borrowed PCs as part of a research project.

Google was named after googol which is the name for number 1 followed by 100 zeros. The search engine was called so because to the google founders the name signified the immense amount of information on the web that a search engine has to sift through.

141. Gravity – Sir Issac Newton

According to a story, Isaac Newton became acquainted with the idea of gravity when an apple fell on his head as he sat under an apple tree. Isaac Newton, one of the greatest scientists, was born in Lincolnshire, England. He was greatly interested in the work of Galileo. Isaac thought that the universe was governed by a few simple laws. Following Galileo, he decided to prove these laws using mathematics.

Newton then formulated the laws of motion and gravitation. His laws explained how objects moved when a force acted on them. Later, he put forth his theory about gravity. Gravity is the invisible force that causes things to fall down. It is always acting and never ceases.

142. Gregor Mendel

Johann Gregor Mendel was a botanist who laid down the foundations of the science of genetics. Born in Czechoslovakia, he left the university to join a monastery and become a priest called Gregor.

There Mendel tended the garden and conducted extensive experiments with pea pod plants, tracking some 28,000 individual plants over several years and focusing his attention on seven basic characteristics of the plants. In his experiments, Mendel crossed peas of different varieties — tall, short, various seed shapes and colours, etc. — and kept detailed records of how these characteristics were seen or vanished in subsequent generations.

Mendel revealed the basic laws of heredity based on his observation. Though his research was ignored at the time but today his research has laid down the foundation for modern genetics.

143. Guglilmo Marconi

The Italian inventor and physicist, Guglielmo Marconi had developed the practical wireless telegraphy.

Marconi was convinced that communication among people was possible via wireless radio signaling. He started conducting experimen in 1895 at his father's home, where he was soon able to send signals over one and a hal miles. He also experimented with reflectors around the aerial in order to concentrate the radiated electrical energy into a beam.

Later, he successfully demonstrated his system's ability to transmit radio signals at various places including across the Atlantic.

144. Guitar – Antonio Torres

Antonio de Torres Jurado was a Spanish guitarist who is considered the most important Spanish guitar maker of the 19th century. He designed the first recognisable modern classical guitars. Most acoustic guitars in use today are derivatives of his designs.

Around 1842, Torres learnt how to make guitars and soon opened his guitar shop. Torres knew that the soundboard was the key to make excellent guitars. To increase a guitar's volume, he made his guitars not only larger but also fitted them with thinner, hence lighter soundboards that were arched in both directions.

Soon, the guitars Torres made were being copied worldwide for they had a clear, balanced, firm and a rounded tone.

145. Gyroplane – Louis and Jacques Breguet

Louis Charles Breguet was a French aircraft designer and builder. In 1905, with his brother Jacques and under the guidance of Charles Richet, he began work on a gyroplane that had flexible wings. This aircraft had an uncovered steel framework with a seat for the pilot. The gyroscope had four arms extending from its central steel framework each having a four-bladed rotors. Two among these rotors moved clockwise and the other two anti-clockwise. It achieved the first ascent of a vertical-flight aircraft with a pilot onboard in 1907. He built his first fixed-wing aircraft, the *Breguet Type I* in 1909 and flew it successfully.

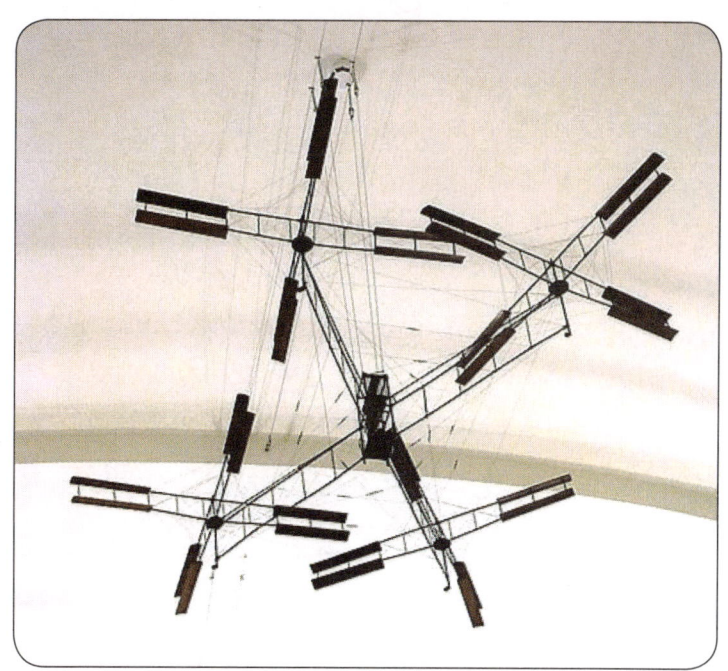

146. Gyroscope – Jean Bernard Leon Foucault

Gyroscope is a device that contains a rapidly spinning wheel or circulating beam of light. It is used to detect the deviation of an object from its desired orientation. It was invented by Jean Bernard Leon Foucault, a French scientist. The device he invented was a wheel or a rotor that was mounted in a set of rings that allowed it to move rapidly in any direction. Using this tool, Leon Foucault studied the Earth's rotation.

Today, gyroscope is used in compasses and in automatic pilots in ships and aircrafts, in the steering mechanisms of torpedoes and even in space launch vehicles.

147. Hair Dryer – Alexander F. Godefroy

Alexander F. Godefroy had invented the first hot air-blast hair dryer, probably in 1890. He created his first model of the hair dryer in his salon in France. Did you know that men and women dried their hair using a vacuum cleaner before the invention of the hair drier! Infact, Alexander had taken inspiration from the vacuum cleaner himself. His hair dryer was large and women had to sit underneath it so that their hair could be dried. A hood made of plastic came down on a person's head. Then, hot air was blown through tiny holes that were inside the dome to dry a person's hair.

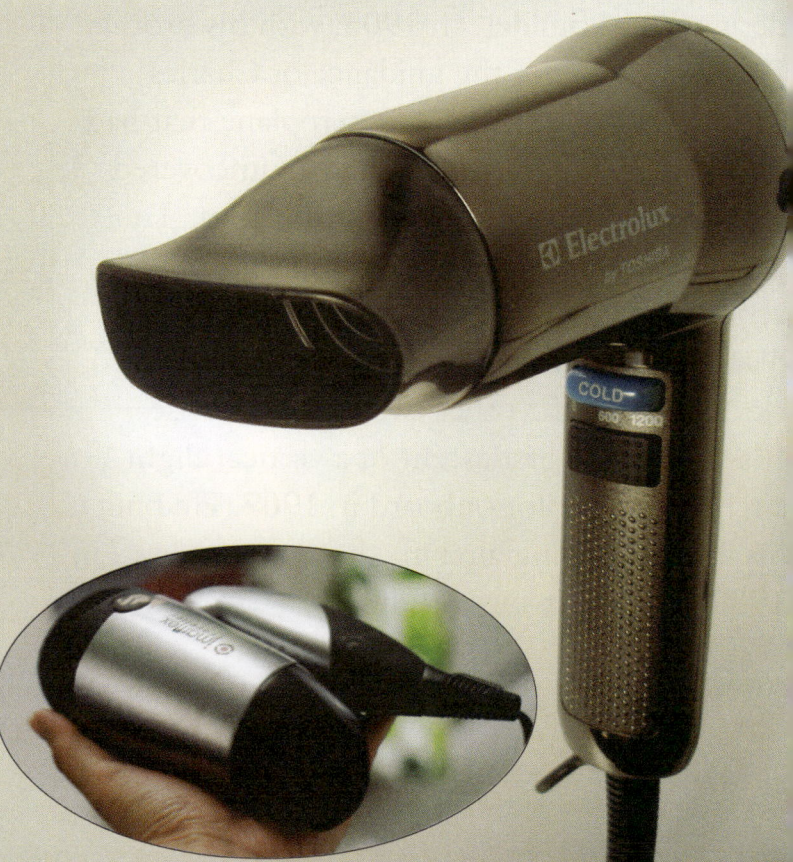

148. Hand-held Metal Detector – Gerhard Fisher

In the 1920s, there was a demand for a device that could detect metal. Among many others, Gerhard Fisher too tried inventing such a device. Already, he had developed a system of radio direction-finding which was used in navigation. Though the system worked very well, Fisher noticed that there were oddities in areas where the terrain contained ore-bearing rocks. He reasoned that if a radio beam could be distorted by metal, then was it not possible that a machine could also detect metal using a search coil resonating at a radio frequency. Based on this idea, he made his hand-held metal detector which was a success.

149. Helicopter – Igor Sikorsky

Igor Sikorsky is considered to be the "father" of helicopters because he had designed and invented the first helicopter on whose design the future helicopters were made. He began working on the helicopters in 1910. By 1940, he had succeeded in making VS-300, the model for all modern single-rotor helicopters. This helicopter had a main lifting engine and an engine mounted at the rear which gave the pilot directional control.

Igor Sikorsky's helicopters had the control to fly safely forwards and backwards, up and down, and sideways.

150. Hole Punch – C.B. Brooks

A hole punch or a paper puncher is a common office tool that is used to create holes in sheets of paper in order that the sheets could be collected in a folder. The first hole punch was invented by Charles Brooke in 1893. He called it the ticket punch. It had two metal pieces attached together with the help of a spring. At the bottom of the lower metal piece was an attached receptable where the round pieces of the waste paper were collected. It was to prevent littering of the waste paper.

This invention was greatly useful and was similar to the modern day hole punches.

151. Hologram – Dennis Gabor

Around 1947, Scientist Dennis Gabor developed the theory of holography while working to improve the resolution of an electron microscope.

A hologram is an image made by exposing film to the interference pattern created when two laser light sources shine on an object. A hologram is a 3-D image that is captured on a 2-D surface. Most people think of a hologram as a three-dimensional image of an object. For his work, Dennis Gabor won the Nobel Prize for physics in 1971.

152. Hot Air Balloon
– Joseph-Michel & Jacques-Etienne Montgolfier

The hot air balloon is the oldest method using which man has taken flight. It constitutes of a large bag which is filled with hot air. Beneath this bag is a wicker basket to carry passengers and an open flame heat source. Joseph-Michel and Jacques-Étienne Montgolfier were pioneers of the hot air balloon.

In 1782, they discovered that heated air when collected inside a large lightweight paper bag caused the bag to rise. Inspired, they publicly demonstrated a hot air balloon they had made. The balloon rose into the air about 3,000 feet, remained there for 10 minutes before settling on the ground more than a mile away. They flew more hot air balloons, sometimes manned, and were successful each time.

153. Hovercraft – Christopher Sydney Cockerell

A hovercraft, a unique vehicle, is supported on a cushion of air supplied by a powered fan mounted on the craft. A hovercraft can move both on water and on land. It was invented by Christopher Sydney Cockerell, British scientist and inventor, in 1955.

Cockerell wanted to make a vehicle that could move over the water surface floating over a layer of air. Doing so would decrease the friction between the vehicle and the water. He experimented by placing a smaller can inside a larger can and used a hairdryer to blow air into them. The smaller can hovered a few inches above the bottom of the larger can as the downward thrust produced was greater. He made the hovercraft based on this idea.

154. Hula Hoop – Richard Knerr & Arthur "Spud" Melin

A hula hoop is a toy hoop that is swirled around the waist, neck and limbs. It was during the early 1800s that British sailors saw the hula dancing on the Hawaiian Islands. Although hoops have always been there in one form or the other, this was something else altogether.

However, the modern Hula Hoop was invented by Richard Kerr and Arthur "Spud" Melin in 1950s. They ran a company called Wham-O where they made the modern plastic hoop which was marked as an 'exercising tool'. In no time, the hoops became popular and remain so even today.

155. Hydraulic Crane – William George Armstrong

A hydraulic crane is a machine for raising and lowering loads. It was invented by William George Armstrong, a British industrialist and engineer. The crane he had invented was dependent for power on water mains or reservoirs. These machines though look simple are very powerful and can fulfill difficult tasks. A hydraulic crane works on a simple principle where force is passed on from one point to another through a fluid. In it, a piston pushes down on the oil, the oil then transmits all the force onto another piston which is then driven up. This is the simple mechanism of the working of the hydraulic cranes.

156. Hydraulic Press – Joseph Barmah

A hydraulic press is a mechanical machine which is used for lifting or compressing large objects. It was invented by Joseph Barmah in 1795. Through this invention, Barmah had given birth to a whole new class of machines. In a hydraulic press, the level of pressure remains contant. This machine is widely used in the manufacturing industry where a large amount of force is required to manufacture metals. Did you know that a hydraulic press can exert a pressure ranging from 1 ton to 10,000 tons or more!

157. Hydrofoil Boat
– Alexander G. Bell & Casey Baldwin

A hydrofoil boat is a vessel that uses foils mounted under the hull to lift the hull above the water. Simply put it is a large boat which gets raised partly out of water when it moves at higher speeds. Alexander Graham Bell and Casey Baldwin had co-invented the hydrofoil boat in 1908.

The American Department of War had called for proposals to build submarine chasers in the form of motorboats. However, Bell argued that a hydrofoil boat was the better option as it could move smoothy over mine infested bay as well as a pond as it barely touched the water. After their first ride, Baldwin described the experience as 'smooth flying'.

158. Ice cream – Jacob Fussell

Ice cream is a frozen dessert usually made from dairy products such as milk and cream and often combined with fruits or other ingredients and flavours. Most varieties contain sugar, although some are made with other sweeteners. To make an ice cream, a mixture of chosen ingredients is stirred slowly while cooling it in order to incorporate air and to prevent large ice crystals from forming. The result is a smoothly textured semi-solid foam that is malleable and can be scooped.

Jacob Fussell is known as the "Father of the Ice Cream Industry" largely because he opened the first ice cream factory in the U.S. in Baltimore in 1851. An unstable demand for his dairy products often left him with a surplus of cream, which he made into ice cream.

159. Infrared Radiation – William Herschel

The electromagnetic spectrum spans a wide range of wavelengths from very short wavelength and highly energetic gamma rays to very long wavelength and low-energy radio waves. Only a small portion of the spectrum is visible. Infrared light part of the spectrum cannot be seen by us.

Infrared radiation was discovered by William Herschel in 1800. While studying the heating effect of different colours of light using a prism and a thermometer, he noticed that the heating effect got stronger as he went from the blue end of the spectrum to the red. Suddenly, he moved the thermometer beyond the visible red end and found that the heating effect was even greater. That was the infrared radiation.

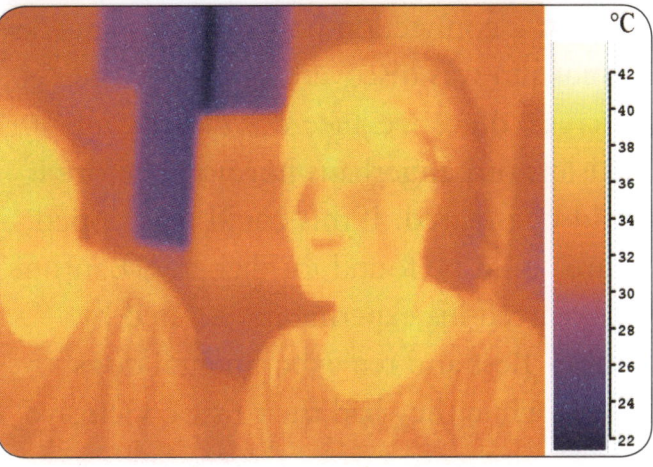

160. Instant Photography – Edwin Herbert Land

Edwin Herbert Land was an American inventor and physicist whose one-step process for developing and printing photographs culminated in a revolution in photography unparalleled since the advent of the roll film.

As a student, he became interested in polarized light where all rays are aligned in the same plane. He experimented and succeeded in 1932 in aligning submicroscopic crystals of iodoquinine sulfate and embedding them in a sheet of plastic.

He then thought of various uses for the Polaroid material including an instantaneous developing film. In 1947, he demonstrated a camera known as the Polaroid Land Camera that produced a finished print in 60 seconds. In no time, Land's Polaroid Cameras became popular the world over.

161. Insulin – Frederick Banting & Charles Best

Insulin, a hormone produced in our pancreas, was isolated by Dr Fredrick Banting and Charles Best.

In 1920, Canadian surgeon Frederick Banting learnt about glucose metabolism and diabetes. He then decided to not only find the cause but a treatment for diabetes. By now, a connection between the pancreas and insulin was discovered whereby the pancreas' digestive juice was destroying the islets of Langerhans hormone before it could be isolated. If this could be stopped, a cure could be found for diabetes. Banting then started his experiments assisted by Charles Best and ten experimental dogs. After a while they had their first conclusive results when they gave extracted insulin to diabetic dogs and their abnormally high blood sugars were lowered. They conducted various experiments with similar results.

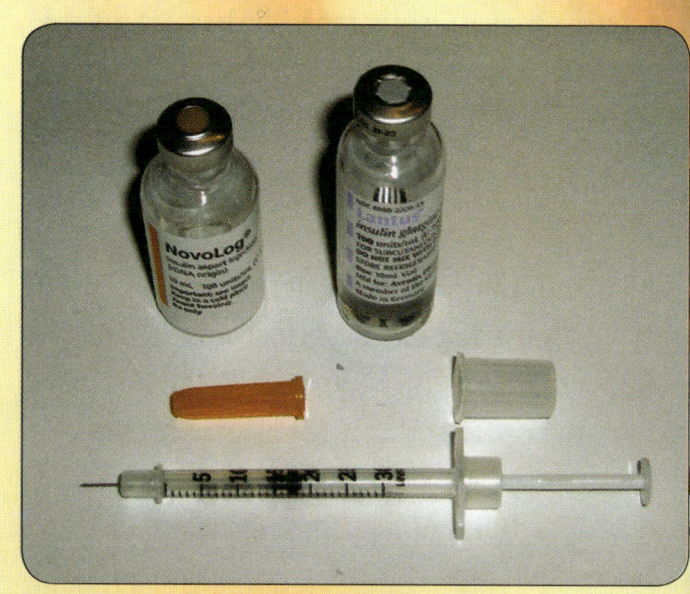

162. Integrated Circuit
– Jack Kilby & Robert Noyce

The integrated circuit was invented by two separate inventors, unaware of each other's activities, at about the same time. An integrated circuit is an electronic circuit that contains many interconnected transistors and other components. It is made on a small rectangle which is cut from a silicon wafer.

Jack Kilby, an engineer with a background in ceramic-based silk screen circuit boards started working on his integrated circuit in 1958. At about the same time, engineer Robert Noyce too had begun making a similar circuit. Kilby used germanium and Noyce used silicon for the semiconductor material. However, it was Robert Noyce who made his circuit first.

163. Integrated Mail System
Dr V.A. Shiva Ayyadurai

In 1978, V.A. Shiva Ayyadurai developed a computer program which replicated the features of the interoffice, inter-organizational paper mail system. He named his program 'EMAIL'.

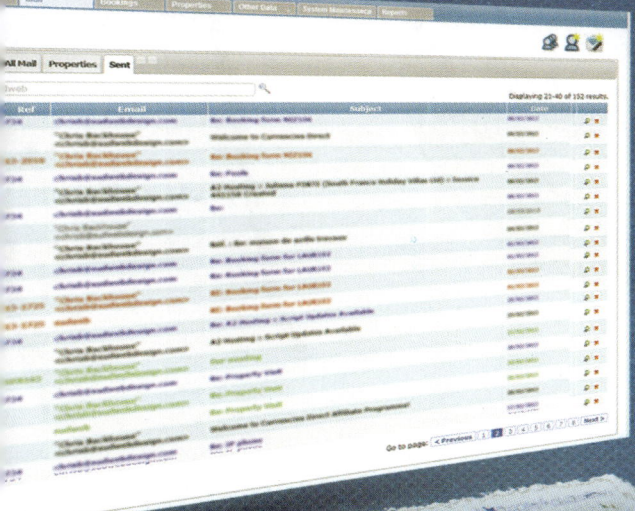

In 1978, Shiva was asked at the University of Medicine and Dentistry to translate the paper-based interoffice communication system to an electronic communication system. Shiva was confident of developing a simple system that anyone could use.

The essential features of his system included "Inbox", "Outbox", "Drafts", "Memo" "Attachments", "Folders", "Compose", "Forward", "Reply", "Address Book", "Groups". This sufficiently simple interface made his software to send and receive mails stand out.

164. Internet – J.C.R. Licklider

The Internet is a global system of interconnected computer networks that serves several billion users worldwide. It is a network of networks that consists of millions of private, public, academic, business and government networks that are linked by a broad array of electronic and wireless networking technologies. It offers the widest range of information resources and services.

In 1962, Dr Joseph Carl Robnett Licklider formulated the earliest ideas of global networking. His original ideas outlined many features the internet offers today. When he first thought of the internet, computers merely speeded up computations. But he wanted to use the computer network to communicate with others.

165. Iron – Henry W. Seely

Hand irons are devices used to press garments. Irons have been of various kinds, some were heated directly by gas flame or heated over stove but today the irons are heated by electricity. The electric irons were invented by Henry W. Seely in 1882. The iron that he had created was about 15 pounds in weight. It also took a long time to warm up. He called the first iron as 'electric flatiron'. After this invention, several irons were invented and these used carbon arc to heat the iron.

166. Ironing Board – Sarah Boone

Sarah Boone, an African American woman had invented the ironing board. The ironing board she had designed was effective in ironing the sleeves and bodice of ladies' garments. She said that the purpose of her invention was "to produce a cheap, simple, convenient and highly effective device to iron ladies garments." The board she had created was very narrow and curved, the size and fit of a sleeve and it was reversible, making it easy to iron both sides of a sleeve. Before she had invented the ironing board, most people ironed clothes using a board of wood that rested across a pair of chairs or tables.

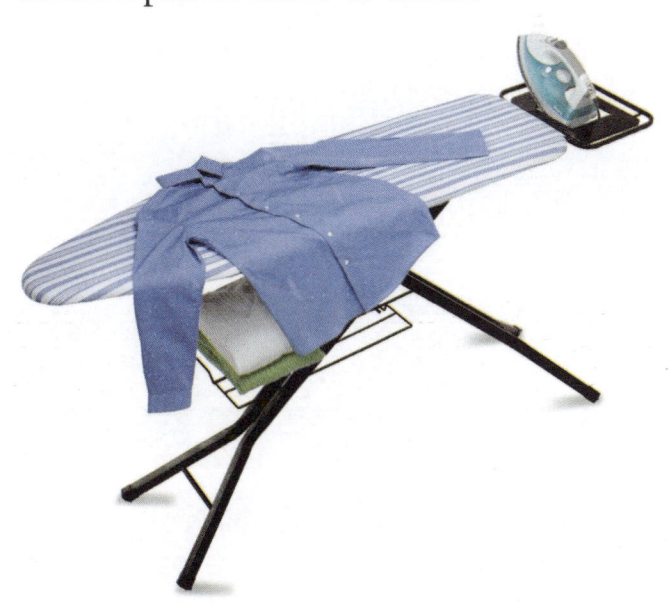

167. Issac Newton

Isaac Newton is among the most important scientists in the world. He is credited with developing the theory of gravity, the laws of motion, a new branch of mathematics called calculus and the reflecting telescope. He was born in Woolsthorpe, England on January 4, 1643.

In 1661, Isaac attended college at Cambridge and later taught as professor of mathematics there. During 1665 to 1667, he developed his theories on calculus, gravity and the laws of motion. In 1687, Newton published his most important work called *Mathematical Principals of Natural Philosophy* where he described the three laws of motion as well as the law of universal gravity. This work defined the principles of modern physics.

168. Jacuzzi – Roy Jacuzzi

Roy Jacuzzi invented the world's first whirlpool bath, known as the Roman, in 1968. This bathtub was the first self-contained, fully integrated bath experience with jets incorporated into the sides of the tub. Each jet contained a venturi, a vented constriction near its opening that injected air into the water. Sensing that Americans were emphasizing on health, fitness and leisure activities, Roy peddled his invention at county fairs and trade shows. While his family members looked on with both surprise and delight, Roy slowly – and nearly single-handedly – created a brand new industry.

169. Jagdish Chandra Bose

Sir Jagdish Chandra Bose, a prominent Indian scientist, proved through experimentation that plants were also sensitive to heat, cold, light, noise and various other external stimuli. Bose created a sophisticated instrument called Crescograph which could record and observe the minute responses of plants against external stimulants. This instrument magnified the motion of plant tissues to about 10,000 times!

Jagdish Chandra Bose was born on November 30, 1858 in Bangladesh. He attended Cambridge and earned his B.Sc degree after studying physics at Calcutta University.

170. James Watson

James Dewey Watson was an American geneticist and biophysicist. He did decisive work in the discovery of the molecular structure of DNA, the hereditary material associated with the transmission of genetic information. He shared the Nobel Prize for the discovery with Francis Crick and Maurice Wilkins in 1962.

He was born in 1928 in Chicago, Illinois. He gained worldwide fame as the co-author along with Francis Crick of four scientific papers that laid down the double helical structure of deoxyribonucleic acid (DNA).

During the 1960s, Watson also became an author with books like, *Molendor Biology of the Gene* and *The Double Helix*.

171. James Watt

James Watt was born in Greenock in 1736 to a prosperous shipwright. Watt initially worked as a maker of mathematical instruments but soon became interested in steam engines.

The first working steam engines called the Newcomen engines were pumping water from mines all over the country since 1698. Around 1764, Watt while repairing a Newcomen engine realised that it was hopelessly inefficient and thought to improve it. He designed a separate condensing chamber for the steam engine that prevented enormous losses of steam.

Soon, this improved steam engine made by Watt became popular. Did you know that a unit of measurement of electrical and mechanical power 'watt' is named after him!

172. Jane Goodall

Jane Goodall grew up in London, loving animals. She dreamt of someday going to Africa to see chimpanzees.

Jane saved money as she grew up to go to Africa. At 23, Jane finally had enough money to visit a friend in Kenya. There, British archaeologist Louis Leakey offered her a job to study chimpanzees. Jane took the offer and moved to Tanzania.

Lacking any formal training, she began studying chimpanzees in 1960 and spent the next forty years doing so. She discovered that chimpanzees like humans used tools like grass and twigs to dig out termites. Secondly, she saw that the chimpanzees also ate meat and that they too showed emotions. Jane won many awards for her work.

173. Jean Piaget

Jean Piaget was a Swiss psychologist who is known for conducting a systematic study of the acquisition of understanding in children. Born in 1896 in Neuchâtel, Switzerland, Piaget showed an early interest in biology and the natural world.

Piaget investigated the methods by which children learn about the world. He based his conclusions about child development on his observations and conversations with his own as well as other children. By asking them ingenious and revealing questions about simple problems he had devised, he shaped a picture of their way of viewing the world by analyzing their mistaken responses. He then forumalted an outstandingly, well-articulated and integrated theory of cognitive development.

He went on to write 70 books and more than 100 articles about human psychology.

174. Jet Engine – Henri Coanda

Henri Marie Coanda was a Romanian inventor, aerodynamics pioneer and builder of an experimental aircraft, *the Coanda-1910* described by Coanda in the mid-1950s as the world's first jet.

In 1910, he graduated at the head of the first class of aeronautical engineers. The same year, he designed and built an aircraft known as the Coanda-1910, which he displayed publicly at the second International Aeronautic Salon in Paris the same year. The plane used a 4-cylinder piston engine to power a rotary compressor which was intended to propel the craft by a combination of suction at the front and airflow out from the rear instead of using a propeller.

175. Jet Engine (turbo jet) – Hans Von Ohain

Dr Hans von Ohain is considered the designer of the first operational turbojet engine. He was also the first to fly his jet propelled engine in 1941.

While working as junior assistant to Hugo Von Pohl, director of a prestigious university, Ohain got an opportunity to make a new airplane propulsion design for German aircraft builder Ernst Heinkel. During this time, Ohain was investigating a new type of aircraft engine that did not require a propeller. He worked hard and designed and constructed a small aircraft based on his new propulsion system - the

Heinkel He178. He flew it for the first time on August 27, 1939. This was the first flight of a jet-powered airplane. Ohain later improved his design.

176. Jet Ski – Clayton Jacobsen

A jet-ski is a relatively recent but immensely popular addition to summertime leisure activities. It is a fast-paced recreation on the open water without the expense of a boat.

Clayton Jacobson, a banker from Arizona was also a dirt bike rider. He wanted to take his hobby of dirt bike riding to water as well. Although fiberglass-bodied propellor-driven "water scooters" were part of the European recreation since 1950s, Clayton's variation was powered by an internal pump-jet and was made of aluminum. Jacobson made his first prototype jet-ski in 1965. A year later, he made a second prototype jet-ski made of fiberglass.

His design had a round hull as opposed to the more conventional V-shaped hull, strakes, a narrow body and a high length-to-beam ratio.

177. Jigsaw Puzzle – John Spilsbury

A jigsaw puzzle is a tiling puzzle. It is also called a picture puzzle. It has irregularly cut pieces of cardboard or anything else that forms the complete picture when all the pieces are fitted together. Each piece of the puzzle usually has a small part of a picture on it.

The jigsaw puzzles were invented by Englishman John Spilsbury in 1767. He was an engraver and a mapmaker. Did you know that the first jigsaw puzzle was a map of the world! In order to make the first jigsaw puzzle, Spilsbury attached a map to a piece of wood and then cut out each country. His jigsaw puzzle was used to teach students geography.

178. Johannes Gutenberg

Johannes Gutenberg invented the printing press. Before the printing press, making a book was a laborious process.

Johannes Gutenberg was born in Mainz, Germany around 1398. In 1450, using some of the available technologies and devising some of his own, he invented the printing press. One key idea he came up with was not to use wooden blocks to press ink onto paper. He instead used moveable metal pieces to quickly create pages. With some further inventions in the printing process, pages were printed more rapidly. He became extremely popular when he printed the Gutenberg Bible and made Bible available to everyone!

179. Johannes Kepler

Johannes Kepler is remembered for his contribution in astronomy. A great mathematician and astrologer, he gave the three laws on planetary motion.

Johannes Kepler was born on December 27, 1571 in Swabia, in southwest Germany. Despite crippled hands and a weak eyesight, Kepler joined the University of Tuebingen in 1589 to study philosophy and theology.

He excelled in mathematics and was a skilled astrologer. In 1600, he met great mathematician and court astronomer, Tycho Brahe in Prague and became his assistant. Together, they worked on planets. In 1601, he succeeded Brahe as imperial mathematician. Then, in 1609 he published his first two laws on planetary motion. In 1619, he published his third law. All his life, he resolutely made discoveries to understand the universe.

180. John Dalton

John Dalton, British chemist, meteorologist and physicist was renowned for formulating the modern atomic theory. He was also the first person to record colour blindness.

Dalton was born in Cumberland, England in 1766. From a young age, Dalton was interested in mathematics and meteorology.

In 1794, John joined the Manchester Literary and Philosophical Society. Soon, he presented his first paper on "Extraordinary facts relating to the vision of colours". He explained that the shortage in colour perception was caused by the discolouration of the liquid medium of the eyeball.

Dalton's greatest interest was in meteorology and he maintained daily records of local temperature, wind, humidity and atmospheric pressure using instruments that he had made himself. In 1803, he published 'Dalton's law.' He also calculated atomic weights of elements. John Dalton's Atomic Theory which has relatively remained unchanged, has laid down the foundations of current science.

181. Jukebox – Louis Glass

Often in a restaurant, in order to listen to a song, one flips a coin into a slot in a machine, chooses a song and it gets played. It is however interesting how these machines came into being. One of the earliest known jukeboxes was the Nickel-in-the-Slot machine. It was invented by Louis Glass and William S. Arnold in 1889. They had placed a coin-operated Edison cylinder phonograph in the Palais Royale Saloon in San Francisco. It was an Edison Class M Electric Phonograph in an oak cabinet that was refitted with a coin mechanism. Did you know that this machine had no amplification and patrons had to listen to the music using one of four listening tubes!

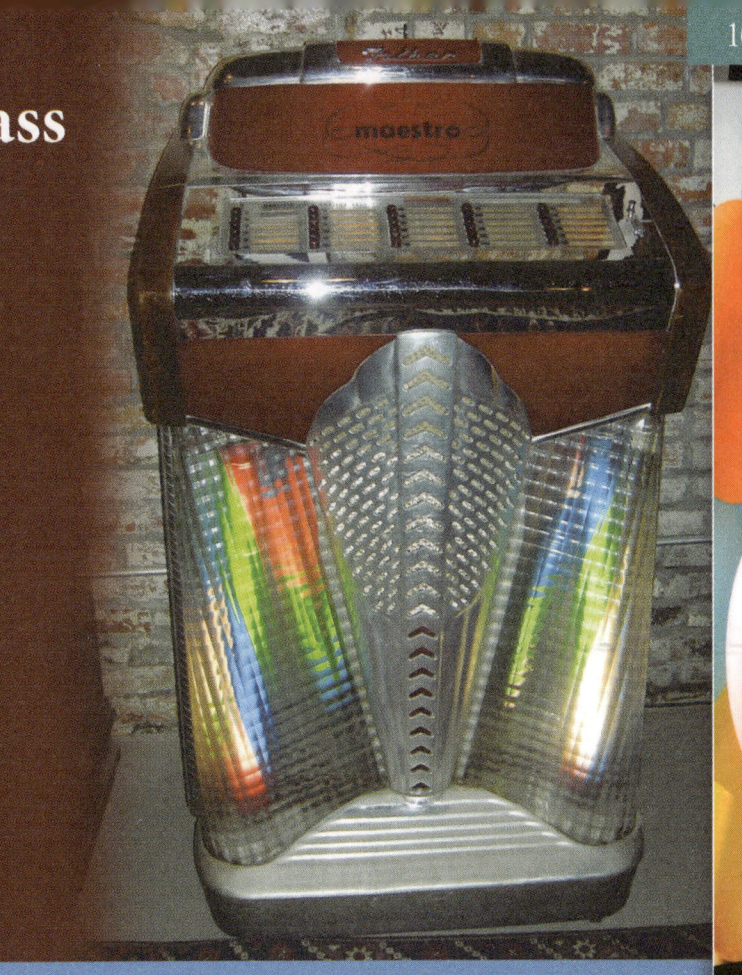

182. Kaleidoscope – Sir David Brewster

The kaleidoscope was invented by Scottish scientist, Sir David Brewster. He named kaleidoscope after three Greek words, where 'kalos' means beautiful, 'eidos' means form and 'scopos' means watcher. So, kaleidoscope means the 'beautiful form watcher'.

Brewster's kaleidoscope was a tube containing loose pieces of coloured glass and other pretty objects, reflected by mirrors or glass lenses set at angles that created patterns when viewed through one end of the tube. A mirror set at 60 degrees will generate a pattern of six regular sectors. A mirror angle at 45 degrees will make eight equal sectors and so on.

183. Karl Benz

In 1885, German mechanical engineer, Karl Benz designed and built the world's first practical automobile to be powered by an internal-combustion engine. Benz built his first four-wheeled car in 1891 after making a three-wheeled vehicle. In 1900, he opened the Benz & Company, which went on to become the world's largest manufacturer of automobiles.

Karl Friedrich Benz was born in 1844 in Baden Muehlburg, Germany. After completing his studies, he founded his first company the "Iron Foundry and Machine Shop" with partner August Ritter in 1871. This company was a supplier of building materials.

After a while, Benz began his work on a two-stroke engine and later on a motor carriage with a four-stroke engine. Benz designed its engine with 958cc, 0.75hp and the body for the three-wheel vehicle with an electric ignition, differential gears and water-cooling. The first gas-fuelled car was driven in Mannheim in 1885. It was in July 1886 that he began selling his automobiles.

184. Karl Landsteiner

Karl Landsteiner was an Austrian-born American immunologist, physician and pathologist. He was awarded the Nobel Prize in 1930 for detecting the major blood groups.

Born in 1868 in Vienna, Karl started studying medicine when he was merely seventeen. After acquiring a degree in medicine, he decided to do research in medicine. During his research, he identified different structures in human blood types which led him to identify different blood groups A, B and C. The C blood group later became O. A year later, he identified a fourth blood group AB. His discovery thus revolutionized the process of blood transfusion.

185. Kelvin Scale – Lord Kelvin

Lord Kelvin had invented the Kelvin scale in 1848. This scale measures the ultimate extremes of hot and cold. It is the most important scale used in science. In the 19th century, scientists were conducting researches to find the lowest possible temperature. The Kelvin scale uses the same units as the Celcius scale but it starts at ABSOLUTE ZERO, the temperature at which everything including air freezes. Absolute zero is at 0° K which is - 273°C. Did you know that the Kelvin scale is based on the energy content rather than on arbitrary temperature values! According to this scale, water freezes at 273.15 Kelvin and boils at 373.15 Kelvin.

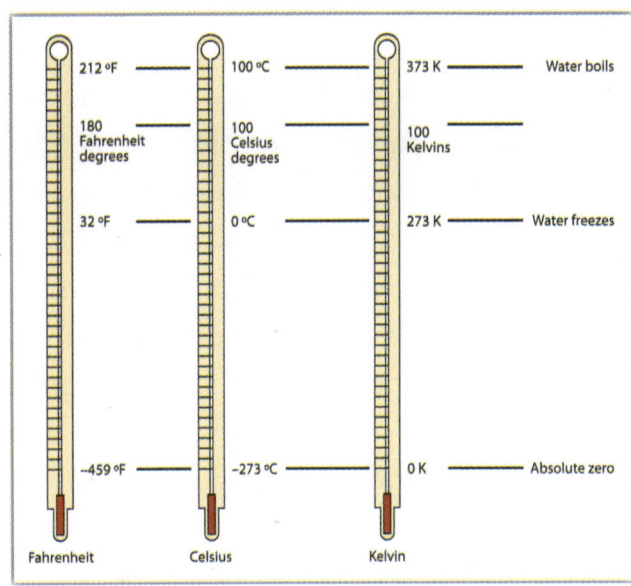

186. Kevlar – Stephanie Kwolek

Stephanie Kwolek, famous woman inventor and scientist, wanted to study medicine. After completing her studies, she took a temporary research position with DuPont. During her research, she discovered long molecule chains at low temperatures. In 1971, she discovered a liquid crystalline polymer solution, later called Kevlar. It has extreme strength and is five times as strong as steel.

Kevlar® is resistant to wear, corrosion and flames and it is the main ingredient in the production of bulletproof vests which have saved countless lives. It is used in products including parachutes, skis, safety helmets and suspension cable bridges.

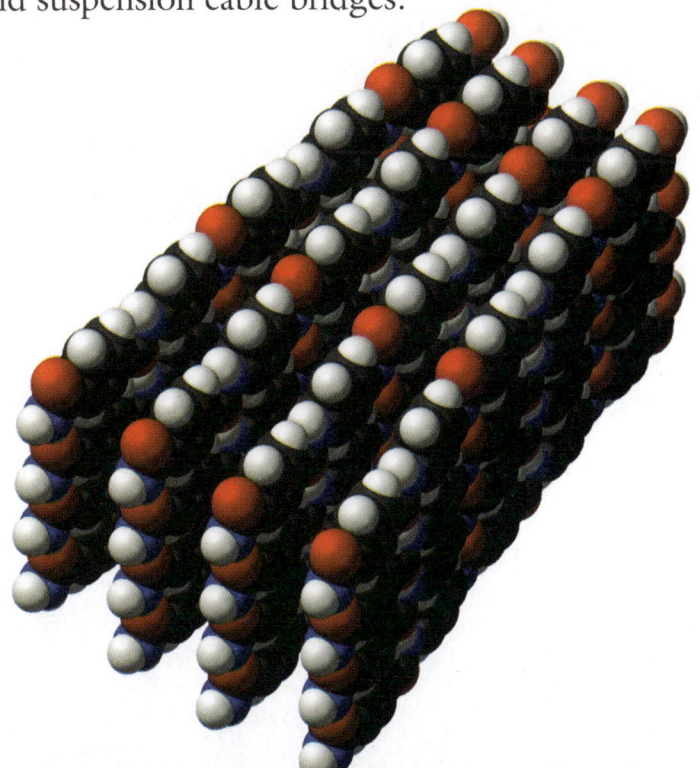

187. Knapsack Parachute – Gleb Kotelnikov

Gleb Yevgeniyevich Kotelnikov was the Russian-Soviet inventor of the knapsack parachute and braking parachute.

In 1894, Kotelnikov graduated from the Kiev Military School and started thinking of a device to make landing safe. Also, the death of a talented pilot which had left him shocked motivated him to save other lives. In 1911, he created his first parachute RK-1. It was a success when he tested it. Later, he modified his parachute design and made new models, including RK-2 with a softer knapsack, RK-3 and a few cargo parachutes. All of these parachutes were used by the Soviet Air Force.

188. Laser – Gordon Gould

Gordon Gould had first coined the word laser after he had invented the laser. Laser is any device that produces a light which is more powerful than ordinary light. It is so because all its rays move together and hence these can be focused in a narrow beam. Do you know that most lasers are used in industrial, commercial and medical applications!

Gould was a doctoral student at Columbia University under Charles Townes, the inventor of the maser. Gordon made his optical laser in 1958. He did so while pursuing his doctorate in optical and microwave spectroscopy.

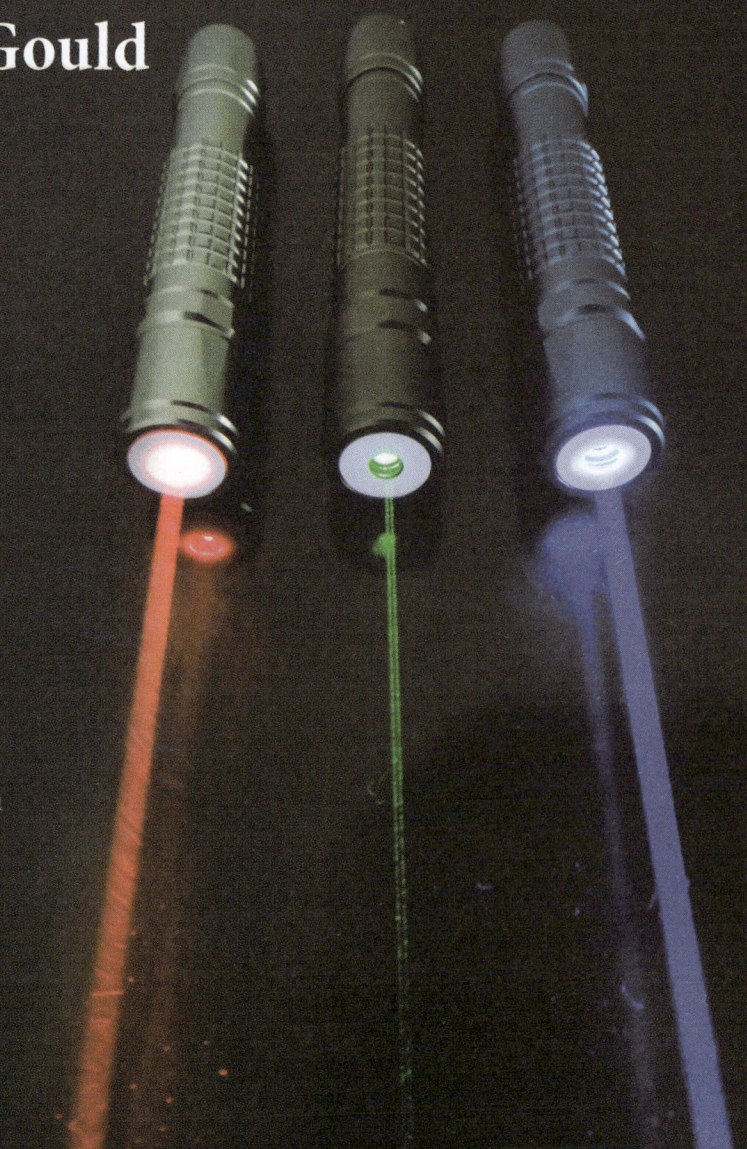

189. Laser Disc – David Paul Gregg

An optical or laser disk is a plastic-coated, transparent disc that can store digital data. There are small dots in the surface of the disc that are read by a laser which scans the disc surface to access the data stored on the disc. The laser disc was first thought of and made by David Paul Gregg in 1958. A laser disc contains a high quality analog video. A single laser disc has a 30mm diameter and is made by combining two single sided aluminium discs which are layered in plastic.

190. Lava Lamp – Craven Walker

The mesmerizing light fixture, called the lava lamp, never fails to catch people's attention. It was invented by a Britiah accountant, Edward Craven Walker. One day, sitting at a certain pub, he saw a homemade egg timer crafted from a cocktail shaker filled with alien-looking liquids that were bubbling on a stove top. He decided to improve the design and to place a light bulb as the heat source.

He then paired two mutually insoluble liquids: one water-based, the other wax-based. A key ingredient he used was the solvent carbon tetrachloride to add weight to the wax. The heat source at the bottom of the lamp liquefied the waxy blob. Interestingly, lava lamps put people at ease.

191. Lawn Mower – Edwin Beard Budding

A lawn mower is used to cut grass in the lawn or garden. In 1830, Edwin Beard Budding invented "a new machinery for the purpose of cropping or shearing the vegetable surface of lawns, grass-plants and pleasure grounds". This was the world's first lawnmower. Budding was a mechanic who built and repaired machinery for textile mills. He first thought of making a lawn mower seeing the cross cutting machines that were used to finish woollen cloth. It was reel-type mower that had a series of blades arranged around a cylinder. Before the invention of the lawnmower, lawns were cut using a scythe.

192. La-Z-Boy Recliner – Edward Knabusch & Edwin Shoemaker

La-Z-boy recliner, an innovative chair design was invented in 1928. Cousins Edward Knabusch and Edwin Shoemaker used orange crates to design a wood slat outdoor folding chair - the first La-Z-Boy recliner. The chair they had made could adjust itself to a person's body as he sat up and when he leaned back. The cousins also found that the chair was very comfortable. Seeing a good business opportunity, the cousins left their jobs in 1927 and invested in their own furniture business. They opened the Floral City Furniture Company. Initially, the La-Z-Boys found it hard to buy buyers as these chairs were considered seasonal chairs. The cousins then designed a new La-Z-boy recliner, a huge success. And till today, the chair has lived up to its name.

193. LED – Nick Holonyak

Nick Holonyak invented the first III-V alloy visible light-emitting diodes (LEDs), today commonly found in applications ranging from traffic lights to consumer electronics.

Holonyak's research in optoelectronics has revolutionized the lighting, communications and entertainment industries. His work is responsible for the technology used to develop lasers in CD and DVD players, the ability to transmit information over the internet and applications in replacing conventional lighting with LEDs. Holonyak also created the basic electronic element of household light dimmer switches.

194. Leonardo da Vinci

Leonardo da Vinci was an artist, scientist and inventor during the Italian Renaissance. He is considered among the most talented and intelligent people of all time. Though he is most well-known for his famous paintings, yet he had done more than that. Leonardo's drawings and sketches in his journals vary from studies of anatomy to scientific sketches.

He made his journals in his pursuit of scientific knowledge. In his journals, he drew designs of hand gliders, helicopters, war machines, musical instruments, various pumps and more. When studying human anatomy, he made drawings of muscles, tendons and the heart, arms and other internal organs.

195. Letter Box – Philip Downing

Long before the letter box was invented, people went all the way to the post office to send their letters. However, Philip Downing changed that by inventing the letter box. The letter box he had created had a hinge on the door that closed to protect your mail from theives and weather.

Philip Downing's letter box featured an outer door and an inner safety door. When the outer door was opened, the safety door remained closed keeping the letters safe. When the outer door closed, the safety door would open so that the dropped letter would join the other letters in the box. This was the first letter box in the world.

196. Letterpress Printing – Johannes Gutenberg

Letterpress printing is the process that involves using movable wooden components with raised letters on them, dipped in ink to produce text or images when pressed onto paper. This type of printing existed before Johannes Gutenberg, invented the printing press. This invention revolutionzed the printing process as now books were mass produced in record time. He had invented a device that put individually cast, reusable metal letters in a frame, then inked and applied the letters with pressure to sheets of paper placed below. The first printed book was the "Gutenberg Bible" in 1455.

197. Levi Strauss

Levi Strauss is the inventor of the world's most famous jeans, Levi's. He was born in Bavaria, Germany but had moved to the United States in 1847. He first moved to New York and then to California. He made his fortune in the California Gold Rush as the maker of sturdy canvas pants that became famous for their durability. With further improvements in his pants based on the shortcoming hinted at by the miners, his pants became the best-selling products in his dry goods store.

To refine his pants further, he imported a fabric from Nîmes in France, dyed his pants blue and made his pants using the fabric. Later, he opened Levi Strauss & Company with Jacob Davis which went onto became one of the world's largest manufacturers of casual clothing in the world.

198. Lie Detector – John Larson

John Larson was the first person who had succeeded in making a lie detector machine in 1921, also called a polygraph machine.

This machine records several different body responses simultaneously as the individual is being questioned.

The theory behind this machine is that when a person lies, the lying causes a certain amount of stress that produces changes in his body. As different sensors are attached to the body and the questioning begins, the polygraph machine starts monitoring the changes in breathing, blood pressure, pulse and perspiration. All the changes in the individual's body are recorded on the graph paper.

199. Light Bulb – Thomas Alva Edison

Thomas Alva Edison was an American inventor. Among his greatest achievements was the development of a practical incandescent, electric light. Interestingly, he did not invent 'light bulb' but rather improved on a 50 year old idea. In 1879, using lower current electricity, a small carbonized filament of carbonized sewing thread and an improved vacuum inside the globe, he produced a reliable, long-lasting source of light. The light bulb he made burned for thirteen and a half hours.

Edison's eventual achievement was in inventing an electrical lighting system that made incandescent light practical, safe and economical. He lit up his Menlo Park Laboratory complex on December 1879 to demonstrate the incandescent light bulb.

200. Lighthouse

A lighthouse is a tower with a beacon light. It warns boats and ships about shallow waters, reefs and other dangers. It also guides boats and ships during stormy or foggy weather. The lighthouse of Alexandria and the Egyptian lighthouse Pharos are among the most famous lighthouses in antiquity. Did you know that the first lighhhouse towers were constructed along the Mediterranean coast around 660 B.C.!

Interestingly, in ancient times, lighthouses were used as entrance markers into ports rather than warning signal markers. In modern times, the construction of lighthouses began in the 18th century as new sea routes were established. But in recent times, due to the improvements in maritime navigation, the usage of lighthouses has decreased.

201. Lightening Rod – Benjamin Franklin

A lightening rod is a metal rod or wire fixed to an exposed part of a building or other tall structure to divert lightning harmlessly into the ground. During the 1700s, lightning was a major cause of fires.

Benjamin Franklin thought of a way to deflect lightening and prevent fires. The lightening rod he created was attached to the roof or outside wall of a building. One end of the rod looked up to the sky while the other end was connected to a electric cable that stretched down the side of a house to the ground. The end of the cable was buried at least ten feet underground. The rod attracted lightning and sent the charge into the ground. Did you know that copper and its alloys are the most commonly used materials to protect against lightening!

202. Lightning Switch – Samuel Face

Lightning Switch is a wireless and batteryless remote control switch technology. It was invented by Samuel Allen Face, Jr. It is used to control appliances. The lightning switch converts the mechanical force placed on the switch into an electrical current when an individual presses it. The lightning switch is based on the piezoelectricity where mechanical stress is used to generate electrical current.

203. Linoleum – Frederick Walton

In 1860, rubber manufacturer Fredrick Walton invented linoleum, floor and wall covering. Fredrick Walton invented linoleum as a cheap substitute to the more expensive Kamptulicon. Walton got the idea for his product by observing the surface of

dried oil produced by oxidized linseed oil on paints.

Linoleum is made of linseed oil, pigments, pine rosin and pine flour. It is made by oxidizing linseed oil and by adding other ingredients to form a thick mixture called linoleum cement. While experimenting, he discovered that linseed oil was unaffected by water, heat or oil unless it was burnt. This property made it more durable.

204. Liquid Helium – Heike Kamerlingh Onnes

Helium is a colourless, odourless noble gas. It has very low boiling and melting points. This gas is used in deep sea breathing systems and also to fill balloons. Heike Kamerlingh Onnes, a Dutch physicist and Nobel laureate, succeeded in transforming helium into its liquid form. It happened while he was exploring how materials behaved when cooled to nearly absolute zero by creating very low temperatures. It was then that he was able to liquefy Helium.

He succeeded in lowering the temperature to the boiling point of helium (-269 °C, 4.2 K). By reducing the pressure of the liquid helium, he achieved a temperature near 1.5 K, the coldest temperatures ever artificially created on Earth.

205. Long Distance Radio Transmission – Guglielmo Marconi

Guglielmo Marconi was a pioneer in the field of long distance radio transmission. He is often credited as the inventor of radio. Marconi did succeed in making the radio a commercial success.

He began experimenting after learning about Heinrich Hertz's discovery of radio waves in 1888. By 1895, he succeeded in transmitting electronic signals from his home to an antennae raised a mile away. After some struggle, his achievement was recognized.

By 1899, his company was providing wireless service between Britain and France. In 1901, he sent signals across the Atlantic and proved that radio waves followed the curvature of the Earth.

206. Long Lasting Alkaline Battery – Lewis Urry

Lewis Urry worked for the Eveready Battery Company in Toronto. At that time carbon-zinc batteries were in use. However, the company wanted to make long-lasting batteries.

Urry tested numerous materials before deciding that manganese dioxide and solid zinc worked well with alkaline substance as an electrolyte to conduct electricity. But there wasn't enough power. Then, Urry used powdered zinc and succeeded.

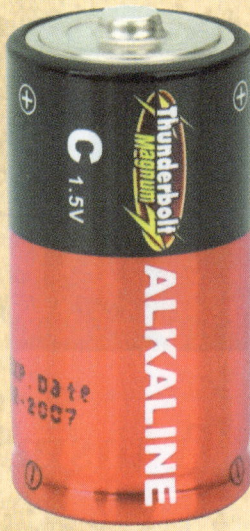

In order to convince his boss, he bought two battery-operated toy cars. He installed his alkaline battery in one and an ordinary battery in the other. The car with the alkaline battery went much farther than the other car. His boss was convinced and the long lasting battery called Energizer was mass produced.

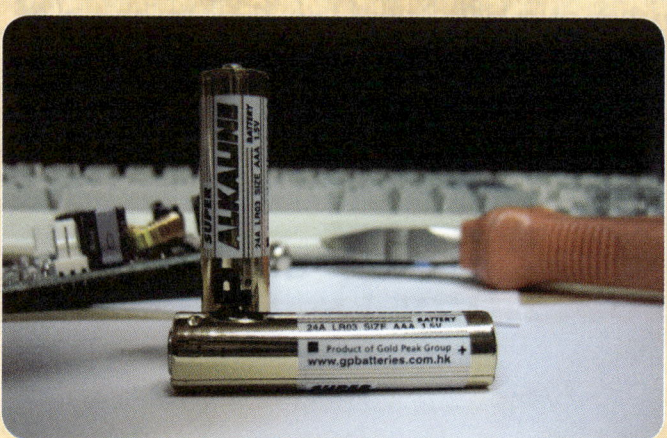

207. Lord Kelvin

Lord Kelvin was born as William Thomson in 1824 in Belfast. After studying in various universities, he became a professor of natural philosophy in Glasgow.

While there, he also created the first physics laboratory in Britain. However there was more to him. He was a pioneer in various fields including electromagnetism and thermodynamics. Together with Faraday, he introduced the concept of an electromagnetic field. In thermodynamics, he worked to put forth his idea of an absolute zero of temperature - the scale based on this is named after him. Despite everything he created, his main goal was to show the practical use of science. He was knighted in 1866.

208. Louis Braille

Louis Braille invented the Braille Language for the blind. Braille, an intelligent and curious child went blind at the age of three when he had an accident in his father's saddle shop.

A few years later, in 1819, he went to the National Institute for Blind Children. There, he soon learnt all that they taught. He now wanted to learn more. Then, he learnt of Captain Charles Barbier's system of sending signals secretly among soldiers. Braille improved this system. In this method, a blind person used a grooved plate and a stylus to punch dots in lines on a page. Also one needed to write from right to left and turn over the paper in order to read the punched holes that formed words.

The Braille system, as it came to be known, opened the world of knowledge to the blind.

209. Louis Pasture

Louis Pasteur was born in Dole, France in 1822. He was greatly interested in science.

Years later, he began investigating infectious diseases in order to find a cure for them. At that time, people believed that microbes like bacteria appeared from nowhere. Pasteur however proved that germs (i.e. bacteria) were living things that came from other living things.

Pasteur used his knowledge of germs to investigate how beverages such as wine and milk were spoiled by microbes. He found that heating liquids killed most of the microbes and allowed the beverages to last longer. This process became known as pasteurization.

He also went on to form a vaccine, which is a weak form of a disease, to create immunity against the disease. His discoveries have led to a great understanding of the microbes.

210. Magnifying Glass – Roger Bacon

A magnifying glass is a glass that produces an enlarged image of an object. It is a convex lens that is usually mounted in a frame with a handle. It is also called a hand lens. When looking through a magnifying lens, all the rays of light are concentrated at the centre which make an object appear large to us than it actually is.

The magnifying lens was first invented by Roger Bacon. During his life, he made many discoveries besides the magnifying glass. His invention was based on optics and he was inspired by the works of the Islamic scientist Alkindus and Alhazen.

211. Marie Curie

Marie Curie, born in 1867, was a bright student with a sharp memory. After graduating from high school, Marie joined Sorbonne University in France. In time, she earned her degree in Physics along with meeting Pierre Curie, a scientist and her future husband. They got married soon after.

After a while, Marie became fascinated by X-rays discovered by Wilhelm Roentgen and Henri Becquerel's discovery that the element uranium gave off certain rays. Curious, Marie experimented and examined a material called pitchblende. To her surprise, many rays emitted from pitchblende proving that there were undiscovered elements in it.

As Marie and her husband examined pitchblende, they found two new elements in it—polonium and radium. The Curies then coined the term 'radioactivity' to describe the elements that emitted strong rays. Together, they won the Noble Prize for their discovery in 1903.

In 1911, Marie won another Noble Prize, becoming the first woman to win two such awards.

212. Maritime Signal Flares – Martha Coston

Martha Coston had developed the rough sketches of signal flares that were drawn by her late husband. She later improved her husband's idea into an elaborate system of night flares. The use of the flares helped ships to communicate with each other even at night by sending signals. These flares were based on colour and pattern. With different colour combinations, these flares made communication between ships and ship and shore possible.

This system was first adopted by the US navy and was later adopted by various other countries. This system helped to save many lives on the sea and also was useful during battles.

213. Masking Tape – Richard Drew

Masking tape or sticky tape is a pressure-sensitive tape. It is made of a thin and easy-to-tear paper and an easily released pressure-sensitive adhesive. It is used mainly in painting to mask off the areas that are not meant to be painted.

The masking tape was invented in 1925 by Richard Drew. He thought of the masking tape seeing the auto-body workers becoming frustrated as they removed butcher paper from newly painted cars, which tore off some of the paint as well. In a masking tape, the key element is the adhesive which allows the tape to be easily removed without leaving behind any residue or damaging the surface on which it had been applied.

214. Max Planck

Max Karl Ernst Ludwig Planck was born in Kiel, Germany, on April 23, 1858. His fame rests on his formulation of the *quantum theory*. This theory revolutionized our understanding of atomic and subatomic processes. Planck won the Nobel Prize in Physics in 1918.

While studying, physics and mathematics, he became deeply impressed by the absolute nature of the law of conservation of energy. As a professor of theoretical physics at the Berlin University, Planck did his most luminous work. He studied thermodynamics in particular and examined the distribution of energy according to wavelength. Soon, he introduced the quanta of energy, a revolutionary idea which marked a turning point in the history of physics.

215. McDonalds – Ray Kroc

The McDonalds chain restaurants were first thought of by Ray Kroc, who was a salesman. In 1954, he received a large order of 8 multi-mixers from a restaurant in San Bernardino, California. Once there, Kroc learnt that the restaurant was run by two brothers Dick and Mac McDonald. He was left stunned seeing the efficiency by which the restaurant was run. He saw that the restaurant had limited items on its menu of burgers, fries and beverages. A limited menu allowed the brothers to focus on quality at every step.

Kroc then told the brothers of his vision of creating McDonald's restaurants all over the U.S. The brothers were interested. In 1955, Kroc founded the McDonald's Corporation and 5 years later bought the exclusive rights to the McDonald's name.

Ray Kroc thus build a restaurant system that would be famous for its food of consistently high quality and uniform methods of preparation. He wanted to serve food that would taste the same on every branch of the chain. And so he did, as the McDonalds chain of restaurants still follow the core McDonald's principles of quality, service, cleanliness and value.

216. Meccano – Frank Hornby

Mr Hornby, who had no formal training in engineering or design, created the best loved toys based on simple mechanics. He began making toys for his sons at his workshop at home. He made these toys by cutting pieces from metal sheets. The toys had interchangeable parts, including nuts and bolts, that could be fixed together to form a wide array of models from one set like cranes, trucks and even cars. Soon, he made these toys for commercial purposes.

"Mechanics Made Easy" went on sale in 1902. Each kit of toys had 16 parts to create 12 different models. In 1908, however, these toys were renamed Meccano. Today, the Meccano kits are sold worldwide.

217. Metal Hull Icebreaker – Mikhail Britnev

An icebreaker is a ship that is designed in such a manner whereby it breaks a channel through the frozen ice. It does so while moving or navigating through ice covered waters. The first predecessor of the modern icebreaker was designed and made by Mikhail Osipovich Britnev. He was a Russian shipowner and shipbuilder. He made the first metal-hull, steam powered icebreaker called *Pilot* in 1864.

Its bow was altered to give the ship maximum ice clearing capacity. As a result, the *Pilot* could easily climb over the ice and break it. With its rounded shape and strong metal hull, the *Pilot* had all the features present in modern icebreakers.

218. Micro-processor
– Gordon Moore & Robert Norton Noyce

A microprocessor is an integrated circuit. In simple words, it is the brain of a computer. It contains all the functions of the central processing unit of the computer. It does all the workings of the computer and also controls all its parts. Gordon Moore is credited with the invention of the microprocessor along with Robert Norton Noyce. Based on Moore's Law, Gordon made the microprocessor. Did you know that the first single chip microprocessor was made by Intel in Nov 1971!

219. Microscope – Hans Janssen

A microscope is an instrument using which one can see objects that are too small to be seen by the naked eye. The invention of the microscope opened new worlds before the humans. It is difficult to determine who had invented the first microscope. The earliest microscope included a tube attached to a plate, where the object to be magnified or seen was kept. At the other end of the tube, a lens which magnified the object was placed.

Do you know that the earliest microscope was used to see fleas and other small creatures! It is therefore that the first microscopes were also called "flea glasses".

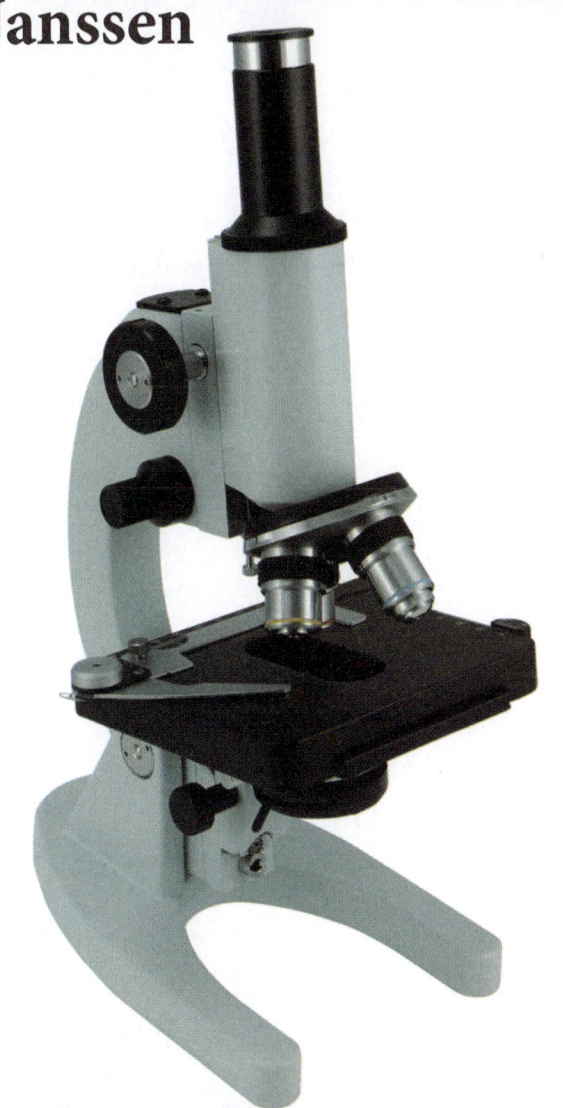

220. Microwave Oven – Percy Spencer

A microwave oven is a kitchen appliance that is used to heat food. It was invented by Percy Spencer, a well-known electronic genius, who was touring one of his laboratories, when he came and stood near a magnetron. A magnetron was a tube that drove a radar set.

Suddenly, he realized that the chocolate bar in his pocket had started to melt. He realized that the microwaves coming out of the magnetron had caused this. This incident gave him the idea for a microwave oven. The Raytheon Corporation produced the first commercial microwave oven in 1954. The first domestic microwave oven was produced in 1967.

221. Miner's Safety Lamp – Sir Humphery Davy

The Miner's safety lamp was invented by Sir Humphry Davy, a famous British inventor, a leading chemist and a philosopher in 1815. During that time, there were a number of accidents in mines due to the presence of methane gas which is highly flammable. Due to the open flames of the lamps, it caused accidents.

Sir Davy, then made a safety lamp. This lamp was a wick lamp where the flame was placed inside a fine mesh screen. This screen allowed the air to come inside for combustion but the flame did not come out.

Did you know that the Davy lamp also indicated the presence of flammable gases by making the flame burn higher with a blue tinge!

222. Miniature Golf – Thomas McCulloch Fairborn

Miniature Golf is a novelty version of golf. It is played on a miniature golf course. It also has various obstacles in the form of alleys, bridges and tunnels. It is played on courses that contain a series of holes like the original game but which are characterized by their short length, usually within 10 yards from tee to cup.

In 1927, Garnet Carter had developed a miniature golf course which he called "Tom Thumb Golf". He developed such a golf course to attract people towards his hotel. His wife had developed all the obstacles in the golf course based on a fairyland theme. He, however, was not the first person to develop a miniature golf course.

It was Englishman Thomas McCulloch Fairborn who had first thought of and made a miniature golf course in Tlahualilo, Mexico in 1922. His golf couse had a surface made from crushed cottonseed hulls mixed with oil, was dyed green and was rolled on top of a sand foundation. Did you know that miniature golf courses are also called minigolf or crazy golf!

223. Modern Calendar – Pope Gregory XIII

The calendar has been used since the Roman times. Over the centuries the calendar has been repeatedly modified. However, the modern calendar, also called the Gregorian calendar is the world's most widely used calendar. It is named after Pope Gregory XIII, who had brought reforms to the Julian calendar. It came into effect from 1582.

The modern calendar has 365 days which are divided into twelve months with unequal number of days. Every fourth year, a day gets added to this calendar, making the month of February with 29 days.

224. Modern Central Heating – Franz San Galli

Central heating is a method that provides warmth to all the rooms in a building from one point in the building. Franz San Galli, a Russian businessman, had invented the modern central heating. He had infact invented a radiator that changed the way the central heating system worked.

The radiator was a great convector of heat which could be plumbed in and placed on walls in people's homes. Due to these radiators, the room was instantly heated up. A typical modern central heating system includes a boiler, a pump and the radiators, forming the backbone of the modern central heating system.

225. Modern Television – Philo T. Farnsworth

American engineer, Philo Farnsworth had invented the modern television. With a great interest in electricity, he had made an electric motor and an electric washing machine by the time he was 12. At the university, while researching television picture transmission, he developed his own ideas to make a television.

After much research and experimentation, he made his first electronic television. The first image that the television transmitted was of a dollar sign. He was able to do so by developing the dissector tube which is the basis of electronic televisions. A camera and a receiver completed his television.

226. Monopoly – Charles Darrow

Monopoly, among the most played games in the world, was invented by Charles Darrow. He was a salesman who lost his job in 1929. While making ends meet, he thought of a game where the object was to buy and sell property. With the help of his son and wife, he devised a game called Monopoly. While he drew the design of the various properties on the game, his wife and son filled in the spaces with colours and made the *title deed cards*, *chance* and *community cards*.

When the final version of the game was complete, he showed it to both the Parker Brothers and to Milton Bradley. It was only the Parker Brothers' company that decided to mass produce this game.

227. Morphine – Frederick Wilhelm Adam Sertürner

Friedrich Wilhelm Adam Sertürner was an outstanding pharmacist. At the age of 21, still an apprentice, Sertürner presented a report on the "sleeping agent" that was found in the poppy plant and which he had isolated from the plant. Though his report was rejected, he repeated his analysis and named the substance 'morphine'. The drug was named after Morpheus, Greek god of sleep and dreams. To know the effects of the drug, he tested it on animals followed by tests on himself and his three friends. Morphine started selling in 1815 and was used as an active painkiller.

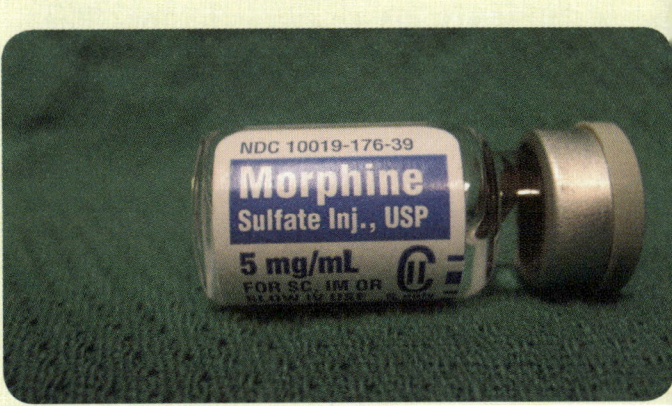

228. Morse Code – Samuel Morse

The Morse Code is a system of representing letters, numbers and punctuation marks by means of a code signal. Samuel Finley Breese Morse had invented the Morse code. His invention revolutionized communication. Though he had little training in electricity, Morse realized that pulses of electrical current could convey information over wires. It was on this principle that the telegraph worked. Assisted by Leonard Gale and Alfred Vail, he developed a crude model of a telegraph that used a one wire system. He improved it with a dot-and-dash code that used different numbers to represent the English alphabet and the ten digits. In 1838, Morse exhibited his Morse Code in New York to great success.

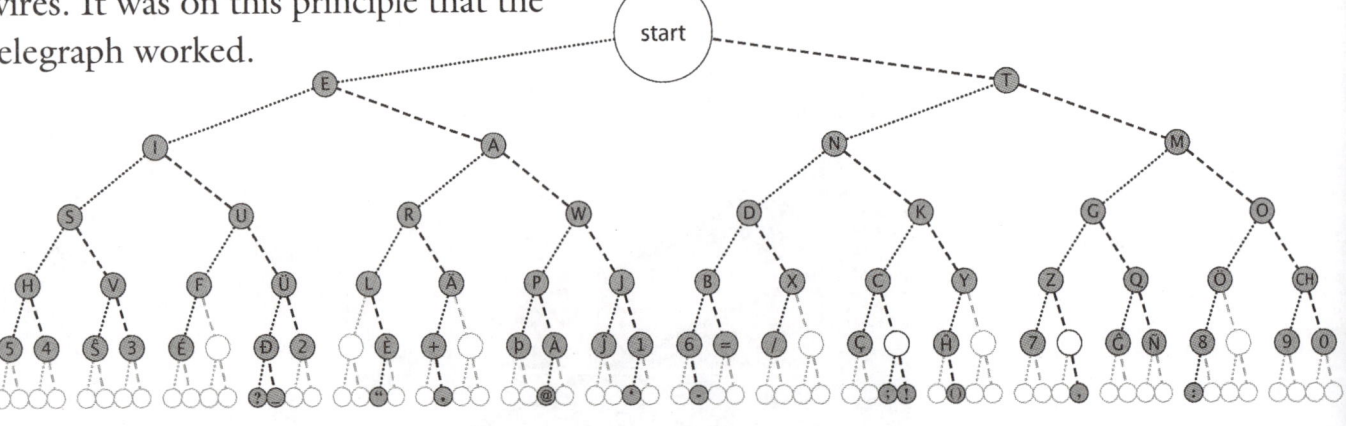

229. Motion Picture Camera – William Kennedy Laurie Dickson

A motion picture camera is a kind of photographic camera that takes a rapid sequence of photographs on a strip of film. William K. L. Dickson had invented the Kinetograph -- the first motion picture camera. This camera could take a rapid succession of photographs which when looked at through a kinetograph created the illusion of motion. Dickson devised the system to chemically treat a film, designed the sprocket and wheel system that advanced film through the camera and he also widened the film stock to 35 mm. It is still the standard size for commercial motion pictures.

230. Motor – Michael Faraday

Michael Faraday, British physicist and chemist, is best known for his discoveries of electromagnetic induction and the laws of electrolysis. His biggest breakthrough was inventing the electric motor.

As a 13 years old, Michael became an errand boy for a bookbinding shop in London. While reading the books he bound, he became interested in energy.

Michael built two devices to produce what he called electromagnetic rotation which is a continuous circular motion from the circular magnetic force around a wire. This was the principle behind the electric motor. Then, in 1831, he began his experiments where he discovered electromagnetic induction, the basis of modern electromagnetic technology. His discoveries have made electricity a powerful force.

231. Motorcar – Nicolas Cugnot

The first self-propelled road vehicle was a military tractor. It was invented in 1769 by French engineer and mechanic, Nicolas Joseph Cugnot. Under the instructions of Cugnot, the first motorcar was built that used a steam engine. It was used by the French Army to haul artillery. It ran on a speed of 2 1/2 mph on three wheels. It stopped after every ten to fifteen minutes to build up steam power. Did you know that the steam engine and the coiler were placed at the front of the vehicle! Later in 1771, Cugnot was also involved in the first motor vehicle accident when he drove the vehicle into a stone wall!

232. Motorcycle Petrol Engine – Gottleib Daimler & Wilhelm Maybach

Gottlieb Daimler, a German mechanical engineer and his co-worker Wilhelm Maybach invented the first petrol engine driven motorcycle. They wanted to create a small engine with a high speed that could be attached to a vehicle. In 1872, Dailmer had invented the four-stroke internal-combustion engine. Then, in 1885, he along with Wilhelm built the first successful high-speed internal-combustion engine and a carburetor that used petrol as fuel. They used the first petrol engine on a bicycle followed by attaching it to a horse driven carriage and a boat. This commercially feasible vehicle had a framework of light tubing, a rear-mounted engine, belt-driven wheels and four speeds.

233. Mousetrap – James Henry Atkinson

James Henry Atkinson in 1879 invented the mousetrap called the Little Nipper. This mousetrap, still used today has a small flat wooden base, a spring trap and wire fastenings. The spring mechanism is triggered by the movement of a mouse as it tries to get to the bait placed on a spike. Atkinson wanted a mousetrap that would not go off prematurely and which made a powerful snapping noise. Did you know that the Little Nipper slams shut in 38,000s of a second and this record has never been beaten!

234. Movie Projector – Charles Francis Jenkins

A movie projector is a device that projects successive frames from a film reel onto a screen. This creates a moving picture on the screen. It has mainly four components — the lamp, spool, lens and audio. Charles Jenkins, an innovator of early cinema is credited with improving the already existing movie projector. He called the projector, he had created 'Phantoscope'.

In 1894, Jenkins showed his parents, friends and newsmen his "motion picture projecting box." Through this projector, he projected a short reel film which he had filmed himself. This film projector illuminated each frame before advancing to the next frame. As the film moved smoothly through the device, it showed the first moving picture.

235. Noam Chomsky

Noam Chomsky was an eminent American theoretical linguist, cognitive scientist and philosopher. His influence on linguistics is similar to what Charles Darwin had on evolution and biology. He gave a new direction to linguistics and strongly influenced the fields of psychology and philosophy.

Born in Philadelphia in 1928, he did his doctorate in linguistics. At that time, concepts regarding the origin of language were inspired by behaviourist ideas. It was advocated that newborn babies had a blank mind and that children acquire language by mimicry and learning.

Chomsky rejected this belief. He said that children are born with the unconscious

knowledge of the principles underlying all languages. He added that children pick up the language spoken around them more quickly and without any instructions.

236. Network Computing – Robert Metcalfe

The ethernet is a system for connecting computers within a building by using hardware running from machine to machine. It differs from the Internet which connects remotely located computers. The Ethernet was invented by Robert Metcalfe.

While working at Xerox, Metcalfe was asked to build a networking system for PARC's computers. It was so because Xerox was building the world's first laser printer and wanted all PARC's computers to be able to print from this printer. Metcalfe made a fast system that not only drove the superfast new laser printer but also connected hundreds of computers within the same building. Today, this technology is used worldwide.

237. Nicolaus Copernicus

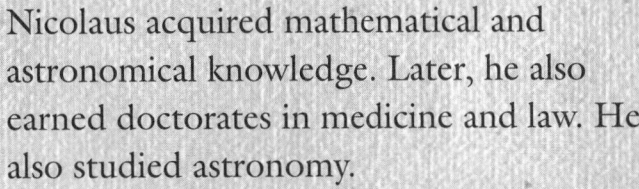

Nicolaus Copernicus was the founder of modern astronomy. He was the first person who had said that the Earth was not the centre of the Universe. He was also a great mathematician, physician, classical scholar, translator and artist.

Born in Prussia and raised by his mother's brother, Nicolaus acquired mathematical and astronomical knowledge. Later, he also earned doctorates in medicine and law. He also studied astronomy.

After completing his studies, Copernicus returned to Poland in 1503 where he began to work as a clerk. However, he continued his astronomical research and medical practice. In 1513, he began working on his heliocentric theory which was a concise description of the world's heliocentric mechanism.

He also wrote a manuscript where he said that the Earth revolved around the Sun. His manuscript was the beginning of modern astronomy.

238. Neils Bohr

Niels Bohr, a Danish physicist, is regarded among the most influencial physicists of the 20th century. He formulated the Atomic Structure and Quantum Mechanics. For his extraordinary work, he received the Nobel Prize in Physics in 1922.

Born in Copenhagen, Denmark, he belonged to a highly influential and well educated family. His father, Professor Christian Bohr taught physiology and his efforts generated Neils' interest in Physics.

After completing his early education, Neils attended University of Copenhagen where he persued Physics and went on to receive his master's and Ph.D degrees in Physics.

In 1913, Bohr's model of atomic structure was published. It became the basis of the *Quantum Theory*.

239. Night Vision Telescope – Dr Vladimir K. Zworykin

A night vision telescope or goggles gives one the ability to see in the dark. These devices use infrared energy along with the visible light to generate an image. It is often used by the military and law enforcement agencies. Night glasses are telescopes or binoculars with a large diameter objective.

Large lenses can gather and concentrate light, enabling the user to see better in the dark. The first practical night vision goggles were invented by Dr Vladimir K. Zworykin and they were meant to be used by civilians.

240. Nikola Tesla

Nikola Tesla was an inventor, an engineer and a physicist. He is best known for his contribution to the design of the alternating current and electricity supply system. He was born in 1856 in Smiljan Lika, Croatia. After studying electrical engineering, he worked in Budapest but later immigrated to the United States and began working at the Edison Machine Works.

During his lifetime, Tesla invented numerous things which made him world famous. Some of his inventions include the Tesla Coil, alternating current and neon lamp. Did you know that because of his wide variety of work, Tesla was termed as the 'mad scientist'!

241. Nuclear Fission – Otto Hahn

Otto Hahn was a German chemist who along with radiochemist Fritz Strassmann, discovered nuclear fission. Nuclear Fission is a process where a heavier and unstable nuclei splits into two or more lighter nuclei. This process also releases huge amounts of energy.

After completing his studies, Otto researched on radioactivity and found a new radioactive substance called radiothorium. Later in 1934, Hahn became interested in the work of physicist Enrico Fermi, who had found that when uranium is bombarded by neutrons, several radioactive products are formed. Otto began experiments with Strassmann. In 1938, they concluded that one of the products from uranium was a radioactive form of barium, indicating that the uranium atom had split into two lighter atoms. They called this process Nuclear Fission.

242. Nuclear Reactor – Enrico Fermi

A nuclear reactor is an apparatus in which nuclear fission chain reactions are initiated, controlled and sustained at a controlled rate. Nuclear reactors are used to generate electricity and to make isotopes. Enrico Fermi along with Leo Szilard is credited with inventing or rather discovering the first nuclear reactor. However, there are some nuclear reactors that are used for research purposes. Fermi was also the first physicist to demonstrate a controlled nuclear chain reaction in a nuclear reactor.

243. Nylon – Wallace Carothers

Nylon is a synthetic polymer. It was first discovered by Wallace Carothers, a chemist and an inventor. Today, Wallace is said to be the father of the science of man-made polymers for his invention of nylon. He discovered nylon while doing research work on the development of artificial materials for the Dupont chemical company. During this research, the team turned their efforts towards finding a synthetic fiber that could replace silk. During the various experiments that were conducted, very large molecules with repeating chemical structures were formed. These large molecules were nylon, a fiber that could withstand solvents and heat. Thus, a replacement to silk was found.

244. Odometer – Benjamin Franklin

The odometer was invented by Benjamin Franklin while he was the Deputy Postmaster-General of North America. By inventing the odometer, he wanted to bring efficiency to the delivery system of mails. While travelling by various routes between Philedelphia and Boston, he attached an odometer to his carriage as he mapped the fastest routes between towns and cities. The odometer was placed near the wheels of a carriage. The device determined the circumference of the wheel and kept a record of the number of revolutions the wheel required to travel a mile. By calculating the revolutions, the device registered the distance travelled.

245. Ophthalmoscope–Hermann von Helmholtz

Ophthalmoscope is an instrument used for inspecting the retina and other parts of the eye. It was invented in 1850 by German physiologist Hermann von Helmholtz. This device allows a doctor to examine the health and the ailments of the eye. The instrument consists of a strong light that can be directed into the eye by a small mirror or prism. The light gets reflected off the retina and goes back through a small hole in the ophthalmoscope, through which the examiner sees a nonstereoscopic magnified image of the structures at the back of the eye.

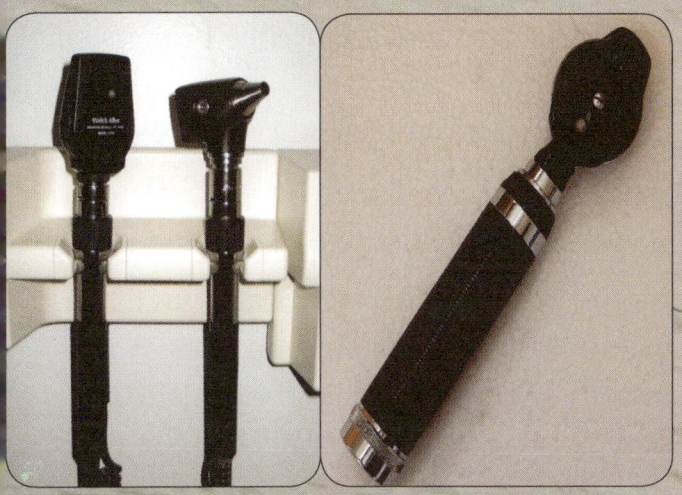

246. Orville & Wilbur Wright

Orville and Wilbur Wright had made and flown the first airplane. The airplane they had designed was powered by an engine and was heavier than air. Their creation was a breakthrough in the field of aviation.

The two brothers loved to invent things. Their passion for flying was ignited when their father gave them a toy helicopter that flew with the help of rubber bands. Soon, they began making their own model planes.

Years later, the two brothers made their first flight on December 14, 1903. This first flight lasted for only 12 seconds. The two brothers flew a number of times that day. Before making their engine powered airplane, they had worked and experimented for years with gliders perfecting the wing design and controls. They had also succeeding in making efficient propellers and a lightweight engine for the powered flight. After the first successful flight, they improved their design. On November 1904, Wilbur took their newly designed airplane, the Flyer II, to air for the first flight that lasted over 5 minutes. This was the first true flight by a human.

247. Pacemaker – Wilson Greatbatch

A pacemaker is a small electronic device which is put inside a person's heart when the natural pacemaker does not work well. It thus allows the heart to beat with its regular rhythm. It was invented by Dr Wilson Greatbatch accidently. It happened while he was attempting to record the sound of a heartbeat but instead created a device that sent electric pulses to the heart.

While building an oscillator with one transistor to record heartbeat sounds, he incorporated the wrong transistor. And instead of recording heartbeat, the device produced a pulse that mimicked the heart's rhythm.

This discovery became a beacon of hope for many heart patients and is considered among the greatest discoveries in medical history.

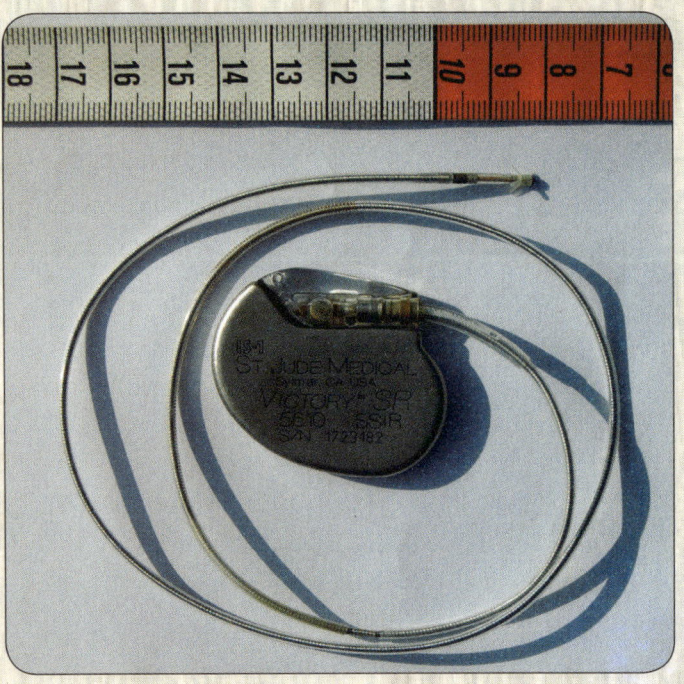

248. Paper Clip – Johann Vaaler

A paper clip is a wire or plastic clasp which is used for holding loose papers together. Johann Vaaler, a patent clerk had invented the paper clip in 1900. It is however thought that perhaps the paper clip was already invented. His design was, however, not perfect as it lacked the two full loops of the wire. As a result, sometimes the loose papers came out of the paper clip. Interestingly, only a limited number of sheets can be held together between the two loops of the paper clip. Today, the paper clips are widely used and are available in a variety of colours.

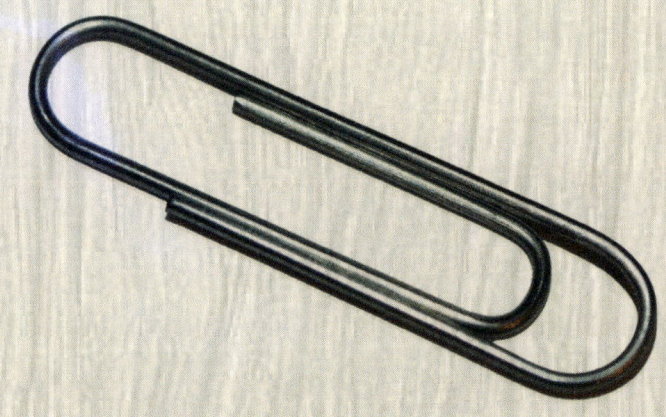

249. Parachute – Faust Vrancic

A parachute is a cloth canopy which gets filled with air and allows the person attached to it with strings to descend slowly towards the ground. It is used by paratroopers and by adventure enthusiasts. It was Leonardo da Vinci who had first thought of a parachute design. However, it was much later that Faust Vrancic put Da Vinci's idea into reality with his modifications. Faust actually jumped from a Venice tower in 1617 wearing a rigid-framed parachute, he had made, to test it. Faust succeeded in his experiment and then made more modifications in his parachutes to make them better.

250. Parking Meter – Carlton C. Magee

Parking Meter was invented by Carlton Cole "Carl" Magee. His parking meter was coin controlled. The city of Oklahoma was facing problems in downtown parking. It was so because people who worked in downtown parked their cars on the parking areas where they stayed the whole day, leaving no space for the shoppers to park their cars. Mr Magee who was also a member of the Oklahoma City Chamber of Commerce traffic committee decided to solve this problem. On his instructions, parking meters were installed in the business district and people were charged for the use of the parking spaces. In this manner, less space was occupied, leaving space for others to park their cars. Also, parking meters generated revenue for a growing city.

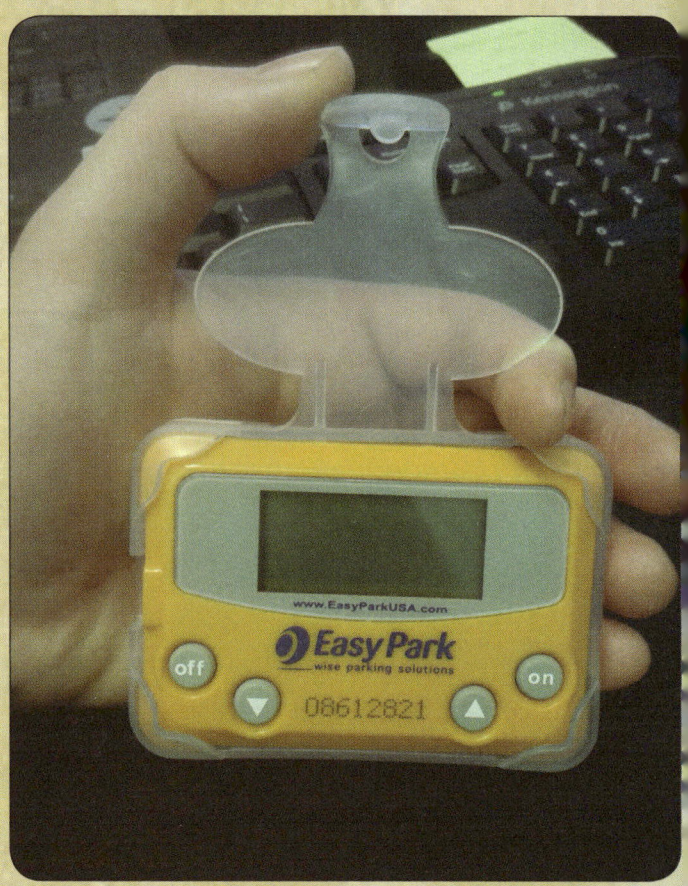

251. Pasteurization – Louis Pasture

Pasteurization is the process of destroying disease producing bacteria and checking the activity of bacteria needed for fermentation by heating the liquid at a specific temperature for a specific amount of time. This process was invented by Louis Pasteur, a French chemist and microbiologist. During his studies, Pasteur realized that specific organisms were involved in fermentation. He also discovered that the fermentation process could be arrested by passing air through the fermenting fluid, a process known today as the Pasteur effect. He concluded that this was due to the presence of a life-form that could function only in the absence of oxygen.

Today, pasteurization is applied to many foods and beverages particularly milk.

252. Paul Ehrlich

Paul Ehrlich, a German scientist, had diverse interests in the fields of immunology, hematology and chemotherapy. He had discovered the first practical treatment for syphilis. For this achievement he was even awarded a Noble Prize.

Born in 1854 into an affluent family, Paul Ehrlich developed an interest in the process of staining cells with chemical dyes as a youth. After earning his medical degree in 1878, he conducted experiments on cellular staining. He noticed that chemical reactions took place in cells and that these reactions caused the cellular processes. He concluded that chemical agents could cure diseased cells and fight infectious agents.

253. Pendulum Clock – Christiaan Huygens

Christian Huygens was a Dutch physicist, mathematician, astronomer and inventor. He is also the inventor of the pendulum clock. The clock he had made was more accurate than the clocks available at that time. Clocks during 1656 deviated from the original time and were based on balance. However, Huygens' pendulum clock was regulated by a mechanism with a "natural" period of oscillation. His clock had an error of less than 1 minute a day. It was the first time that such accuracy in time was achieved. With further modifications, the error was reduced to less than 10 seconds a day making his clocks the most accurate clocks back then.

254. Penicillin – Alexander Fleming

Penicillin is one of the earliest discovered and widely used antibiotic agents. Antibiotics are natural substances that are released by bacteria and fungi into their environment, as a means of inhibiting other organisms. In 1928, Sir Alexander Fleming observed that a plate culture of Staphylococcus had been contaminated by a blue-green mold and that colonies of bacteria adjacent to the mold were being dissolved. Curious, Fleming grew the mold in a pure culture and found that it produced a substance that killed a number of disease-causing bacteria. He named this substance Penicillin. Interestingly, the usage of penicillin did not begin until the 1940s!

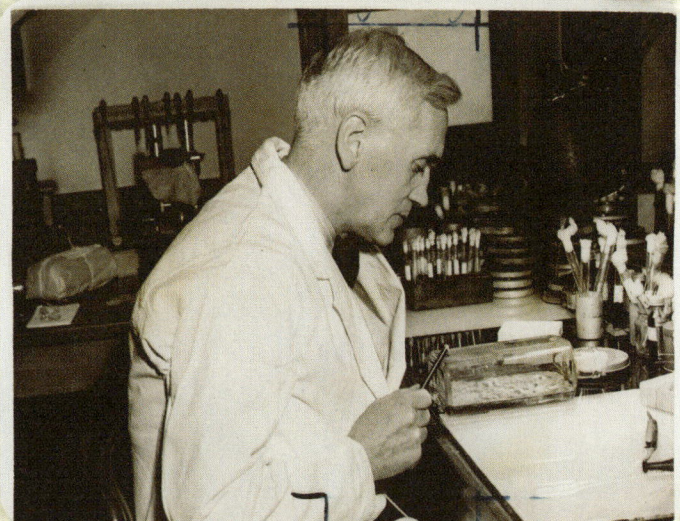

255. Percy Spencer

Percy Spencer is the inventor of microwave oven. In his teens, deeply interested in electric power, he worked as an electric installer. Later, he joined the Navy, where he was sent to radio school. In the 1920s he joining Raytheon and became the company's expert in tube design. He also oversaw the company's exponential increase in manufacturing tubes for military applications and the production of magnetrons, devices that power radar equipment.

His discovery of microwave cooking was utterly accidental. In a Raytheon laboratory in 1946, he felt the chocolate in his pocket melting as he stood near a magnetron. Curious, he brought raw popcorn that started popping near the magnetron. Spencer then built a rudimentary metal box with a magnetron in it -- the first microwave oven. By 1954, Raytheon began selling microwave ovens for industrial use.

256. Periodic Table – Dmitri Mendeleev

The Periodic Table was first thought of and assembled by Dmitri Mendeleev. He was a highly distinguished professor at the University of St. Petersburg. As a professor of chemistry, he wanted to classify the various known elements according to their chemical properties and thus began assembling them. In his first Periodic Table, he arranged the elements in ascending order of their atomic weight and grouped them by the similarity of their properties. He also hinted at the existence of other elements. The table Mendeleev had assembled, however, did not include the noble gases which are now part of the Periodic Table.

257. Petroleum Jelly – Robert Chesebrough

Petroleum Jelly, known by the name Vaseline was invented by Sir Robert Augustus Chesebrough. He was a chemist who clarified kerosene from the oil of sperm whales. However, the discovery of petroleum greatly affected his job so he decided to extract something useful from petroleum.

He then took the unrefined black material that the drillers dislike, to refine it in his laboratory. As he refined it, he realized that this substance healed his wounds and cuts. Encouraged, he decided to sell this material which he called 'petroleum jelly' as the cure against all kinds of cuts and wounds. It was due to a firm belief in his product that he managed to sell it.

258. Petroleum Refining – Edith Flanigen

Petroleum refining is a process where crude oil is refined into more useful products in a refinery. Edith Flanigen, a gifted chemist had invented the process of petroleum refining. While working on developing technology of molecular sieves, which are crystalline structures that work like strainers, she discovered that these sieves had pores that could be used to refine, filter and separate the components of highly complex compounds. The sieves could be widely used in the petroleum industry for refining.

She had also developed a substance called 'Zeolyte Y', a sieve that could break crude oil into its various components. This discovery allowed petroleum products to be used in a variety of ways.

259. Photography – William Henry Fox Talbot

Never good at making sketches, William Henry Fox Talbot, made a machine that used a light sensitive paper to make sketches.

At that time, pictures were either produced on bitumen or by using daguerreotypes. Neither were satisfactory. Meanwhile, Talbot succeeded in creating an 'art of photogenic drawing'. In this process, he took pictures on a light sensitive paper and saw that an image formed on the paper after being exposed to light. He decided to chemically develop this image into a negative by fixing it with a solution. By doing so, the light sensitive silver got removed and the picture could be viewed in bright light and printed from a negative. He had thus developed the three primary elements of photography: developing, fixing and printing.

260. Play-doh – Noah & Joseph McVicker

Play-doh was originally used for cleaning wallpapers. It is a plastic which is soft and squishy and can be made into anything. It was developed by Noah and Joseph McVicker. Later, when they learnt that the modelling clay which children used to play was hard to manipulate, they thought of the squishy material used for cleaning wallpapers. Then a supply of the doh was sent to a school and the children loved it. This soft clay was easy to modify and did not stick to the child's hands. This clay was then renamed play-doh. Do you know that September 18 is National Play-doh Day!

261. Pocket Watch – Peter Henlein

Pocket Watch was invented by Peter Henlein, a clockmaker from Nuremberg, Germany. Clocks during the 1400s were large. Henlein however managed to create small watches that could be worn in chains or kept in one's pocket. His key invention was the balance spring that improved the accuracy of the spring-driven clockwork. His watches ran for 40 hours before they needed rewinding and chimed after every hour. Interestingly, his watches only had the hour hand. It is due to his expertise and invention of the balance spring that he is regarded as the father of modern clocks.

262. Postage Stamp – Rowland Hill

A postage stamp is a small, printed and gummed label that is put on a letter or a mail. It is a sign that the letter and the mail has been paid for. Before the use of paper stamps, which were invented by Rowland Hill, letters were hand stamped or postmarked with ink. These postmarks marked the day and month the letter was sent in.

The 'Penny Post' was the first issued postage stamp in the world. The system of postage stamps began in Great Britain in May 1840. The Penny Black Post showed the image of Queen Victoria's head. Did you know that Rowland Hill had not only created the stamps but also the uniform postage rates which are based on the weight of the mail rather than its size! Interestingly, the postage stamp allowed the payment for the mail to be done before it is sent and brought sending mails within the reach of everyone.

263. Postage Stamp-adhesive – James Chalmers

James Chalmers, a Scotsman is thought to have invented the adhesive postage stamp. Trained as a weaver, he later worked as a bookseller and a newspaper publisher.

He is also known to have fought to make postage less expensive along with inventing an adhesive postage stamp. The adhesive stamp had a strong gum rubbed on its back, which allowed the stamp to stick itself on the letter or envelope. This was a step ahead from the method where stamp was stappled or tied with a string to the letter or envelope. He also suggested that stamps could be used to seal the letter or envelope.

264. Postcard – John P. Charlton

The first postcards were invented by John P. Charlton in 1861. Charlton had invented a plain card. Its one side was plain and was completely reserved to write the message. The other side of the postcard, the reverse side, was for the address and the stamp. Neither side of this postcard had a picture or image as modern postcards do.

The copyright for these postcards was later sold to H. L. Lipman. He made and sold the Lipman's Postal Card. These cards too had no picture or image on them. Later, Lipman cards were used to print messages and illustrations. He is considered the father of modern postcards.

265. Post-it Notes – Arthur Fry

A Post-it Note is a small piece of coloured paper which has an adhesive put at one of its sides. It sticks to a paper surface without damaging the paper. It was first thought of and invented by Arthur Fry. During the 1970s, Arthur Fry wanted a bookmark to place inside his church hymnal which would neither fall out nor damage the hymnal. It was then that he thought of the adhesive which his colleague at 3M, Doctor Spencer Silver had invented. This adhesive was strong enough to stick to surfaces but left no residue after it was removed. Interestingly, any object with the adhesive on could be repositioned. With this idea, he placed some of this adhesive at one end of a sheet of paper and put that sheet inside his hymnal book. This was the first Post-it Note.

266. Power Loom – Edmund Cartwright

A loom is a machine used in the textile industry to weave yarn into textile. The hand loom used by weavers was modified and made mechanical by Edmund Cartwright. This loom was called a power loom. He got the idea to make a power loom after a visit to the cotton-spinning mills of Richard Arkwright.

His power loom combined threads to weave cloth. Also he used water to provide power to his loom instead of steam. However, his designed looms were not a success.

267. Power Steering Wheel – Francis W. Davis

When the automobile industry was in its beginnings, the steering wheel of early cars was wooden. It was very difficult to navigate using the wooden steering wheel. Several attempts were made to introduce power steering in cars but none of them were successful.

Then in the 1920s, Francis W. Davis, an engineer with the Pierce Arrow Motor Car Company, began working on a power steering system. While working on a steering system for truck drivers, he ended up inventing the first power steering system that could be fitted into a car. His steering wheel was based on the system used in ships which he modified using hydraulics. Did you know that the first steering system was fitted into a Cadillac!

268. Pressure Cooker – Denis Papin

A pressure cooker is a closed container inside which food is cooked using steam pressure. It was invented by Denis Papin in 1679. He called his invention the steam digester. It was a closed vessel that had a tightly fitting lid. The lid confined the steam inside the container only to come out until a high pressure was generated. This high pressure also raised the boiling point of water considerably, thus cooking the food. Papin had also invented a safety valve to prevent any explosion while the steam was generated.

269. Punch Card – Hermann Hollerith

In 1881, Herman Hollerith thought of a machine that could count the census more accurately and speedily instead of the traditional methods. He called this machine a punch card tabulation machine. His machine using electricity could read, count and sort punched cards whose holes represented data gathered by the census-takers. He got the idea to make a punch card machine after seeing a train conductor punch tickets. For his tabulation machine, he used the punch card invented in the early 1800s by French silk weaver Joseph-Marie Jacquard. His machines were used to count the 1890 census and these machine counted the census in one year, a task completed using hand tabulation in 10 years.

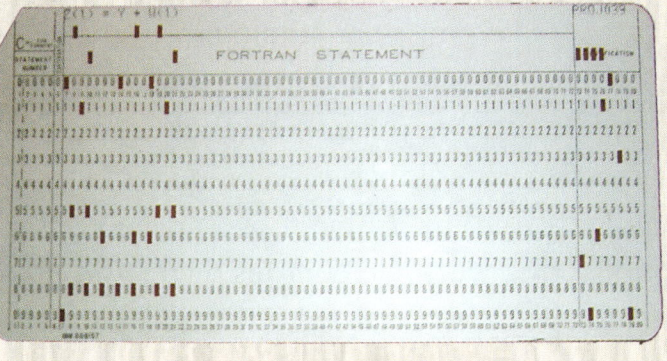

270. Quartz Clock – Warren Marrison

As telephone wires carried more messages and radio broadcasting became better in the early 20th century, it became difficult to maintain and moniter stable electrical frequencies. It was during this time that Warren Marrison, a telecommunications engineer at Bell Laboratories, started searching for more reliable frequency standards.

In 1925, he developed a very large, highly accurate clock based on the regular vibrations of a quartz crystal in an electrical circuit.

Accidentally, in his pursuit, he had also produced the first quartz crystal clock. He further improved his quartz clocks and by 1940s, the world had switched from mechanical clocks to quartz clocks.

271. Radio Telescope – Grote Reber

A radio telescope is used in astronomy to detect radio emissions coming from the sky. The emissions can either come from artificial satellites or from natural celestial objects. Grote Reber was a pioneer of radio astronomy. Inspired by Karl Jansky's pioneering work, he built his own radio telescope in his backyard. His telecope was far more advanced than the one built by Jansky.

Reber's telescope consisted of a parabolic sheet metal mirror 9 meters in diameter, focusing on a radio receiver 8 meters above the mirror. The entire assembly was mounted on a tilting stand which allowed it to be moved in different directions. After successive attempts, he succeeded in proving Jansky's attempts by setting the radio telescope's frequency at 160MHz. He then went onto develop an elaborate radio frequency sky map by 1941. He further discovered that a constant stream of radio waves emanated from the stars.

272. Radium – Marie Curie

Radium is an extremely rare element found on earth. Marie Curie, a French-Polish physicist and chemist, had discovered radium. Fascinated by radioactivity, Marie and her husband began working on an element called pitchblende and realized that there were more elements hidden in it. They conducted experiments and Marie was finally able to isolate radium from pitchblende. Today, radium is used in clocks, watches and other objects as radium glows in the dark. It is also used to treat cancer. However, it is not used in the industry because it is highly radioactive.

273. Razor – King Camp Gillette

King Camp Gillette thought of and developed the world's first disposable safety razors. Gillette's invention made shaving safer and convenient.

Before the invention of disposable razor blades, men used expensive razors to shave. These razors were sharpened after every use and due to their cost were used for a long time. Gillette, tired of the available razor blades, thought of making a blade which was inexpensive and could be disposed off when the blade became dull. He sought inventor William Nickerson, who helped improve Gillette's design and build a machine that would harden, hone, grind and sharpen the blades. After first entering the market, the Gillette razors have never looked back.

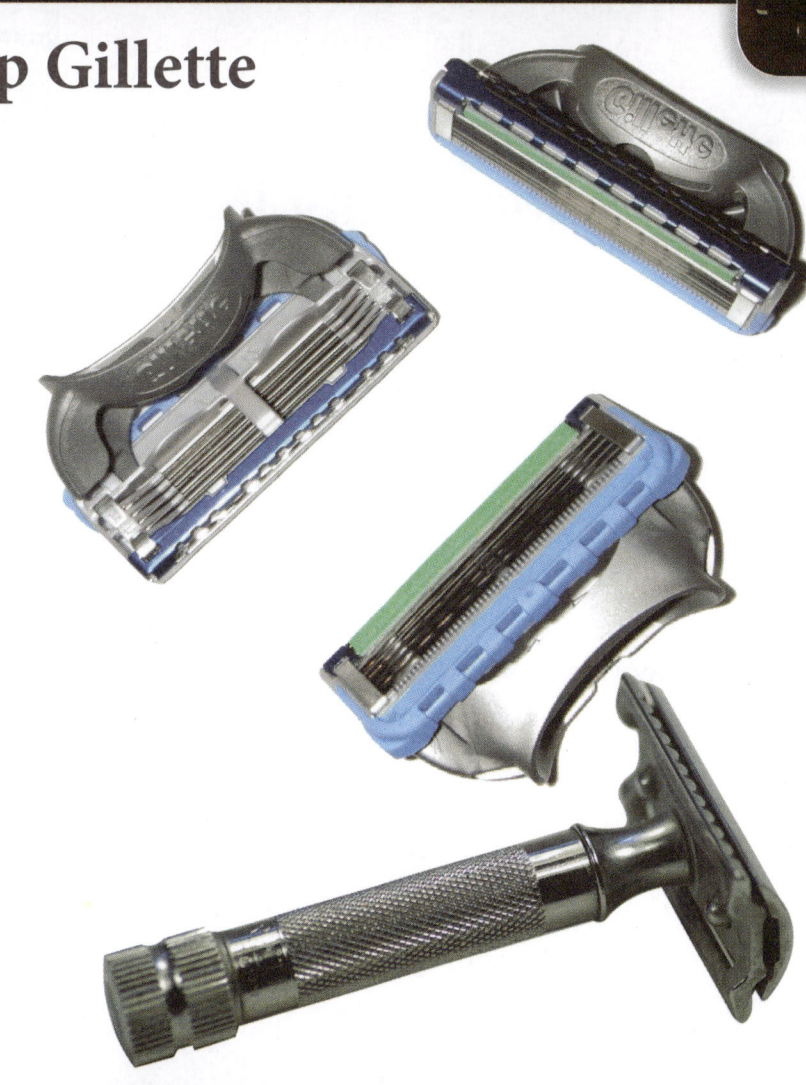

274. Refrigerator – James Harrison & Alexander Catlin Twining

A refrigerator is a large appliance that artificially maintains cool and is used to store food and drink. It preserves food by lowering the production of bacteria. Before the invention of refrigerator, icehouses were used to store food. Though there had been attempts to make a refrigerator like appliance, it was James Harrison who made the first refrigerator. He had made an ice making machine using ammonia and an ether compressor. Meanwhile, American professor Alexander C. Twining had made an early vapor-compression refrigerator in 1853 capable of producing a ton of ice each day. These were the first refrigerators.

275. Revolving Door – Theophilus Van Kannel

Revolving Doors are seen at the entrance of various large buildings and hotels. These doors prevent the cool or hot air inside the building to escape and at the same time, it prevents the outside dust to come inside the building or hotel. The revolving doors were invented by Theophilus Van Kannel in 1888. The doors thus created were airlocked. These doors were also useful as they helped in maintaining the pressure differences inside and outside the buildings without causing any difficulty in opening and closing the doors.

276. Richter Scale – Charles Richter

The Richter Scale is used to measure the magnitude or the intensity of an earthquake. It does not mean that it measures the damage done by an earthquake. The Richter Scale was developed by Charles F. Richter. He was an American physicist and seismologist.

This scale is based on the instrumental recording of ground motion which is recorded by a seismograph and thus provids a quantitative measure of the size of the earthquake. Richter also mapped out quake-prone areas in the United States, though he disparaged attempts at earthquake prediction. Do you know that there is no lower or higher limit to Richter Scale!

277. Robert Goddard

Robert Goddard, an eminent American physicist and inventor is considered the father of modern rocketry. It is because he had first created the liquid-fueled rocket and had published important and influencial work on rocket science.

He was the first scientist who shifted the attention of other researchers from the substance to be used as a fuel for rockets to oxygen, the essential element needed for combustion. He established that rockets without any oxygen in space would not be able to go on their course. Goddard also discovered that the rate of combustion depends on the amount of oxygen. It was later on his solution that rockets fuelled by gasoline and liquid oxygen were sent into space.

278. Rocket Launch Complex – Vladimir Barmin

Vladimir Barmin was a well-known Soviet designer who is credited with designing the rocket launch complexes. An area that can be used as a base to launch a rocket into space is called a rocket launch complex. Such an area may contain more than one launch sites. Do you know that a rocket launch site is established as far away from human habitation as is possible! It is done to avoid any catastrophy that the rocket may sustain during the launch.

Barmin had first designed the Katyusha barrage rocket system in 1941 that was used by Soviet forces to a great extent during World War II.

279. Rocket Liquid Fuel (first launch) – Robert H. Goddard

The first man to give hope of space travel was American Robert H. Goddard, who had successfully launched the world's first liquid-fueled rocket on March 16, 1926. The rocket travelled for 2.5 seconds at a speed of about 60 mph and reached an altitude of 41 feet. This 10 feet tall rocket was made out of thin pipes and was fueled by liquid oxygen and gasoline.

Before the use of liquid oxygen and gasoline, the rockets were powered by gunpowder. And it was only after making a liquid fuel rocket that scientists were successfully able to send man into space.

Goddard was able to prove to his peers that rockets could propel in an airless vacuum-like space. He had also explored the energy and thrust potential of various fuels including liquid oxygen and liquid hydrogen before choosing a rocket fuel.

280. Roller Skates – James Leonard Plimpton

The first roller skates were used on the London stage in 1743. However, these were neither comfortable nor stopped efficiently or at the right time. Then, James L. Plimpton decided to make better roller skates. His skates were the forerunner to modern skates and made roller skating a popular sport.

In January 1863, Plimpton successfully made four-wheeled roller skates that could turn. He had added a rubber cushion to his roller skates that allowed the roller skater to curve by leaning in the direction he wanted to travel. As these roller skates became more and more popular, skating rinks were opened. In the summer of 1866, the first roller skating rink was opened in the United States.

281. Rollercoaster – L.A. Thompson

A rollercoaster is an amusement park ride where small, open carriages move over sharp twists and turns on a track. The first rollercoaster was made by LaMarcus Adna Thompson in 1885. He got the idea for the rollercoaster seeing the downhill rail track called the Mauch Chunk Gravity Railroad. He thought that such a ride would be highly entertaining for the youth of New York City. His rollercoaster had a bench that was situated on a track that went downhill after starting at a tower which was 600ft up. This first rollercoaster was opened on January 20, 1885. Interestingly, the speed of this rollercoaster was only 6mph!

282. Rotary Printing Press – William Bullock

A rotary printing press is a printing press where the images to be printed are curved around a cylinder. The rotary printing press was invented by William Bullock in 1863. This invention was the beginning of modern newspaper press. This press worked using curved plates and printed on both sides of the paper which are passed through a machine. The machine used a continuous roll of paper to print. The rotary printing press put an end to the hand-feeding that was needed in early presses. Bullock's printing press printed 10,000 copies of sheets on both sides each hour. Do you know printing presses that use continuous rolls are sometimes called 'web presses'!

283. Rubber Vulcanization – Charles Goodyear

Vulcanization is a process where rubber is treated with sulphur to improve its elasticity and strength along with hardening it. The process of rubber vulcanization was first thought of by Charles Goodyear in 1839. The usage of this process increased the use of rubber to manyfolds and changed the industrial world. Do you know that the process of vulcanization is named after Vulcan, the Roman god of fire! Today, however, the process of vulcanization is further refined by adding carbon black and zinc oxide along with sulfur.

284. Rubik's Cube – Enro Rubik

The Rubik's Cube is undoubtably the most popular puzzle in the world. Interestingly, there is only 1 method to solve it and 43 quintillion wrong ones. This cube was invented by Erno Rubik.

Rubik's Cube has twenty-six individual little cubes or cubies that make up the six sides of a cube. Each side has nine cubies that twist and the layers that overlap. When Rubik himself began to twist the cubies, he realized that he could not realign the six colours on its six sides. Did you know that it took him a month to solve it! To this day, millions of these cubes have been sold in the world.

285. Samuel Morse

Samuel Morse was an American inventor and painter. He is well-known for inventing the Morse code. He became interested in arts in his early years and learnt to paint. However, it was years later that he decided to dedicate his life to improve long distance communication. He went on to understand the relationship between electricity and magnetism. He then developed a telegraph with a single wire over which messages could be sent. This invention now known as the Morse code is widely used to transmit data. He also authored the Morse code signaling alphabet. His invention was adopted as the standard of telegraphy in 1851.

286. Sawmill – Cornelis Corneliszoon

A sawmill is a factory where logs of wood are cut or sawed into boards. The concept of the sawmill was first thought of by Cornelis Corneliszoon. His sawmill used wind power to run the saw. With this invention, wood could be cut up to thirty times faster when compared to cutting wood by a hand-saw. In this sawmill, a windmill provided energy to the saw through a crankshaft and multiple gears. Interestingly, this sawmill built in 1594 floated on water on a raft and moved over various water bodies. The invention of sawmill greatly improved the industry in Netherlands.

287. Scanner – Rudolf Hell

A scanner is an electronic device that is used to create a digital likeness of an image for data input into a computer. The first scanner was invented by Rudolf Hell. A scanner has a glass surface over which the document which needs to be scanned is placed. Today, different kinds of scanners are avaliable including hand held ones and camera scanners. A flatbed scanner mostly found in offices uses three rows of sensors of red, blue and green filters to scan an image or text.

288. Scrabble – Alfred Mosher Butts

Alfred Mosher Butts, an architect, was out of work when he invented a board game that combined the vocabulary skills of crossword puzzles and anagrams. He searched through the newspaper to see how often the 26 alphabets of the English language were used.

He discovered that vowels appeared more often than consonants with E being the most frequently used vowel. He placed different point values to the 26 alphabets and decided how many times each letter would appear in the game. He also made sure that the letter 'S' was used only 4 times in the game. The boards for the game were hand drawn. The tiles were similarly hand-lettered, then glued to quarter-inch balsa and cut to match the squares on the board. He called the game 'Criss Cross Word Game' but later it became known as Scrabble.

289. Transparent Scotch Tape – Richard Drew

A scotch tape is among the most practical inventions found in every house and office. It was invented by Richard G. Drew in 1923. While testing 3M's "Wetordry" sandpaper at auto shops, Drew saw that the two-tone auto paintjobs were difficult to manage at the border between the two colours. He decided to invent something to prevent the two colours from merging. Two years later, he invented the first masking tape, a two-inch-wide tan paper strip backed with a light, pressure-sensitive adhesive.

This tape had adhesive running along its sides. When used for the first time, the tape fell off the car without any promising result. Drew then improvised his masking tape which became his greatest invention.

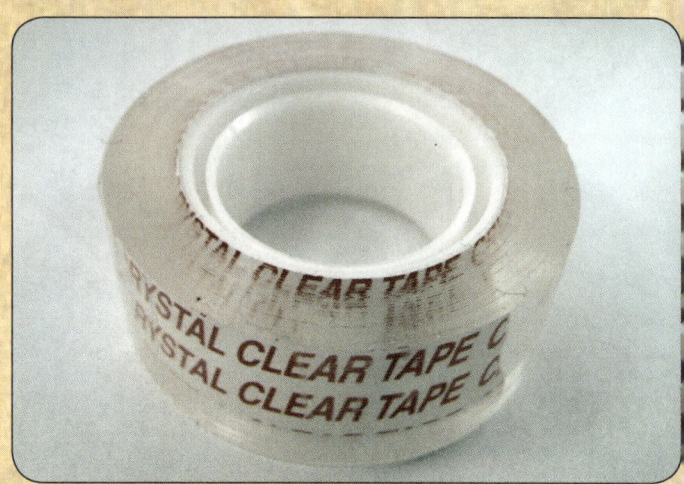

290. Seaplane – Glenn Curtiss

The seaplane is a plane that can land both in water and on land. It was invented by Glenn Curtiss. He owned a bicycle shop where he manufactured his own vehicle motors.

Fascinated by speed, he joined hands with Alexander Graham Bell who was trying to make a stable flying machine. It was then that the idea of a seaplane occurred to Curtiss. He built his hydroaeroplane and showed it at the 1911 aviation meet in Chicago.

The fact that this invention was of importance was proved when an airplane at the meet while in flight became out of control and fell into Lake Michigan. Glenn flew in his hydroaeroplane to rescue the pilot.

291. Segway Human Transporter – Dean Kamen

The Segway Human Transporter is an electronic vehicle with two wheels. This vehicle can balance itself and it can be used in any sort of environment or surface. It was invented by Dean Kamen, owner of Segway LLC.

This vehicle is environment friendly and has zero emissions. The word "Segway" is taken from the word segue which means, 'to transit smoothly from one state to another.' It allows a pedestrian to go farther quickly, without using a car. This invention was made keeping in mind Dean's belief that science and engineering can be harnessed to improve people's daily lives and community.

292. Seismograph – John Milne

A seismograph is an instrument which is used to measure and record the intensity and duration of an earthquake. The most widely used and reliable seismograph, called the horizontal pendulum seismograph, was invented by John Milne, an English geologist and seismologist. A seismograph has electromagnetic sensors that convert the ground motion into electrical changes which are read by the instrument circuits. Did you know that seismographs are also used to moniter volcanic activity in petroleum extraction and to explore the Earth's crust!

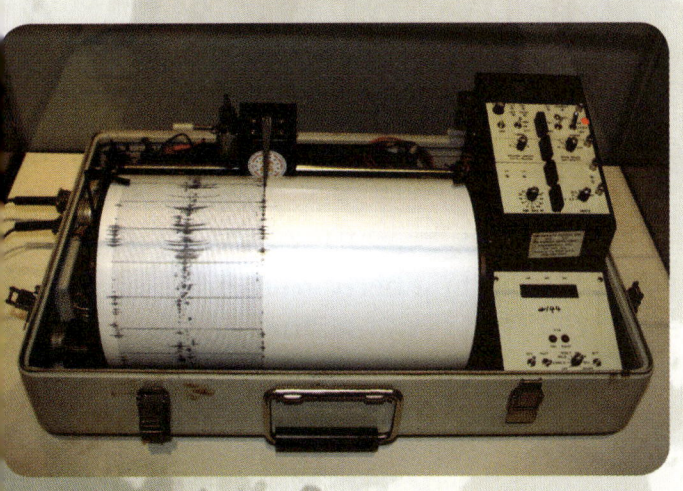

293. Sewing Machine – Isaac Merritt Singer

The precursor to the modern sewing machine was invented in 1851 by Isaac Merrit Singer, an American inventor. He was a machinist who worked on and repaired various machines over the years. In 1851, he was asked to repair Lerow and Blodgett sewing machine. The sewing machine had many errors in it. So, 11 days later Singer showed an improved sewing machine that he had designed. His machine allowed continuous and curved stitching. This improved machine had an overhanging arm which held the needle bar over a horizontal table making it easier to sew on any part of the work. The machine also embodied the basic eye-pointed needle and the lock stitch still used today.

294. Shampoo – Sake Dean Mahomed

A shampoo is a hair care product widely used to remove dirt and dust from the hair and also to provide nourishment. It is believed that shampoo was introduced to the world by Sake Dean Mahomed, an Indian traveller. Initially, shampoo was merely used to massage the head. It was much later that the word 'shampoo' meant to apply soap to the hair instead of a head

massage. Before the invention of shampoo ordinary soaps were used to wash hair. The first shampoos were made by boiling soap flakes and adding herbs to them to provide fragrance. It was in the 20th century that commercially manufactured shampoos became available.

295. Silicone – Frederic Stanley Kippling

Silicones are polymers (a naturally occurring synthetic substance) that contains alternate silicon and oxygen threads. Silicones can remain stable in extreme temperatures and are exceptionally water resistant. They were first discovered by British chemist Frederic Stanley Kipping in 1900 who was working on silicon.

Today, silicones are used in a variety of ways as synthetic rubber, water repellents, hydraulic fluids, to make cookware, in the medical industry and greases. Silicones are also widely used as synthetic rubber and in the lubricant industry.

296. Silly Putty – James Wright

Silly putty is a modelling substance which can be moulded, stretched and made into a ball. It was invented by James Wright, an engineer working with GE. He created Silly Putty when he mixed silicone oil with boric acid. The substance he created could rebound almost 25 percent higher than a normal rubber ball. It was soft, malleable and did not tear even when it was stretched many times. Interestingly, he also found that when Silly Putty was pressed on an object, it could copy the image of that object. Silly Putty was sold publically in 1949. Did you know that Silly Putty, is among the fastest selling toys in history with over $6 million sold in the year 1949.

297. Skateboard – Bill & Mark Richards

A skateboard is a toy in the form of a short, oblong board of wood or plastic with a pair of small wheels attached at either of its ends. It is used for riding while balancing as one stands on the board. Though it is not clear who had first thought of the skateboard but they were manufactured and sold by Bill and Mark Richards. Did you know that the first skateboards were called sidewalk surfers! They were made by attaching a pair of wheels to a wooden board. The first skateboards immediately caught the attention of surfers and teenagers.

298. Sliced Bread – Otto Frederick Rohwedder

In the beginning, bread was sold as a loaf and was not sliced. However, Otto Frederick Rohwedder, owner of three jewellery shops invented a mechanical bread slicer in 1928. Rohwedder was sure that sliced bread would change the baking industry for the better.

He first thought of a bread slicer in 1912. He sold his three shops and made the first bread slicer. This prototype held the bread slices together by metal hat pins but the pins fell out often. Then, in 1917, a fire destroyed his creation along with the blueprints of the bread slicer.

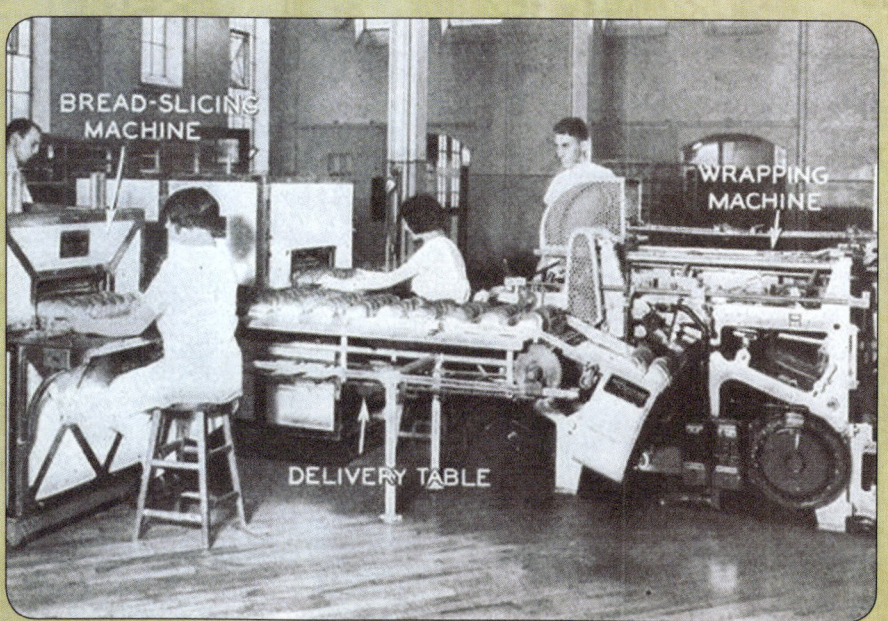

Despite the setback, Otto designed another bread-slicing machine in 1927 which not only sliced bread but also wrapped them in paper to keep the bread fresh. With some initial hiccups, sliced bread became so popular that bread sales skyrocketed.

299. Sliding Automatic Door – Dee Horton & Lew Hewitt

Sliding automatic doors are moveable doors. They open and close automatically when a person is about to enter or exit. This happens due to the sensors present on the door. These doors were invented by Dee Horton and Lew Hewitt in 1954. Their company Horton Automatics developed and sold the first automatic sliding door in 1960. They had thought of such doors because swinging doors were of no use in the winds of Corpus Christi. The sliding doors proved strong, durable and did not damage property.

300. Smallpox Vaccine – Edward Jenner

The Smallpox Vaccine was developed by Edward Anthony Jenner. It is the only effective and preventive vaccine against the fatal Smallpox.

During his apprenticeship, he had overheard a girl say that she would not get Smallpox as she already had Cowpox. Years later, a medical practitioner himself, he remembered this information, when the Smallpox epidemic struck in 1788. Jenner then observed his patients who worked with cattle and found the girl's words to be true.

Jenner experimented on an eight year old James Phipps, his patient. He put in Cowpox puss in the boy's wound. The boy had slight fever for a dew days and then he was healthy again. A few weeks later, when Jenner repeated the vaccination using Smallpox matter, the boy remained healthy. This experiment led to the birth of the Smallpox vaccine.

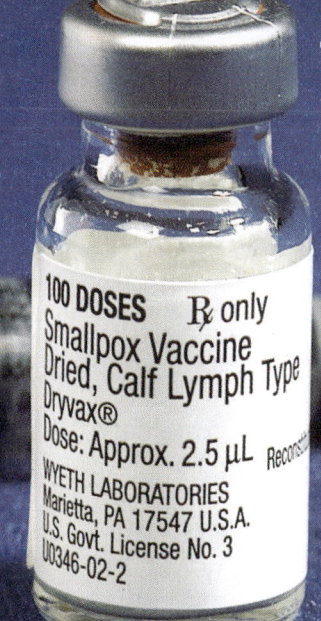

301. Smoke and Heat Detector Alarm – Sidney Jacoby

Protection against smoke and fire is among the prime concerns while buying a house. Perhaps, Sidney Jacoby, had the same concerns for he is credited with inventing a combined smoke and heat detector alarm system. The device invented by him also had its own energy source in the form of a cylinder filled with compressed gas. This device was sensitive to both smoke and heat in a room as it had separate gas conduit systems to detect smoke and heat. Though this was not the first detector but it was the first combined detector invented to secure homes and buildings.

302. Sneakers – Bill Bowerman & Phil Knight

Sneakers are shoes that are worn while playing sports. They are very comfortable. The first sneaker in the world was made in 1917 and it had a rubber sole. But the combined efforts of Bill Bowerman and Phil Knight elevated the humble sneakers.

Over the years, they made innovations in their sneakers and the company became what it is today.

In 1958, Phil Knight, a miler on the track team told his coach Bill Bowerman that the running shoes available in the market were uncomfortable. Bowerman took this seriously. He then designed and made shoes for Knight which Knight liked greatly. Later, they started a company in 1964 to market a lighter and more comfortable shoes designed by Bowerman. Four years later, they named their company NIKE, Inc.

303. Snow Blower – Arthur Sicard

A snowblower is a vehicle that removes snow from the roads, driveways or any other unwanted areas. It was invented by a Canadian called Arthur Sicard in 1925. Sicard worked as a delivery man for his dad's dairy farm. However, in winters it was a difficult task to deliver milk. Then, one day Sicard saw his neighbour using a threshing machine to harvest wheat. The swirling blades on the machine made Sicard think if he could create a similar machine to clear the roads. After a lot of hard work, Sicard made a working snow blower in 1925.

He called it Sicard Snow Remover Snow Blower. To test the machine he took it to the streets of Montreal. His machine was a success as it cleared the snow off the road and tossed it away.

304. Snowmobile – Joseph-Armand Bombardier

A snowmobile is a light vehicle which is designed to travel on snow. The modern snowmobile was designed by Joseph-Armand Bombardier in 1958. It took him many years to build such a vehicle. As a youth, he saw that many villages in Quebec were cut off from the cities during winters.

He developed a variety of prototypes by adapting automobiles year after year. Then in 1933, he built a lighter 45 kg motor which he fitted on new prototypes for one or two persons. But the new motor got overheated easily.

Finally, in 1935 Joseph-Armand used a cogged gear wheel, the sprocket made of wood covered with rubber, to pull the track. The latter is comprised of two rubber bands connected by steel cross-links. This did the trick and Joseph had finally made a sprocket wheel/track system that led him to invent the snowmobile.

305. Soda Fountain – Samuel Fahnestock

A soda fountain is a counter where one gets served soft drinks, sodas and even ice creams. It was hugely popular during the 1960s as it was a place where people met around a large counter equipped with swivel chairs and talked as they enjoyed soft drinks and ice creams. The soda fountain was first invented by Samuel Fahnestock in 1819. As years passed by, the popularity of the soda fountain did not decline until the coming of fast food chains. Did you know that a pharmacy was often adjacent to a soda fountain!

306. Sonar – Paul Langevin

Sonar is a system that is used to detect objects underwater by sending high frequency sound waves through the water. The time taken by the sound waves to reach the object and their return is calculated and in this manner the location of the object is determined. This technique of detecting objects underwater was developed by Paul Langevin in 1916. He was a professor of physics in Paris. Interestingly, the term sonar is also used for the instrument that sends the sound waves and receives their echo.

307. Spinning Jenny – James Hargreaves

The spinning jenny was amongst the most important inventions during the Industrial Revolution. This invention, made by James Hargreaves, revolutionized the textile industry. Hargreaves was a carpernter and a weaver. It is said that Hargreaves' wife knocked over a spinning wheel and as Hargreaves watched the spindle roll across the floor the idea for the spinning jenny came to him. The spinning jenny invented by him used eight spindles instead of the one found on the spinning wheel. The eight spindles created a weave using eight threads spun from a corresponding set of rovings. It took a while before the spinning jenny was used by all the weavers.

308. Stainless Steel – Harry Brearley

Harry Brearley, an English metallurgist is credited with the invention of stainless steel. He grew up working as an apprentice in his father's steelworks and became specialized in steel production techniques and other chemical analysis.

During that time, the steels used easily became coated with rust if not cleaned and polished often. Brearley decided to make steel that would get rid of rust caused by high temperatures. He began his experiments by added chromium to steel. As was expected, chromium raised the melting point of steel and made them very resistant to chemical attack. He also thought that this new stainless steel could be used for making cutlery among its many other uses.

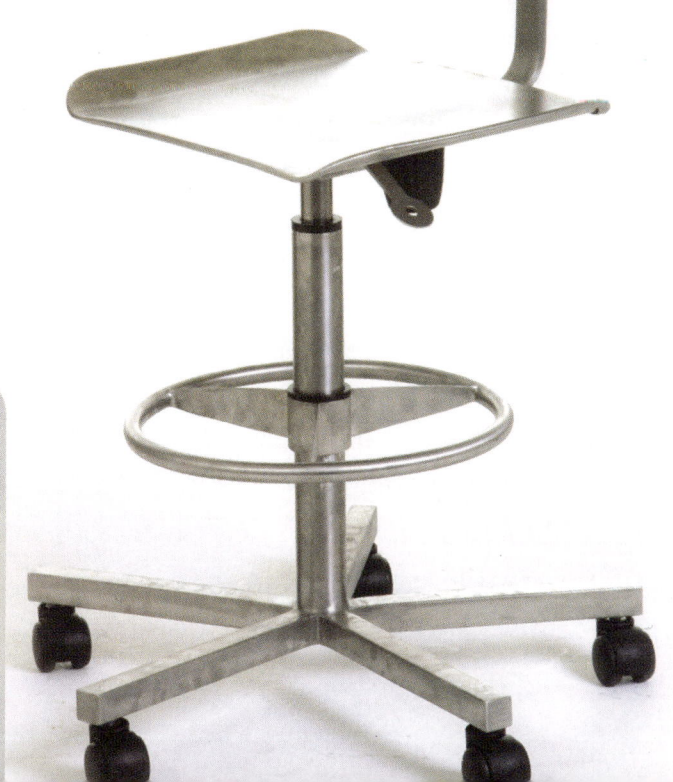

309. Steam Engine – James Watt

Steam can be a great energy source. Its potential was seen long ago but it was James Watt who put steam power to good use and made the first practical steam engine. His steam engine was an improvement on the previous steam engines that wasted a lot of power.

His steam engine had a separate vessel where the steam was condensed. As a result, it was possible to keep the condensing vessel cool and the cylinder hot at the same time. This separation did not allow any wastage of power generated by the steam.

310. Steamboats – John Fitch

The invention of the steamboat revolutionized water transportation. The steamboat made it easier to transport people and to carry goods across the waterways from one place to another. Also, sailors and people no longer had to depend on the wind to propel ships.

After the invention of steampowered boat in 1769 by a Scottish engineer, inventors in Europe and the United States soon tried to use steam to power boats. In 1787, John Fitch, an American inventor, demonstrated the first workable steamboat in the United States. And for the next 50 years, steamboats ruled the waterways of Europe and America.

311. Stephen Hawking

Stephen Hawking was born in Oxford, England on January 8, 1942. He is among the most well-respected scientists in the world. He did groundbreaking work on black holes and space-time theories. He demonstrated that black holes emit radiation which is now known as Hawking Radiation.

He was diagnoized with a disease called ALS (Lou Gehrig's disease) while he was working on his Ph.D. As a result, he is confined to a wheelchair and is unable to speak. However, he communicates using a computer touch pad and a voice synthesizer. Hawking has decided his life to research and is the author of several books including *A Brief History of Time*.

312. Stethoscope – René Laënnec

A stethoscope is a hearing instrument which is used to examine heart and lungs by listening to the sounds they make. The stethoscope, an instrument used by doctors was invented by René-Théophile-Hyacinthe Laënnec, a French physician.

Laënnec's stethoscope had a hollow tube of wood that was 3.5 cm in diameter and 25 cm long. Also it could be easily disassembled and reassembled. It used a special plug through which the sounds from the patient's heart and lungs could be heard. His instrument replaced the inconvinent method where the physician laid his ear on the chest of the patient to listen to the chest sounds.

313. Stove – Lloyd Groff Copeman

While working for the Washington Electric Company in 1906, Lloyd Groff Copeman developed a design for an electric version of the gas stoves.

The electric stove he invented was developed from a thermostat he had made himself. During that time, women cooked food over a device called a "fireless cooker." It was an awkward wooden box which enclosed heated soapstones over which pans of food were placed. Copeman applied the idea of his transformer thermostat to a fireless cooker and substituted electrical units for the soapstones.

314. Styrofoam – Ray McIntire

Polystyrene is a strong plastic that can be injected, extruded or blow molded. It is therefore a very useful variety of plastic. Most of us recognize polystyrene as Styrofoam. It is used in building materials like light switches and also to manufacture disposable cups and plates.

This unique plastic was first discovered by German apothecary Eduard Simon in 1839. However, it was another German Hermann Staudinger, an organic chemist who understood the potential of polysterene. Later, it was Dow Chemical Company scientist, Ray McIntire who had invented foamed polystyrene aka Styrofoam. Interestingly, styrofoam is about 98% made of air.

315. Submarine – David Bushnell

A submarine is a warship designed in such a manner that it can lie and move completely submerged in water. It is equipped with a periscope to look outside and is also loaded with weapons. It was invented by David Bushnell, a Yale graduate in 1776. The vessel designed by him was a one-man vessel that submerged underwater by admitting water into the hull and came on the surface by pumping the water out using a hand pump. It was powered by a pedal-operated propeller and was armed with a keg of powder. It was on this basic design that future submarines were constructed.

316. Subramaniyam Chandrashekhar

Subrahmaniyan Chandrasekhar was an Indian born American astrophysicist. He won the 1983 Nobel Prize for physics along with William A. Fowler for making key discoveries on the later evolutionary stages of massive stars. He concluded that a star having a mass of more than 1.44 times that of the Sun does not become a white dwarf but instead continues to collapse, blows off its gaseous envelope in a supernova explosion before becoming a neutron star. An even more massive star continues to collapse until it becomes a black hole. His studies led to the understanding of supernovas, neutron stars and black holes.

317. Sunglasses – James Ayscough

The first vision aid called a reading stone was invented in 1000 AD. It was just a glass sphere which was laid on top of the material that needed to be read as the letters got magnified by the glass. Then, the first wearable eyeglasses were invented in Italy in 1284. But the eyeglasses which became the precursors to modern eyeglasses and sunglasses were designed and made in 1752 by James Ayscough.

These spectacles had double-hinged side pieces and the lenses were made of clear, tinted glass. He also advised that since white light reflected sunlight, green and blue glasses should be used. Ayscough's glasses were the first sunglass like eyeglasses but instead of shielding the eyes from the sun, these glasses corrected vision problems.

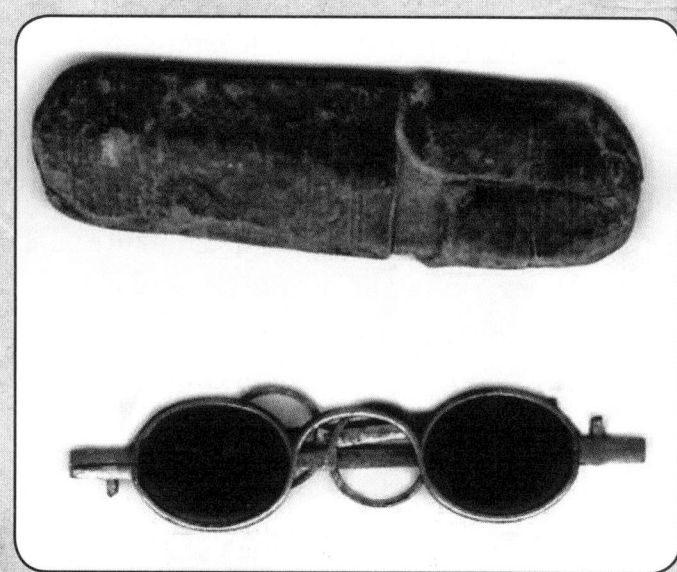

318. Suspenders – David Roth

Suspenders are used to hold up trousers. The first suspenders, invented in France, were merely strips of ribbon that were attached to the buttonholes of trousers. Did you know that suspenders were thought to be a part of man's undergarment! However, the modern suspenders with the metal clasp were invented by David Roth in 1894. Interestingly, though men wore belts but these were used merely as ornaments on the outside of coats and clothing. The job of holding up the trousers was left in the care of suspenders.

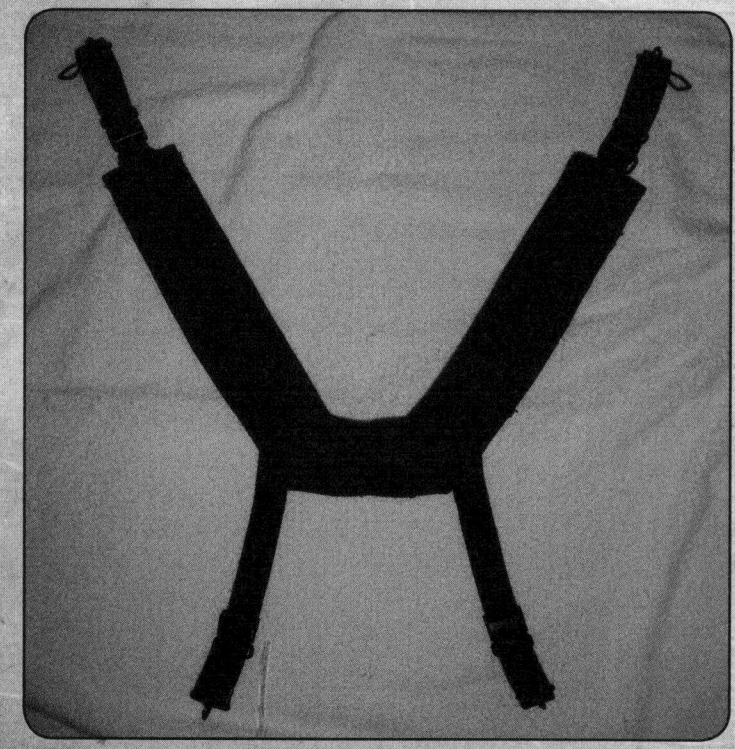

319. Swiss Army Knife – Karl Elsener

A Swiss army knife is a penknife that has several different blades and other tools including scissors, can openers and screwdrivers. It was invented by Karl Elsener in the early 1900s. The knives were invented for the Swiss Army who wanted a knife that could not only act as a knife but also cut cheese; open cans and help the soldiers clean their rifles.

The first knife Karl made had a wooden handle, a large blade, a screwdriver to clean the gun and a tin opener. Later, with several modifications, these knives were named Victorinox in 1921, after his mother. Did you know that a Swiss Army Knife usually comes with a red handle and the coat of arms of Switzerland is featured on it! Interestingly, these world famous knives were popularized by the American GIs who took them home as gifts for their friends and relatives.

320. Swivel Chair – Thomas Jefferson

Thomas Jefferson, the third president of the United States, is credited with the invention of the swivel chair. A swivel chair is one where the seat can be turned on its base to face any direction. Modern swivel chairs have wheels at their base which allow the user to move the chair in any direction without getting down.

Jefferson bought an English-style Windsor chair and modified it by incorporating top and bottom parts connected by a central iron spindle, enabling the top half known as the seat to swivel on casters of the type used in rope-hung windows. Today, swivel chairs are used in offices around the world.

321. Synthetic Dye – William Perkin

A synthetic dye is any of the organic dyes that are produced using chemicals or their derivatives. The synthetic dye, especially the colour purple, was invented by William Perkin in 1856. At the age of 15, he read August Wilhelm von Hoffmann's hypothesis where he had said that it might be possible to synthesize quinine.

Curious, Perkin started his experiments in 1856 and made an accidental discovery proving that aniline could be partly transformed into a crude mixture which when extracted with alcohol produced a substance of intense purple colour. This discovery scaled up the production of the purple substance which was commercialized into a dye, mauveine.

322. Tape Measure – Alvin L. Fellows

A tape measure is a flexible ruler which is used for measurement. It can be made of cloth, plastic, fiber glass or a thin metal strip with linear measurements marked on its one side and metric measurements marked on its other side. A tape measure because of its small size is used with ease by tailors, architects, engineers for measuring.

Do you know that surveyors use tape measure in lengths of over 100 metres! Though the tape measures have a long history but the first known tape measures were invented by Alvin L. Fellows in 1868 in Conneticut.

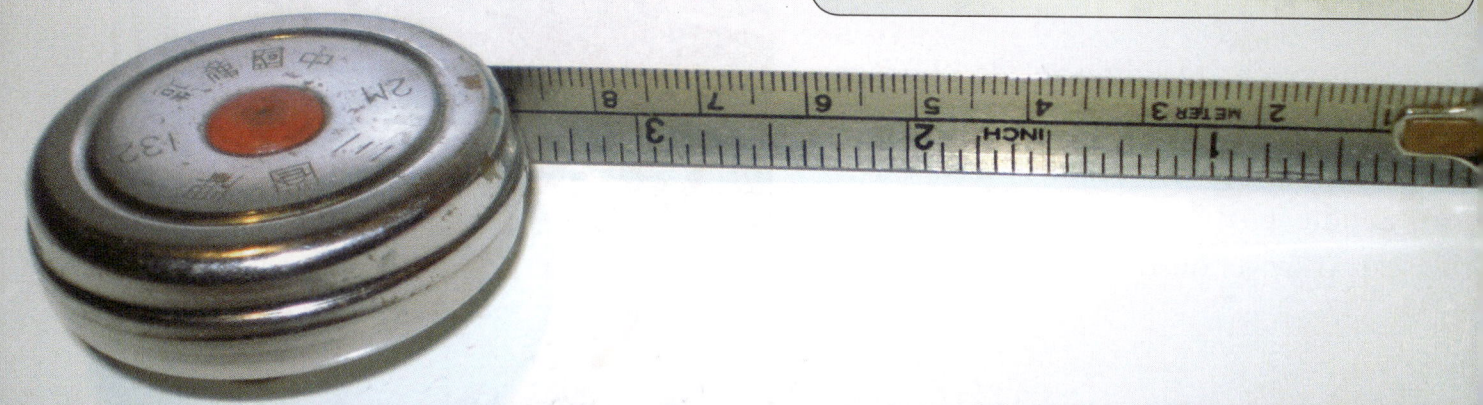

in the service of the British Empire. James Watt, a Scotsman, improved the steam engine that propelled mankind into the industrial era. In the latter half of the 19th century Alexander Graham Bell, another Scotsman who emigrated to America, invented the telephone, and Andrew Carnegie became an American steel magnate.

As the British colonial empire expanded into China, Scottish nationals arrived in the country as naval officers, consular and customs officials, engineers, doctors, architects, merchants, bankers, and accountants, and settled in China's opening trading ports. Scottish missionaries reached into the Chinese interior to seek new converts for the Lord.

In 1834, when the British Parliament removed the East India Company's monopoly on trade with China, Jardine Matheson & Company, a partnership between Scotsmen William Jardine and James Matheson, saw great business opportunities and entered into the tea and opium trade. From 1872, Jardine Matheson & Company invested in the construction of railways, dockyards, factories, mines, shipping and banking companies in Hong Kong and mainland China.

During the First Opium War, the wooden boats of the Qing navy were no match for Scottish-built steam-engine ships. After 1860, most of the Royal Navy's warships patrolling the Yangtze River were built in shipyards on the Clyde in Glasgow. Gabriel James Morrison, a Glasgow University graduate and railway engineer, came to Shanghai in 1876 to build China's first railway from Shanghai to Wusong, but the engine was seen by many as a "monster". The Qing government bought the railway and dismantled it. Morrison then set up his own construction and engineering company in Shanghai and became vice president of the Bureau of Public Works of the Shanghai

/ Jardine Matheson Scottish Thistle Mark

Public Concession, responsible for the day-to-day management of the concession. Thomas Sutherland, a Scot, initiated the establishment of the Hong Kong Shanghai Banking Corp. (HKSB) in Hong Kong in 1864, and opened the Shanghai Branch in 1865, introducing modern banking to China. In 1898, when Weihaiwei became a British concession, two Scotsmen became the city's administrators. The first was John Stewart Lockhart, who served from 1902 to 1921, and the second Reginald Fleming Johnston, who served from 1927 to 1930 when the city was returned to China. Johnston was the English teacher of China's last emperor, Pu Yi.

After the mid-19th century, Scottish nationals became the backbone of the British Empire's presence in China. As they became residents in China's trading ports, they brought along their national game of golf. Almost without exception, early Chinese golf courses and clubs appeared first at China's trading ports. Those behind the golf courses and clubs were overwhelmingly Scots, with some key figures coming directly from the birthplaces of modern golf such as St. Andrews and Carnoustie.

According to our research, the earliest golf course in China appeared in Hankou (Hankow) in 1870 and the earliest golf club was the Hankow Golf Club incorporated in 1878. Later, golf courses and clubs appeared in other Chinese ports: Hong Kong (1889), Yantai (Chefoo, 1890), Shanghai (1894), Tianjin

(Tientsin, 1895), Yingkou (Newchwang, 1895), Xiamen (Amoy,1897), Yichang (Ichang, 1899), Beijing (Peking, 1900), Weihai (Weihaiwei, 1901), Fuzhou (Foochow, 1900), Shenyang (Mukden, 1904), Zhenjiang (Chinkiang, 1905), Qingdao (Tsingtao, 1908), Guangzhou (Canton, 1910), Jiangzi (Gyantse, Tibet, 1912), Dalian (Dairen, 1915), Danshui (Tamsui, Taipei, 1919), Nanning (1919), Tangshan (Tongshan, 1919), Qinhuangdao (Chinwangtao, 1921), Dandong (Antung, 1921), Harbin (1921), Nanjing (Nanking, 1920s), Wuzhou (Wuchow, 1920s), Fushun (1920s), Jiaozuo (Chiaotso, 1920s), Anshan (1930s) and Changchun (Hsinking) (1934). The history of golf in Hong Kong and Taiwan is not covered in this book.

The pioneer of the Hankow Golf Club was a Scotsman, James Ferrier, from Carnoustie, Angus. His father John had been the founder and captain of the Carnoustie Golf Links. James played at Carnoustie from an early age and had honed his golfing skills to the level of a zero handicapper when he arrived in China in the late 1860s. He was a marine engineer employed by the China Merchants Steamship Company Ltd.

Ferrier travelled with his ship up and down the Yangtze River between Wuhan and Shanghai. In 1870, together with a few Scottish friends, he built China's first rudimentary golf course with only a couple of holes in Hankou and started playing the Royal & Ancient game. Eight years later, Ferrier was one of the founding members of the Hankou Golf Club when it was established in 1878. Ferrier also built Shanghai's first golf links of a few holes inside the Shanghai Race Course in 1871. After he settled in Shanghai, Ferrier was one of the 18 people who founded the Shanghai Golf Club in 1894. From then, he personally facilitated the close relationship between the Hankou and Shanghai golf clubs during his lifetime.

In late 19th century Shanghai, half of the expatriates were from Scotland. On June 2, 1893, right before the founding of the Shanghai Golf Club, a reader wrote to the editor of the Shanghai-based English-language weekly newspaper, *North-China Herald*, asking city officials to consider building a park and a golf course to cater to the golfing needs of Scottish expatriates living in Shanghai. The reader, apparently from Scotland, wrote: "A public place is needed where any and everybody can go and play any game they like. Golf is played everywhere and by everybody, old and young, in the British Isles now. It is popular in India and in all the colonies. Even in the south of France now John Bull has introduced his golfing clubs and balls, but in Shanghai where half the community is Scotch there is nowhere for them to indulge in their splendid national pastime. Grazing is very much needed here too, and a park would help to provide that."

/ James Ferrier

Duncan Houston Mackintosh, from Inverness-shire, Scotland, joined the Hong Kong Shanghai Banking Corp. in 1880 and worked in Singapore, Hong Kong, Hankou, Kobe, Saigon and Xiamen before becoming manager of

HSBC in Tianjin in 1895. Mackintosh was one of the founders of the Tianjin Golf Club.

The earliest golf course in Beijing was built in 1900. The driving force behind the construction of the course was Nigel Oliphant, a cadet interpreter from the British Legation in Beijing. A native of St Andrews, Oliphant had an ancestor who was knighted in the 12th century after having saved King David I of Scotland. Oliphant was born in the very house of his parents in which Mary Queen of Scots stayed when she visited St Andrews. In 1897, Oliphant's brother David went to Beijing and became secretary to Claude MacDonald, the British Minister to China. David was killed in 1900 during the Boxers' attack on the Legation grounds. In 1899, Nigel was invited by Robert Hart, the Qing Dynasty government's top Customs officer, to take up a position at the Chinese Post Office in Beijing. He saw first-hand the siege of the Legation quarters by the Boxers during the four months from June 1 to September 30, 1900 when. A golf enthusiast, Oliphant, along with several representatives of the British Legation Sports Club, personally built the first golf course in Beijing on the outskirts of the western city. In his diary published in 1901,

/ Shanghai Race Course

Oliphant documented in detail how he had found an open area and constructed Beijing's first rudimentary golf course.

After Weihai was leased to Britain in 1898, the city's Liugong (Liukung) Island became a training base for the British Royal Navy. In 1901, the Royal Navy built a 9-hole golf course on the Island. The Weihaiwei Golf Club President was James Stewart Lockhart, the city's Chief Administrator. A second golf course was built in 1907 on the mainland outside of the East Gate, and

/ Tientsin Golf Course 1900s

the Port Edward Golf Club was formed.

In 1920, Ian Macnair, a Scottish Royal Navy officer, came to Weihai as third mate of the L15 submarine and played golf at the 9-hole course on the east end of Island. Seven years later, Macnair, now captain of the L27 submarine, again visited Weihai. Macnair's father, who won two championships at the Calcutta Golf Club, was once Club captain and life vice president. Macnair's wife, Ruth, took a number of photographs of the Weihaiwei Golf Club on the island.

Under the Treaty of Lhasa in 1904, the British were allowed to do business in Yadong, Jiangzi (Gyantse) and Gedake (Gartok) and set up trading offices there. Most of the personnel for the trade houses were selected by examination from the Indian Civil Service of the East India Company, or were members of the British Army. They were mostly single men, many from Scotland. For these trade representatives in Tibet, life was extremely hard and monotonous. Hunting, cricket, hockey, football and wrestling became hobbies for the bachelors. The young men from Scotland then set up a simple golf course at Jiangzi, bringing this Royal & Ancient sport to Tibet on the roof of the world.

/ 3rd Green at Paomachang Golf Course in Beijing 1928

One of the organizers of the Zhenjiang (Chinkiang) Golf Club, founded in 1905, was a Scot called A. G. Elder from Edinburgh. Elder worked for almost 39 years as a customs assessor in Shanghai, Jiujiang and Zhenjiang.

In 1912, Richard Graham from Scotland was selected by the Shanghai Golf Club to be the club's first resident professional. Graham arrived in Shanghai by ship on October 8 and went to work immediately on arrival. He played with great skill, shooting 33 on the 9-hole course at the

/ Liugong Island Golf Course 1920s

Race Course and 78 on the Jiangwan (Kiangwan) course. But unfortunately, a little over a month later, the first professional golfer in China died in his sleep due to a heart attack.

Like James Ferrier, Walter Hughes Corsane, from St Andrews, was a steamship engineer who came to Hankou in 1902 and worked for the China Merchants' Steam Navigation Co. In 1904, he co-founded the Hankou Ice Works, and in 1921 he invested in the Hankou Aerated Water Co. A low handicap amateur golfer, he won the Shanghai Challenge Cup for the first time at the Hankou Golf Club in 1907. He won it a second time in 1912 as club captain, and a third time the following year as vice-captain, thus winning outright the beautiful silver trophy presented by the Shanghai Golf Club in 1897.

On the evening of October 21, 1920, Peking Golf and Country Club hosted a dinner at the Peking Club to celebrate the transfer of member A. H. Ferguson to the Standard Chartered Bank in Hong Kong. Ferguson, a Scot, was captain of the Beijing Golf Club for two consecutive years in 1917-1918 and made an unparalleled contribution to the Club's development. On leaving, Ferguson donated the Ferguson Cup to the newly formed Beijing Golf and Country Club as the club's annual competition trophy. From 1921, the Club hosted several successive Ferguson Cup invitational tournaments.

Scotland's close relationship with the early

/ Macnair (right) and Players on the Liugong Island

days of golf in China can also be seen in the golf trophies named after Shanghai and China at the Scottish golf clubs as well as a Scottish golf association named after China.

The Carnoustie Golf Links, home of golf "veteran" James Ferrier, had two trophies in the 1920s for annual club competitions. One was called the "Shanghai Cup" and the other the "China Cup". The Dumbarton Golf Club in Scotland also played a "Shanghai Cup" competition starting in the 1930s.

The China Golfing Society originated in Turnberry, Ayrshire, and has been in existence for over 100 years. First named "China Golf"

/ Jiangzi Golf Course in the 1910s

association in June 1914, it was formed so that British citizens who had worked in China and the Far East could meet and associate on the golf links. The association's second meeting did not take place until June 1921 due to the First World War. In 1922, members met at Cruden Bay in Scotland, and after that, annual meetings of the "Old China Hands" were basically fixed at Aldeburgh. In April 1936, China Golf was officially renamed the China Golfing Society and by the end of the Second World War, membership had grown to over 150. After the war, the Society established representatives in Shanghai, Hong Kong and Singapore. On May 21, 1949, 32 delegates attended the annual meeting and decided to donate £50 to the Hongqiao (Hungjao) Golf Club in support of its restoration. Today, China Golfing Society has up to 300 members and holds two events a year, one in Scotland and one in Hong Kong. The Society has a close relationship with the Hong Kong Golf Club and has a Hong Kong branch.

/ *Shanghai Challenge Cup (Gerard Corsane)*

British Empire thanks to pioneering Scottish golfers and enthusiasts. Second, almost all of the early golf courses and clubs in China's open ports were set up and operated by Scots and Englishmen. Third, early golf activities in China were closely related to horse racing, also brought over to China by the British. Fourth, the history of golf courses and clubs in China predates that of North America, most European countries, and Asian and Oceanian countries. Fifth, almost all golf courses and clubs in China prior to 1950 were only open to foreigners, with only a few clubs taking in Chinese as honorary members. Sixth, most of the golf courses in early China were primitive, simple and rough, starting with only a few holes or at most up to nine holes. The courses in the north had almost no grass greens, making them inexpensive to build, maintain and play. And seventh, during the 1920s and 1930s, a number of golf clubs were established by the invading Japanese in the puppet Manchuria State.

Looking back at the 80-year history of early golf in China, we can draw the following conclusions.

First, the modern game of golf spread around the world with the expansion of the

There may very well have been more golf courses and clubs which may have escaped our attentive eyes and which may not have been covered in this book. For example, although the authors have failed to find any written records about golf in Wuhu, Anhui Province, a trophy owned by a collector in Shanghai proves the existence of a golf club in the city. The trophy is a silver cigarette ashtray on which are inscribed the words: "Wuhu Golf Club 1923 Record Score for Course." Similarly, on August 4, 1923 a report in *North-China Herald* says that the St. Paul High School in the city of Anqing (Anch'ing), Anhui Province, built a 5-hole golf course for students due to the closure of the tennis courts during the flooding rainy season. Another report by the same newspaper on September 20, 1924 writes that the summer resort at Zhalantun (Chalantun), Inner Mongolia, was planning to build a golf course in order to attract more travelers during the summer. Likewise, other trading ports such as Ningbo (Ningpo), Shantou (Swatow), Jiujiang (Kiukiang), and Wenzhou (Wenchow) may also have had golf activities. We encourage interested golf historians to conduct further studies and research in order to dig out more facts about early golf in China.

In addition to the Nanjing (Nanking) Golf and Country Club built by the government of the Republic of China, there was also report of provincial-level government efforts in developing the game of golf. An interesting report from Hangzhou (Hangchow) was published on April 11, 1934 in *North-China Herald* with the headline *Playground of All China: Ambitious Scheme Drawn up for Chekiang*. The story says that with the completion of the 1,000 km of highways in Zhejiang (Chekiang), the provincial government had drawn up a plan to build a race course, a golf course, a swimming pool, and six hotels along the highways. Generalissimo Chiang Kai-shek and the young marshal Chang Hsueh-liang reportedly supported the plan and promised to donate funding. The Japanese invasion of China and continued civil wars rendered such a plan only a dream on paper.

Even though the first 80 years of history of golf in China started earlier than in most countries, it was a largely a history of foreign nationals playing golf on the Chinese soil. The clubs were funded, built, owned and enjoyed by expatriates living in China.

After the founding of the People's Republic of China in 1949, golf was outlawed as a resource wasting bourgeois pastime. In 1984, amidst China's economic reform and opening up to the outside world, the first golf course emerged at Zhongshan, Guangdong Province, with investment from Hong Kong businessmen. After a golfing void of more than 30 years, Zhongshan Hot Spring Golf Club opened to the public in 1984. Modern golf has finally been reintroduced in China as an outdoor sport. Following

/ *1923 Wuhu Golf Club Trophy*

Zhongshan, hundreds of golf courses and clubs have been built by the Chinses and serve both foreigners and Chinese.

Although an Olympic sport and a popular game globally for people of all ages, golf in China is not yet a sport for the common people. The limited number of only a few hundred golf courses is insufficient for a country of 1.4 billion people. In contrast to most countries, the game of golf in China struggles to support the country's national goal of "developing sports and enhancing people's physical fitness." China needs to change the current policy of only building expensive championship golf courses that cater to the rich. What the government needs is to consider how to utilize public resources, such as mountainous areas, waste lands, coast areas and other open spaces, to build a large number of simple and public golf courses. Municipal public golf courses built and maintained at minimal cost and operated as part of municipal sports and recreation programs should be the goal of all levels of governments. The popularization of golf as a sport and recreation for common citizens in China will be a touchstone to measure whether China has truly become a well-off society.

A number of scholars, Chinese and foreign, believe that China's ancient game of *Chuiwan* was the world's earliest form of golf. With its origins in China's Sung Dynasty more than 1,000 years ago, this ancient game of the high court boasted clubs, balls and rules of the game similar to those of modern golf. We believe, however, that *Chuiwan* was only one of many earlier stick and ball games which resembled modern golf. There is not yet sufficient evidence to establish a direct connection between *Chuiwan* and the modern game of golf that we know and play today. Our focus in this book, therefore, does not involve the history of *Chuiwan*. Instead, we have dedicated our research to the history of modern golf in 19th and 20th Century China that was introduced directly from Scotland.

The goal of *Early Golf in China 1870-1950* is to interest historians and golf enthusiasts in our preliminary research and findings about the history of early golf in China contained in this volume. We welcome comments, suggestions, new leads and stories about the Royal & Ancient Game in China. Together, we hope that we can help promote the history and culture of modern golf.

The images used in this book, unless otherwise noted, originate either from the public domain or are owned by the authors. In order to reflect history, we have decided to use the Wade-Giles spellings for the names of Chinese cities and golf clubs in this book.

The authors thank Jeff Wu (Wu Yifei) for his article, "*Chronology of Golf History in Modern China*," published in 2017 and 2022 in the Chinese edition of *Golf Magazine*. Our sincere thanks go to Gerard Esplin Corsane, former scholar of Heritage, Museum and Gallery Studies at the Newcastle University, for his information and images of the Shanghai Challenge Cup featured on the cover of this book. This beautiful silver trophy presented in 1897 to the Hankou Golf Club is a true testimony to China's early golf history. Wayne was fortunate to meet with Gerard on May 15, 2022, in Newcastle upon Tyne and witness this exquisite piece of art work handed down from his grandfather, Walter Hughs Corsane, who in 1913 won it outright. David Ferguson, Honorary Chief English Editor of Foreign Languages Press, kindly read and edited the Foreword. We thank Xiling Huang, Senior English Editor of the Beijing Foreign Language Teaching and Research Press, for her professional editing. We also thank Ji Chen for his hard work on the graphic design and layout of the book.

Wayne Xing waynexing2017@yahoo.com
Christoph Meister cnmeister@t-online.de
June 2025

Hankow Golf Club

Golf courses and clubs that emerged in China during the late 19th and early 20th centuries were mostly built, formed and operated by the British expatriates living in Chinese open port cities. Until recently, most golf historians believe that the earliest golf club established in mainland China was the Shanghai Golf Club incorporated in 1894.

According to Jeff Wu, golf collector and secretary of China Golf Heritage Society (formerly China Golf Collectors' Society), Shanghai was the birthplace of both China's first golf course and golf club. In his article, "You Should Not Only Remember the Image of Pu Yi Playing Golf" published in the January 2017 issue of the Chinese edition of *Golf Magazine*, Wu wrote a chronology of the history of modern golf in China.

Wu wrote in the article: "Around 1865, the Shanghai Sports Foundation was formed by British commercial establishments and it rented a vacant space inside the Shanghai Race Course and set up a rudimentary golf links. Due to the limited number of British expatriates at the time and lack of funding, the course made use of existing creeks and grave mounds as natural hazards. Because golfers often clashed with horse racers due to stray golf balls, some British expatriates organized a 'country club' in 1879 along Jing'an Temple Road and built a simple golf course. Golf was played there, as well as other sports, but participants were few. In 1882, Augustus White became one of the first members of the Shanghai Golf Club. In his diaries White described golf enthusiasts playing at the rudimentary golf links inside the Shanghai Race Course."

Shanghai was one of the first five Chinese ports open to foreign trade after the signing of the Treaty of Nanking in 1842 during the 1st Opium War. The city established a British concession as early as in 1846. It is therefore logical to assume that golf should was played in Shanghai earlier than other open ports of China. However, Wu's statement that a golf links was set up inside the Shanghai Race Course around 1865 remains to be substantiated by historical data.

Available historical information proves that the Shanghai Golf Club was incorporated in 1894. It is therefore questionable to claim that Augustus White could have become "one of the first members of the Shanghai Golf Club" in 1882.

Based on our research, the Hankow (Hankou) Golf Club was China's earliest golf club instituted in 1878, much earlier than the Shanghai Golf Club. Over the years until the 1920s, the Hankow Golf Club built three golf courses. The earliest one was located to the west of the Hankow Railway Station, today's Golf Course Street (Qiuchang Jie). It started in 1870 with only one or two holes and later expanded to 9 holes. The second was built in 1905 inside the Hankow Race Course, which was a short 9-hole. The third was an 18-hole course built around 1920 on the outskirts of the Race Course.

The Golf Course Street still existing in Hankow today is testimony to the fact that China's first golf course was built in Hankow, part of today's City of Wuhan, Hubei Province, over 153 years ago.

Hankow Golf Club

After several years of digging into published records in English and Chinese, we have found out that China's first rudimentary golf links appeared in Hankow in 1870. The Hankow Golf Club was instituted eight years later in 1878, 11 years earlier than the former Royal Hong Kong Golf Club and 16 years earlier than the Shanghai Golf Club.

After the 2nd Opium War, China was forced to sign the Treaty of Tientsin in 1858. Ten additional ports were opened to foreign trade, including Newchwang (Yingkou), Taiwanfu (Tainan), Swatow (Chaozhou), Chefoo (Dengzhou), Tamsui (Danshui), Kiungchow (Qiongzhou), Hankow (Hankou), Kiukiang (Jiujiang), Nanking (Nanjing) and Chinkiang (Zhenjiang). Following the Treaty of Peking (1860) and Treaty of Chefoo (1876), Tientsin (Tianjin), Taku (Dagu), Ichang (Yichang), Wuhu, Wenchow (Wenzhou), Peihai (Beihai) and Chungking (Chongqing) were also opened. The British and other powers flocked into these open ports to establish consulates and settlements, opened up commercial facilities, churches and schools, and in the meantime, started to promote Western cultural and sports activities.

The modern game of golf was soon introduced into the port cities by Scottish and English expatriates living there and became a popular outdoor sport. Starting in 1861, the UK, Germany, Russia, France, Japan, etc., opened consulates in Hankow one after another. In a settlement area about two square kilometers along the bund of the Yangtze River, there were soon more than 100 foreign government agencies, banks, trading companies, factories and other commercial facilities established.

Our main source of materials about early golf in China comes from China's longest-published English newspaper, *North-China Herald*, which began in 1850 in Shanghai. Searching the weekly newspaper archives of the late 19th Century, we came across the name of Mr. James Ferrier, who was often referred to as China's golf "Veteran." Born in Carnoustie, Angus, Scotland, Ferrier was a scratch handicapper. As early as in 1870, it was reported, Ferrier and a few friends from Scotland built a simple golf course with a couple of holes in an open space in Hankow and started playing the Royal & Ancient game. In 1878, Ferrier became a founding member of the Hankow Golf Club. Interestingly, the "Veteran" did the same in Shanghai: building a simple course inside the Shanghai Race Course in 1871 and becoming a founding member of the Shanghai Golf Club in 1894.

A report by a Hankow correspondent appeared on pp. 91-92 of the January 23, 1884 issue of *North-China Herald*. After reviewing the origin of the Royal & Ancient game in Scotland, the author writes about the recent activities at the Hankow Golf Club: "So much for the game, then; and it is not so well-known as might be expected that a flourishing club exists in Hankow, and I am happy to say the chief report of this letter is to inform the outside world of the latest development of the latent energies of the members of this Club in a social way." The correspondent was referring to a complimentary tiffin offered by members of the Hankow Golf Club to thank Alex Leith Esq., manager of the Hankow branch of the Hongkong and Shanghai Banking Corp., for his service as Honorary Secretary on the day he was leaving for home on a 12-month holiday. Club members gave Mrs. Leith a beautiful gold bracelet as a present in appreciation of Mr. Leith's contribution to the Club.

Captain Price then proposed 'Mr. Ferrier;' going over the history of the Club from its birth, Price said they were all indebted to Mr. Ferrier for the many able hints he gave them in regard to every detail of the game. Of course everybody knew Mr. Ferrier was the best player, and although he had not so far been successful in any of the handicaps, that was due to the 'weight which he carried;' and while bearing testimony to the efficient manner in which Mr. Leith had acted as Hon. Sec., he hoped Mr. Ferrier would be long spared to guide and instruct them in the mysteries of the Royal and Ancient game." After lunch, a game was played and Mr. Ferrier won after two rounds with a 76, 8 below. Captain Price was second, 83.

A report of Hankow Golf Club's annual meeting was published on pp. 181-182 of the February 7, 1898 *North-China Herald*. The annual meeting was held on January 25 and the report ended with the words: "Hankow Golf Club, Instituted 1878." It was signed by Honorary Secretary W.I. Mason. The paper also printed the Club balance sheet for the year ending December 31, 1897 signed by the Honorary Treasurer Stuart Smith.

/ *Hankow Golf Club Instituted 1878*

The online *History of Wuhan Timeline* compiled and updated by Konrad M. Lawson (*http://www.froginawell.net/reference/wuhan-timeline.html*), indicates that the Hankow Golf Club was instituted in 1878.

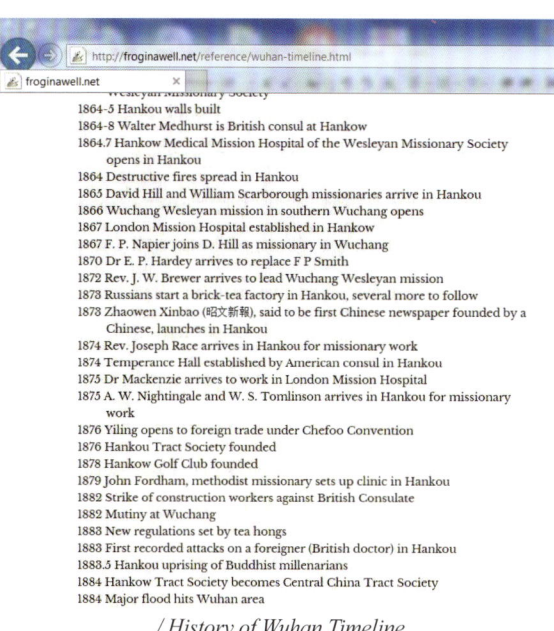

/ *History of Wuhan Timeline*

In fact, the Hankow golf course was first built by James Ferrier, the "Veteran", with only one or two holes. This was mentioned in an article titled "Golf in China: The Shanghai Course" in *The Dundee Courier* on February 2, 1899. The article, written "By an Old Carnoustie Player," had a sketch drawing of a club house with a handwritten note that reads "Shanghai Golf Club House opened 19/11/98." After a description in the first paragraph of the 9-hole golf links inside the Shanghai Race Course, the author points out that China's earliest golf links came into being in 1870 and a golf club was established in 1878. The rudimentary golf course was built by James Ferrier and a few "canny" Scottish friends.

The article reads: "It might not be out of place here to say a word or two on the introduction of golf into China, and I am glad to say, as an old player on the Carnoustie links, that the pioneer of the Royal and Ancient game in the Far East was Mr. James Ferrier, whose parent's name is associated with a cup played for on the popular links of the East Coast. So far back as in 1870, Mr. Ferrier, together with a few other canny

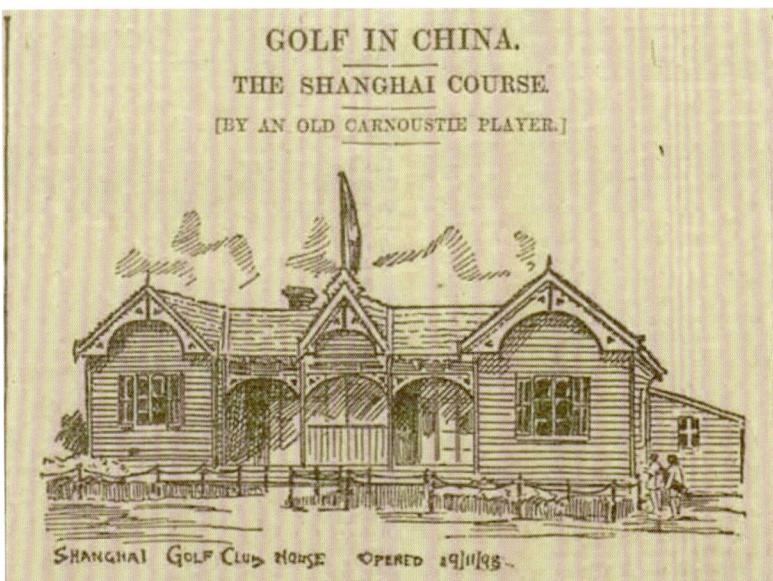
/ Golf in China

Scots, had one or two holes made on an open piece of ground at Hankow, and here at various intervals they enjoyed, as much as circumstances would permit, their favourite pastime. It was not until 1878 that the Hankow Club was founded, Mr. Ferrier being one of the founders; since then, it has flourished, and today its links on the race course are noted for their perfect greens. For some years past, Mr. Ferrier has been resident in Shanghai, and five years ago, he took a prominent part in establishing the golf club here. Known as the 'Veteran,' he has well-earned the name, and is indeed the Tom Morris of the Far East, for to-day he is as active and enthusiastic as ever, and holds the record of 79 strokes for the Shanghai course. Mr. Ferrier must be proud to observe how, in recent years, the interest in his pet game has ever been on the increase, and the opening of the new pavilion at Shanghai this autumn has, I know, afforded him the keenest sense of satisfaction. The pavilion stands an ornament to the Shanghai Recreation Ground, and forms a fitting crown to the labours of Mr. Ferrier and his 'blither Scots,' who have assisted him in thoroughly acclimatising, though far from the scene of its birth, the national game of the land o' cakes."

This important piece of historical document confirms the following:

1. James Ferrier, the "Veteran" golfer from Carnoustie, started the "one or two holes" golf course in Hankow in 1870 "with a few canny Scots."

2. The Hankow Golf Club was formed in 1878 and Ferrier was "one of the founders."

3. Ferrier "five years ago" (1894) took "a prominent part in establishing the golf club" in Shanghai, and held "the record of 79 strokes for the Shanghai course."

The "Old Carnoustie Player" that penned the article, we believe, was a native of Carnoustie and a friend of Ferrier. He might have also been one of the founders of the Shanghai Golf Club.

James Ferrier

James Ferrier was born on October 26, 1847. According to *Transactions of the Institution of Engineers and Shipbuilders in Scotland 1903-04*, young James Ferrier was apprenticed to the firm of Messrs. Goulay Brothers Engineers at Dundee. After the completion of his apprenticeship, he went to sea for a voyage or two as engineer of a Dundee whaler. Ferrier went to China in 1869 and joined the China Merchant Steam Navigation Company as a marine engineer. He eventually became engineer-in-chief of the extensive fleet of vessels owned by the Chinese company. Ferrier became a member of the Scotland Institution of Engineers and Shipbuilders in 1896.

As early as in September 29, 1883, the Hankow golf course had grown into 9 holes, though comparatively short. A correspondent from Hankow reported the monthly competition for a "Subscription Cup" in the October 10, 1883 issue of *North-China Herald*. On pp. 405-406 it is written: After two rounds of 9-hole playoffs participated by 10 members on September 29, Captain Martin won the Cup with a score of 96, a net of 10 below. Mr. Ferrier "played a remarkably steady game: first round, 38; second round, 37; total, 75 strokes." The report gave a hole-by-hole recount of the playoff between Mr. Ferrier and Mr. Price in medal play. After a heated competition over the 9 holes named Starter, Stand, Stone, Straight, Pond to the Mountain, Consulate, Gully, Grog and Gate, Ferrier scored 4, 4, 5, 5, 3, 4, 5, 4, 5, a total of 39 and Price 4, 3, 4, 6, 6, 4, 4, 5, 5, a total of 41.

As a scratch player and founder of golf courses and clubs in both Hankow and Shanghai, Ferrier spent his life time in China actively promoting the inter-club activities between Hankow and Shanghai.

On p. 53 of the January 11, 1895 *North-China Herald* was a letter from Honorary Secretary H.J.H. Tripp of the newly established Shanghai Golf Club. He wrote about the Club's 2nd handicap competition played on January 3 and suggested that new members learn from Mr. Ferrier: "The Ancient and Royal Game has now fairly started in Shanghai, and long may it flourish. We new beginners at the game must not be disappointed at our failures in putting-out, driving, etc., but practice hard and try and work up the best

Jas. Ferrier
/ James Ferrier

on record at present held by Mr. Ferrier with 86 for the 18 holes."

Ferrier was Captain of the Shanghai Golf Club in 1896. The Club's annual meeting held on January 27 was reported on pp. 211-212 of the February 7, 1896 *North-China Herald*. Ferrier said at the meeting: "The last of which was the Hankow Challenge Cup, so generously presented by the members of the Hankow Golf Club, and which we trust will eventually lead to inter-port matches." In celebration of the founding of the Shanghai Golf Club, Hankow Golf Club presented the new club a Challenge Cup in 1895.

Ferrier went back to Carnoustie for vacation after the annual meeting. When he returned the following year, he came back with a silver trophy named after his father. The Ferrier Cup became a new competition trophy for the Shanghai Golf Club. At the Club's annual meeting reported on pp. 785-786 of the October 29, 1897 *North-China Herald*, it was stated that "Mr. Ferrier, the Nestor of the Club, has lately returned from home and as you are aware he has not only a correct eye for golf but an eye for the beautiful as well, and he has selected the handsome cup you see on the table for presentation to the Club. It will give a zest to at least one of the competitions during the coming season. The Club highly appreciates Mr. Ferrier's graceful act. He helped to found the Club and has taken a strong interest in its welfare and this last act is another proof of his enthusiasm (Cheers)."

The Club in the meantime made a decision to return a favor to the Hankow Golf Club for its Challenge Cup: "It was decided to return the compliment received from the Hankow Golf Club by presenting them with a Cup, and the new Committee was requested to get a suitable trophy." The trophy, named Shanghai Challenge Cup, was made in late 1897 and presented to the Hankow Golf Club for its annual competition. The names of the winners would be inscribed on the trophy.

A report published on p. 141 of the January 28, 1898 *North-China Herald* described the year's Captain's Cup competition at the Shanghai Golf Club as follows: "Although several members availed themselves of the China New Year holidays to get away from Shanghai, a very large field entered on Saturday last for the most important 'to-be-won-outright' event of the season–the handicap for the Cup presented by the Captain, Mr. Wade Gard'ner." "Playing from scratch the 'Veteran' made a good bid for the Trophy with 84, but his was beaten by Mr. Molloy, an old Hankow golfer of note, with his best round on these links of 80 net."

A report in the November 21, 1898 issue of the *North-China Herald* says that the season's Opening Handicap Competition on November 5 was again won by "Veteran" James Ferrier with a score of 40 and 46 over two rounds. Ferrier was now Club president and he presided on Saturday (November 19) over the opening of the Club's new pavilion clubhouse. This confirms the handwritten date under the sketch of the new clubhouse in the *Golf in China* article published in *The Dundee Courier* mentioned earlier: "Shanghai Golf Club House Opened 19/11/98."

On behalf of the Club, Ferrier presented Miss Welch, daughter of J. Welch, Chairman of the Municipal Council, with a pretty little padlock and key as appreciation of her work and as master of ceremony for the opening. Mr. J. Welch said at the end of the ceremony: "Although this Club has only been established since 1894 we must not forget that your worthy President played the 'Ancient and Royal Game' on this same ground with some of his friends in 1871 and we rejoice to find him yet to the lore and as ready to compete for the honours of the game as ever he was."

The Hankow Challenge Cup competition was held on December 3-5, 1910 and the result was published on pp. 593-594 of the December 9, 1910 *North-China Herald*. With a net score of 81, W.J. Hawkins won the competition. The report reads: "This being his second consecutive victory, Mr. Hawkings wins the cup outright. The Cup was presented to the Shanghai Golf Club in 1895, to be played for under the conditions mentioned above and to be won twice in succession, or three times in all."

The report listed the names of the 30 winners of the Hankow Challenge Cup over the past 15 years from 1896 through 1910 as follows:

The Shanghai Challenge Cup was also played annually at Hankow Golf Club since 1898. A report from Hankow Golf Club published on p. 665 of the November 29, 1913 *North-China Herald* said: "The cards returned for the Shanghai Challenge Cup, Golf Handicap, Stroke Competition, have been examined and Vice-Captain W.H. Corsane declared the winner with 36, 36 plus 8 = Total 80. The runner-up being D.

/ 1912 Ch'ing Army Soldiers at Hankow Golf Course
(Bristol University WS01-065)

Aikman with 81. This being the third win for Mr. Corsane, the Cup becomes his property."

The report writes: "The Shanghai Challenge Cup, which is a handsome piece of plate, standing some 20 inches high, was presented to the Hankow Golf Club by the Shanghai Golf Club in the year 1897, and has been regularly contested for, with the exception of the period during the Chinese Revolution when the Club House was occupied and devastated by the Imperial troops and the Links became a battlefield."

/ 1896-1910 Hankow Challenge Cup Champions

The report gave a list of the winners of Shanghai Challenge Cup from 1898 through 1913:

Carnoustie and the Ferriers

The institution of the Carnoustie Golf Club in the mid-19th Century was almost a century later than the Royal and Ancient Golf Club at St. Andrews. However, the earliest golf links appeared in Carnoustie in 1527, 57 years earlier than the Old Course at St. Andrews, ranking the 4th oldest golf links in Scotland. According to https://www.carnoustiegolflinks.com, "St Andrews can rightfully lay claim to being the Home of Golf in Scotland but it was Carnoustie, across the water in Angus, which provided many of the game's earliest ambassadors. At the start of the 20th century around 300 of Carnoustie's sons emigrated, many of them westwards to America, spreading the golfing gospel as they went." Herbert Warren Wind, renowned American golf writer, wrote: "St. Andrews may be the home of golf, but Carnoustie is the home of American and Australian professional golf."

For several generations, the Ferriers from Carnoustie were not only guardians of the Scottish game of golf but also vanguards that introduced the Royal and Ancient game into China and Australia. As a marine engineer, James Ferrier spent his life for more than three decades in China. Ferrier learned the game of golf at Carnoustie before going to China. He also learned the ins and outs of how to build and maintain a golf course and how to organize and manage a golf club. He pioneered the game of golf in Hankow and Shanghai, becoming a pioneer of modern golf in China.

David Valentine, MBE, is a friend of Wayne Xing and International Trade Ambassador for China of the Scottish Chamber of Commerce. As the owner of the Simpson Shop in Carnoustie, he kindly provided some information about the Ferrier family. There is a Ferrier Street in Carnoustie that used to lead to the Ferrier Inn owned by James' parents, John and Isabella Ferrier. John was a founding member of the

/ 1898-1913 Shanghai Challenge Cup Winners

Carnoustie Golf Club instituted in 1842. Their son James was born five years later. Isabella was the proprietor of the Ferrier Inn, which was a popular meeting place for golfers. The Inn was demolished in 1882 and later became the 19th Hole Inn, which continues to be frequented by golfers today.

Learning the game of golf from his father, young James honed his playing skills while back home. He was a member of the Carnoustie Golf Club when he was 16. In 1868 at the age of 21 he became secretary of the Carnoustie Golf Club, according to David Ford's book, *The Carnoustie Golf Club 1842-2017*. This gave him the knowledge and experience of golf club organization and explains why he was able to build golf courses and organize golf clubs in Wuhan and Shanghai soon after he started working in China. The Ferrier Inn was run by his mother, Mrs. Ferrier, who donated a gold medal for the Carnoustie Golf Club's annual championship competition.

/ Mrs. Ferrier's Gold Medal (The Carnoustie Golf Club)

/ Ferrier Street, Carnoustie (David Valentine)

/ The Ferrier Inn (The Carnoustie Golf Club)

After a long career as marine engineer in China, James Ferrier decided to retire in 1900 and planned to take a leave with his family back in Carnoustie for two years. After the sudden death of his 18-year-old daughter in Shanghai in December due to diphtheria, Ferrier boarded a ship from Shanghai in April 1901 to sail back home. Unfortunately, the ship was wrecked on April 24 on its way to Scotland and although Ferrier and family were safe, he lost his life's savings, which included "a large quantity of Oriental finery and artistic ware." Back in Carnoustie, Ferrier soon decided against returning to China and lived at the Retreat Cottage, Links Parade in Carnoustie and continued playing golf at his home course.

On April 5, 1903, Ferrier suddenly died during sleep due to several weeks of influenza. He was 56 years of age. The Carnoustie *Evening Post* published an obituary on April 6, which reads: "The deceased was a well-known golfer in his early days and had been connected with the Carnoustie Golf Club for over forty years. In many ways he manifested his interest in that club, and it was only ten days before his death that he was presented with a handsome medal by the members as a token of the honorary life membership conferred upon him. In China he was the foremost golfer in all matches and tournaments."

The *Celestial Empire*, an English publication in Shanghai, printed an obituary on p. 76 on April 15, 1903, which reads: "It is with extreme regret we learn of the death of Mr. James Ferrier, who died at his residence at Carnoustie, Forfarshire, Scotland. The sad news came by telegram on Tuesday. According to late letters, Mr. Ferrier was enjoying his great health and his favourite game—golf. He was well-known in Shanghai and the outports and he was respected by a large circle of friends in China, who will be sorry to hear of his death."

Ferrier's son, John Bennett Ferrier, was born in Shanghai and worked as an accountant at the British Cigarette Co., Ltd. and British American Tobacco Co. J.B. Ferrier was a low handicapper and on February 23, 1910, he was elected as a member of Shanghai Junior Golf Club's General Committee, according to a report on February 25's *North-China Herald*. In 1911, J.B. Ferrier won the annual championship of Shanghai Golf Club and in November 1920, he won the third championship of Shanghai GC's annual competition. After marrying an Australian girl, J.B. Ferrier lived in Australia for six years starting in 1913.

J.B. Ferrier's son, James Bennett Elliott Ferrier or Jim Ferrier, was born in 1915 in Australia and came back to Shanghai when he was four. Jim Ferrier went back to Australia when he was 11 as his father became a secretary of the Manly Golf Club outside of Sydney. Young Jim learned the game of golf through his father at Manley and became a noted amateur golfer in Australia. He immigrated to the U.S. in 1940, turned professional in 1941 and became a U.S. citizen in 1944. Jim participated in 36 PGA games and won the 1947 PGA Championship.

To commemorate its long and close ties with China, members of the Carnoustie Golf Club presented a Shanghai Cup and a China Cup for annual competition in the 1920s.

Hankow Golf Club in the 20th Century

Hankow Golf Club was listed on p. 283 of the 1899-1900 *Golfing Annual* published in London. It was also listed on p. 781 of *The Directory & Chronicle of China, Japan, Straits Settlements, Malaya, Borneo, Siam, the Philippines, Korea, Indo-China, Netherlands Indies, Etc.* published in 1906 by the Hong Kong Daily Group, with the names of members of its board.

/ Hankow Golf Club Board Members

J.M. Robb was an engineering consultant of a Shanghai partnership. H. Bass was an assistant to the president of a Hankow company. W.H. Clearsby was manager of a Hankow company and A. Schultze was assistant to the president of another Hankow company.

The 1906-1907 *Golfing Annual* published in 1907 in London listed Hankow Golf Club with the following note: "The course is a short one of nine holes near the foreign settlement."

/ Hankow Golf Club Board Members

There was a story published in the June 17, 1911 issue of the *Exmouth Journal* in England about the home visit of a native E. Harris. Harris was the master of a passenger steamship in China and a member of the Hankow Golf Club. Over the years, he had won two trophies in Hankow, the Shanghai Challenge Cup and the Crosbie Cup. He was on the list of the Shanghai Challenge Cup winners mentioned earlier for 1911.

During the Wuchang Uprising in 1911, D.J. Claris, Captain RN of HMS Thistle stationed in Hankow, took a photograph of the golf links inside the Race Course with the caption that reads: "Shells bursting on the 1st tee on the golf course inside Hankow race course." The photo is now with the Imperial War Museum (#Q114765) in London.

On July 18, 1913, the *Yorkshire Evening Post* published a story by Alec Taylor on p. 4 about his travel to Hankow after the 1911 Revolution. He writes: "Ever since the Chinese revolution, eighteen months ago, there has been a constant feeling of unrest at all ports up the Yang-tze. At Hankow, when the Imperial soldiers from Peking captured it, the officers made the golf club premises their headquarters. They made a fire on one of the billiard tables to boil their stock pot on, and found the composition balls, cues, and golf clubs made an excellent fire to cook with. They afterwards played billiards, using their rifles with fixed bayonets for cues, and golf balls took the place of the real things, which were all burned. After the trouble and things got a bit settled the club executive sent in a compensation bill to the authorities. As they anticipated getting about a tenth of what they asked they named a ridiculously large sum, and much to their amazement were granted all they

/ Shells Bursting on the 1st Tee

asked. The principal battle at that time was fought on the Hankow golf links."

Chinese historians in Wuhan have published articles about the history of Hankow golf links. A blogger on www.sina.com.cn named Yijianzhai wrote several articles about *Stories of Old Wuhan*. A 1902 map of the *Plan of Hankow* concession that he provided had a notation of "Golf Club" in English.

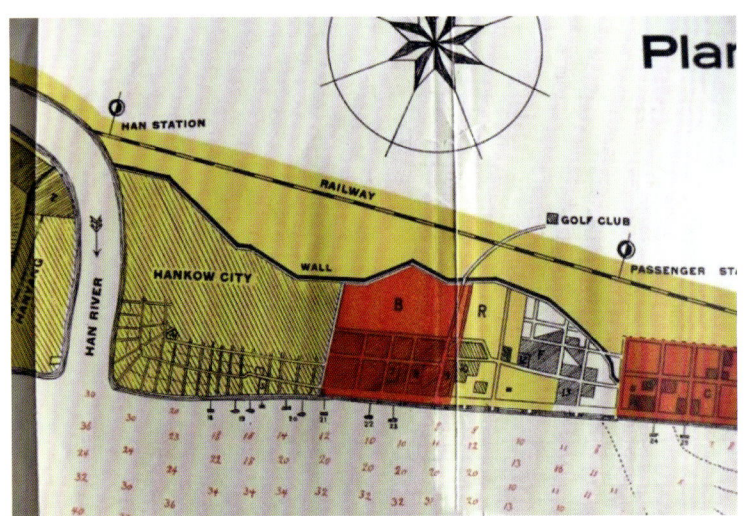

/ 1902 Plan of Hankow

Yijianzhai wrote in his blog that historical records indicated that when the Race Course was built at today's Liberation Park, an 18-hole golf course was also built. But looking at the 1902 map, the area noted as Golf Club near Golf Course Street "does not look like an 18-hole golf course, not even a 9-hole." Reading about the history of the first golf course built in Taipei by the Japanese in 1914 which started with only three holes, he came to the judgement that the earliest golf course in Hankow started also with only a few holes. The Golf Course Street was named because of this golf course. As already mentioned earlier, the Hankow Golf Club expanded into 9 holes in 1883, even though it was a short 9-hole.

Yijianzhai also offered a photograph of German marines playing golf inside the German concession in 1912, using a simple tree branch as club.

Yijianzhai also provided a map used by the Japanese soldiers stationed in Hankow in 1912. The " ゴルフ倶乐部 " is Japanese for Golf Club and the Peking Street close to the Club is now Golf Course Street.

Another 1915 map of the Hankow Settlement in English clearly listed the 9-hole golf course and club in Hankow.

The Chapter on "Xu Enzeng, Head of the Central Investigation and Statistics Bureau" in the Chinese book, *The Rise and Fall of the Central Investigation and Statistics Bureau*, published in May 1989 mentioned a "small golf course in the 3rd Special District of Hankow." The Chapter reads: "In April 1928, Cai Mengjian received intelligence that an important Communist Party member was in Wuhan pretending to be a

/ 1912 German Marines Playing Golf

magician (Gu Shunzhang was using his 'Shanghai Hua Guangqi Magician' for street advertisements). Cai immediately sent out You Congxin and other traitors to roam the streets trying to identify the Communists so as to prove their loyalty. On April 24, You Congxin discovered Gu Shunzhang in front of the small golf course in Hankow's 3rd Special District and shouted 'Here is the General Director of the Shanghai Uprising!' Gu was therefore arrested." The 3rd Special District refers to the British Concession in Hankow.

An article titled "Touring Wuhan to Discover the Whereabouts of the Old Golf Course" was published in the July 25, 2013 issue of the *Chutian Metropolitan Newspaper*. The author mentioned Shi Jun and his collection of old maps of Wuhan. One map was titled "Hankow Complete Street Map" published in 1920 by the Wuhan Book Trade. The Golf Club in the map was changed to "Throw Ball Course" (Paoqiuchang). In a later map of 1938, titled "The New Detailed Street Map of Hankow," it was labeled as "Golf Course." The "Hankow Wuchang Street Map" dated 1938 retained the name of "Golf Course" until 1949. But some other maps dated 1945, 1946 and 1949 referred to it as "Golf Course Main Street" or simply "Golf Course Street."

According to the Golf Course Street neighborhood committee in Hankow, its jurisdiction before the liberation was adjacent to 1,875 kilometers of the Beijing-Guangzhou Railway. In 1914, German residents at the German Concession in Hankow built a road 10 meters wide from Dazhi Road along the Railway close to the golf course. After Hankow fell into the hands of the Northern Warlords, the authorities further extended and widened the road all the way to the front gate of the golf course and named it "Golf Course Main Road." In

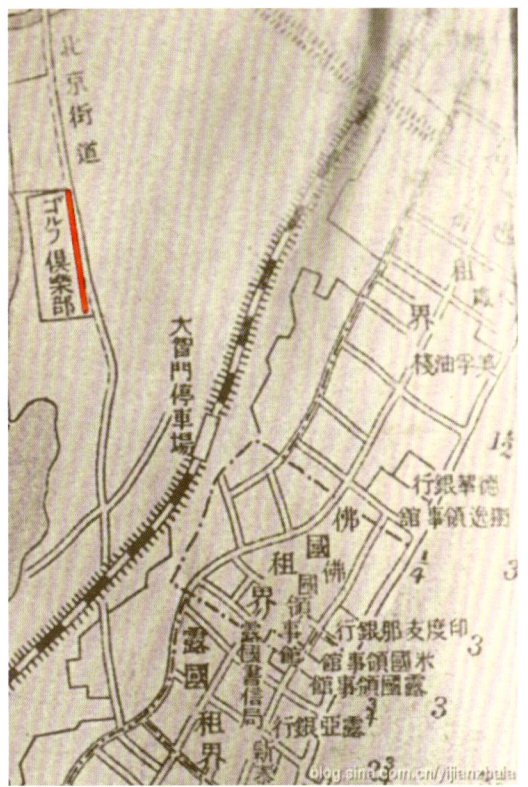

/ 1912 Hankow Map (Yijianzhai)

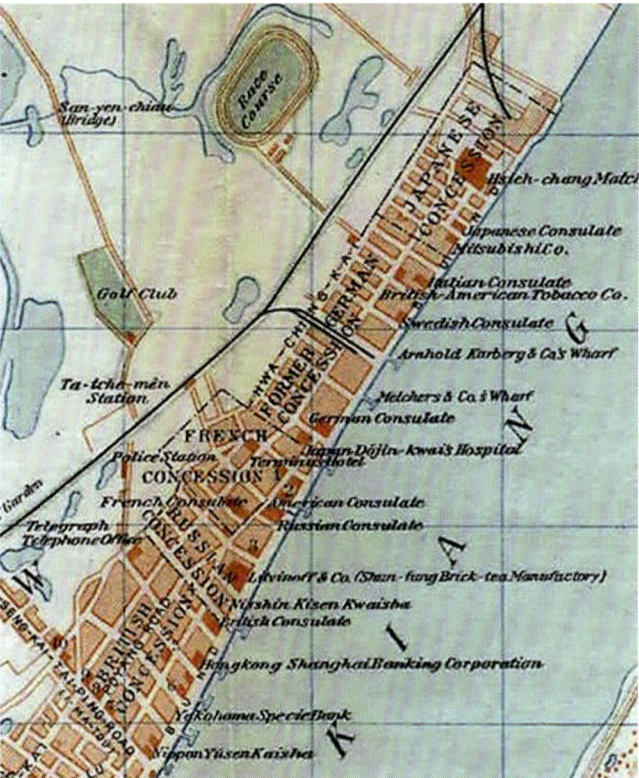

/ 1915 Hankow Settlement (Yijianzhai)

1946, the Hankow government renamed the road Golf Course Street, which is used until today. "Naturally," said a neighborhood committee official, "our committee decided to use the old and famous name of Golf Course Street."

These Chinese sources confirm that the earliest golf course in Hankow was located in today's Model New Village area along the Golf Course Street. Built in 1870 with just a few holes, it expanded to a formal 9-hole course in 1883. The course was the earliest one in China built by James Ferrier and became the formal course for the Hankow Golf Club after it was established in 1878.

Golf Links at the Hankow Race Course

According to an article by Xiao Zhihua and Shi Yuwen published in Volume 75 of *Hubei Culture and History*, the Hankow Race Course was started by the British expatriates in 1895. French, German, Russian, American and Japanese concessions also participated in its construction and was referred by locals as the Race Course of the Six Foreign Concessions. The Race Course was located in the northeast suburbs of Hankow (today's Liberation Park) and used to be a swamp area of 800 *mu* (53.33 acres). The Race Course, the earliest in Wuhan, was registered with the British government in Hong Kong in 1902 and started operating in 1905. After the National Revolutionary Army took over the British Concession in 1926, the Race Course business started to decline but recovered in 1928. It was taken over by the Japanese in 1941 after the Pearl Harbor attack and was turned into a storage facility of cannons for the Japanese army. Even though the British Concession opened again after the surrender of the Japanese, the Race Course never resumed operation.

/ *Hankow Race Course (Bristol University bl03-006)*

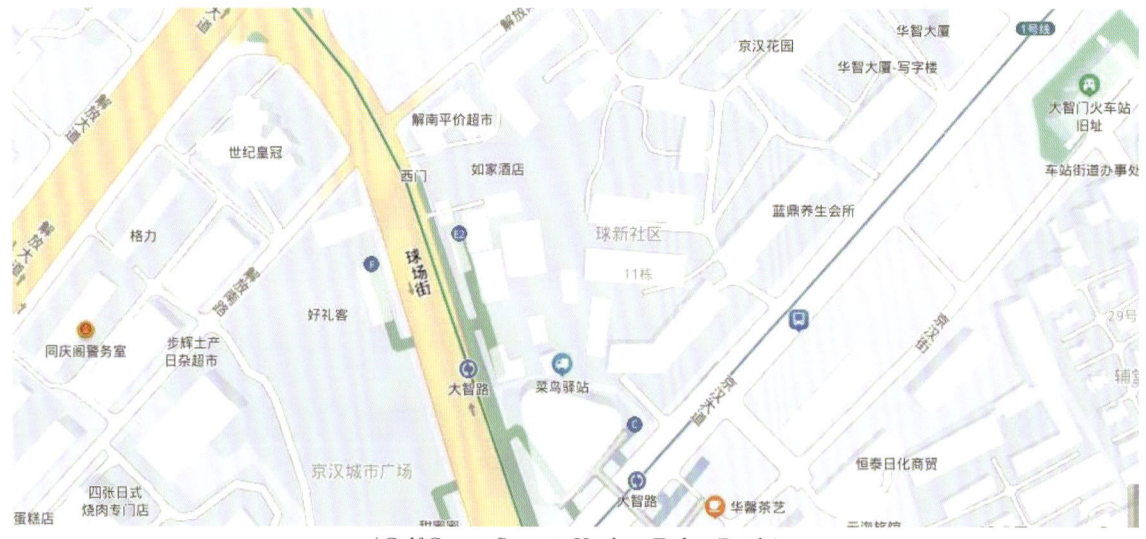

/ *Golf Course Street in Hankow Today (Baidu)*

A small 9-hole golf course was built inside the race track after 1905. Volume 51 of the *Journal of the Royal Asiatic Society Hong Kong Branch* published in 2011 has an article by Kim Salkeld titled "Witness to the Revolution: Surgeon Lieutenant Bertram Bickford on the China Station 1910-12." The article said that Bickford had an old photograph of the Hankow Race Course. The article writes on p. 120: "To the north of the foreign concessions was a large racetrack with a prominent clubhouse next to it, a picture of which is in Bickford's collection." It then quotes D.J. Claris, Captain RN of HMS Thistle on which Bickford also served, as saying: "One can obtain plenty of exercise at Hankow. Riding is cheap and proves very well in fact they go too well sometimes. There is an excellent Recreation Club whose grounds are inside the circular Race Course. Golf is going all the year round. The course is a short 9 holes course and is usually in very good conditions. Naval officers are non-members and pay no subscription."

The 18-hole golf course outside of the Race Course was built around the early 1920s. The Chapter on Hankow in the 2nd Edition of *Seaports of the Far East* published in 1925 described the history of the Race Club and Recreation Ground, with a picture of the Race Course and Club. It writes: "The race course is a little over a mile, with both cinder and sand training tracks; and the grounds comprise also a golf-course of 18 holes, tennis courts, and sections for lawn bowls, base-ball, polo, cricket, football, hockey, and basket-ball. The club is run by a general committee of seven stewards, and there are sub-committees for every branch of sports."

Today, there is still a place called Race Course Corner (Machangjiao) in Hankow.

/ Hankow Race Course and Club

In 2015, Robert Nield published his book *China's Foreign Places: The Foreign Presence in China in the Treaty Port Era, 1840-1943*. On p. 113 of the Hankow chapter, Nield writes: "The Hankow Race Course and Recreation Ground was opened in 1905 and was an instant success. In addition to the race tracks (an inner cinder track and an outer grass one), by the early 1920s it boasts two golf courses, cricket and football fields, twelve tennis courts, a bowling green, and a clay-pigeon shooting range." "Golfers were well looked after; in addition to the Race Club courses, there was to the west of the railway station of the Hankow Golf Club, founded in 1878 and latterly with a membership of over 100."

An anonymous letter was published on p. 525 of the March 28, 1925 *North-China Herald* with the title: "Germans and the Hankow Club." Writing about the fact that German residents in Hankow had not paid the backlog of their fees due to the Hankow Race Club, the author writes: "The Race Club at Hankow occupies, as many know, a unique position in the port. Races are but a small part of the Club's attractions which consist of several thousand *mow* of land devoted to golf (two courses), riding, pole, football, cricket, hockey, tennis, baseball, and kindred sports."

On p. 5 of the May 6, 1927 *Belfast Telegraph* we find the following news about British officers golfing in Hankow during the Northern Expedition of China's National Revolutionary Army: "The sailors of the foreign warships are ready for any emergency. The Japanese Concession (next to the British) is in the hands of 1,000 Marines, who at many points behind banks of sandbags, walls, and wire, are feverishly digging themselves in, while two miles inland on the Hankow golf course Rear-Admiral J.E. Cameron and other Naval officers of the Powers are digging themselves out—of bunkers."

/ British Officers Golfing

The *North-China Herald* published numerous reports of inter-port matches between the Hankow and Shanghai Golf Clubs during the 1920s and 1930s. A report on p. 927 of the September 29, 1923 issue reads: "Hankow Golf Club defeated Shanghai today by 27 shots to 15."

The China amateur open championship to be held in 1924 was announced by the Shanghai Golf Club in a story published on p. 262 of the May 17, 1924 issue. Hankow Golf Club was among the 17 participating clubs from China, South Asia and Japan to be invited. The open championship was tentatively scheduled for October 19 or 26 and it would be an annual competition of 72-holes. A trophy would be presented by a member of the Shanghai Golf Club.

The October 2, 1925 issue of *North-China Herald* printed a story about an inter-port match in Hankow between Shanghai Golf Club and the Hankow Customs Team, with a 29 to 13 score in the former's favor.

The Foreign Affairs Oral History Project of the Association for Diplomatic Studies and Training recorded an interview dated March 25, 1993 by Charles Stuart Kennedy with Richard P.

Butrick, a U.S. consular officer in Hankow from 1926 to 1932. Butrick recalled the days of his Yangtze River Patrols by saying on p. 11: "They were a lot of fun. Sometimes the wives would come out and stay in Hangzhou (sic., should be Hankow), so we got to know the ladies quite well. We would see them at the club, playing golf. We had a very nice club in Hangzhou (Hankow). The most unusual club I have ever seen in the world, for a country club. We had a race track, a nine hole golf course inside the race track, an eighteen hole golf course outside the race track, 12 or 15 tennis courts on grass, a swimming pool which was indoors and in winter was covered over and made into a ballroom." Lewis Clark, a U.S. diplomat stationed in a number of cities in China, including Wuhan, remembered playing golf in Hankow in the early 1930s. He was interviewed in 2012 by Susan E. Palsbo and the story was published in *Diplomacy as a Career: Hard Work, Hardship, and Happy Times*. Clark arrived in Hankow with his bride in early 1930. The new couple was able to find a house near the Race Course about two miles from the U.S. General Consulate. The house looks over the 6th Green of the 9-hole golf course. According to Clark: "Life in Hankow centered around the Race Club. In addition to the racetrack, the Hankow Race Club had a polo field and a 9-hole golf course inside the racetrack, an 18-hole golf course around and behind the track, 52 grass tennis courts, a cricket field, lawn bowling greens, a swimming pool and badminton courts." As the office was overstaffed, Clark said, his wife Anne used to come by the Consulate sometimes early in the afternoon and entice the Consular Chief, Frank Lockhart, out for nine holes of golf on the small course inside the racetrack. "The minute they were on their way, I and another officer, usually George Graves, would slip out also and go to play on the big course."

Clark and his friends invented a game of Monkey Golf. He said: "We played it on the little 9-hole course located inside the racetrack. The names of the various iron clubs were written on pieces of paper and placed in a hat. Each player drew a piece of paper out of the hat, and he had to play the entire nine holes with the club stipulated thereon. I might draw a putter and be matched against a naval officer or his wife playing with a mashie. These competitions did not offer a very high caliber of golf, but they were occasions of hilarity. The trophy was a large locally-produced silver cocktail shaker. Each player was required to drink two martinis from that cocktail shaker before he was allowed to tee off. Afterwards, there was general refreshment and dinner at the Race Club. It didn't make much difference who won; everybody had a good time."

On p. 3 of the *Western Daily Press* dated November 2, 1934 was news from Hankow titled: "Chinese War Lord's Golf Triumph." It reads: "Marshal Chang Hsueh-Liang, formerly ruler of Manchuria, has gained another victory. Competing here for the first time in a golf tournament he

Western Daily Press - Friday 02 November 1934

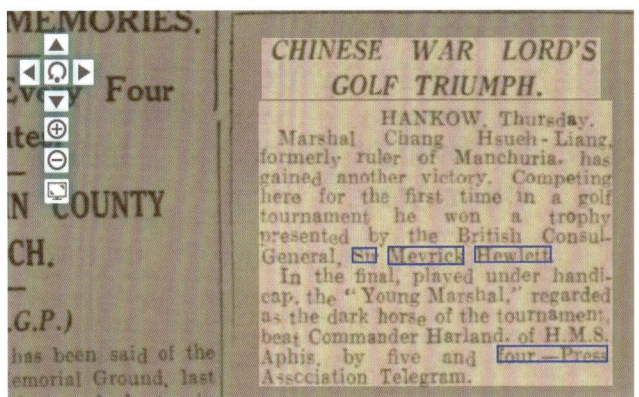

/ *Chinese War Lord's Golf Triumph*

won a trophy presented by Sir Meyrick Hewlett. In the final, played under handicap, the 'Young Marshall,' regarded as the dark horse of the tournament, beat Commander Harland, of H.M.S. Aphis, by five and four."

The *Singapore Free Press & Mercantile Advertiser* published a story about Hankow Golf Club championship on December 19, 1934 on p. 15, which reads: "The replay for the Hankow golf championship at the Race Club resulted in a win for W.J. Allan by one stroke, his opponent, J.S. McEachran, making a very fine recovery in the afternoon after being nine strokes down on the morning's play. In the morning Allan returned a 73 and McEachran an 82, while in the afternoon the former's card showed an 85 and the latter a 77, making a total for the 36 holes of: Allan 158 and McEachran 159."

The following two photos of the Hankow Race Course Golf Club were taken in 1936 and are a collection of the Studienwerk Deutsches Leben in Ostasien e.V. in Munich. One shows workers maintaining the fairway in the morning, together with a foreigner. The other shows Edith Heinisch, a German resident, playing golf accompanied by a caddie.

Sir Meyrick Hewlett, British diplomat in China, published his book, *Forty Years in China*, in 1943. Hewlett had a vivid description of his friendship with local caddies at the Hankow Golf Club during his time as Consul General in 1932-1935. Hewlett played golf almost daily at the Race Course. He would use a caddie to carry his bag, and in addition hired two other fore-caddies to spot where his balls went. When the caddies shouted "outerboundza," Hewlett often cursed in Chinese which triggered hearty laughter from the caddies. At year end, Hewlett would give a feast to all the caddies at the golf club, and on p. 254 he writes: "It was a happy night to see a hundred and twenty children sitting down to the only feast they had ever had, as much rice as they could eat, a bowl of soup and five dishes of various

/ *Maintaining the Race Course Fairway at 6 am in 1936*

/ *Edith Heinisch at the Race Course Golf Club in May 1936*

meats and vegetables. When I entered the room the Caddie Master tapped on the floor with a stick and all stood up in perfect unison, and at the word 'Salute' hands were smartly raised. I used to remind them that they were important members of a big club, that if those who smote the ball cursed them they must not lose their tempers, rather must they admire them as good players. Then, after saying 'one, two, three,' they were allowed to yell 'outerboundza' and again 'one, two, three,' when they called out 'Hao' (all right) and sat down." The Hankow Golf Club had as many as 120 caddies in the 1930s, which showed the popularity of the game in the city.

During the 1930s, there appeared in Hankow, like in Shanghai, a number of mini golf courses or putting grounds. The following are photos of mini golf courses in Hankow taken by naval officers of the HMS Berwick during the Royal gunboat's visit. Two Chinese ladies dressed in cheongsam are seen putting at a mini golf course.

By 1936, members of the Hankow Golf Club shrank to 85. H. Brownlow was the Honorary Secretary and G. Hall the greenkeeper. Caddies were allowed to play on Sunday.

The golf courses in Hankow were forced to close after the Japanese occupied the city of Wuhan in 1938. After the Japanese surrendered in 1945, the city, known as the "Pittsburg of China," was still in ruins. A *Reuter*'s report on p. 5 of the August 7, 1946 *The Straits Times* reads: "Although almost a year has elapsed since Japan's surrender, the big Yangtze port of Hankow, the 'Pittsburgh of China,' is still a crippled rubble-strewn, ghost town." "The city's only golf course is overgrown and neglected; and the Race Club, one of the most famous in China, which the Allied authorities used as an internment camp for the Japanese after the surrender, is a shambles."

Post-war issues of *The Golfer's Handbook* no longer listed any information about the Hankow Golf Club, indicating the closure of China's oldest golf club after operating for close to 70 years.

Hankow Golf Club Trophies

As China's earliest golf club, the Hankow Golf Club has left numerous medals and trophies over the years, including trophies of its billiard section. A number of these medals and trophies have been seen at auctions in the U.K. and U.S., which testifies its long history of close to 80 years.

A silver trophy competed for in 1897 at the Hankow Golf Club was auctioned in the U.K. on December 9, 2022 and was acquired by the Golf Heritage Museum in Shenzhen, China. The trophy, made by Hung Chong, a famous Shanghai silversmith, stands 26.5 mm high and weighs 642 g. Two dragons are etched on the trophy, which

/ 1932-1934 Hankow Mini Golf Course

sits on the base with three bamboo sticks. On the front of the trophy are the words: "HANKOW GOLF CLUB," beneath which are two crossed golf clubs. Further down are the words: "ST. ANDREWS CUP." On the other side of the trophy are the words: "WON BY J. SHEARER 1897." This trophy once again proves that the Hankow Golf Club was China's earliest golf club.

/ 1897 Hankow Golf Club St. Andrews Cup

On August 18, 2024, the Golf Heritage Museum purchased another Hankow GC St. Andrews Cup dated 1906 from an antique store at Penang, Malasia. The silver trophy was made by Luen Wo and weighs over 500g. Two reliefs of flying dragons are made on the cup, with two dragon handles. Clearly etched on the bottom of the trophy are the words: "Hankow Golf Club St. Andrews Cup 1906 Won by Walter Hughs Corsane."

The Great Western Auctions at Glasgow in 2012 sold a 1908 silver trophy of billiard competition of the Hankow Golf Club. Inscribed on the trophy are words: "A. Crosbie RUNNER-UP 1908 BILIARD CHALLENGE COMPETITION HANKOW GOLF CLUB." The trophy cup has flowers etched on the cup and sits on the base with three bamboo sticks. The trophy is now owned by a Wuhan collector.

/ 1908 Hankow Golf Club Billiard Trophy

In 2010, eBay sold a 1910 Hankow Golf Club trophy: China New Year Cup. Inscribed on the cup are words: "HANKOW GOLF CLUB 1910 CHINA NEW YEAR CUP 1st Prize WON BY WAT. CROSBIE." This silver trophy has a gold inlay, with a dragon on the cup. The trophy measures 7.3 inches high, 3.25 inches wide and weighs 10.6 ounces. It sits on the base with three bamboo-shape sticks. The trophy was made by Tuck Chang of Shanghai, one of the major manufacturers of export silver

/ 1906 Hankow GC St. Andrews Cup

in 1785-1925. The trophy is now owned by the same Wuhan collector.

/ 1910 Hankow Golf Club China New Year Cup

Three silver trophies of the Hankow Golf Club were auctioned in March 2012 by the Great Western Auctions. The two trophies on the left were won by Wat. Crosby and the one on the right by A. Crosby. We estimate that the trophies were presented to the winners around 1910.

It was reported on p. 665 of the November 29, 1913 *North-China Herald* that the Hankow Golf Club's Vice-Captain Walter Hughes Corsane won for the third time the Shanghai Challenge Cup in the handicap stroke competition. "The Cup becomes his property," the paper reads. Made by the famous Shanghai silversmith Luen Wo, a manufacturer of export silver of Canton (Guanzhou) origin, the beautiful silver trophy was characteristic of relief design and craftsmanship. When the Shanghai Golf Club decided to return a favor from the Hankow Golf Club, it chose this Chinese design of a silver pot with two handles in the shape of dragons and a cover with a dragon head. The silver pot is connected with three dragons to the base. This trophy is a rare piece of

/ Hankow Golf Club Trophies Around 1910

silver artwork that combines Chinese and western cultures. In the middle of the pot is inscribed the words: "CHALLENGE CUP Presented by the Shanghai Golf Cub to the Hankow Golf Club 1897."

/ Walter Hughes Corsane (Gerard Corsane)

of the Hankow Golf Club in 1912 he won the Challenge Cup a second time. In 1913, as Vice-Captain of the Club he won the Challenge Cup a third time, winning it outright. From 1898 to 1913, the Hankow Golf Club organized a total of 24 competitions for the Shanghai Challenge Cup.

McTear's, an auction house in England, sold a 1914 Hankow Golf Club Billiard Trophy. The silver trophy is 14 cm high and weighs 115.6 grams. It was presented for D. Maitland, the runner-up of the billiard competition. The trophy is also with the collector in Wuhan.

/ Shanghai Challenge Cup (Gerard Corsane)

/ Hankow Golf Club Trophies Around 1910

According to Gerard Corsane, his grandfather Walter Hughes Corsane was a steam ship engineer and in 1902 served as the 3rd Mate of the Hankow-based Anping ship owned by the China Merchant Steam Navigation Company. In 1904, Walter invested in a partnership of the Hankow Ice Works, and in 1921, he made another investment in the Hankow Aerated Water Co. Born in St. Andrews, Walter Hughes Corsane was a skilled amateur golfer. He first won the Shanghai Challenge Cup in 1907. After becoming Captain

Jacobs & Hunt Auctioneers had on its website a group of five Hankow Golf Club gold medallions, which were sold in a past auction for £1,000 at hammer price. The front and back of the medals have Hankow Golf Club on them with a pair of crossed golf clubs underneath. The front of

/ Hankow Golf Club Gold Medallions

the medals has designs of a city wall, a pavilion and a pavilion and a pagoda. The back of the medals displays the Chinese character Fu (meaning fortune). The five medallions weigh a total of 50.5 g.

In 2012, Dominic Winter Auctions of the U.K. sold a Hankow Golf Club Billiard Handicap Trophy. Inscribed on the trophy cup are the following words: "Hankow Golf Club 1920 Billiard Handicap Champion J.W.E. Radford." The trophy cup sits on three cues and a billiard ball on an ebony base.

Conclusion

Based on historical sources mentioned above, we are able to make the following conclusions: The earliest golf course in China appeared in 1870 in Hankow. The earliest golf club in China, the Hankow Golf Club, was instituted in 1878, 11 years earlier than the Hong Kong Golf Club (1889) and 16 years earlier than the Shanghai Golf Club (1894).

During the late 19th Century and up to the 1920s, Hankow built three golf links. The first one was built in 1870 west of the former Dazhimen Railway Station, starting with one or two holes and expanding into a short 9-hole course in 1883.

/ 1920 Hankow Golf Club Billiard Trophy

The second was built inside the Race Course in 1905, a short 9-hole. And the third was outside the Race Course built around 1920.

The Hankow Golf Club was established thanks to amateur and "Veteran" golfer James Ferrier from Carnoustie, Scotland. As a marine engineer in China, the zero-handicapper also initiated the Shanghai golf links and founded the Shanghai Golf Club. During his life time in China, Ferrier contributed to the growth of golf in both Hankow and Shanghai. James Ferrier was the Scottish ambassador that introduced the Royal and Ancient game to China. Ferrier was not only the Tom Morris of the Far East, more accurately, he was the Tom Morris of China.

Chefoo Golf Club

After Chefoo (Yantai) opened to foreign trade in 1863, about 400 expatriate residents registered with foreign consulates in the city, and half of those were missionaries. There was no formal concession area designated for foreign residents. Foreigners were under the administration of a General Purpose Committee and chose to build their residence on the coastal areas.

According to the book, Westerners and Modern Yantai, by Professor Wei Chunyang of the Shandong College of Industry and Commerce, one of the first important companies set up in Yantai was Cornabé, Eckford and Co. (Ho Kee in Chinese), a partnership between W.A. Cornabé and Andrew Eckford. Benefiting from their privileged position as British citizens and to the envy of other foreign businesses, the company went into ocean shipping and transportation business in addition to the trading of yarn, handicrafts, peanuts, etc.

/ 1920 Hankow Golf Club Billiard Trophy

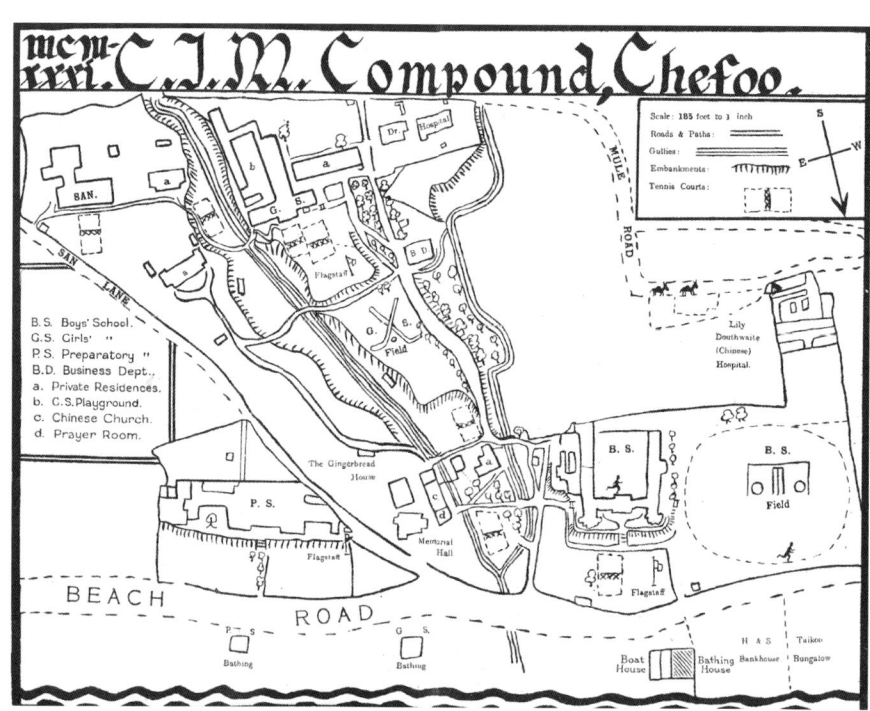
/ Early Chefoo Map

W.A. Cornabé came from Amoy (Xiamen) and after forming the partnership with Andrew Eckford, the company expanded into Weihaiwei, Tsingtao and Dairen. According to the 20th Century Impressions of Hongkong, Shanghai, and Other Treaty Ports of China, Cornabé started the Chefoo Club in 1865 and it was housed in one of his premises. There were about 50 members that represented eight to nine different nationalities. An international chamber of commerce was formed in 1867.

/ Chefoo Horse Race 1904

/ The Chefoo Club

On February 15, 2018, Professor Wei published an article, "Modern Horse Racing in Yantai," in Yantai Evening News. He pointed out that Cornabé and Beckford initiated the formation of the Chefoo Race Club in March 1864 and organized the city's first horse race on May 4th. By 1868, horse racing attracted a large number of visitors from both foreigners and local residents.

Vivvy Eckford, stepson of Andrew Eckford, built Chefoo's first golf links around 1890. This was mentioned in a biography written by Frances Osborne about her great grandmother, Lilla Eckford who was born in Chefoo. The book, Lilla's Feast, was published in 2004, and on p. 148 Osborne writes: Lilla's oldest brother, Vivvy, "was a keen golfer and built Chefoo's first and only golf course– playable only at low tide."

As early as in 1893, there were reports in the English press about golf in Chefoo. The June 9, 1893 issue of the North-China Herald reprinted on p. 827 an article written by Lord George Curzon published in The National Review. Titled "The Destinies of the Far East," Britain's Minister of Foreign Affairs described the life of British expatriates in the Far East.

/ British Settlement at Chefoo

Curzon writes: "In his passion for games, which keeps him healthiest of all the foreign settlers in the East, while the German grows fat and the Frenchman withers, the Englishman plays lawn-tennis under a tropical sun; he has laid out golf-links at Hong Kong and Chefoo; cricket matches are as frequent and excite as keen an interest as the doings of a county team at home; nay I have even heard of football and hockey at Singapore, within seventy miles of the Equator. A race course must be constructed outside every town where there is a sufficient settlement, the annual race meeting in which the owner frequently buys or breeds, trains, and rides his own ponies, is one of the events of the year, the winner of the Hong Kong or Shanghai 'Derby' enjoys a more than ephemeral renown."

Judging from the year Curzon's article was published in the U.K., the golf course in Chefoo must have been built before 1893, which verifies Osborne's statement in her book. Vivvy Eckford was born in 1877 and he might have built Chefoo's first golf course when he was still a teenager.

/ The Destinies of the Far East

On July 30, 1904, a writer named J.A.T. published a story titled "Life in Chefoo" on p. 190 of The Field, The Country Gentlemen's Newspaper in England. The author writes: "The European community numbers about 300 of all nationalities, the majority living in what is known as the foreign settlement. Chefoo, for a small place, is one of the most cosmopolitan that it is possible to find."

About golfing, the author writes: "Golf I played occasionally in Chefoo, but with small success or pleasure. There is no proper course, and the so-called 'Greens' are merely patches about 12ft. in diameter of dry mud hammered down hard. Approaching and putting under these conditions was truly a fine art, much too fine for me, 'through the green' being nothing but a series of fine ruts; to get a lie at all we had to invent a rule allowing the ball to be lifted and placed without penalty! Needless to say, the fullest advantage is taken of this benevolent rule, but golf of this

/ Chefoo in 1899 (Queen's University Belfast)

/ Chefoo to the Northwest 1908 (Arnold Wright)

kind becomes a farce."

On p. 275 of the May 3, 1919 North-China Herald, a correspondent from Chefoo writes: "The scheme for the formation of a Golf and Country Club at Chefoo is at length maturing and arrangements have been made to lease a suitable piece of ground on the hillside. The idea at present is to lay the ground out for golf, and, then, if circumstances permit, erect a pavilion or clubhouse. Certain public-spirited men have come forward with a guarantee of the first five-years' rent."

Chefoo businesses discussed the prospects of building a Recreation Ground in the early 1920s. A report from Chefoo was published on p. 730 of the March 19, 1921 North-China Herald about a private meeting held at the Chefoo Club. A Mr. Railton said at the meeting that three local Chinese businessmen had quietly purchased a piece of land for the purpose of building an International Recreation Ground and were ready to form a partnership with foreign businesses for that purpose. The report writes: "Mr. Railton described the uses to which it could be put, and mentioned that there was no reason why the golf enthusiasts should not start playing there at once. The Ground is to be laid out so that golf, football, cricket, baseball, horse racing and later on polo may be played on it, and tennis, if it is thought necessary. The whole community is to be invited to use it; and Mr. Railton asked that the Chinese themselves as well as the missionaries should do their best to advertise the ground and make its attractions fully know." Mr. Railton said that once a company was formed, it would work with the foreign and local community to make the International Recreation Ground the best sports and recreation play in Northern China. The report also said that the American Navy in Chefoo would contribute to the upkeep of the Recreation Ground.

But by 1923, the planned Recreation Ground was still in slow progress. According to a report on p. 84 of the January 19, 1924 North-China Herald, the Chefoo Hotels, Ltd., had already almost completed the outer structure of the hotel. The report reads: "Chefoo will also be in a position to advertise a new attraction this summer and that, a golf course. The Hotel Company has secured a very nice piece of property on the Bluff where it is their intention to construct a nine-hole course. The ground has already been surveyed and the general opinion is that a very sporting course can be made. A large clubhouse, where if enthusiasts desire, they may spend the week-end, forms part of the scheme while there will be regular ferry

/ D.F.R. McMullan

boats plying at intervals between the mainland and the course. Other resorts have, in the past, had a distinct pull over Chefoo by virtue of their having a golf course but Chefoo can now enter into the battle of competition fully armed with attractions equal to all and better than most."

North-China Herald again quoted a Reuter's report on p. 373 of the September 6, 1924 issue that the Racing Club was reorganized in preparation for the fall race meeting. "Plans are in progress for the laying out of a golf course in Chefoo."

Due to the chaotic wars among warlords starting in 1925 and the limited number of foreign expatriates at Chefoo, the planned golf course and club failed to materialize.

The September 13, 1933 issue of North-China Herald published a caricature sketch of D.F.R. McMullan, manager of the James McMullan Co. at Chefoo. The caption of the sketch reads: "One of the Promoters of Chefoo Golf Club."

In 1938, Japanese invaders captured Chefoo and the eastern Shandong Peninsula. Westerners living there were thrown into concentration camps at Weixian. The history of golf at Chefoo finally came to an end.

Golf in Chefoo was at best an on and off activity due to the limited number of foreign expatriates living in the city.

Shanghai Golf Courses and Clubs

As we have pointed out in the chapter on Hankow Golf Club, James Ferrier from Carnoustie, Scotland was the key person who introduced modern golf into China. Ferrier, a scratch amateur golfer, best known as the golf "Veteran," arrived in China in the late 1860s and worked as a marine engineer at the China Merchants Steam Navigation Co. headquartered in Shanghai. In 1870 Ferrier, together with some of his Scottish friends, built a rudimentary golf course of a couple of holes on an open space in Hankow. Eight years later, in 1878, he became a founding member of the Hankow Golf Club. The Scotsman did the same thing in Shanghai—building a rudimentary golf course in 1871 and organizing the Shanghai Golf Club in 1894.

The Shanghai Golf Club was incorporated later than the Hankow and Royal Hong Kong Golf Clubs. However, as the largest port city open to foreign trade after the Opium War, Shanghai became the first choice of entry to China by British and Western powers in the mid-19th century, attracting missionaries to build schools and hospitals, merchants to trade and industrialists to set up manufacturing facilities. As the number of expatriates living in Shanghai expanded, golf as an outdoor sport developed much more rapidly here compared to Hankow, Hong Kong or any other trading ports in China.

After the first golf links was built inside the Shanghai Race Course in 1871, a number of golf courses were constructed in later years. These included golf links at Hongkew (Hongkou, 1911), Kiangwan (Jiangwan 1912), Hungjao (Hongqiao 1916), Seekingjao (Sijingqiao 1926), Kiangwan Country (1926), Standard Oil Co., etc.

A number of golf clubs also came into being after the Shanghai Golf Club was instituted in 1894, such as the Shanghai Ladies Golf Club (1905), Shanghai Junior Golf Club (1909), Hongkew Golf Club (1909), Kiangwan Golf Club (1912), Hungjao Golf Club (1916), Japanese (Kiangwan Country) Golf Club (1920) and Seekingjao Golf Club (1926).

Shanghai Golf Club and the Golf Links at the Race Course

Prior to the formal incorporation, the Shanghai Golf Club had organized inter-club competitions with the Royal Hong Kong Golf Club. A report on p. 339 of the September 11, 1891 *North-China Herald* said that members of the Hong Kong Cricket Association were on their way to Shanghai, arriving on Saturday. Two of the members would like to arrange a golf challenge competition with Shanghai. A follow-up story on the September 18 issue said Shanghai had yet to select two golfers for the competition but encouraged all golfers in Shanghai to practice and get ready.

At this time the golf links inside the Race Course was still a rough one. Residents of the Shanghai settlement suggested building a park inside the Race Course so that expatriates could walk inside the park and participate in various games and sports. In 1893 a reader wrote a letter to the editor of the *North-China Herald*, suggesting the building of a public park and a formal golf course. On p. 807 of the June 2 issue, the letter reads: "A public place is needed where any and everybody can go and play any game they like.

Golf is played everywhere and by everybody, old and young, in the British Isles now. It is popular in India and in all the colonies. Even in the south of France now John Bull has introduced his golfing clubs and balls, but in Shanghai where half the community is Scotch there is nowhere for them to indulge in their splendid national pastime. Grazing is very much needed here too, and a park would help to provide that."

/ Early Golf Course at the Shanghai Race Club

By the end of 1893, the golf course at the Race Club had only 6 holes.

On the evening of Wednesday, January 10, 1894, 18 golf enthusiasts met at the Shanghai Club presided by Brodie Augustus Clarke, chairman of the Shanghai Horse Bazaar. Attendants, including James Ferrier, unanimously agreed to constitute a Golf Club. The event was reported on p. 36 of the January 12 issue of *North-China Herald*: "Hopes were expressed that six greens inside the Race Course would be obtained, no difficulty being anticipated with the Horse Bazaar or the Recreation Fund. The following committee was elected: Messrs. E.F. Alford, Wade Gard'ner, E.A. Arbuthrot, J. Ferrier, B.A. Clarke, A.G. Rowand (Hon. Treasurer) and R. Carr (Hon. Secretary)."

Clarke was born in 1844 in Nairn, Scotland and came to Hong Kong in 1863. After working at the Taiwan Customs, he became 3rd Mate at a cargo ship under Jardine Matheson & Co. in 1864-1865. Afterwards he worked at the shipping office of Jardine Matheson Shanghai and then for 10 years at Jardine Matheson Hankow. Clarke was one of the founders of the Masonic Lodge St. Andrews and started Masonic Lodge China. He returned to Shanghai in 1891 and became partner of Messrs. Hopkins, Dunn & Co.

According to *A Brief History of the District Grand Lodge of the Far East*, Clarke loved sports and was an oarsman for the Scottish "Eight" in both Shanghai and Hankow. We believe that Clarke should have been a friend of James Ferrier and a member of the Hankow Golf Club.

Shanghai Golf Club held its first general meeting at the Shanghai Club on the evening of March 15, 1894, according to a report on p. 392 of the March 16 issue of *North-China Herald*. Brodie A. Clarke presided the meeting and a draft set of rules was approved. It was decided to limit the number of members to 75, to fix the entrance fee from the 31st instant at $5, and the annual subscription of members joining after that date should be $10. "The Chairman said there were 72 members at present, and it was estimated that the expenses for the first year, including the cost of putting the greens in order, would be about $750. The assistance of the Hankow Golf Club in lending gear was acknowledged, and it was stated

/ North-China Herald January 12, 1894

that the gear which had been ordered from home was expected shortly."

Club activities started to increase after the founding of the Shanghai Golf Club. A mixed foursome was played in early December 1894, participated by 19 couples. On January 11, 1895, *North-China Herald* published on p. 53 a letter from the Club's new Hon. Secretary, H.J.H. Tripp about the Club's 2nd handicap competition held on January 2. Tripp writes that the competition "was even more successful than that on Boxing-day. The weather was simply a perfect day for golf – bright and clear and little or no wind." Twenty-four golfers "teed off." "The Ancient and Royal Game has now fairly started in Shanghai, and long may it flourish."

On the same page of the issue was another letter from a St. Ninlan, a member of the Shanghai Golf Club, written on December 29, 1894. The writer complained he had found little notice taken by the newspaper "of an event which took place on Boxing-day on the interior of the Race Course, namely the Golf Handicap. The Ancient and Royal Game has of recent years taken such hold of all and sundry all over the civilized world that I could hardly believe the first handicap of the Shanghai Golf Club should have come off with merely a passing notice in the *N(orth) C(hina) Daily News*."

The writer continues: "It is now nearly a year since a meeting of golfers was held to start a Club, and though the game has been played at odd-times during the interval, the handicap which took place on boxing-day may be looked upon as the opening day of the Shanghai Golf Club, and I trust the success which attended it is an omen of the good look for the future. I believe twenty-

/ *Close-Up View of Early Golf Course at the Race Club*

nine members, enthusiastic golfers, entered for the Christmas Cup presented by Mr. Gard'ner." "The handicap was a sealed one, as no one knew who had won until all the cards had been handed in. When the box was opened, it was found that Mr. Ferrier, a veteran golfer, one of the scratch men, had won the cup with the fine score of 46 and 40 = 86; a record which will, I know, take some beating. Mr. Gampert took the second prize, Mr. Pike the 3rd and Mr. Reith the 4th. The Cup was christened with good Scotch wine and the health of the winner drunk in proper golfer's style, as also success to the Shanghai Golf Club." The author then thanked the Municipal Council for what they had done in improving the links and Mr. Tripp for the time and trouble he had spent in getting the greens in order.

On February 11, 1895, Shanghai Golf Club convened an annual general meeting to elect a new board of management. Brodie Augustus Clarke was elected captain and it was decided to increase the number of members to 100. On pp. 235-236 of the February 15 issue, the *North-China Herald* published a formal report of the Club delivered by Clarke at the annual meeting. The report reads: "During the year a course of nine holes has been laid out, and the links were formally opened on 1st of October. Since then, the Municipal Council have leased the property of the Recreation Fund

Trustees, and have done so much towards its improvement that the links are now probably the best in the Far East from a golfer's point of view, there being plenty of hazards, bunkers and ditches, etc., to delight the old and experienced, and the reverse to the novice."

After the founding of the Shanghai Golf Club, James Ferrier, founder of both the Hankow and Shanghai Golf Clubs, worked tirelessly to develop a close inter-club relationship between the two Clubs. Thanks to a trophy given by Hankow, the first Hankow Challenge Cup was played in Shanghai on January 2, 1896, attracting 42 entries. The January 10 issue of the *North-China Herald* reported on p. 53 that two golfers came out tied with a score of 82 net and a playoff would be arranged to decide on the winner of the Challenge Cup. James Ferrier, now Captain of the Shanghai Golf Club, "warmed up on his second round and broke the record with the top score of 39 for nine holes."

At the Club's annual general meeting held on January 27, Captain Ferrier thanked the Hankow Golf Club for "generously presented" the Hankow Challenge Cup "which we trust will eventually lead to inter-port matches."

Ferrier left Shanghai in February 1896 for Scotland on vacation. When he returned the following year, he brought back a silver cup in the name of his farther for Club competition. It was reported on p. 786 of the October 29, 1897 issue of *North-China Herald* that "Mr. Ferrier, the Nestor of the Club, has lately returned from home and as you are aware he has not only a correct eye for golf but an eye for the beautiful as well, and he has selected the handsome cup you see on the table for presentation to the Club. It will give a zest to at least one of the competitions during the coming season. The Club highly appreciates Mr. Ferrier's graceful act."

In 1897, Shanghai Golf Club presented a Challenge Cup to Hankow Golf Club in return for the trophy they had presented. The Shanghai Challenge Cup started to be competed for in 1898 at Hankow and the names of winners would be inscribed on the Cup.

A report in the November 21, 1898 issue of the *North-China Herald* said that the season's Opening Handicap competition on November 5 was again won by Veteran James Ferrier with a score of 40 and 46 over two rounds. Ferrier was now Club president and he presided on Saturday (November 19) over the opening of the Club's new pavilion clubhouse.

On behalf of the Club, Ferrier presented Miss Welch, daughter of J. Welch, Chairman of the Municipal Council, with a pretty little padlock and key as appreciation of her work and as master of ceremony for the opening. Mr. Welch said at the end of the ceremony: "Although this Club has only been established since 1894, we must not forget that your worthy President played the 'Ancient and Royal Game' on this same ground with some of his friends in 1871 and we rejoice to find him yet to the lore and as ready to compete for the honours of the game as ever he was."

/ *1899 Shanghai Golf Clubhouse*

SHANGHAI

On January 6, 1899, *Golf Illustrated*, the weekly organ of the Royal & Ancient Golf Club, published an article, "Golf in China," which described the founding of the Shanghai Golf Club. The article featured a photograph of the new clubhouse and said the Club now had 150 members.

As was mentioned in the Chapter on Hankow, the article, "Golf in China," published in the February 2, 1899 issue of the *Dundee Courier* had a subtitle "The Shanghai Course." The article had a sketch of the new pavilion clubhouse built at the Race Course.

In the first paragraph, the author gave a detailed description of the 9-hole golf links inside the Race Course: "Just exactly a mile from the busy Bund of Shanghai, traveling by the Maloo, or Nanking Road, there is an open space which the casual observer would at once remark, was a race course, and a race course it truly is; but within this open space there are many more sporting interests centred than that of testing the merits of the China pony. The race course is about a mile and a quarter round, and in the centre, there are two cricket pitches, polo, football, hockey, lawn tennis, and baseball grounds, and, last but not least, our golf course. One could hardly express that all of these sports could be carried on at the same time within such a limited space, but each has its own season, and there is little clashing. To those who have been accustomed in the open breezy links of most of the old home courses, it may appear that only a poor game of golf can be had within the circumference of a mile and a quarter, but such is

/ *Golf in China*

not the case. Our course does not certainly boast its eighteen holes, but it has nine holes, which take a lot of doing in 45 strokes. The longest hole is 283 yards, and the shortest 163 yards. To three of the holes, the lofting iron has to be brought into requisition, as ditches have to be crossed, and at others steeple chase jumps have to be negotiated; so, taken all in all, we have hazards capable of drawing out the dry humour of the home caddie, had he the opportunity of witnessing many of the attempts made to get out of the bunkers by those who have had the misfortune to 'top' or 'setoff' in their endeavour to lie dead upon the green."

The February 27, 1899 *Greenock Telegraph and Clyde Shipping Gazette* published a news story about Shanghai, which reads: "Golf in China is pursued in a very comfortable manner. The Country Club at Shanghai is composed chiefly of Englishmen and Scotsmen. The links are made on the race track course and infield, and are provided with artificial bunkers, water hazards, and sand ditches. The ground in Shanghai is level, and the course at the Chinese club is necessarily devoid of picturesque effects. The holes are well arranged, and spectators can view matches from the grandstand as well as from the clubhouse. The Chinese caddie is a bright fellow, who says 'floo' where the Prestwick article would shout 'fore.' High winds that sweep over Shanghai prevent the golfers from making low scores."

The Golf Heritage Museum in Shenzhen, Guangdong Province has a silver trophy from the Shanghai Golf Club on display at the China Hall. It is a Consolation Cup won by G.F. Lanning at the April 1901 competition. The cup was made by Luen Wo of Shanghai, with two flying dragons etched on the cup, sitting on three golf clubs attached to the base. On the cup are the words: "SHANGHAI GOLF CLUB CONSOLATION

/ *Golf Course to the North of Race Course*

CUP APRIL 1901 WINNER G.F. LANNING." The silver cup, 17mm high and weighs 255g, is the earliest Shanghai GC golf trophy found so far.

/ *Shanghai Golf Club Consolation Cup April 1901*

In an open competition of the Shanghai Golf Club held on May 5, 1901, A.J. Wicks defeated J.C. Dyer to win the championship. The two were tied after 36-holes. In the playoff, they were still tied in the first 8 holes. At the last hole, a par-four, both golfers were on the green with three shots. Wick's ball was closer to the edge of the green. He putted first and holed his ball, winning the game one up. The medal Wicks won is China's earliest golf gold medal found so far. The front of the medal reads: "SHANGHAI GOLF CLUB AD 1901 OPEN CHAMPIONSHIP." The name

/ 1901 Shanghai GC Gold Medal (Jeff Wu)

/ 1902 Shanghai GC Members with Caddies

"A.J. Wicks" is etched on the back of the medal, which is now in the collection of Jeff Wu, secretary of the China Golf Heritage Society.

The *Golf Illustrated* published a photograph of the Shanghai Golf Club on the front page of its August 29, 1902 issue. The photo shows Shanghai Golf Club members in front of the clubhouse after a match, with two Chinese caddies holding bags of golf clubs.

On p. 163 of the same issue, there was a full-page story about a caddie's competition held at the Shanghai Golf Club in 1902. The story, with four photographs, was reprinted from the July 2 *North-China Herald* report. This was the first known caddie's competition in China, and 16 caddies participated. They played one round over the ladies' course using only irons in the presence of a foreign umpire. The report says: "it was generally thought that any card returned under 60 would win, but, as will be seen from the scores below, the play proved of a higher standard than was anticipated."

/ Shanghai Caddies' Competition Scores

The two top scores were 52 and 53, the first one by Li Sung, but his score was void because Li was not a regular caddie. Lali Sung became the champion, winning four silver dollars. The runner-up and 3rd place scored 60 and 61, winning two and one silver dollar, respectively. Two caddies tied at fourth place, were each given 50 cents.

Three of the four photos featured runner-up Siau Pa-tsze driving, chipping and putting. One photo showed champion Lali Sun putting.

The August 27, 1902 issue of *The Tatler* carried a story by Garden G. Smith titled "Golf and Golfers." With the article was a photograph of Lali Sun driving gracefully at the Shanghai course. The photo caption reads: "In Far Cathay Caddies at Shanghai GC." The article praised the caddies by saying: "It is only fair to state, however, that the small competitors appeared to be imbued

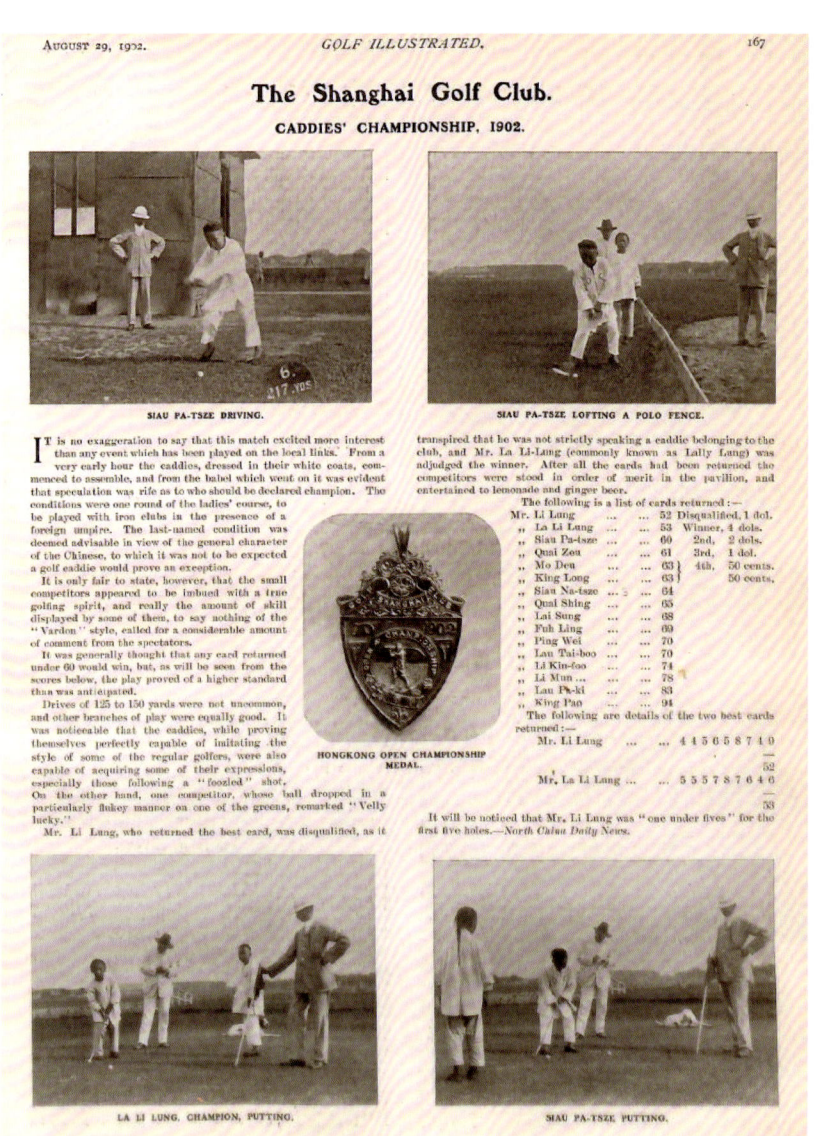

/ 1902 Shanghai GC Caddies' Competition

with a true golfing spirit, and really the amount of skill displayed by some of them, to say nothing of the 'Vardon' style, called for a considerable amount of comment from the spectators."

According to a report on p. 223 of the February 4, 1903 *North-China Herald*, the final round for the "handsome cup" presented by Captain, Mr. H. G. Gardner, was played on February 2 between J.H.T. McMurtrie, ex-champion of Hong Kong and J.A. McGill, ex-champion of Singapore. McMurtrie, a scratch player, conceded strokes for three holes and beat McGill by 3 up and 1 to play.

The Captain's Cup presented by Gardner was made by the famous Shanghai silversmith Luen Wo. It is a Chinese style silver cup 17.5 mm in height and 963 g in weight, with three dragons as handles. On the cup are inscribed the words:

/ *In Far Cathay Caddies at Shanghai GC*

"SHANGHAI GOLF CLUB 1903 CAPTAIN'S CUP PRESENTED BY H.G. GARDNER WON BY J.H.T. MCMURTRIE." The silver trophy is now in the collection of the Golf Heritage Museum in Shenzhen.

The Golf Heritage Museum also owns an interesting silver spoon trophy presented by the "Golf Handicap Country Club Shanghai" on January 16, 1904. Judging from the time of

/ *1903 Shanghai GC Captain's Cup*

/ 1904 Shanghai San Duo Silver Spoon

this silver spoon, we suspect that the "Country Club Shanghai" might very well be the Shanghai Golf Club. The design of the spoon features the auspiciousness of fortune in the Chinese culture: "Three Many's and Nine Like's (Sanduo Jiuru)." The spoon handle tip has the Chinese characters Sanduo, which means "Many Fortunes, Many Years of Life and Many Sons." Jiuru refers to "Like a Mountain, a Mound, a Hill, a Hillock, a Creek, a Moon, a Sun, a Pine and a Southern Mountain." The spoon itself is in a shape of gourd. Gourd in Chinese is pronounced Hulu, simulating another two Chinese characters Fulu, meaning fortune and prosperity.

It was reported on pp. 546-547 of the December 8, 1905 *North-China Herald* that an interesting competition was organized in early December. During the one round medal play, 60 players were allowed using only one club. In the three-day event, all players chose an iron club except one golfer who played with a wood. Mr. H.M. Little won the trophy of a silver cigarette box with a net score of 43.

Descriptions of early Shanghai Golf Club can be found in the 1908 edition of the *20th Century Impressions of Hongkong, Shanghai, and Other Treaty Ports of China: Their History, People, Commerce, Industries, and Resources*. The 800-page book was edited by Arnold Wright and featured detailed introductions of major treaty ports in China. A paragraph about golf was written in the Shanghai Chapter, which reads: "It was not until fifteen years ago that any attempt was made to organize a golf club in Shanghai. In the late eighties a few ardent Scots used to knock the balls about in the open country to the west of the recreation ground, but it was not until January 1894 that anything was done in the way of laying out golf links."

According to the book, after 18 enthusiasts met and decided to form the Shanghai Golf Club in 1894, "the Golf Club holds numerous competitions throughout the season, including mixed foursomes and monthly cup competitions." "A Challenge Cup, which carries with it the championship of the Club, is also competed for each year. This cup can never be won outright, but the winner receives a miniature replica. The holders have been as follows: A.J. Wicks, 1901; J. Mann, 1902; J.H.T. McMurtrie, 1903; A.W. Walkinshaw, 1904; J.H.T. McMurtrie, 1905; A.W. Walkinshaw, 1906; A.W. Walkinshaw, 1907; G.M. Wheelock, 1908."

A photograph news was published in the June 18, 1909 issue of *Golf Illustrated* titled "Open Championship of China at Shanghai." The caption reads: "Group of Competitors and Caddies. Mr. J.B. Ferrier (marked with an X), who won the championship, is the son of the first honorary life member of Carnoustie Club and

SHANGHAI

/ 1908 Shanghai Golf Club

learned his golf on Carnoustie Links. He is 21 years old."

North-China Herald reported on p. 754 of the December 24, 1909 issue about Shanghai Golf Club's decision to donate a special inter-port golf cup. Named the Shanghai Golf Cup valued at $1,000, it would be competed for in competitions between golf clubs in China, Hong Kong and Japan. The competition would be annually held on the links of the club holding the Cup. The format would be 36-hole medal play. Each team would consist of no more than five men, and the three best scores would count. The team returning the lowest score in the aggregate would be declared the winner. In the event of a tie, a further 18 holes would be played. The first match was planned for April 1910 in Shanghai. The organizer also suggested that in connection with this Cup, the "Individual Golf Championship of the Far East" might be played. On March 24, 1910, an inter-port competition between Shanghai and Hong Kong was played. Shanghai won easily.

The competition for the Shanghai Golf Championship in 1911 took place on April 7 at the Shanghai Golf Club, reported by *North-China Herald* on April 8. The match was between J.B. Ferrier and A.T. White, and the former won the match and the championship on the 27th hole, with 10 holes up and 9 to play. As mentioned

/ 1909 Shanghai GC Open Championship

/ The 9th Green at the Shanghai Race Course Golf Links

earlier, J.B. Ferrier was the son of the late golf Veteran James Ferrier and he had been elected captain of the Shanghai Junior Golf Club earlier in the year. This was the second time he won the Shanghai Golf Club championship. The championship trophy, a silver bowl, is now in the collection of the Shanghai Museum.

J.B. Ferrier was five times champion of the Shanghai Golf Club and also the winner of the 1924 China Amateur Golf Open Championship. At the 1912 Shanghai Golf Club Championship, he lost to H.R. Honeyman. The March 15 issue of *Golf Illustrated* published a photograph of about 60 golfers participating at the 1912 competition. Honeyman and Ferrier were seated

/ 1911 Shanghai GC Championship Trophy

in the center to the left and right of the trophy, respectively.

Since the founding of the Shanghai Golf Club, members were only able to play over the

/ 1912 Shanghai GC Championship, Honeyman and Ferrier Sitting in the Middle

9-hole links inside the Race Course. After the Hongkew (Hongkou) Recreation Ground to the north of the city was completed, a new 9-hole golf course was built, which only briefly helped relieve the crowdedness of the Race Course links. A growing number of engineers living in the northern district, most of them from Scotland, met and decided to form a Junior Golf Club and use the Hongkew links as its home course. So, both golf courses continued to be crowded. Shanghai urgently needed a new 18-hole golf course to alleviate the crowdedness of the two existing 9-hole courses.

China's First 18-Hole Golf Course — Kiangwan

For the history of the Shanghai Golf Club, two dates stood out prominently. One was January 10, 1894, when 18 people met and decided to form the Shanghai Golf Club. The second was August 10, 1911, when the Club decided to lease part of the property of the International Recreation Club at Kiangwan (Jiangwan) for the purpose of laying out China's first 18-hole golf course.

In 1908, Ye Yi-ch'uan, son of famous Shanghai industrialist Ye Ch'eng-chung, and shipping magnate Yu Ch'ia-ch'ing had pooled funds to purchase 1,200 *mu* of land at Kiangwan Village to build Shanghai's second race course in an effort to compete with the existing Shanghai Race Course. Due to poor management, the project did not go well as planned. Owners of the Kiangwan Race Course first delegated management to the International Recreation Club and later sold out their ownership.

Learning about the spacious Race Course

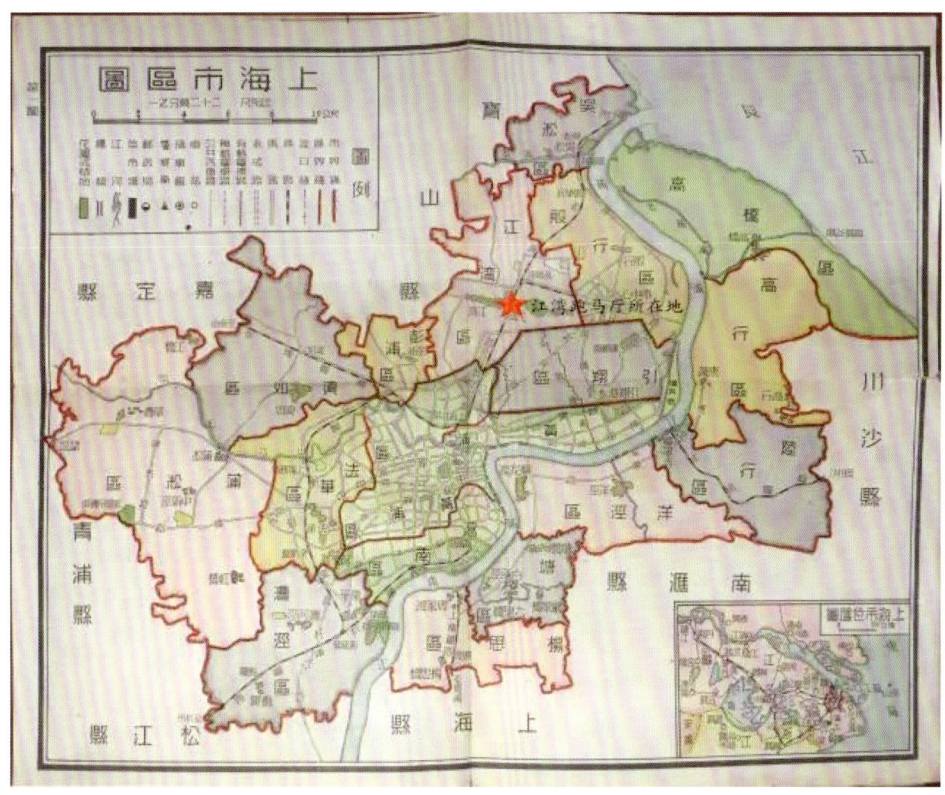

/ *Kiangwan Race Course*

when it opened in May 1911, the Shanghai Golf Club organized a special committee to negotiate with the International Recreation Club about the possibility of renting the space inside the track to build an 18-hole golf course. A general meeting of the Shanghai GC was held on August 10 and it was unanimously decided to proceed with the construction. The distance of Kiangwan to the Shanghai Golf Club was about 45 minutes of drive. A new road was planned and once completed, it would take even less time to get to the course.

/ *Kiangwan Race Course*

A detailed report published on p. 454 of the August 19, 1911 issue of *North-China Herald* discussed the progress of the new race course at Kiangwan. According to the report, the race track was completed by June 1911, but little was done to the interior. There were enough ingredients for the making of a good golf links. A few houses still remained, but they posed no serious obstacles to overcome, and with trees, a few creeks, and a sprinkling of grave mounds, there were natural hazards.

"The ground is not altogether flat," the author writes, "it rather undulates in places, and although not to anything like the extent to be found on a home course, it is an improvement on the absolute flat surface of the present courses. In addition to the land lying inside the race track, the surrounding country for some fifty or a hundred yards, or even more, is available, and in the laying out of the course this will be utilized. With all this ground to work upon it will be possible to lay out a full eighteen-hole course, and many of the holes will be of a length calling for a brassie shot to follow the drive, and a short approach. On the old Race Course only one hole gives this, namely the ninth, so that in addition the advantage of possessing double the number of holes, the new links will beat the old in length as well. Further, the putting greens, as at present intended, will be much more in the style of the home courses than anything seen here so far. It is expected that they will be a hundred feet by a hundred, thus affording a thorough test in the gentle art of putting." The new golf course intended to import Australian seed for the turf, and 18 months should see the opening of the links. A pavilion would be erected and people believed that in years to come "this will be the home of golf in China."

By September 1912, the Kiangwan course was almost completed, with the structure of the new clubhouse built. Shanghai GC Committee members already played some holes of the new course. The length of the front nine is

1,991 yards, and back nine 3,144 yards, a total of 5,135 yards. *North-China Herald* published a course layout on p. 666 of its September 7, 1912 issue, and the length of each of the 18 holes.

At the start of planning for the Kiangwan golf course, Shanghai Golf Club decided to invite a professional golfer from Scotland to help manage and finish the construction of the new Kiangwan course. The Committee searched for possibilities and eventually chose Richard Graham who at the time was working as an assistant to Tom Ball, a noted professional at the Raynes Park Golf Club at Wimbledon. Graham arrived in Shanghai on October 8, 1912 and started to work as soon as he arrived. As a skilled professional, Graham scored 33 at the Race Course's nine holes and 78 at Kiangwan. However, on the night of November 12, just a little over a month after arriving in Shanghai, 24-year-old Graham suddenly died during sleep due to a heart attack. Just a day earlier, he had played at the Hongkew links scoring 33 and 35, breaking the course record. The bogey score for Hongkew was 37.

On November 30, 1912, Scotland's National Holiday, St. Andrew's Day, the Kiangwan 18-hole golf course was formally opened, according to a report in the *North-China Herald* on December 7. Sir Havilland de Sausmarez, Judge of His Britannic Majesty's Supreme Court for China, chaired the tiffin before the opening and drove the first ball, which was followed by a foursome match play.

/ *Kiangwan Course Design (not proportionate)*

The holes have now been chained, and their distances are as follows:—

1.	220 yards	10.	233 yards
2.	133	11.	293
3.	388	12.	354
4.	264	13.	130
5.	90	14.	283
6.	213	15.	487
7.	113	16.	547
8.	415	17.	495
9.	155	18.	322
	1991		3144

/ *Kiangwan Course Yardage*

On January 10, 1913, *Golf Illustrated* published a photographic news story about the opening of the Kiangwan course. Titled "Golf in China, New Course Opened at Shanghai," the report on p. 89 reads: "Since 1894, when the Shanghai Golf Club was inaugurated, golf has steadily grown in favour among the foreign community of this great Treaty Port, and especially during the last few years has the question of congestion been a difficult one. For long the only course at Shanghai was the nine-hole one on the Race-course, and upon it many famous battles have been waged, but Shanghai outgrew it at least a lustrum ago. Then, with the opening of a new park in Hongkew – the northern district of the Settlement – another nine-hole course was laid out, but it failed to help matters, rather creating a new class of golfers – at first principally engineers from the banks of the Clyde, but now all and sundry, including not a few Japanese residents. A score of men, with the interests of the game at heart, made an effort to start another course at Hungjao, three or four miles from the Settlement, but through lack of facilities for reaching it – for, in spite of the abled wealth of the East, not all have motor cars at their disposal – this scheme did not succeed, and it was left until the year 1912 before Kiangwan, the new links of the Shanghai Club, came into existence as a home of the Royal and Ancient game."

The article continues: "Kiangwan is situated perhaps four miles from the heart of Shanghai. And while it is now reached by a road, it has the advantage of railway facilities. Three years ago, the ground was under cultivation, to say nothing of having such picturesque attributes as a village in the middle and innumerable grave mounds." Two members of the Shanghai Golf Club, P. Peebles and R.E. Wilson designed and laid out the 18-hole golf course. A spacious pavilion stood in front of the first tee, which led to the first green, 220 yards in length. For the lack of enough funding to turf the entire golf course, the Club decided to leave a space of some 100 yards from the tee unturfed but covered with native grass. It was expected that by the next winter, it would be possible to play the championship course.

The following photograph shows club members in front of the clubhouse at Kiangwan after a game. The Chinese on both sides were employees of the golf course.

The 1912 edition of the *Nisbet's Golf Guide* listed the following information about the Shanghai Golf Club: "Instituted 1894. Members—736, and 100 Ladies. Station—Shanghai, 1 mile. Hon. Secretary—G.D. Main. Entrance Fee—50 dols. Subscription—30 dols.

/ 1912 Shanghai GC Members at the Kiangwan Clubhouse

Holes—9. Visitors—Yes, on introduction by members, for one month. Sunday play, with caddies."

In late 1912, Shanghai Golf Club decided to invite professional golfer Samuel Green, assistant professional at Worplesdon Golf Club in Woking, near London, to become the Club's professional. Arriving in Shanghai on March 17, 1913, the 24-year-old professional started working on the maintenance and improvement of the Kiangwan course. As a golf architect, Green during his tenure in Shanghai was invited to work in Dairen on the Hoshigaura Golf Course as well as in Japan on designing a few Japanese golf courses. Green was a skilled golfer and a three-handicapper. He was an enthusiastic and patient coach and taught many golfers while in Shanghai.

On March 29, 1919 the *North-China Herald* reported that there was a shortage of golf equipment in Shanghai due to the 1st World War. Green made an effort to hand make wooden clubs in Shanghai and also tried to teach workers there how to forge iron heads. He was able to order quite a number of golf clubs from Scotland for golfers in Shanghai. These iron heads were stamped "S. Green Shanghai China." The Golf Heritage Museum owns a number of S. Green irons and a wood. The story about the history of these golf clubs made in Scotland for Shanghai will be discussed later in the Chapter.

Again, it was unfortunate that after a short six years in Shanghai, Green died, like his predecessor, on March 21, 1919 of pneumonia. His death came after a severe attack of influenza, according to an obituary published in *North-China Herald* on March 29. Green was only 30 years of age. Close to 100 people from the Shanghai GC, the Shanghai Ladies Golf Club, the Shanghai Junior Golf Club, the Shanghai Recreation Club and the Shanghai Masonic Lodges attended his funeral on March 23 and mourned for the loss of a great golf teacher who had "raised the standard of the game generally in Shanghai."

SHANGHAI (CHINA).
SHANGHAI GOLF CLUB.
Inst. **1894.** *Members*—**736,** and **100** Ladies. *Station*—Shanghai, **1** mile. *Hon. Sec.*—G. D. Main. *Entrance Fee*—**50** dols. *Subs.*—**30** dols. *Holes*—**9.** *Visitors*—Yes, on introduction by members, for one month. Sunday play, with caddies.

/ *1912 Nisbet's Golf Guide*

/ 1Samuel Green's Shanghai Golf Irons

On April 19-20, 1913, Shanghai Golf Club organized the first competition on the Kiangwan Links playing out the cup presented by President Sir Havilland de Sausmarez. Fifty-four golfers participated in a 36-hole medal play, with a maximum handicap allowance of 12.

By the end of 1913, the new Kiangwan Golf Course was already crowded. In a letter written to *North-China Herald* published on p. 348 of the November 1 issue, a member of the Shanghai Senior Golf Club said that due to the crowdedness of the Kiangwan course on Sundays and holidays, his Club was seriously considering limiting its membership at an upcoming annual meeting on the 30th. As an alternative, he proposed that the Senior Club members be divided into three batches. The first batch would comprise members with a handicap of six or lower and they could play all days of the month. Batch II were members with sir names starting from A to J, who would be allowed to play on the 1st and 3rd Sundays every month. And Batch III were members with sir names starting from K to X, who could play on the 2nd and 4th Sunday every month.

The opening of the Kiangwan 18-hole golf course provided plenty opportunities for young kids to work as caddies. P. 421 of the September 5, 1925 *Illustrated London News* had two photographs of the Kiangwan golf links, with traditionally dressed European golfers and quite a number of caddies.

/ *Kiangwan Golf Links, Upper Left Corner*

/ *Golfers and Caddies at Kiangwan*

The Shanghai Sports Museum has a 1926 silver golf trophy in the shape of a tall cup. On the cup are inscribed the words: "PAOMACHANG (RACE COURSE) GOLF CLUB, MEN'S KNOCKOUT FOURSOMES, E.H. CARTWRIGHT, DECEMBER 1926."

In 1932, the Japanese invaders expanded its military operation in China and the Kiangwan golf course became a battlefield. A report in the March 23, 1932 issue of the *Singapore Free Press and Mercantile Advertiser* said that the clubhouse at Kiangwan was damaged by bombs and much of the members' golf equipment was destroyed.

Shanghai GC and the Seekingjao 18-Hole Golf Course

Since its inception, Shanghai Golf Club was open only to foreign nationals. This changed in 1923 when Chinese members were admitted, even though only as honorary members. The April 21, 1923 issue of *North-China Herald* reported on p. 146 that "the Shanghai Golf Club has taken a wise, liberal and far-sighted step in deciding to admit Chinese members." The decision was announced at a dinner on April 16 at the Union Club which was featured on p. 172 of the same issue. The dinner was attended by 50 Chinese, British and American dignitaries, including Shanghai Golf Club Committee members. The dinner, presided by Fu Siao-en, director and general manager of the Commercial Bank of China, was arranged for two purposes. One was to bid farewell to Alfred Sze, who was resuming his diplomatic mission in Washington D.C. And the other was to introduce the game of golf to the Chinese guests.

General Ho Feng-ling, Defense Commissioner of Shanghai and Sungk'iang, was

/ *1926 Paomachang Golf Club Trophy*

already an honorary member of the Shanghai Golf Club. Ho spoke at the dinner, saying that although he would probably not have time to play golf, he would always do anything that would help the Club along. Shanghai GC president R.G. MacDonald talked about the current situation of the Club and said that "a golf course needed a considerable area of ground, and so they had to go beyond the Settlement limits. Their membership was increasing so greatly that in addition to the International Recreational Club they required additional courses." He learned that General Ho had promised to be one of the patrons of the Club and said "it would be the first sporting club in China to have such a distinguished General as a member. With the support of their Chinese and foreign friends he was sure that they would soon have a new course."

According to the April 3, 1926 *North-China*

Herald, Shanghai Golf Club's 3rd golf links at Seekingjao formally opened on March 27. The new 18-hole golf course was the result of the dinner meeting at the Union Club two years earlier and of the coordinated efforts of the Chinese and foreign communities. The opening of the Seekingjao Golf Course signaled a bright future for golf in Shanghai as well as in China. A large number of people attended the opening, which included Shanghai GC President R.G. MacDonald, British Consul-General Sidney Barton, U.S. Consul-General Edwin S. Cunningham, Shanghai GC Vice-President J.B. Ferrier, Captain C.W. Porter, Hon. Secretary R. Haves, Fu Siao-en, Hsu Yuan, etc.

/ *Shanghai GC Clubhouse at the Race Course*

Shortly after 12:30 pm, MacDonald led the participants to the clubhouse and gave a silver key to Barton and asked him to perform the ceremony of opening the building. Barton said that "he would like to remind those present of a meeting held two years ago at the Union Club when Chinese and foreign residents of Shanghai met with a view to obtaining another open space where the Royal and Ancient game could be enjoyed by them. The result of the endeavors then set on foot could be seen today in the opening of the new course, and they hoped that it would not be very long before the Chinese came there and played golf."

Barton talked about his belief that golf was best suited to the Chinese and was "essentially a game which ought to appeal to Chinese." The Chinese, he said, had for many many years been blessed with a proper appreciation of deportment and demeanor, and he was sure that there was no game more calculated to improve deportment and demeanor than was golf. The idea of the stance in golf fitted the idea of the Chinese as to how to carry oneself, and golfers would realize how very important was the way they moved the body. Then as to demeanor, it was especially important from the Chinese point of view to conduct oneself without showing anger. A man who could conceal his anger at certain stages at golf was calculated to secure a high degree in the Chinese estimation of demeanor and deportment. Barton again expressed the hope that the Chinese residents would very soon become players of golf.

After luncheon, MacDonald on behalf of the Club welcomed all the ladies and gentlemen present and took the opportunity of mentioning that it was only owing to the work of their Chinese friends that they were able to golf at Seekingjao. While none of the Chinese honorary members at present played golf, he hoped that they would do so before long. He thanked Mr.

Stewardson and Mr. Spence for the design of the clubhouse. He also thanked Philip Peebles for his many years of contribution to the Shanghai Golf Club. MacDonald then proceeded to the first tee and officially opened the links by driving off. The newspaper carried a photograph of the Seekingjao Clubhouse.

/ Seekingjao Clubhouse

A story about a caddie strike at the Seekingjao Golf Course was published on p. 13 of the June 26, 1930 issue of *The Singapore Free Press and Mercantile Advertiser*. The report said that about 300 people at Seekingjao were affected. Golfers obliged after Club Secretary Colam appealed to them to carry their own bags. Faced with the prospective that they would lose their salary for an entire week because the strike was unjustified, the caddies in the afternoon offered to resume work unconditionally.

Shanghai Golf Club in the 1930s and 1940s

The Shanghai Golf Club held its annual meeting on November 4, 1927 at the Race Course Clubhouse to elect officers for 1928. The following people were elected according to a report in *North-China Herald* on November 12: President A. Gray and Vice-President R. Bailey. General Committee members: Gray, Bailey, Budd, Downs, Holland, Pilcher, Pettit, Denison and Porter. Balloting Committee members: Bowerman, Lester, Arnold, Cobb, Cousins, Cumming, Farman, Hutchinson, Lancaster,

/ Seekingjao Clubhouse

Malcolm, Banham, Noxon and de Berry. Thompson & Co. was re-elected as auditor. Captain E.L.M. Barrett paid tribute to retiring president R.G. MacDonald and proposed that he be elected a life member in recognition of the very great services he had performed for the good of the Club during his term of office. C.W. Porter seconded the motion, which was carried unanimously.

According to the 1928 edition of the *Port Directory of the Principle Foreign Ports* published by the Office of Naval Intelligence, U.S. Navy Department, "public recreation ground at race course and the Kiangwan golf course have been used for landing purposes" and "two flying units of the British Royal Air Force temporarily stationed here are using the race course as a

/ *1927 Shanghai Race Course*

flying field."

An aerial photo of the Shanghai Race Course dated 1928 shows a baseball game being played on the golf links. The Shanghai GC Clubhouse is visible in the center.

By the early 1930s, the old 9-hole golf links

/ *1928 Shanghai Race Course Baseball Game*

at the Race Course was handed over to the Race Club. Shanghai GC no longer used the course. It was now open to the public at low cost and became very crowded on weekends.

In the November 1930 issue of *Golf Illustrated*, Walter Buechler authored an article titled "Golf in China," in which he commended the work at Shanghai Golf Club in training caddies to make sure that they offer the best of services. Specific regulations for caddies and fore caddies were drafted, including not allowing caddies to take tips. Members who violated the rule and offered tips to caddies would face suspension of membership and caddies would be suspended for service. As tips for caddies added up to almost as much as their salaries, such regulations met resistance from caddies, and they went on a strike. The Club had to hire women to serve as temporary caddies.

According to a 1937 edition of *Golfer's Handbook*, the address

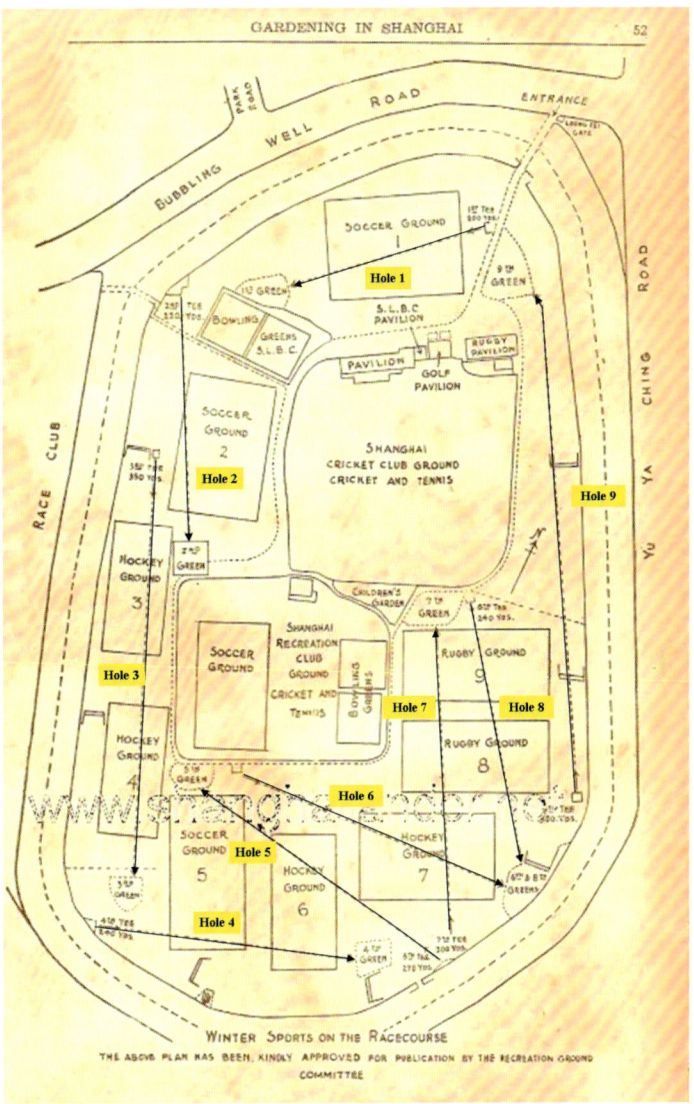

/ Race Course 9-Hole Golf Links in the 1930s

of Shanghai Golf Club was 20 Canton Road, Shanghai. Membership included 762 gentlemen and 181 ladies. Club Secretary was Royal Navy's retired Lt. Commander J.B. Wooley. The two courses were 18 holes at Seekingjao and 18 holes at Kiangwan. Visitors pay $3 on weekdays and $5 on Saturday and Sunday.

/ Shanghai Race Course in 1935

/ 1937 Golfer's Handbook

/ 1937 Shanghai GC Member Booklet

The 1939 *Shanghai Hong List* has the following information about Shanghai Golf Club: Shanghai Golf Club, Clubhouses and Courses at Kiangwan and Seekingjao, Secretary's Office: 20 Canton Rd (Room 305), Tel 13386. President Dr. W.E. O'Hara, Vice-President C.E. Harber, Captain A. Henderson and Secretary J.B. Woolley.

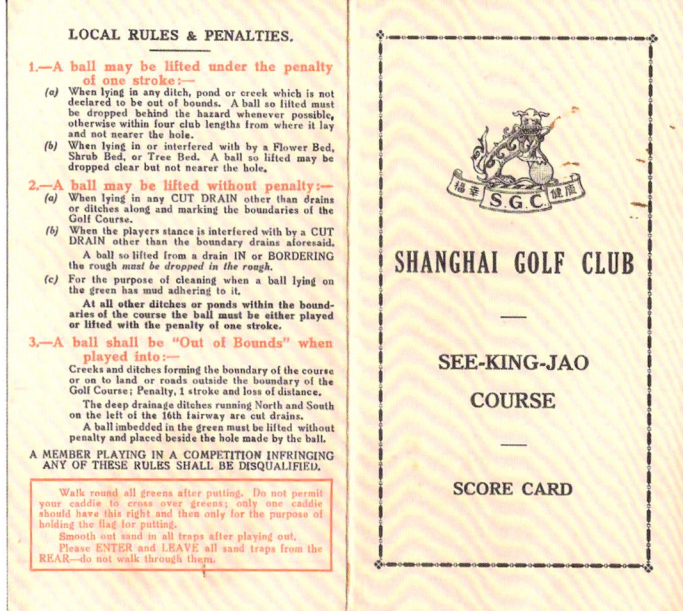

Shanghai Golf Club

Clubhouses and Courses at
Kiangwan and Seekingjao
Secretary's Office:
20 Canton-rd (Room 305)
Tel 13386

O'Hara, Dr. W. E., pres.
Harber, C. E., vice-pres.
Henderson, A., capt.
Woolley, J. B., sec.

/ 1939 Shanghai Hong List

In an article published in the March 2016 issue of the Chinese edition of *Golf Magazine*, Jeff Wu wrote about former Shanghai Golf Club member John Rigg as well as his father Bill Rigg. Bill was a manager at the Hongkong and Shanghai Banking Corp. in Hong Kong and was transferred to Shanghai in 1936. A noted athlete and a member of both the Shanghai GC and Scottish Rugby Team in Shanghai, Bill had a handicap of seven. He won numerous trophies at golf competitions in Shanghai, including a monthly bogey competition in September 1939 for the A Class. He was also a champion of Malaysia Open Competition.

/ 1930s Shanghai GC Seekingjao Course Score Card

/ *Bill Rigg 1939 Trophy (Jeff Wu)*

/ *Bill Rigg's Membership and Handicap Card (Jeff Wu)*

Hungjao Golf Club

On the afternoon of Saturday, October 21, 1916, the Hungjao (Hongqiao) Golf Club formally opened. Located at the corner of the Hungjao and Rubicon (today's Hami) Roads, the land was formally owned by George Dallas of the Dallas Horse Repository. The Dallas family was a shareholder of the Shanghai Race Course and owned 100 or so horses on a land area of 67,000 square meters.

In 1910, 16 British residents decided to purchase a piece of land from Dallas to build a private 9-hole golf course. But the deal failed to go through due to the 1911 Revolution, the opening of the Kiangwan Golf Course and refusal of some of the land owners to relocate. After the death of George Dallas in 1914, the land once again was on the market. A consortium of another 16 British investors was formed to purchase the land in October 1915. The golf links and the clubhouse went into construction and were completed by the summer of 1916.

As was reported on p. 193 of the October 28, 1916 *North-China Herald*, Hungjao was a "proprietary British Club, the membership of which will be limited to 100, exclusive of shareholders, and it is the intention to purchase more land as opportunity offers and eventually to have an 18-hole course." "The surroundings of the Club are delightfully pretty. Wide stretches of open country, free from any suspicion of the noise and dust of town, flat, of course, yet from a golfing point of view exceedingly sporting,

Gate of the Hungjao Golf Club

make an ideal site for the Club, which in days to come will probably be one of the most popular in Shanghai."

A foursome competition was played on the opening day of the Club. The first group composed of Club President R.J. Marshall and Sir Havilland de Sausmarez against Robert Macgregor and T. Forrest. A lady's putting competition was held on the green close to the clubhouse. Members of the Club Committee were R.J. Marshall (President), Robert Macgregor, Edward White, F.H. Crossley (Secretary), R.E. Wilson, P. Peebles, T. Forrest and L. Walker.

By the end of 1916, the golf course had been improved and the Club renamed Hungjao Golf Club. By 1920 a changing room, office, meeting room and a bar were built in the Clubhouse. The Club was only open to expatriates but employed over 30 locals and had at least 10 local caddies.

Hungjao Golf Course expanded to 12 holes by December 1917, according to a report on p. 553 of the December 1 issue of *North-China Herald*. The Club hosted the first of its inter-club match on November 24 against 16 golfers from Shanghai Golf Club. Team Hungjao lost by three points in the individual match in the morning but caught up with Team Shanghai during the foursomes in the afternoon. The result of the inter-club match was listed as follows:

According to a report on p. 324 of the May 5, 1923 *North-China Herald*, Hungjao's match in November 1922 with a visiting team from Manila was played again on the 12-hole course. The course was extended to 18 holes in 1923. At the annual general meeting of the Club in 1923, R.J. Marshall was re-elected as President and C.M.G. Burnie Captain.

According to a report in the *North-China Herald* in October 1926, the names of the 18 holes at Hungjao were as follows: 1, Bamboos;

HUNGJAO G. C.		S. G. C.	
Dr. Marshall	0	L. Evans	1
R. Macgregor	0	A. G. Stephen	1
H. M. Little	0	C. W. Porter	1
W. W. Cox	1	A. Gray	0
C. M. G. Burnie	½	O. Crewe-Read	½
J. C. Dyer	1	E. M. Ross	0
F. W. Godfrey	0	G. F. Browne	1
P. Peebles	1	J. C. Macdougall	0
Sir H. de Sausmarez	0	A. Wilson	1
Ed. White	1	R. G. Macdonald	0
Skinner Turner	1	C. Knight	0
G. A. Richardson	0	A. W. Macphail	1
J. W. C. Bonner	0	E. L. Arnold	1
E. F. Mackay	0	T. Harborne	1
F. S. Gibbings	0	Dr. Neild	1
C. J. G. Hill	1	H. Payne	0
	6½		9½

HUNGJAO G. C.		S. G. C.	
Dr. Marshall and R. Macgregor	1	L. Evans and A. G. Stephen	0
H. M. Little and W. W. Cox	1	C. W. Porter and A. Gray	0
C. M. G. Burnie and J. C. Dyer	½	O. Crewe-Read and E. M. Ross	½
E. W. Godfrey and P. Peebles	1	G. F. Browne and J. C. Macdougall	0
Sir H. de Sausmarez and Ed. White	0	A. Wilson and R. G. Macdonald	1
Skinner Turner and G. A. Richardson	0	C. Knight and A. W. Macphail	1
J. W. C. Bonner and E. F. Mackay	1	E. L. Arnold and T. Harborne	0
F. S. Gibbings and C. J. G. Hill	1	Dr. Neild and H. Payne	0
	5½		2½

Totals: Hungjao, 12; S. G. C. 12.

/ 1917 Hungjao vs. Shanghai GC

2, Second; 3, Hole Across; 4, Mrs. Liddels; 5, Dead Man's Pool; 6, Punch Bowel; 7, Creek; 8, Village; 9, Ginger Beer Hole; 10, Tenth; 11, Red Joss House; 12, Graves; 13, Pond; 14, Death or Glory; 15, Road; 16, Corner; 17, Second Last; 18, Home.

The size of the golf course expanded to 277,000 square meters by 1930 and the membership of Hungjao increased to 175 during the second half of the 1930s, according to *Golfer's Handbook*.

On November 4, 1930, *North-China Herald* reported that K.M. Cummings, twice champion of the Royal Hong Kong Golf Club, onetime champion of Canton Golf Club, had won his fifth champion of the Hungjao Golf Club. The following is a runner-up trophy for the B-Class Cup competition at Hungjao in 1930.

/ 1931 Hungjao Golf Club Trophy

A photograph published in the July 1933 issue of *Die Deutsche Golfzeitung* shows grave mounds at the Hungjao Golf Course. The caption of the photo reads: "Hungjao Club Golf Course. The only obstacles, apart from the water ditches, are the Chinese tombs. The red-painted bridges, which can be found everywhere, liven up the flat, somewhat monotonous course."

The photo was taken by Freiherr von Schertel during his visit in Shanghai. Von Schertel was somehow impressed by the local rule allowing the golfer to pick up the ball and drop it without penalty if it lay within three club lengths of a brick or wooden grave or a coffin. There were another nine local rules and seven out-of-bounds areas, he wrote, and he was therefore wondering how studying all these local rules would delay the game during a well-attended medal competition. Von Schertel later became President of the Wiesbadener Golf Club in 1945.

/ Hungjao Golf Club Rules

/ 1933 Grave Mounds at Hungjao

/ *Hungjao Golf Club Rules*

In a Captain's Cup competition in March 1932, F. Thoroughgood won the championship and the silver cup presented by Captain R.G. MacDonald.

A small silver plate with a silver coin in the center dated May 21, 1933 was a competition prize at Hungjao.

John Rigg, former member of the Shanghai Golf Club wrote an article in the September 2004 issue of *Through the Green*, official publication of the British Golf Collectors Society. Titled "Pre-War Golf in China," the article mentioned a report of Hungjao's 1936 annual general meeting, in which the problem of maintaining the green and fairway was discussed. The report said that climatic variances in China created difficulties in green keeping. It was stated that the fine Bermuda on the Ninth and Tenth holes was not proving successful and that on the Third, Twelfth, Thirteenth and Fourteenth greens the mix of Bermuda and Soochow grasses was very slow in greening up after the winter. Imported Japanese turf was to be laid on the First, Fourth, Fifth, Eighth and Eleventh as a possible solution and an experiment of New Zealand grass would be tried on the Sixteenth.

In the collection of the Golf Heritage Museum in Shenzhen there is a silver prize plate offered at a Hungjao competition in 1938. In the middle of the plate is a 1914 Yuan Shih-k'ai silver dollar. On the plate are the words "HUNGJAO GOLF CLUB SHANGHAI HONG FOURS 1938 WON BY L.B. & M. PRESENTED BY H.R. CLEALAND AND D.R. GLASS."

/ *1932 Hungjao Captain's Cup*
  (Adrien von Ferscht)

/ *1933 Hungjao Silver Plate (Jeff Wu)*

SHANGHAI

/ *1938 Hungjao Hong Fours Silver Plate*

G. Warren Swire of the Shanghai Butterfield & Swire took a number of photographs of the company's golf competition at Hungjao in April 1938.

Among the Golf Heritage Museum's collection is a Taikoo (Butterfield & Swire) Challenge Cup presented by Henry Wallace Robertson, manager of Butterfield & Swire

/ *Butterfield & Swire Golf Competitions*

67

Shanghai (1906-1907) and Hong Kong (1910-1912). The Challenge Cup competition started in June 1911 and ended in April 1919, when H.A. Lawson won it a third time and outright. Names of the 27 champions over the years were inscribed on four silver plates fixed on the base.

On p. 79 of the 1939 issue of the *China Hong List*, both Hungjao Golf Club and Hungjao Ladies Golf Club were listed.

According to the April 26 issue of *North-China Herald*, an annual general meeting of the Hungjao Golf Club was held on June 21, 1940. A new club committee was elected to include General Committee members Captain F.S. Gibbings, H.R. Cleland, C.O. Cumming, W.J. Hawkins, N.E. Kent, A.P. Nazer and K.E. Newman; and Ballot Committee members L.R. Andrews, G.F.H. Bichard, W.C. Bond, F.G. Harrison, C.C. King, Martin Little, H.E. Reynell and R.D.K. Silby.

/ Taikoo Trophy Cup

In 1946, shareholders of the Hungjao Golf Club set up the Hungjao Golf Club Ltd. in Hong Kong in an effort to save and transfer the Club assets. But the Hong Kong entity was dissolved in 1953. The Club closed during fighting in

/ 1939 China Hong List

/ 1940 Hungjao Annual Meeting

1949 but opened again with 9 holes in June, with increasing activities. The *Malaya Tribune* reported on June 21 that the Club had been in preparation, though unsuccessful, for the China Amateur Open Championship, which was last held in Hungjao in 1948.

At the annual dinner held near London on May 21, 1949, 32 members of the China Golfing Society (www.chinagolfingsociety.com) decided to donate £50 to Hungjao to help with its continued operation. The fund was transferred via Hong Kong. After Shanghai was liberated, the Hungjao Golf Club was taken over by the Shanghai People's Municipal Government. In 1954, it was converted into the Western Suburban Park. In 1980, the Park was renamed Shanghai Zoo.

Walter Hagen's "Greatest Show in Golf" at Hungjao

On April 14, 1938, noted U.S. professional golfer Walter Hagen and his partner, Joe Kirkwood, were invited to play an exhibition match at the Hungjao Golf Club.

Walter Hagen won the U.S. Open in 1914 at the age of 21, and again in 1919. He continued to win five PGA championships in 1921, 1924-1927. In 1922, he became the first U.S.-born golfer to win the British Open Championship, to be followed by clenching three more Open Championships in 1924, 1928 and 1929. Six times Hagen was the captain of the U.S. Ryder Cup team, in 1927, 1929, 1931, 1933, 1935 and 1937.

With his many world-class wins in golf competitions, Hagen became a golf celebrity and started to play exhibition golf traveling around the U.S. and the world. The fashionably dressed Hagen played a total of no less than 2,500 exhibition matches all over the world. This not only helped popularizing the game globally but also greatly enriched his purse. In the midst of the Japanese military invasion into East China and Shanghai, Hagen arrived in Shanghai in April 1938 as part of his world tour that had started in 1937. He reportedly put on "the greatest show in golf" at the 18-hole golf links at Hungjao which had been bombed the day before.

Hagen's China trip during the war had never been reported, not even mentioned in his own autobiography. The story was first retold in the biography of professional golfer Joe Kirkwood, who was Hagen's travelling companion. As Kirkwood noted, the war in Shanghai was suspended on April 14, 1938 for one day, to accommodate their exhibition match at the Hungjao Golf Club.

Early in 1937, Hagen started his 18-month global tour, visiting 32 countries and regions playing exhibition golf with former Australian professional and trick-shot golfer Kirkwood as partner for the tour. After visiting New Zealand, Australia, Fiji, Singapore, Egypt, Malta, France, England, Scotland, Wales and Ireland, Belgium, Germany, Switzerland, South Africa, Kenya, India, Ceylon (Sri Lanka), the Philippines and Japan, they arrived in Hong Kong in April 1938.

The long journey had already taken more than one year. The two golfers were planning to

/ *Walter Hagen with the Claret Jug*

take a break in Hong Kong before word came from Shanghai that the Hungjao Golf Club would like to invite them to play an exhibition on April 14. Shanghai then was in the war zone, with Japanese invaders expanding their operations inside China to East and Central China after they attacked the Marco Polo Bridge in Beijing in 1937. Hungjao Golf Club was under Japanese occupation, with 600 fully armed Japanese soldiers stationed on the golf links.

Formally opened for business on October 21, 1916, Hungjao was Shanghai's fourth golf links after the Race Course, Hongkew and Kiangwan. Hungjao, which started as a 9-hole course, expanded into 12 holes in 1917 and 18 in 1923.

It was obviously not a good idea to play golf in wartime Shanghai, Kirkwood stated. But attracted by a sizeable fee already paid and the fact the Japanese and Chinese sides agreed to a one-day truce, Hagen and Kirkwood decided to take the chance and arrived in Shanghai on April 13 and stayed at the elegant Cathay Hotel.

The next morning Hagen and Kirkwood were driven to the Hungjao Golf Club. According to Dale Concannon's article published in 1972 in the *HK Golfer Magazine*, Walter Hagen had a bad feeling, driving through the gates of Hungjao Golf Club in war-ravaged Shanghai in April 1938. "Months of conflict between the occupying Japanese forces and the Chinese militia had left the city in disarray. The roadway was badly pocket-marked and soldiers stood guard every fifty yards up to the bomb-damaged clubhouse. Greeted by a welcoming party which included the Japanese Commanding Officer and various British dignitaries, the American star was invited to view the golf course he was due to play a few hours later. Looking at the eighteenth green, he noticed the freshly turfed grass and unfilled bunkers. 'They were shelled a few days ago,' explained Anthony 'Frank' Hastings George of the British Consulate. 'They rebuilt it especially for your visit!'"

Informed that a ceasefire had been agreed just for the day and the possibility of causing a diplomatic incident if he refused to play, Hagen "reluctantly" agreed to walk a few more holes and agreed to go ahead with the play.

After nine holes, Hagen and Kirkwood squared off. Their performance drew warm applauses. Lots of photographs were taken during tea after the game.

As Hagen and Kirkwood waited for a car to pick them up, they received an unusual and slightly disturbing request from the Japanese Commander. He would like to film both professionals hitting iron shots down the first fairway. "Not wishing to

/ *Hagen and Kirkwood at Cathay Hotel (Dale Concannon)*

/ Hagen Driving Off in Japan

Kirkwood Playing Out of a Bunker at Hungjao (Jack Ephgrave)

be unhelpful," Concannon writes, "Hagen and Kirkwood each grabbed a five-iron and began to fire away. Suddenly a group of Chinese soldiers appeared from the opposite direction running toward them with bayonets fixed! Hagen and Kirkwood prepared to bolt but were quickly assured this was merely simple playacting by Japanese troops. This was confirmed moments later as the so-called Chinese troops suddenly threw down their rifles and fled in mock terror under a modest barrage of golf balls hit by a bemused Hagen." Later Kirkwood realized that this was simply a Japanese propaganda tool to show the cowardice of Chinese troops. "How could they face guns if they ran away at the sight of golf balls hit by a decadent golf professional, he later conjectured?"

Concannon continues: "A few months later in June 1938 the Philadelphia Chewing Gum Company published a series of trading cards for an American audience entitled 'The Horrors of War.' Showing the bayoneting of a Chinese peasant by a Japanese soldier at Hungjao Golf Course, a green with a flag in it could be seen plainly in the background."

/ *Japanese Soldier Bayoneting Chinese Peasants (Dale Concannon)*

Hagen never mentioned his Hungjao trip after he returned to the U.S. Neither did he mention it in his autobiography. Asked if he would ever plan another similar trip to play exhibition golf, Hagen answered: "Hell no!"

Shanghai Ladies Golf Club

As early as in 1900, there were reports of the popular "putting golf" competitions among women in Shanghai. The *North-China Herald* had a story on p. 1285 of the December 19 issue quoting *Vogue* magazine about such "mini golf" events, which reads: "One of the most popular and enjoyable variations of golf this season are the putting matches which have been held weekly at almost every club, the contestants as a rule being women. Some simple prize is given, such as a box of balls, the winner in any one match being thereby debarred from further entry for the weekly competitions, but by such winning qualifying for the final match of the season between all winners, a cup of considerable value then being offered in competition. The play is either a round of 6 holes varying in length from ten to twenty yards, so that a bogey score can be put fairly from 30 to 33 for three rounds of 18 holes. Another mode of play is known as 'Clock Golf,' the tee being supposedly the center of a clock face, and the holes arranged around at the hour marks, but at uneven distances from the tee." Such putting matches can be played in any series and by any order of sequence. "There is, in fact," the report said, "no prettier assemblage than a number of women in garden-party gowns on a smooth lawn, the day being fair, the sky clear, and the near-by clubhouse supplying a solid background to an array of colour, sunlight, and beauty."

The story shows that before the founding of the Shanghai Ladies Golf Club, there had been weekly putting competitions among women at the Shanghai Golf Club. The Shanghai Ladies Golf Club was formed in 1905 and it became Shanghai's earliest and most important ladies' athletic organization.

According to a report on p. 802 of the December 14, 1921 *North-China Herald*, a few women members of the Shanghai Golf Club proposed in 1902 to organize an inner-club for ladies with authority to arrange its own fixtures and set its own handicaps. The request was approved. A special meeting was held in 1904 at the Shanghai Golf Club to discuss members of the Ladies Club playing on the Race Course links.

The first general meeting of the Shanghai Ladies Golf Club was held on November 2, 1905 by 19 founding members, according to a report in *North-China Herald* dated November 14. The following Committee was elected: Captain Mrs. Winston, Vice-Captain Mrs. E.O. Cumming, Hon. Treasurer Miss Ivy, Hon. Secretary Miss Hunt, Mrs. Pemberton, Miss Buyer, and Miss Mann.

At a bogey competition held by the Ladies Golf Club on November 27, 1905, Miss Ivy won with five strokes down. At a Club competition for the longest drive and putting held on January 18, 1906, Miss Buyer won the prize for longest drive and Miss Ivy won the prize for putting.

Shanghai Ladies Golf Club held its annual general meeting on October 23, 1912 at the Shanghai GC clubhouse, according to a report in the October 26 *North-China Herald*. Captain Mrs. J. Valentine delivered the annual report, which said the Club's financial condition was very satisfactory. The Club had a much bigger balance than at the beginning of the year, was able to buy a handsome cup, the "Challenge Cup," which had been won outright this year. The Club had increased the prize for the Captain vs. Secretary Competition from $2 to $5 and the entrance fee for it was reduced from $1 to ten cents. The Club had also changed the medal prize for the monthly cup to a spoon, which "was really very handsome, and cost even less than the medal."

The British Women's Association in Shanghai decided to move out of its headquarters at the Bund to a new address at Kiukiang Road, according to a report in the May 21, 1921 *North-China Herald*. The report said that a garden party was held on May 17 at the house of Mr. and Mrs. Pearce on Kiaochou Road. The Pearces made a generous decision to provide sport and recreation ground free of charge to the members of the Sports Section and a monthly fee of $120 towards expenses in support of the events. The Pearce house had four tennis courts, a clock putting ground and a miniature 9-hole golf links. The British Women's Association currently had 70-80 members in its Sports Section.

According to the annual meeting of the Shanghai Ladies Golf Club reported on p. 802 of the December 17, 1921 *North-China Herald*, the Club since its founding had organized a number of competitions. In addition to the annual Club championship on December 1-23, there were: Kiangwan Season Medal (November-May), Club Cup Shanghai (November-April), Sprat Competition Shanghai (November 1-30), Sprat Competition Kiangwan (November 1-30), Club Foursomes (November 14), Captain's Cup (April), Eclectic Competition Shanghai (January and February), Eclectic Competition Kiangwan (January and February), Challenge Cup (January) and Bogey competition (February and March). Members of the Shanghai Ladies Golf Club had been increasing to a total of 286 in 1921.

It was reported in the same issue of *North-China Herald* that Shanghai Ladies Golf Club and Hungjao Ladies Golf Club had their first challenge match at Kiangwan Golf Course on December 5. Shanghai won with a score of 4:2. At another match a week later at Hungjao, Hungjao beat Shanghai by 3.5:2.5.

The annual club championship of the Shanghai Ladies Golf Club started in 1903 and was held continuously until 1921. Past champions were listed on the December 17, 1921 issue of *North-China Herald*. Also listed were members of the original committee that started out the Ladies Club: President Mrs. Armstrong, Vice-President Mrs. Winslow, Treasurer Miss Ivy (Mrs. E. E. Parsons), Secretary Miss Mann, Mrs. Ayacough and Mrs. Jackson.

According to the 1922 annual meeting published on p. 95 of the October 14 issue of *North-China Herald*, Shanghai Ladies Golf Club added 37 new members in the year, bringing the total number of memberships to 300. Since 1921, Shanghai Ladies Golf Club initiated an annual inter-club competition with the Hungjao Ladies Golf Club. The meeting proposed a gift of $200 to be sent to the Shanghai Golf Club for its many

Ladies' Championship.

Season	Champion	Runner-up
1903-04	Mrs. Keswick	Mrs. Armstrong
1904-05	Miss Ivy (Mrs. E. E. Parsons)	Mrs. Pemberton
1905-06	Mrs. Armstrong	
1906-07	Miss Butler	Mrs. G. W. Noel
1907-08	Mrs. Winslow	Mrs. Parsons
1908-09	Mrs. Winslow	Miss Butler (Mrs. Drakeford)
1909-10	Mrs. Winslow	Miss Macdougall
1910-11	Miss Stevenson	Mrs. Winslow
1911-12	Mrs. Godfrey	Mrs. Parsons
1912-13	Mrs. Parsons	Miss Brown
1913-1914	Miss Brown	Mrs. Parsons
1914-1915	Mrs. Ryde	Mrs. Godfrey
1915-1916	Mrs. Ryde	Mrs. Johnstone
1917-18	Mrs. Ryde	Mrs. Shaw
1918-19	Mrs. Drakeford	Mrs. Grundy
1919-20	Mrs. Fowler	Mrs. Parsons
1920-21	Miss Coutts	Mrs. Muriel

/ *1903-1921 Shanghai Ladies GC Champions*

years of support to the Ladies Golf Club. With regard to the motion of becoming a member of the Ladies Golf Union in the U.K., it was not possible because the Shanghai Ladies Golf Club was not on British soil.

On January 8, 1923, the Shanghai Ladies Golf Club organized an "international" competition between Scotland/Ireland and England, according to a report on p. 106 of the January 13 *North-China Herald*. The Scottish/Ireland team won by 7.25:2. It was reported on p. 690 of the June 9 issue that the Shanghai Ladies Club decided to lower the Club bogey score from 86 to 77. At a competition during the season, Mrs. Tweedie Stodart scored a Club record of 82 strokes for 18 holes. During the two other rounds, she scored 82 and 83 to win the championship. Mrs. Stodart was elected Captain of the Club for the coming year.

The *North-China Herald* reported on p. 114 of the October 13, 1923 issue that Hungjao beat Shanghai by one point at the annual inter-club competition. It was decided at the Shanghai Ladies Golf Club annual meeting held in October to organize a Ladies Open Championship since all lady golfers in Shanghai were now members of the Hungjao Ladies Golf Club.

The first Shanghai Ladies Open Golf Championship was held on November 30 in 1923, according to a report on p. 623 of the December 1 *North-China Herald*. Mrs. Burton and Mrs. Enticknap squared off in the final competition. Mrs. Burton finished the morning round of 18 holes with a score of 76 and defeated Mrs. Enticknap in the afternoon by 15 up and 13 to play. The report reads: "Mrs. Burton did the morning round in 76 and it would appear that her consistency of playing, to round about that figure would cause the leading men players in Shanghai to look to their laurels." Mrs. Burton's morning score was as follows:

Out: 4, 5, 5, 4, 5, 3, 4, 4, 3: 37
In: 4, 3, 4, 6, 6, 3, 4, 3, 6: 39

The 1925 Shanghai Ladies Open Championship was played at the Hungjao Golf Course in February, according to a report on p. 49 of the February 26 *London and China Express*. The final competition of 36 holes was played between Mrs. Enticknap and Mrs. Lofting. Mrs. Lofting won by 2 up and 1 to play.

Mrs. John H. Lofting was a scratch amateur golfer who came to Shanghai with her husband three and a half years ago, according to a report on p. 171 of the April 25, 1925 *North-China Herald*. Titled "Mrs. Lofting Leaving for Home," the report reads: "Mrs. John H. Lofting, who left on Monday by the Str. Empress of Australia, for a holiday of six months at Home, will be very much missed not only by her many friends but also on the links where she has spent so much of her time. Coming to Shanghai some three and a half years ago, Mrs. Lofting immediately justified the golfing reputation she brought with her, by winning the Shanghai Ladies Challenge Bowl within a few weeks of her arrival, and that playing as backmarker in the competition from a handicap of Scratch. She also won the cup for the best scratch score in her first season and has gone on accumulating trophies ever since. This year her triumphs have culminated in a record of which she may well be proud. She won the Championship of the Shanghai Ladies' Golf Club, was runner-up in the Hungjao Ladies Championship and, finally, won the Ladies Open Championship of China, all in the same season. Mrs. Lofting has served as Captain of the Shanghai Ladies' Golf Club during the past season and has been indefatigable in her efforts to promote the best interests of the Club and the game of golf. Her advice and judgement in golfing matters will be missed during her absence, but she takes with her the best wishes of the Committee and members for many good games at home and a speedy return to Shanghai."

/ Mrs. Lofting

The February 26, 1925 *London and China Express* also reported that in the recent match between teams of Scotland and England at the Shanghai Ladies Golf Club, 32 players participated, and Scotland won by one point. In the same year, Shanghai Ladies Golf Club obtained the right to play at Kiangwan.

On January 6, 1927, the *London and China Express* published a report on p. 8 about the result of the year's Club Championship, which was won by Mrs. Tweedie Stodart. Stodart beat Mrs. F.G. Harrison with three up and one to play.

It was also reported in the same newspaper on June 23, 1927 (p. 146) that Mrs. J.B. Ferrier, the Club's Honorary Secretary, would leave with her husband for Australia. The Club held a farewell party for her and presented to her with a silver cigarette box in appreciation of her hard work for the Club over the past two years.

In the collection of the Shanghai History Museum there is a silver trophy of the Shanghai Ladies Golf Club Captain's Cup. It was awarded to a Mrs. A.J.P. Coghlan, wife of a Shanghai Municipal Council employee. She was the runner-up for the 1929-1930 Captain's Cup competition. On the trophy are inscribed the words: "SHANGHAI LADIES GOLF CLUB CHAMPIONSHIP 1929-30 Runner-up Mrs. A.J.P. COGHLAN." The inside of the trophy is gilded, showing the style of a Western modern trophy.

At the Club Championship held on January 3, 1931, Mrs. Case defeated Mrs. Philips and won the champion, according to a story published on p. 22 of the *London and China Express* on February 5, 1931.

In his article mentioned earlier, John Rigg provided a group photograph of lady golfers after a competition in 1937 between the Shanghai St. Andrew's Association and the Shanghai St.

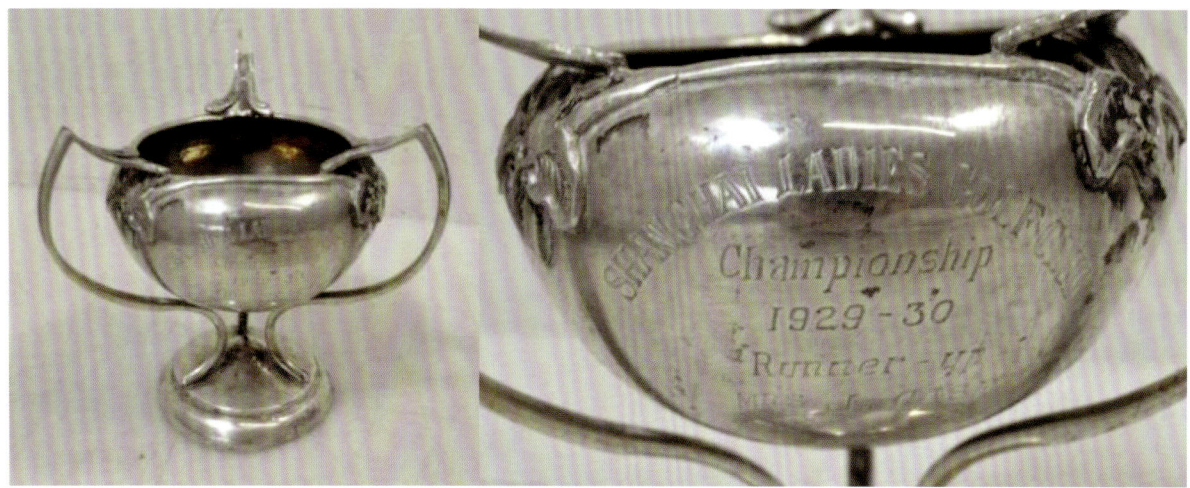

/ 1929-30 Shanghai Ladies GC Trophy

George Association.

The first round of the semi-annual golf competition between lady associations was played over the Hungjao Golf Club on November 28, 1940, when the St. Andrew's team won by a small margin of ¾, with a score of 5¾:5. In the second round played on December 1, 1940 St. George's team turned the

/ 1937 Lady Golfers of St. Andrew's and St. George's Associations

/ 1940 Shanghai Ladies GC Association Competition

tables and won by a big margin of 45:34, according to a report on December 4 in the *North-China Herald*.

The final round of the 1940 China Ladies Amateur Golf Championship was held at Hungjao on November 25, as reported by the *North-China Herald* on December 4. Mrs. Reynell defeated Mrs. Piercy on the 37th green winning the championship.

Shanghai Junior Golf Club and Hongkew Golf Course

Membership of the Shanghai Golf Club steadily increased after 1894 and reached 600 by 1909. Many of the Club charter members as well as Committee members were advanced in age, and therefore the Club was referred to by young Scottish engineers living to the north of the city as a "Senior Club."

In 1895, the Shanghai Municipal Council rented 200 *mu* of land at North Szech'uan Road to build a shooting ground, which was later expanded into a sports and recreation park. The park, named "Hongkew Recreation Ground," started construction in 1905, modeling on the Glasgow Sports Park. In 1922, the Recreation Ground was renamed Hongkew Park. It was Shanghai's second largest public park after Jesffield (today's Zhongshan) Park. The two parks were outside of the foreign settlements in Shanghai but were administered by the Shanghai Municipal Council on behalf of the expatriates.

/ Hongkew Park

A reader named "Niblick" wrote a letter to the editor of *North-China Herald* on December 18, 1906 suggesting that the new Hongkew Recreation Ground consider building a 9-hole golf course in order to relieve the over crowdedness of the Race Course Links. The reader writes: "Can nothing be done to utilize the new Hongkew Recreation Ground? This large piece of land is not yet laid out, and if some comprehensive scheme was adopted, the position of flower beds and planted clumps could be so arranged, as to allow of some excellent links being laid out, and some relief given to the Race Course Game. If someone interested in furthering this idea would come forward and start a new Golf Club, or if the present Club would open a branch links, on which their present members would be able to play, considerable relief would be accorded, and more persons able to have a round."

Niblick's letter seemed to be working. It was reported in the August 19, 1911 issue of *North-China Herald* that as the Hongkew Recreation Ground was near completion in 1908, a new 9-hole golf course went into construction with the approval of Scotsman MacGregor, who was head of municipal parks under the Municipal Council.

Members of the Shanghai Golf Club had hoped that the opening of the new Hongkew Golf Links would help relieve the crowdedness of the Race Course links. But soon engineers from Scotland living in the Hongkew area decided to form a new club and make the Hongkew Golf Links their home course.

A report published on pp. 556-557 of the September 4, 1909 *North-China Herald* discussed a recent meeting of the Shanghai Junior Golf Club in which Club president Crawford D. Kerr talked about how the Club had been organized. The President said that the Club was originally formed on April 14, 1909, by several enthusiasts who elected a Provisional Committee of six people to arrange the formation of the Club. At a general meeting on April 23, a balloting committee was elected, and entrance fees and subscription fees were agreed upon. Kerr said: "It was resolved that a clubhouse should be built in the Hongkew Park at a cost of about Tls 6,000 of which Tls 4,000 have been lent by the trustees of the Recreation Fund at 5 per cent and the remaining Tls. 2,000 has to be raised by 7 per cent debentures to be taken up by the members themselves." The meeting decided to adopt the same rules and regulations as those of the Shanghai Golf Club subject to such local bylaws as would be found necessary.

The meeting said that the clubhouse had been under construction and would be ready for members by the end of October. The number of members had already reached sixty-five and "it is confidently expected that before the next annual meeting this membership will be largely increased. As the senior club, which plays on the Race Course, is ten times as large as our new club it is evident there is a demand for further facilities for golfers."

The meeting reported that the Municipal Council had laid out excellent links of nine holes with properly raised and drained greens and tees. The committee hoped that the forty debentures of Tls. 50 each would be subscribed by members in order to complete the building of the clubhouse and add furniture and fixings. The entrance fees already collected would suffice for furnishing the building. And the subscriptions will be required for current expenses. Additional revenue would be received from hire of lockers, profits on bar and sundries.

On the evening of February 22, 1910, Shanghai Junior Golf Club held an annual meeting in the pavilion at Hongkew Park, according to a report on p. 427 of the February 25 *North-China Herald*. Captain S. Barton who chaired the meeting said that as of October 31, 1909, the cost of the clubhouse was Tls. 5,500, and the furniture, light and water fittings, roughly, $2,700. A supply of golf clubs and balls had been purchased and the building insured. Tls. 4,000 had been borrowed from the Recreation Fund and Tls. 2,000 had been obtained by debentures. A total of $8,000 was raised, which more than covered the expenses of the building. The expenses of the furniture had been met out of the first year's entrance fees and subscriptions. The bar had been sub-let for the first year at all events, to the boy at a rental of $200. The prices at which he should sell the drinks were based on those in force at the Recreation Club. The balance of accounts showed $500, but it was less because of ongoing payment of expenses. The membership of the Club was ninety but by now it should be around 100.

The meeting decided to retain the name of Shanghai Junior Golf Club. The entrance fee was fixed at $30 instead of $20. The annual subscription of $10 remained the same. The meeting elected a 10-member general committee

/ Hongkew Park

for the new year, which included Barton and J.B. Ferrier and an 11-member balloting committee.

By the time of the 1911 annual general meeting, the number of members of the Shanghai Junior Golf Club had increased to 105. Captain J.B. Ferrier presided the meeting, according to a report on p. 207 of the January 27 *North-China Herald*. The Club organized its first championship in 1910 and created a trophy worth of $80. The annual meeting resolved to revise Rule 20 so that the wives and daughters of members should be entitled to make use of the Club free of charge. Other ladies may be given similar privileges if introduced by wives of members as honorary members on payment of an annual subscription of $5 each.

The Shanghai Junior Golf Club purchased a small boat, called "Foozle," in 1911 to be used on the lake near the 9th hole to help retrieve lost balls in the water, according to reports in the April 8 and April 15 issues of the *North-China Herald*. This was for the purpose to prevent golfers, especially non-members, from spending too much time trying to retrieve lost balls, causing a delay. The boat would replace the current raft. The Club committee decided to hire a worker with a monthly salary working on the boat. To partially pay for the boat's running expenses, the Club sold books of tickets, each containing 100 tickets, at $1 each book. The books were also sold by the park-keeper to non-members. This was a reasonable arrangement because 100 balls might be recovered from the lake at less than the cost of one new ball.

By the end of 1911, Shanghai Junior Golf Club added 56 members, a net increase of 46 minus 10 withdraws. The annual general meeting held on December 15, 1911 discussed the issue of caddie salaries, according to a report on p. 807 of the December 23 *North-China Herald*. Captain J. Ross Young discussed a trial negotiation with 10 caddies about paying them a monthly salary of $3, but it was refused. Caddies did not even agree to a monthly pay of $3.50. Young hoped that members would stick to paying caddies five cents a round, not 10 or 20 as some members did. If members stick to the five cents tip, the Club should be able to hire caddies at $3.5 per month, A Committee member pointed out that the Hongkew course was shorter than the Race Course links and there were fewer creeks.

Shanghai Junior Golf Club held an extraordinary meeting at the clubhouse on April 10, 1912, according to a report on pp. 103-104 of the April 13 *North-China Herald*. The meeting passed a resolution to invest Tls. 1,000-1,200 to add an addition to the current pavilion, which would comprise a workshop, kitchen, servants' quarters, caddies' room, etc., to be erected as a lean-to-against the present building.

At the annual general meeting held on October 21, 1912, it was decided that the entrance fee would rise to $50 from $30, annual subscription to $12 from $10 and for ladies to $6 from $5. It was also decided to hire a paid secretary to be in charge of daily work. Members of the Shanghai Junior Golf Club reached 225 in 1912, according to a report in *North-China Herald* dated November 23. As golfing activities were increasingly affected by other sports at Hongkew Park, especially football, Club members decided to complain to the Municipal Council about the dangerous situation when football game was played on fairways.

The 5th annual general meeting of the Shanghai Junior Golf Club was held at the clubhouse on October 24, 1913, according to a report of the November 1 *North-China Herald*. Members proposed that the Club should apply to the Municipal Council to extend playing time.

The current rule that golf could be played prior to 3:00 pm prevented members who work until 5:00 pm. By this time, two branches had been formed under the Junior Golf Club, a lawn tennis branch and a lawn bowling branch.

A Junior Golf Club member wrote a letter to the editor of the *North-China Herald* on November 18, 1913 about a group of Japanese baseball players removing the hazards on three golf holes the previous Sunday, according to a report on November 22. The writer, pen named "One Day A Week," writes: "A competition of the Junior Golf Club was completely disorganized on account of the removal by the said Japanese of certain of the artificial bunkers. Baseball is a summer game, and has finished for the season on the other public playing grounds of Shanghai. Golf is a winter game, and it seems hard that players, who only have an opportunity of playing on one day in the week, should be deprived of their game."

On June 10, 1915, 40 members of the Shanghai Junior Golf Club met at the Palace Hotel and discussed the proposal to purchase land and build a new golf course at Woosung Forts, according to a report on pp. 764-765 of the June 12 *North-China Herald*. Two Club committee members had met with A.C. Clear, general manager of the railway. Clear asked for a guarantee of out-of-pocket expenses and any compensation for the existing tenants of the land at Woosong. In addition, the railway company would get the contract of leveling the course and other works, and that they would build a pavilion to be leased to the Golf Club. The Club originally planned to sell shares to raise Tls. 10,500 for the project. But the sum was only sufficient to meet preliminary expenses and would not meet the requirements of the railway authorities. As going forward with the scheme would entail high financial liabilities, the meeting proposed the possibility of reaching out to the public and explore the possibility of forming a Woosong Golf Course Co. But the entire proposal about a new course fell through.

It was reported on p. 309 of the November 1, 1919 *North-China Herald* that by October 30,

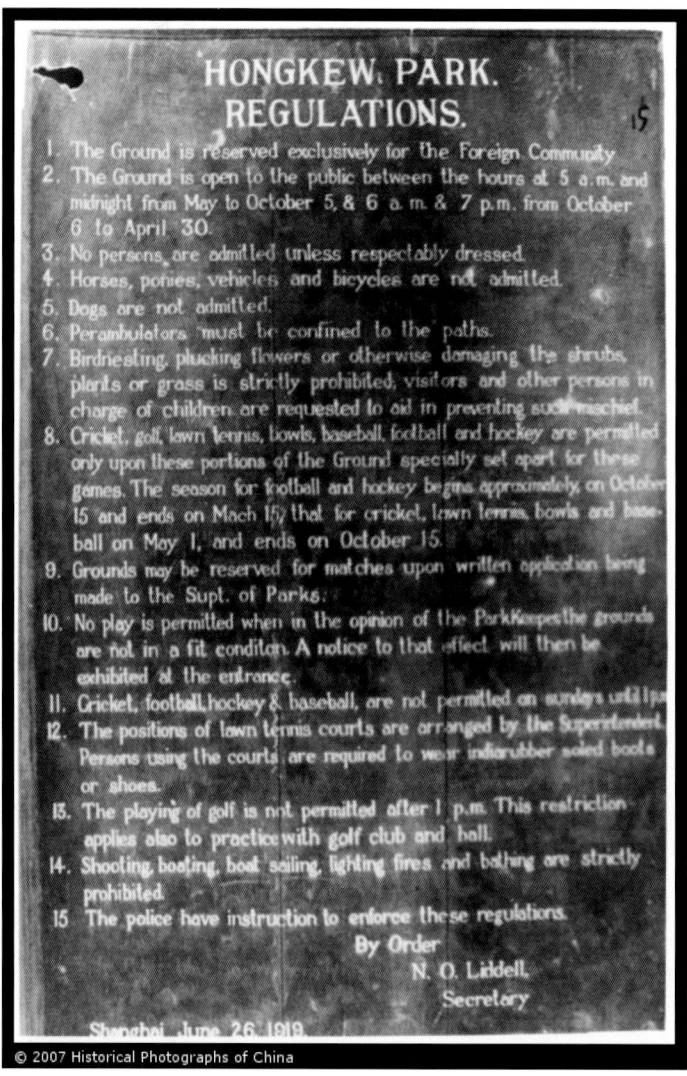

/ Hongkew Park Regulations

Club membership reached 261. The annual general meeting reported that Club competitions in 1919 were "far from successful, this being due to a great extent to the persistently bad weather, with the results that the entries little more than covered the expenses." Competitions included the annual Club Championship, Monthly Medals, President's Cup, Captain's Cup, Boyes Cup, Engineers' Trophy and War Funds Competition. The annual report thanked the Marine Engineers' Institute for the use of their room for committee meetings.

At the 13th annual general meeting held on November 10, 1921, Club members suggested to request that the Municipal Council Parks Committee consider extending the opening hours of the Golf Course from 1:00 pm to 3:00 pm on days when football was not played from the months of November to March, as reported in the November 12 *North-China Herald*. Their reasoning was that except on Saturdays and Sundays, "there was hardly a soul to be seen in the Park during any afternoon between November and March."

Club membership increased to 277, with a net increase of 59, in 1922, according to a report in *North-China Herald* on November 25. At the 14th annual meeting, Sidney Barton, British Consul-General, was elected a life member. Barton was the Club's founding member and Captain in 1910. The subject of a new course was brought up again for discussion. This was because the Hongkew Golf Course was open to the public and became growingly congested. A newly elected committee would be responsible to look into feasibilities of finding a new home for the Club.

The annual championship of the Shanghai Junior Golf Club for 1923 was held on January 7, according to a report on p. 106 of the January 13 *North-China Herald*. The finalists, like last year, were again A.M. McGregor and Chas. H. Hopkins. Hopkins, a Canadian, led by two holes in the first two rounds of nine holes. But

/ 1922 Hongkew Golf Links

Scotsman McGregor caught up in the third round and led by three holes at the 33rd hole in the fourth round. Hopkins clenched back two holes but tied with McGregor for the last hole, thus losing by one hole. It was an impressive play for Hopkins because he had been playing golf for only two years. To McGregor, this was his third championship win, the first in 1915 and the second in 1922.

The January 27 *North-China Herald* reported an inter-club match between the Shanghai Junior Golf Club and the Shanghai Japanese Golf Club at Hongkew links. Thirty members from each club participated in the competition, with Japan winning by 1¾ points. A Japanese golfer presented a silver cup to be won by the best player. The Junior Golf Club hosted a tiffin at the pavilion after the game.

At the 1925 annual meeting held on November 20, Captain Hopkins told members that the Japanese Golf Club was building its own golf links, according to a report in the November 25 *North-China Herald*. Once it was completed, it would relieve the congestion at Hongkew.

/ *Hongkew Park Postcard*

Hongkew Golf Course was occupied by the Japanese army in 1938. A news story published in the September 2, 1938 issue of *The Singapore Free Press and Mercantile Advertiser* said that on September 1, "the Japanese flag flying over the main building of the Hongkew Golf Club was torn down by Chinese guerillas."

Shanghai Junior Golf Club was listed in the 1939 *China Hong List*. The Club's address was Public Park, Hongkew, Tel. 46647, President W.J. Gande, Captain P.J. Kano, Vice-Captain K.L. Swartzell, Honorary Secretary and Treasurer M. Benton.

Shanghai Junior Golf Club

Public Park, Hongkew
Tel 46647

Gande, W. J., pres.
Kano, P. J., capt.
Swartzell, K. L., vice-capt.
Benton, M., hon. sec. and treas.

/ *1939 China Hong List*

Kiangwan Country Club

Japanese golf enthusiasts in Shanghai built a 9-hole golf course to the northeast of the Kiangwan Race Course and the Kiangwan Country Club formally opened on October 2, according to the report on p. 76 of the October 9 *North-China Herald*.

The report reads: "The formal opening of the new Kiangwan Country Club (otherwise the Japanese Golf Club) took place on Sunday morning in delightful weather. The opening ceremony was very brief. Mr. M. Nodaira, the president, driving the first ball in the presence of some 50 members and declaring the course open. Among those present were Mr. T. Tanabe, the Vice-President, and Mr. H. MacAndo, the honorary secretary. The opening of the course was the occasion of a competition for a beautiful silver cup, presented by the *Osaka Mainichi*. The conditions were 18 holes, medal play, under handicap." The result of the competition was tied between Agawa and Kunnouni and the two would replay next Sunday.

"This is the first time that local Japanese golf players have had a course of their own," the report says. "The club was started on the suggestion of some of the leading Japanese golf enthusiasts when it was known that there were in Shanghai no fewer than 150 players of the Royal and Ancient game. Membership is to be limited to 100 but already 70 have been admitted. The club is now the possessor of approximately 235 *mu* of fine land to the northeast of the Kiangwan Race Course. More than $20,000 was expended for the laying out of the links and another $1,000 for the building of an excellent, spacious and well-lighted clubhouse. All expenses are borne by members."

The report said that members of the club had invited their Chinese friends to play free of charge. Despite ample investments and great efforts in building the links, the greens had not yet matured and the fairways were still not in good condition. The clubhouse was not yet ready to entertain a large number of members and their families until probably the end of November or early December.

The 9-hole Kiangwan Country Club course was 2,260 yard long, which comprised four par-4s, two par-3s and three par-5s. The report had a scheme of the course in which the length of each hole was listed:

The Japanese Golf Club in Shanghai was formed in 1920 and had since used the Hongkew Golf Course for their Club championship competitions. MacAndo, the Honorary Secretary won the 1925 championship. He again won the championship in 1926, according to the report on p. 364 of the November 20, 1926 *North-China Herald*. So far, the Japanese Golf Club had organized seven club championships at Hongkew. The Club decided to invite members of the Shanghai, Hungjao, Junior and Hongkew golf clubs to participate at an invitational open competition at the Kiangwan Country Club on November 27.

In an inter-club competition on May 13, 1929, Shanghai Golf Club beat the Kiangwan Country Club by 15:10 at the Seekingjao Golf Course.

The 1935 *Shanghai City Guide* listed the address of the Kiangwan Country Club at "295 Boone Road," together with the other golf clubs in Shanghai:

Hongkew Golf Club: Hongkew Park

Hungjao Golf Club: Hungjao & Rubicon Roads

Hungjao Ladies Golf Club: Hungjao & Rubicon Roads

Kiangwan Country Club: 295 Boone Road

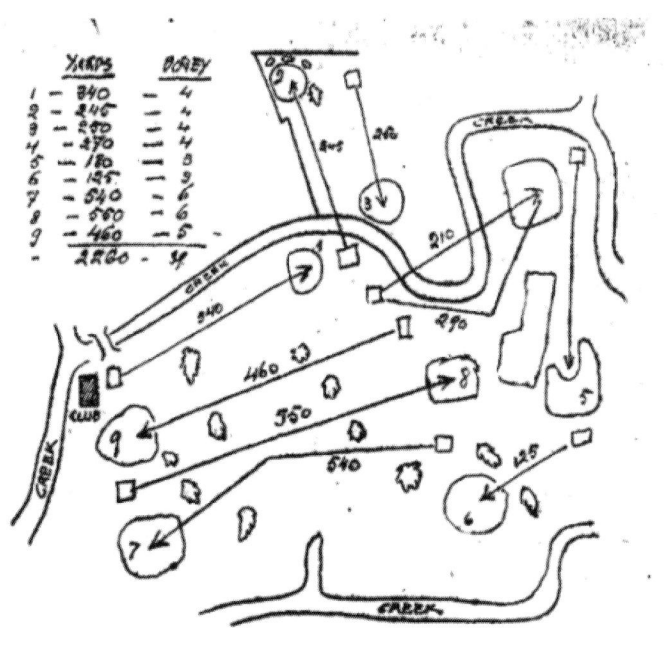

/ Scheme of Kiangwan Country Club

EARLY GOLF IN CHINA

(c/o Japanese Club)

Shanghai Golf Club: Seekingjao, Kiangwan

```
92              ALL ABOUT SHANGHAI
                       GOLF
Hongkew Golf Club           Hongkew Park
Hungjao Golf Club           Hungjao & Rubicon Roads
Hungjao Ladies' Golf Club   Hungjao & Rubicon Roads
Kiangwan Country Club       295 Boone Road
  (Golf)                      (c|o Japanese Club)
Shanghai Golf Club          Seekingjao, Kiangwan
```
/ 1935 Shanghai City Guide

The information of Kiangwan Country Club was listed in the 1939 *China Hong List*: "Kiangwan Country Club (Golf) c/o Japanese Club, 295 Boone Road, Tel. 43807, President T. Tanabo, Vice-President K. Tanaka, Captain B. Hashimoto, Hon. Secretary H. Takata, Hon. Treasurer S. Asada."

Kiangwan Country Club (Golf)

C/o Japanese Club,
295 Boone-rd
Tel 43807

Tanabo, T., pres.
Tanaka, K., vice-pres.
Hashimoto, B., captain
Takata, H., hon. sec.
Asada, S., hon. treas.

/ Kiangwan Country Club (Golf)

Standard Oil Golf Course

The Standard Oil Company of New York purchased land in Pootung (Pudong) along the Huangpu River and set up its Shanghai facilities in the 1910s. The company built a simple 9-hole golf course inside the facilities for use by its employees. Expatriates living in Pootung found it too far away playing golf at the Race Course links and chose to go to the Standard Oil links instead. A British engineer who lived in Pootung in the 1920s wrote: "The golf club at Hungjao was too far away to interest us, but Pootung residents were always welcome to use a home-made nine hole course at the Standard Oil Company's installation a mile down river from our place." (http://www.talesofoldchina.com/shanghai/image/cfm)

Paul French in his 2011 book, *The Old Shanghai A-Z*, mentioned this 9-hole golf course: "The boat services between Pootung and the Bund provided a lifeline to the more exciting side of the river but there were entertainment activities in Pootung too, including hunting, fishing, boating as well as a nine-hole golf course at the Standard Oil Company's installations."

The Standard Oil Co. golf course should have been operating until the 1930s.

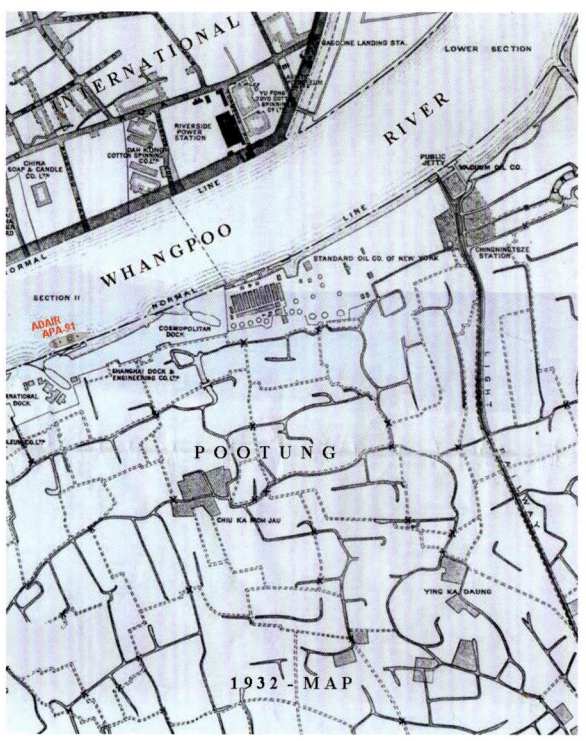

/ 1932 Standard Oil Co. in Pootung

China Open Amateur Golf Championship

In May 1924, Shanghai Golf Club decided to organize a China Open (Amateur) Golf Championship to be held in late October, according to an announcement in the May 17, 1924 issue of *North-China Herald*. It would be an annual tournament and clubs invited to participate included Hungjao, Royal Hong Kong, Amoy, Mukden, Tientsin, Weihaiwei, Port Edward, Hankow, Nanking, Peking, Tsingtao, Foochow, Manila, Tokyo, Yokohama, Kobe and Hodogaya Golf Clubs. Entry deadline was October 15. A trophy was presented by a Shanghai resident and the names of the champions would be inscribed on the trophy. But the trophy would remain in Shanghai and the winner would receive a commemorative cup. The entrance fee would be $5.00 and conditions would be 72 holes medal play.

The first China Amateur Open Golf Championship was played at Hungjao Golf Course on November 1-2, 1924. In a medal play of 72 holes similar to the Open Championships of Great Britain and the United States, J.B. Ferrier won the game with a score of 77, 78, 73 and 78.

According to a report on p. 28 of April 17, 1926 *North-China Herald*, the permanent trophy for the China Amateur Open Golf Championship was made of gold and had an excellent design. "On the left is the caddie standing at the hole and holding the pin, while the player is in a semi-kneeling position close to the ground studying the line of his putt. The attitude of both player and caddie are remarkably true to life." The trophy was presented by the late A. E. Algar, who unfortunately passed away before he could witness the trophy's formal presentation.

The 3rd annual China Amateur Open Golf

> **CHINA OPEN GOLF CHAMPIONSHIP**
>
> **An Annual Tournament to be Held at Shanghai in October: A Trophy Presented**
>
> It has been decided to establish an Open Amateur Golf Championship of China, to be played for annually at Shanghai. The following clubs are asked to send in their entries before October 15, on which date the list for this year will be closed:—
> Hungjao Golf Club, Royal Hongkong Golf Club, Amoy Golf Club, Mukden Golf Club, Tientsin Golf Club, Weihaiwei Golf Club, Port Edward Golf Club (Weihaiwei), Hankow Golf Club, Nanking Golf Club, Peking Golf Club, Tsingtao Golf Club, Foochow Golf Club, Manila Golf Club, Tokio Golf Club, Yokohama Golf Club, Kobe Golf Club, Hodogaya Golf Club.
> Any member of any recognized club staying in Shanghai when the competition takes place will be eligible to enter. The actual date of the competition will be communicated in due course, but it is anticipated that either October 19 or 26 will be the date selected.
> A trophy, which has been presented by a Shanghai resident, will be inscribed with the name of the winner but will remain in Shanghai and the winner will receive a cup to commemorate the event. Entrance fee $5.00; conditions, 72 holes, medal play.

/ *1924 China Open Golf Championship*

Championship was held on October 9-10, 1926 at the Kiangwan Golf Course. A total of 34 golfers, including golfers from Japan and Hong Kong, participated in the 72-hole medal play competition. "With a gale blowing on Saturday while on Sunday it was very showery at times," reported *North-China Herald* on the October 16 issue, the championship was won for the second time by M.W. Budd "by only one stroke."

Again, at the China Amateur Open Golf Championship held in October 1927 at Kiangwan Golf Course, M.W. Budd took the trophy, beating Colonel A.G. Barry, champion of the 1905 British Open, according to a report in the October 15, 1927 *North-China Herald*.

The 1934 China Amateur Open Golf Championship was played at the Seekingjao and Hungjao Golf Courses on October 20 and 21, respectively, according to a report in the October 24 *North-China Herald*. J.B. Broadus of the U.S. Marine Corps stationed in Shanghai won the championship. Broadus beat famous Shanghai golfer F.D. Hunter. On Saturday morning Hunter broke the Seekingjao course record with a score of 69. Broadus, however, shot another record in the afternoon of 67. Hunter once again broke the course record on Sunday at the Hungjao course, by shooting a 71.

The 1940 China Amateur Open Golf Championship was held on October 20 and 21 again at Seekingjao and Hungjao respectively, according to a report of the October 23 *North-China Herald*. Tony Ricketts, the defending champion, came out to be the winner. Lew Carson was the runner-up and Davis Gains won 3rd place.

According to the 1950 *Golfer's Handbook*, the China Amateur Open Golf Championship started in 1924 and continued until October 24, 1948. A total of 17 competitions were held (except 1937, 1941-1947). Tony Ricketts won four times in 1938, 1939, 1940 and 1948, consecutively.

The China Ladies Amateur Open Golf Championship started in 1923 and continued until 1948, running at least about a dozen times.

/ J.B. Broadus Champion of 1934 China Amateur Open

/ Winners of the 1940 China Amateur Open

CHINA OPEN AMATEUR CHAMPIONSHIP.

Year	Winner	Club	Venue	Score
1924	J. B. Ferrier	Shanghai	Shanghai	306
1925	M. W. Budd	Shanghai	Shanghai	305
1926	M. W. Budd	Shanghai	Shanghai	318
1927	M. W. Budd	Shanghai	Shanghai	293
1928	M. W. Budd	Shanghai	Shanghai	289
1929	J. L. Humphreys	Selangor	Shanghai	302
1930	H. S. Mitchell	Royal Hongkong	Shanghai	306
1931	J. W. Harrison	Shanghai	Shanghai	315
1932	J. W. Harrison	Shanghai	Shanghai	307
1933	J. W. Harrison	Shanghai	Shanghai	305
1934	J. B. Broadus	(Unattached)	Shanghai	290
1935	J. W. Harrison	Shanghai	Shanghai	309
1936	A. Ricketts	Hungjao	Shanghai	302
1937	No championship.			
1938	A. Ricketts	Hungjao	Shanghai	304
1939	A. Ricketts	Hungjao	Shanghai	—
1940	A. Ricketts	Hungjao	Shanghai	304
1948	A. Ricketts	Enfield	Hungjao	—
1949	Not played.			

/ 1924-1948 Winners of China Amateur Open

Hickory Golf Clubs Made for Shanghai

Golf developed rapidly during the first half of the 20th century in Shanghai, witnessed by the growing number of golf courses and golf clubs in the city. The growing number of golfers led to increased demand for golf equipment. In the history of modern golf, gutta percha balls gave way to the new rubber core golf balls in the early 20th century. As a result, golf clubs also underwent evolutionary changes to better suit the new golf balls. Hickory wood drivers and brassies changed from the traditional spliced neck joint to socket head style and club heads started to become shorter, bulkier and thicker. As to hickory irons, manufacturers started to number them from the mid-1920s instead of using the old-style names such as Mid-Iron, Mashie, Mashie Niblick, Niblick, etc.

Expatriates living in Shanghai and other trading ports depended on imported golf equipment from Scotland. A growing number of golfers in Shanghai started to custom make their own clubs in Scotland and stamp "Shanghai" or "China" on their clubs. Sports companies in Shanghai became importers of golf clubs and company names were stamped on club heads and shafts. Two of these China related golf clubs were at one point owned by Scottish collector and historian Douglas MacKenzie, who gave the clubs to a Canadian collector and member of the U.S. Hickory Championship Hall of Fame Bob West. Some of the Shanghai clubs are now in the collection of the Golf Heritage Museum or private collectors like Jeff Wu and Ge Li.

Bob West was given two Shanghai clubs about 20 years ago. One had the name of Richard Graham, the first professional at the Shanghai Golf Club, who died of a heart attack just a little over a month on the job. The other was made by Samuel Green, who followed Graham as professional in Shanghai. Both clubs are stamped "Shanghai" on the club heads.

Jeff Wu owns four hickory clubs made for Shanghai: a brassie, a lady's brass putter, a goose-neck putter and a lady's mid-iron.

Brassie was the name of the most popular fairway wood that was to be found in every golfer's bag in the early 20th century, equivalent to a modern 2 or 3 wood. Wu's brassie head is

/ Graham and Green Shanghai Irons

made of persimmon and a brass plate was fixed underneath to protect the club as well as add some weight. On the club head there is an oval shaped cleek mark "C. Carter." Underneath are the words Kiangwan and Shanghai GC. Kiangwan was Shanghai GC's first 18-hole golf course that opened in 1912. The club was made in the 1920s.

During a trip to Las Vegas in 2015 to participate at the U.S. Golf Collectors Society (now Golf Heritage Society) annual meeting, Jeff Wu and Ernie Wang, publisher of the Chinese edition of *Golf Magazine*, spent more than an hour digging into a U.S. collector's box of golf clubs to find a brass hickory putter related to China. The club is 72 cm long and the club head 9.9 cm wide. Although the leather grip was replaced over the years, it still constitutes a 100-year-old golf memorabilia with a rich history. On the back of the club head is marked "Made by Hong Kee Co. Shanghai." According to Jeff, two leading U.S. experts on antique golf clubs, Jeff Ellis and Peter Georgiady, said that the club should have been made by a local Chinese clubmaker. Quite different from the clubs made in the U.K., U.S., Canada and Australia, they said, the club has an especially long hosel and the mouth of the hosel does not have the usual sawtooth nicking. If this were true, the club could

/ Kiangwan Brassie (Jeff Wu)

be an extremely rare find in the golf collection world. And Hong Kee might have been the only Chinese company that made its own golf clubs.

Jeff Wu's goose neck putter, with "Shanghai" on the club head, was imported by Squires Bingham, an import/export company owned by U.S. businessmen Roy Squires and William Bingham in Shanghai. Richard Graham, the first professional in Shanghai was in fact invited by the company in 1912, according to Wu. Based on the company's import record and the cleek mark of an arrow through a heart, the club was made around 1912. The club face has irregular dots, which were standard face marks for clubs made in 1905-1915. Also clearly marked on the club head are the words "Made in Scotland" and "Hand Forged." The club bears an arrow through a heart, cleek mark by Walter Reginald "Wattier" Hewitt of Carnoustie, Scotland, an Englishman originating from Liverpool who started his club making business in 1895.

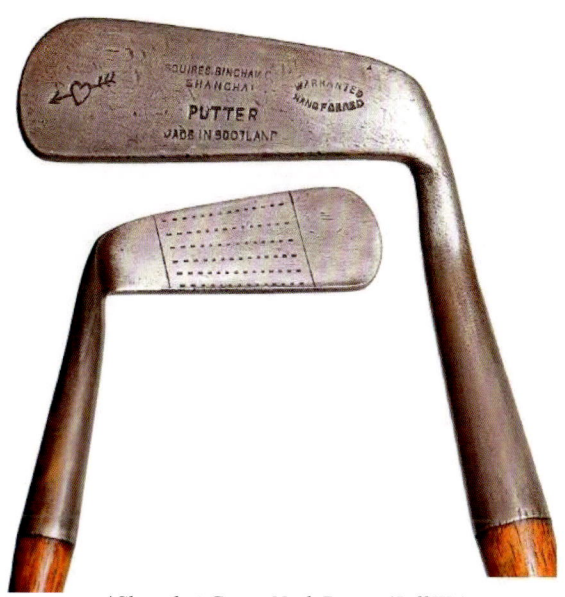

/ *Shanghai Goose Neck Putter (Jeff Wu)*

The marks on the head of the mid-iron in Wu's collection are fading due to the many years of its history, but still recognizable. It is a "mid-iron," corresponding to a modern 2 or 3 iron. The letter "L" on the club head indicates it is a lady's club. "Made in Scotland" and "Warranted

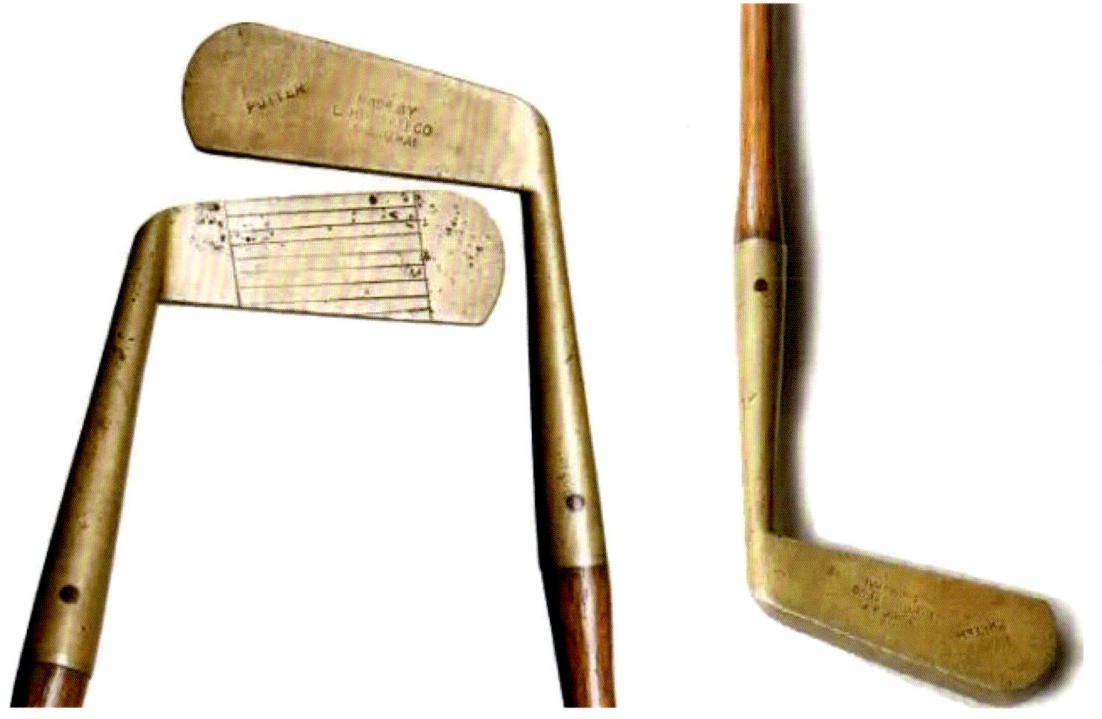

/ *Hong Kee Co. Putter (Jeff Wu)*

Hand Forged" are marked close to the neck of the club head. In the middle of the club head is "Shanghai." The knot below the letter "L" is the well-known cleek mark of James Pringle Cochrane of Edinburgh.

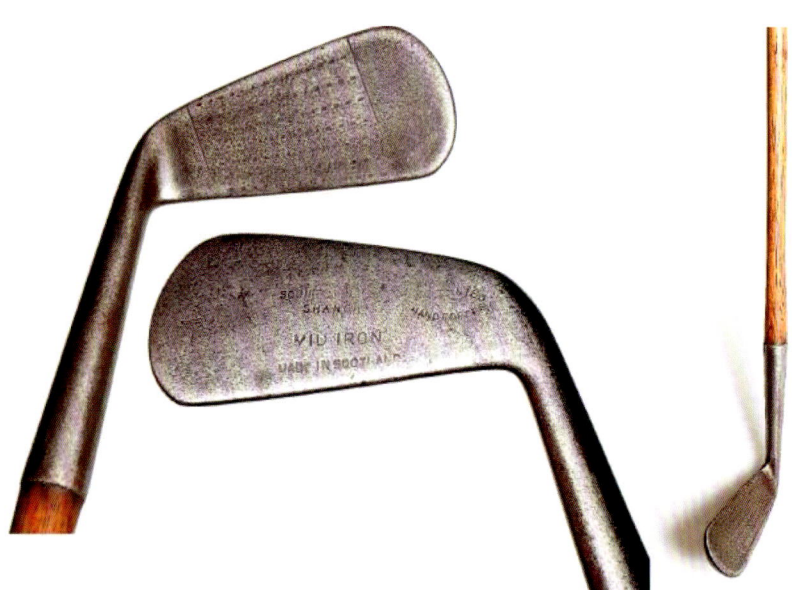

/ Shanghai Lady's Mid-Iron (Jeff Wu)

Ge Li, member of China Golf Heritage Society's Beijing Branch, purchased an iron on a trip to California in 2010. The hickory club is a "Deep Face Mashie," with a rustless steel head hand forged and made in Scotland. The hickory shaft has a brown leather grip. On the club head is a five-star, cleek mark of Scottish clubmaker William Gibson. In the middle of the club head is the name James Braid, five-time British Open champion who authorized the production of the club. What is special about this club is the mark of a Chinese company in Shanghai, Sun Co., which sold the club. The mark reads in English: "Sun Co. Ltd. Athletic Goods," with four Chinese characters xinxin gongsi (Sun Company) in the middle of the mark.

One of the Shanghai clubs in the collection of Golf Heritage Museum is a brassie made by Scottish clubmaker Jack White. White was the runner-up in the 1899 British Open Championship and won the Claret Jug in 1904. The Jack White drivers and brassies won silver medal at the 1909 Deal International Golf Exhibition. White worked as professional at the Sunningdale Golf Club from 1901 to 1926. He returned to his hometown Gullane and opened a Jack White club shop, which is still operating under his name today. The

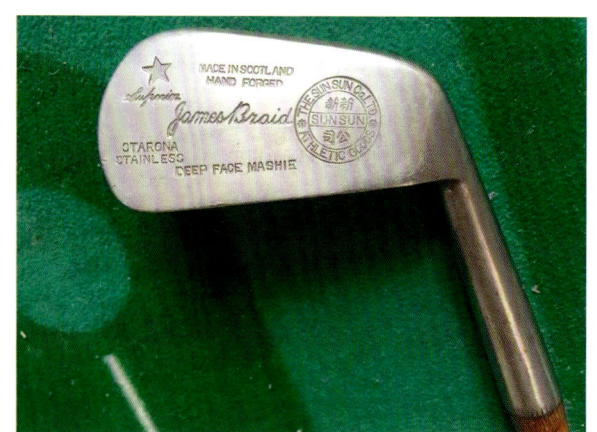

/ Sun Sun Mashie (Ge Li)

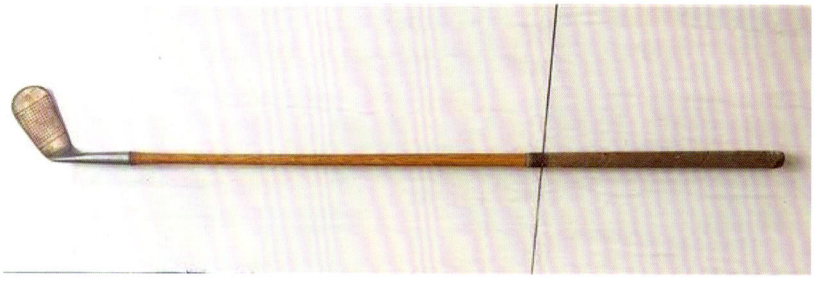

/ Sun Sun Mashie (Ge Li)

brassie was made around the 1920s and was a product of Sports Ltd. in Shanghai.

The Golf Heritage Museum owns three irons with the name of S. Green on them. One is a Cleek, similar to today's 1 or 2 iron; one is a lofting iron, similar to a wedge and one a putting cleek, similar to a putter or a 1 iron.

As discussed earlier in this Chapter, S. Green was Samuel Green, club professional of the Shanghai Golf Club from 1913 to 1919. He was also a golf course architect and club maker. He ordered golf clubs from Scotland bearing his name and Shanghai, China.

Inside the oval mark to the right of the S. Green Cleek club head are the words: "Shanghai GC, China, Special, Made in Scotland." On the upper left side of the club head are "Warranted Hand Forged." The cleek mark is a "hand of friendship" used by clubmaker George Nicoll of Leven. Nicoll opened his shop in 1881 and

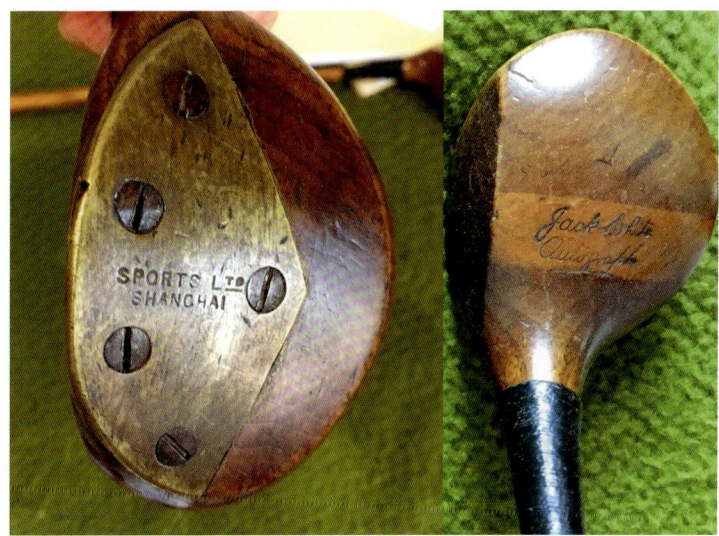

/ Jack White Brassie

continued for 102 years. Different styles of the friendship hand were used over the years. The cleek marks on this club as well on the putting cleek were used for products made between 1910 and 1920. The short lines on the face of the clubs indicate that they were made before 1920.

The lofting iron was used to hit high approaching shot near the green before the invention of the modern pitching wedge. On the back of the club head are words: "Hand Forged

/ S. Green Cleek

/ *S. Green Lofting Iron*

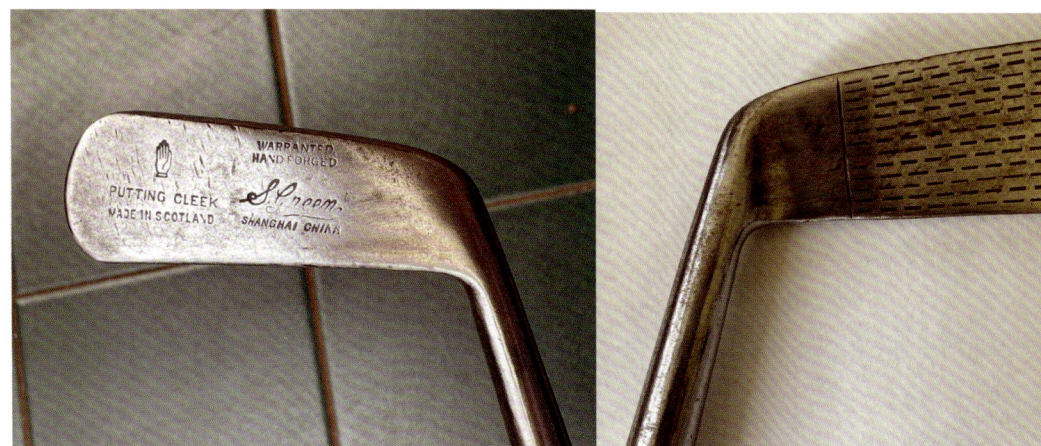

/ *S. Green Putting Cleek*

in Scotland, S. Green, Shanghai China, Lofting Iron." The five-star mark shows it was made by Willian Gibson of Kinghorn. A blacksmith himself, Gibson started his club making shop at Edinburgh in 1887 and moved to Kinghorn in 1903. Starting from 1913, he began using the five-star as his cleek mark until the 1920s. The clubface design of dots and short cross lines were standard to clubs made in the 1920s.

The putting cleek was used either for putting or approach shots. On the club head are "Warranted Hand Forged" with S. Green's signature underneath followed by "Shanghai, China." On the left of the club head is the "Hand of Friendship" mark for George Nicoll, followed by "Putting Cleek" and "Made in Scotland." The short line design on the club face shows it was a product made before 1920.

Chinese Golf Club

An interesting article was published in the May 25, 1929 issue of *North-China Herald* titled "Chinese Interest in Golf." The article said that local sporting circles were contemplating forming a Chinese golf club, acquire a course in Shanghai vicinity and inviting Charlie Chung, the former Honolulu champion, to China to teach golf. Chung, a Chinese American, was the first Chinese to become a professional, and was working at a golf club in Los Angeles at the time. He had expressed his readiness to come to Shanghai, as he had never visited China before.

The article listed a score of Chinese golf enthusiasts in Shanghai, which included Foreign Minister C.T. Wang, Minister to Italy Quo Tai-chi, former Commissioner of Foreign Affairs and Superintendent of Customs S.T. Wen, K.Y. Woo. Arthur Lee, Gordon Pao-hwn Lum, Andrew Ma, K.S. Lee, W.Y. "Nick" Char, etc.

Arrangements were being made to secure a course and a clubhouse, but it was yet too premature as no official negotiations had been started. These Chinese golfers currently were playing golf at the Race Course, Hongkew, Kiangwan and Kiangwan Country courses. Nick Cha at 6 Kiukiang Road would be interested to hear from Chinese golfers if they were interested in starting a club.

The report said that Chinese golfers were proposing to hold a tournament, possibly beginning on June 1, in which all golf players of Chinese nationality were invited to join, handicap to be given. Applications were to be sent in to Nick Char no later than the 31st of May. Thomas Goon Wong, general manager of A.B.C. Underwear Weaving Mills had offered to present a silver cup for the winner. Wong was an all-round sportsman and interested in all forms of sports.

Unfortunately, there was no further news about either the tournament or a Chinese golf club.

/ Charlie Chung

Tientsin Golf Club

For many years, students of golf history in China and overseas believed that the Tientsin Golf Club was founded in 1901. This conclusion was based on a 1925 book, *Tientsin, an Illustrated Outline History*, by British author O.D. Rasmussen.

Rasmussen, from Kent, England, came to Tientsin in 1906 and worked as reporter and editor for *The North China Commerce*, *The North China Star* and *The Far Eastern Times*. He wrote a number of books about Tientsin in the late Ch'ing and early Republican periods.

Rasmussen writes on pp. 319-320 of *Tientsin, an Illustrated Outline History*: "The Tientsin Golf Club, organized in 1901, owes its first course of nine holes on the site it still occupies on the ex-Russian concession to the efforts of Dr. J. O'Mallry Irwin, and Mr. E.F. Mackay, assisted by Mr. Adams of the firm of Adams and Knowles. The course was later extended to the south and south-east of the present adjoining lumber yard. In 1904 the Club had, as its first Club House, a movable military barrack, purchased from the German troops. It was erected on the site now occupied by the lumber yard. The same year the course was increased to 18 holes, five of which were situated inside the old mud wall (Sankolinsin's Folly), now demolished. The holes previously laid out south and south-east of the club house were abandoned because of their sandy nature. Municipal and industrial developments later forced the course in 1920 to be developed in an easterly and northerly direction, where it has remained ever since."

"The old mud wall" mentioned in the book was a 13-mile mud wall built by General Prince Sankolinsin during the Second Opium War in an effort to stop the British and French forces. The wall, which was useless, was mocked as "Sankolinsin's Folly."

/ Post Card of Tientsin Golf Club 1900s

The *Overland China Mail* dated October 21, 1901 printed a story on p. 290 that says: "A Polo Club has been formed at Tientsin, and a Golf Club is to be inaugurated also at an early date."

A report in *The Straits Times* on April 2, 1903 said that a member of the Tientsin Golf Club broke the club's Colonel Bogey record of

TIENTSIN

40 by scoring a 39 for the nine holes.

The *Overland China Mail* reported on May 7, 1904 that in a golf competition on April 23, Peking beat Tientsin by 11 up and 3 to play. The report did not mention where the competition took place.

The Sphere dated July 16, 1910 published a photo story on p. 62 titled "On the Golf Links at Tientsin." It reads: "The popular Scottish pastime of golf now seems to have its advocates in every civilized corner of the globe, and in most cases the associations are governed by the rules laid down by the Royal and Ancient Golf Club of St. Andrews. The above illustration shows a golfer in the act of putting on the eighteenth green of the Tientsin golf links in China. The tallest figure on the right is presumably his opponent with two native caddies behind him, while on the left is another native holding the flag which marks the green until the player has holed off."

At the 1912-13 Tientsin Golf Club medal play competition, W.W. Hogg won the championship in the A Class. The silver trophy cup has a larger opening at the mouth, but shrinks slightly in the middle, with flowery decorations at the bottom. On the cup are the words: "TIENTSIN GOLF CLUB, 1912-13, Medal Competition, CLASS A, Won by E.W. Hogg." The trophy is now with the Golf Heritage Museum.

/ *1912-13 Tientsin Golf Club Trophy*

According to Rasmussen, Tientsin Golf Club started an annual Open Championship in the spring of 1905 and was held every spring until 1924. It was decided in 1922 to change the event to the fall starting in 1923. However, since a spring competition had already been scheduled, two Open Championships were held in 1923. Rasmussen listed the winners of the Open Championships from 1905 to 1924:

/ *Tientsin Golf Links*

1905 : E. P. Allen	1912 : Capt. Chaldecott	1919 : A. B. Lowson
1906 : Major Thurston	1913 : A. B. Lowson	1920 : D. B. Walker
1907 : G. S. Knowles	1914 : Capt. B. A. Hill	1921 : E. L. MacCallie
1908 : J. Lee	1915 : P. D. Bolland	1922 : Dr. J. O'M. Irwin
1909 : G. S. Knowles	1917 : Capt. K. W. Kinard	1923 : Capt. H. S. Oldham
1910 : G. B. Walker	1916 : G. S. Knowles	1923 : G. P. Douglas*
1911 : Colonel Dewing	1918 : E. H. Rigby	1924 : J. M. Venters

/ *Winners of Tientsin Open Championships 1905-1924*

/ 1917 Tientsin Golf Club Championship Trophy

Adrien von Ferscht, an expert on Chinese silver at the University of Glasgow, published an article on March 29, 2013 on his website http://chinese-export-silver.com.gridhosted.co.uk/ titled "Gleneagles: Scottish or Chinese?" The article writes: "Chinese Export Silver has always been a wonderful medium to create trophies and golf trophies are no exception." Von Ferscht's article featured a few silver golf trophies in China. One of them was a trophy for the 1922 handicap competition at the Tientsin Golf Club. On the cup are the words: "1922 GOLF HANDICAP WON BY CAPT. A.J. McCHRYSTAL TIENTSIN CHINA."

/ Pu Yi Playing Golf in Tientsin
(https://ppfocus.com/sg/0/b341543.html)

/ 1922 Tientsin Handicap Competition Trophy (Adrien von Ferscht)

Von Ferscht writes: "The Tientsin Golf Club was popular in the 1920s, with initiation fees of $50 and an annual $25 membership fee. The club had an 18-hole course 'on the flat where Chinese graves constitute most of the hazards. Only a real enthusiast can obtain much of a thrill from the rather uninteresting course, but the fact that the luxury of two caddies may be enjoyed for 40 cents is a compensating feature.'"

China's last emperor, Pu Yi, played golf while he was living in Tientsin.

According to our recent research, however, Tientsin Golf Club was founded much earlier than Rasmussen's book claimed. The date could go back to 1895. Our proof is an article published in the *Weekly Sun* of Singapore. On p. 6 of the November 8, 1913 issue there was an article titled "Opening of New Tientsin Golf Club." The article reads:

"This afternoon at 3 o'clock the New North China Golf Club was started on its career, says the *China Critic* of October 11. The weather which looked bad in the morning, turned out finer, and there was a large gathering of members, both of the new and the senior golf clubs, present to witness the opening ceremony, which was performed by Mr. Macintosh, the President of the Club, who said:

"'Ladies and Gentlemen, before we start on the more interesting business of this afternoon, I would ask for your indulgence by allowing me to say a few words. I would call the attention of those guests who have honored the club with their presence today that although it has already been played over we are met here to baptize this infant Golf Course.

"'With the bestowal of care, sympathy and support of all its friends, I am convinced that this child will more than repay all debts of kindness to its friends by giving in return healthy recreation. For this purpose it is now dedicated.

"'A Saturday, or for that matter a Sunday afternoon in the open air works wonders for those and they are the great majority, who have to lead sedentary lives during the rest of the week. For these reasons I warmly commend this infant child to your blessings. The club has now a membership of 50 or more, a signal enough proof of the gap that it fills. I recall the fact as an interesting one that, when a few of us started the senior golf club, now close on 18 years ago we had under a score of members. The total membership of the two clubs to-day numbers over 200 I think.'"

As the oldest member of the Tientsin Golf Club, Macintosh thanked the Russian Consul, Mr. Kristy, and his predecessor for allowing the Club to use ground in the Russian Concession.

After the remarks, members moved to the first tee and the President made a splendid drive. Mrs. Willis, wife of the British Consul General, declared the new Club open. A four-ball game was started between Messrs. Stevens and Powney and Maj. Bliss and Lowsen. During the game tea was served in the new clubhouse.

Going back by 18 years from October 1913, it would mean that the Tientsin Golf Club was founded in 1895.

Scotsman Duncan Houston Mackintosh was then manager of the Tientsin Hongkong and Shanghai Banking Corp. Born in Inverness, Mackintosh joined the Bank early on and had worked in Singapore, Hong Kong, Hankow, Kobe, Saigon and Amoy. He was transferred to Tientsin in 1895.

O May 8, 2018 Chinese writer He Yuxin wrote an article on https://kknews.cc/history/vkvlbqq.html about old Tientsin and mentioned the 18-hole golf course at the Russian Concession during the late Ch'ing Dynasty. He writes: "Outside of the Russian Park was a standard 18-hole golf course built on brown sandy ground. Often people could see funeral or wedding processions crossing through the golf links. During the fall, residents nearby would use the golf course to make and dry coal balls."

Pan Ding, Class of 2002 at the Institute of Environmental Resources at Beijing Forestry University, wrote about the history and growth of the Tientsin Golf Club in his graduation thesis "Investigation and Research of Modern Golf Development in China." During his research at the Tianjin Library, he discovered a 1917 Map of Tianjin, in which on the southeast corner of the Russian Concession, a place was marked "Wild Ball Course." He believed that it was the local reference of the golf course. Around the "Wild Ball Course" were walls made of dirt, which could be the "old mud wall" mentioned earlier.

This confirms Rasmussen's description in his book that the Tientsin Golf Course moved close to the lumber yard and the additional five holes were situated inside the old mud wall.

As mentioned earlier, the Tientsin Golf Course was built on a graveyard, a fact of which was vividly written about by famous British golf writer Bernard Darwin. In his article, "Golf in the Far East," published in the January 1910 issue of *C.B. Fry's Magazine*, Darwin wrote about golf courses and clubs in Tientsin, Peking, Yokohama and Egypt. Tom Browne painted interesting sketches for the article.

Darwin writes: "The chief hazards on the

/ *A Tientsin Caddie*

links of Tientsin are of rather gruesome character, since they consist of the graves of deceased Chinamen. The modern golfing architect is rather in favour of mounds as hazards, and, as will be seen from the picture, he might glean some ideas from the graves at Tientsin."

He continues: "The golf course being situated on a large, flat plain close to the town offered a convenient burial-ground, much to the inconvenience of the golfers." "However," Darwin said, the Chinese "proved an accommodating people, and a bargain was struck whereby, for a payment of four taels, a coffin could be removed and dumped down somewhere else, and the green committee could flatten down the impeding mound."

/ *Playing Off a Grave on the Tientsin Course*

New York Times published an article on April 7, 1914 titled "Golf Links Laid in Chinese Graveyard: Tientsin Club Uses Grave Mounds as Bunkers." The article described the experience of Major Palmer E. Pierce who just returned to the U.S. after two years of service at the 15th Infantry in China.

Pierce was director of athletics at West Point and helped organize the National Collegiate Athletic Association, serving for several years as its president with distinction. The article quoted Pierce as saying: "The golf course in Tientsin was unquestionably without an equal anywhere. The mode of burial in China is to place the coffins just below the ground and build large mounds over them. These mounds dot the course, and no additional bunkers are necessary. In fact, there are bunkers everywhere, and to a golfer accustomed to playing on a fairly open course, it takes some time to get accustomed to the numerous bunkers and hazards."

Major Pierce said that one of the ground rules at the Tientsin Club was that "if a ball rolls into an open grave it may be lifted without penalty. The greens are laid out between the grave mounds, and are as smooth and well-kept as the greens in America." Pierce also said that "the Chinese caddies are the most interesting in the world. The fee is about 5 cents for the 18 holes, and the youngsters are so numerous and so anxious to caddy that competition is very keen. The club house at the course is surrounded by graves."

Grave mounds, in fact, gave tips to golf course architects in designing bunkers and hazards. Keith Cutten in his book *The Evolution of Golf Course Design*, stated on p. 61 that hazards in the shape of grave mounds were choices of many course architects in the 20th century, and they are called "chocolate drops."

Sir Meyrick Hewlett, former British consul in China, wrote on p. 49 in his book *Forty Years in China* that his short stay in Tientsin during the winter of 1905 or 1906 was "memorable for excellent golf on a cruel course composed chiefly of mud fields and graveyards."

Starting in 1914, according to Rasmussen, Tientsin Golf Club began organizing inter-port golf matches with the Shanghai Golf Club and the Royal Hong Kong Golf Club. Tientsin reportedly did not win any of the matches. Rasmussen said that the North China Golf Club, a junior club with a course to the north of the senior club, was absorbed by the Tientsin Club in 1922.

In 1920, Rasmussen wrote that the Tientsin Golf Club had an inter-port match with Peking Golf Club and Peking won. But a return match later in the year resulted in a win for Tientsin. An Inter-Port Cup was presented by members of the Tientsin Golf Club in 1921, to be played for semi-annually. The 1925 book listed the results of the matches from 1921 through 1924:

1921; May; Tientsin.	1922; Nov.; Tientsin.	1924; Apr.; Tientsin.
1921; Nov.; Peking.	1923; May; Peking.	1924; (no match).
1922; May; Tientsin.	1923; Nov.; Tientsin.	1925;

/ *Tientsin and Peking Inter-Port Matches*

According to Rasmussen, Tientsin Golf Club organized a Championship of North China in 1924 "open to all amateur members of any recognized golf club in the world. The championship carries with it the Dickinson Challenge Cup presented by J.M. Dickinson." Dickinson was president of Tientsin Chamber of Commerce. Today's Xuzhou Dao in Heping District was originally named Dickinson Road.

According to the *London and China Express* published on May 29, 1924, "the first competition of the Ladies' Section of the Tientsin Golf Club since its reorganization, with Mrs. P.C. Young as Captain, has been held. It was against bogey and was won by Mrs. Oldham, handicap 9 three down."

Rasmussen mentioned that the first Championship of North China was held in the spring of 1925 and was won by D.B. Walker of the Tientsin Golf Club. L. Schmertz of Peking Golf Club was runner-up.

In a competition between the Tientsin and Peking Japanese Golf Clubs held on October 4, 1925, Peking beat Tientsin by 9:5, according to *North China Standard* dated October 6, 1925.

Pan Ding also mentioned in his graduation thesis that a British Country Club was founded at 188 Machangdao (Horse Race Road). The Club was divided into two sections: recreation and horse racing. The recreation section included a dining hall, teahouse, ballad room, theater, ballroom and a swimming pool. Outdoor facilities included a ball court, tennis courts, a golf course and a pond for boating or ice skating.

The 1925 *Comacrib Directory of China* published in Shanghai and Hong Kong listed the committee members of the Tientsin Golf Club as follows:

TIENTSIN GOLF CLUB.
H. S. Oldham, *Captain*.
A. Harvey, *Hon. Sec.*
F. A. Hanish, *Hon. Treas.*
Committee:—
F. Hussey-Freke.
A. R. Blinks.
A. J. Miller.
P. C. Young.
Major Gullian.
E. J. Nathan.
Capt. R. P. Sands.
J. Hayes.
A. P. McLaughlin.
R. A. Foster.

/ *1925 Tientsin GC Committee*

In an article titled "Tientsin," published in the April 1925 issue of *The American Foreign Service Journal*, former consul in Tientsin David C. Berger wrote about the Tientsin Golf Club and its links. To golfers who were new in the city, the golf course looked somewhat strange, Berger wrote. There were numerous grave mounds, some very tall. "If you hit a ball from the fairway and it landed among the graves, you would be confronting a huge hazard. If you sometimes hit a ball into the broken grave, the Club had no specific rules to go by. Golfers were at a loss as to whether they should continue with the game or move the ball without a penalty. Often a golfer would flatly refuse to climb inside a grave either to play or to move his ball."

The August 4, 1928 *Illustrated London News* published a photograph of Tientsin on p. 222, in which U.S. Colonel Newill and K. Oldham, Superintendent of British Police in Tientsin, were playing golf beside trenches. The caption of the photo reads: "GOLF BESIDE THE TRENCHES IN DISTURBED CHINA: A PEACEFUL ROUND IN WARLIKE CONDITIONS."

There was a report in the *Aberdeen Press and Journal* on p. 5 of January 10, 1930 about sporting life in China. At a weekly luncheon hosted by the Aberdeen Rotary Club, R.G. Buchan, a trader on home leave from Tientsin where he had lived for many years, talked about golf in northern China. He was quoted as saying, "There are some fine golf courses, even if the greens in the north were made up of sand and mud, owing to difficulty in getting grass to grow. To the ordinary hazards of the game, however, there must be added the numerous graves which are often scattered over the course, as is the case at Tientsin."

/ Golf Beside the Trenches in Tientsin

A story published on p. 24 of *The Lowell Sun* in Massachusetts on September 19, 1935 described how William Lawson Little Jr., champion of the 1934 U.S. Amateur and the 1935 British Amateur Open Golf Championships, played golf at a graveyard course in Tientsin. The report reads, "There are tales about Little learning the game among the decaying tombs of an ancient Chinese cemetery. The truth is that Lawson played just one round during the 12 months that his father was stationed at Tientsin in 1921 and 1922."

The *Golf Illustrated* of the U.S. published a report about Tientsin Golf Club on June 1, 1933 and mentioned some special rules at the Club. If a ball fell inside an open grave, the golfer can pick up and drop the ball without a penalty. The author wrote a short poem describing such a special rule.

By 1936, membership of the Tientsin Golf Club reached 350. The golf course was situated about three miles from the Tientsin East Railway Station. Up to 1936, Tientsin was one of the few cities in north China that had an 18-hole golf course.

According to the 1939 *China Hong List*, the Captain of Tientsin Golf Club was P.H. Cobb. The secretary was G.K. Wallington of Kent & Mounsey. The treasurers were Lowe, Bingham & Matthews.

Tientsin Golf Club
Cobb, P. H., captain
Wallington, G. K., sec., c/o Kent & Mounsey
Lowe, Bingham & Matthews, treasurers

/ 1939 China Hong List

Mini Golf in Tientsin

Pan Ding in his graduation thesis described mini-golf activities in Tientsin based on his research through the city's *Peiyang Pictorial*

EARLY GOLF IN CHINA

/ *Peiyang Pictorial News, September 7, 1931*

News. This Chinese language newspaper started on July 7, 1926 and continued until 1937 with a total of 1,578 issues. It was invested by Feng Wu-yue and Tan Peiling and edited by Wu Kui-ch'en. Starting as a weekly, it later increased frequency to every three days and finally to every other day. The content of the newspaper included current affairs, social news, personalities, theater, film, travel, literature and arts. The goal of the periodical was to "publish public affairs, promote arts and culture, and propagate knowledge." It brought out 20 Supplements in July-September 1927, which featured novels, literary notes, famous paintings and cartoons.

Through the research of the *Peiyang Pictorial News* with the help of Wang Xiangfeng, historian at the Tianjin Library, Pan concluded that during the 1930s there were five major mini-golf clubs in the city.

Tienhsiang Golf (otherwise known as Tienhsiang Wild Ball) opened at the southern gate of the Tienhsiang Market (now north gate of Quanyechang or Shopping Center) on April 21, 1931. The club course was rectangular, only one-third the size of a regular mini-golf court. There were 10 holes and the fee was 20 cents per round. Tea was five cents. The club opened from 10:00 am to 12:00 midnight. It became crowded if 30 people were playing at one time. The club advertised in 27 issues of the *Peiyang Pictorial News*, from No. 661 dated August 8, 1931 through No. 687 dated October 8, 1931.

A mini-golf club opened on the top floor of the Six Nation Hotel at No. 10 Street inside the French Concession on June 7, 1931. It cost 40 cents per round, and $3 for 10 rounds. Customers were mainly foreigners at the hotel. It advertised the service in 168 issues of the newspaper from No. 633 on June 4, 1931 through No. 828 on September 8, 1932.

Mei Kee Golf Club opened for business on June 16, 1931 on the 3rd floor of Yong'an Hotel (now near Binjiang Road). It charged 50 cents per round, with a 50 percent discount for students between 9:00 am and 5:00 pm. The club had the best decorated holes among the mini-golf clubs. With an investment of $7,000 to build it, the club advertised in 18 issues of the newspaper, which included Nos. 647-648, 656-661 and 662-671.

A Wee Golf Club opened on the ceiling garden of the Huichung Hotel on July 1, 1932. It had 18 holes and the cost was 50 cents per round. Foreigners comprised three quarters of the customers and one quarter was local Chinese. Business hours were from 10:00 am to 12:00 midnight. This was an outdoor course of a fairly large size, which had sandy play areas with hazards, bunkers or creeks in each hole. It provided lighting at night, which attracted many more customers than the other clubs. The highest score of local Chinese was made by a Chu Wen-kee, 49 strokes. Any customer who scored under 50 would no longer be charged to continue to play.

Around the same time in 1931 or 1932, a Midget Golf Club was opened at the lobby of the Victoria Hotel, formerly the site of the British Club. A 9-hole course was designed. But the club only existed for a short time before it was closed.

Newchwang Golf Course

The *Treaty of Tientsin* between China and Britain was signed on June 26, 1858, in which nine additional treaty ports were opened. These included Newchwang (Niuzhuang), Tengch'ow (Dengzhou), T'ainan (Tainan), Chawchow (Chaozhou), Kiungchow (Qiongzhou), etc. Newchwang opened in 1861, and the U.K. became the first foreign power to establish a consulate office in the city. Then came British business companies such as Butterfield & Swire, Jardine Matheson and Bush Brothers, which soon monopolized trade at Newchwang and controlled the shipping lines to Shanghai, Amoy and Hong Kong.

/ 19th Century Port of Newchwang

According to the *20th Century Impressions of Hong-Kong, Shanghai, and Other Treaty Ports of China* published in 1908, Western powers such as France, the U.S., Japan, Russia, Sweden, Norway and the Netherlands followed the U.K. in setting up consulate offices in Newchwang. Trading companies and other businesses were soon established, making Newchwang the most prosperous commercial city in northeast China. It was considered the "Shanghai outside of Shanghai Fort." Before Japan reopened Dairen in 1905, Newchwang was the only trade port in Manchuria. In 1906, Newchwang had a population of 60,000, of which 7,699 were foreigners and Japanese expatriates numbered 7,408.

/ Newchwang Club

The earliest golf course appeared near the Western Fort at the mouth of Liao River. It was a rudimentary course built around 1894 during the Newchwang Battle of the Sino-Japanese War. This historical fact was confirmed by William F. Tyler in his 1929 book, *Pulling Strings in China*. According to Tyler, Newchwang was one of the few cities where the British expatriates built golf links towards the end of the 19th century.

In describing an interesting incident during the 1894-1895 Sino-Japanese War, Tyler writes on pp. 61-62:

"At Newchwang, the northern most treaty port of China, an old Major was considering the situation. He had charge of the fort commanding the entrance to the Liao River. The fort was old and dilapidated; it was only made of mud, and its armament consisted of a few old cast-iron guns. But it was a fort and there was war; so on his shoulders rested great responsibilities; quite plainly he must pull up his socks, eschew opium and keep his weather eye lifting. Yet he hoped with earnestness that great issues would not fall on him for settlement.

"But luck was not his way; for on the wide mud flat which lay between his fortress and the sea, on which hitherto he had rarely seen a soul, there now appeared each evening a group of foreigners, whose actions were undoubtedly mysterious and suspicious.

"He watched them with his telescope, and in the morning when the place was clear, he scrutinized the little holes and the larger banks which they had made and the flags that they had left behind. Then he sat down and wrote a formal letter to the Tao-tai, reporting what had happened.

"He would have felt it his duty to report in any case, but doubly so in these crucial times. The foreigners had made small cylindrical holes in the ground and carefully and skillfully lined them with metal; they had dug short trenches here and there -- a most suspicious fact. They were each armed with various shaped weapons, with which they propelled white projectiles for long distances. The whole proceeding was most mysterious and he could form no opinion as to what it meant. He could not say for certain that these operations were connected with the war, but he begged the Tao-tai to instruct him what to do.

"On receipt of this letter, the Tao-tai sent it to the Senior Consul, with a covering dispatch, referring to the war and the need for utmost caution. He concluded by saying that whatever might be the purpose of the operations on the mud flats, they must be stopped. Would the Senior Consul please take note and the necessary action.

"The Senior Consul was an Englishman. He would reply very formally and politely: 'What my nationals are doing is playing a well-known game which is played at every other port. It is usually done on grass, but as none exists here they are making the best they can of the deserted mud flat. They are merely amusing themselves; that is all.'

"The Senior Consul's letter was now sent to the Major with instructions from the Tao-tai for a further report in light of the information given in it. So once more the old man took his brush in hand and wrote those upright columns of complicated characters: 'I am an ignorant soldier, and this problem is beyond me. If these operations have no military significance, I have wondered whether they might not be connected with prospecting for minerals. It is the only suggestion I can make. As for the Senior Consul's so-called explanation, I have admitted that my ignorance disables me from saying what they are doing; but it is not so great as to disable me from saying, quite positively, and without a shadow of doubt about the matter, that they are not amusing themselves.'"

The first person in the circles of golf collectors and historians that mentioned Tyler's

/ The Mouth of Liao River

description of this early Newchwang Golf Course was Ralph Elder. In his article, "Early Golf in China," published in the December 2002 issue of *Through the Green*, official journal of the British Golf Collectors Society, Elder mentioned Tyler and his book, *Pulling Strings in China*.

Elder wrote in the article that he was a frequenter of a local bookstore and sometimes chatted with the bookseller's wife. He did not believe that she thought collecting golf books was a proper reason to visit a bookstore, which normally sold literary books. "It surprised me," he writes, "when she greeted me warmly one day and declared that she had found a tale about golf in *The Last Empress*." The book was written by Daniele Varèi and published in 1936. Varèi quoted the above passages by William F. Tyler about the incident during the 1894-95 Sino-Japanese War.

Interestingly, the story about the Newchwang Golf Course appeared in about two dozen British newspapers in December 1894, most of them quoting a report by a Newchwang correspondent published in the November 12 issue of the *North-China Herald*. On December 3, 1894, for example, *Homeward Mail from India, China and the East* published the following news on p. 3:

"The authorities discovered the plot on Friday last, November 12. On the previous day two foreigners had measured out piece of ground about a mile in circumferences. In seven different places they had chosen level spots to draw mysterious circles; in the centre of each circle they dug a small hole, and sunk sinister looking canister in each hole. Fortunately information of these proceedings reached the general in charge of the defense of this port, and when next day four foreigners appeared on the ground, and placed a small flag on each level spot, a General rode out with his officers, and halting about 200 yards off the nearest foreigner, sent one of the officers to see what the foreigners were doing. The following report we suppose was made: that the foreign devils were armed with huge clubs, some of which had irons which they were propelling over the ground a mysterious round object, which doubtless was a shell of some kind. Presently, when the foreigners were at distant part of the ground, General Gyiang and his staff dismounted and carefully approaching one of the level spots and cautiously inspected it. That night soldiers were sent out with lanterns and dug up the level spots, and removed the mysterious canisters. They were taken to the Taotai's office where they remain as proof of the evil designs of the foreign devils. The Taotai immediately wrote to the British Consul, who was informed by the suspected parties that they had been marking out golf links, and that the level spots of brown mud were the putting greens; and the sinister-looking canisters were empty jam tins, with the bottoms knocked out, and were used to keep the putting holes clear of mud. The native population and soldiers are greatly excited, and crowds visit the spots where the subterranean mines were discovered. Imagine the splash an acre or two of Newchwang mud would make."

A report from Newchwang published on p. 452 of the June 2, 1905 *North-China Herald* discussed the city's sports and recreation activities as follows: "With the return of Dr. Daly, a great revival in the way of general sport is taking place. Our cricket, tennis, golf, and football clubs have been languishing for some years and all in a sad state of approaching bankruptcy. With the idea of 'buking up things,' a general meeting was called. The community turned up in force and after due discussion, it was unanimously decided to amalgamate all the existing sport clubs into one, to be known as 'The General Sports Club.' A committee of five was there and then elected, to work out the scheme in detail and with power to nominate sub-committees for each branch of sport."

Sir Meyrick Hewlett, who was acting British Consul at Newchwang in 1913-1914, remembered in his memoir, *Forty Years in China*, that the city had a cricket club as early as in 1894. A British Club was also established before then. During the short seven-month stay in Newchwang, Hewlett said on p. 79 that "with the help of local Chinese authorities I secured a golf course and a site for the local club."

According to a report in the October 22, 1914 *Manchuria Daily News*, Newchwang Golf Club would send a team of six golfers on October 25 to visit Mukden Golf Club for an inter-port competition. Mukden defeated Newchwang in individual match by half a point and later again beat Newchwang in the foursomes by 3:0, according to a report in the October 27 issue of the newspaper.

Based on these historical facts it is safe to conclude that the earliest Newchwang Golf Links and Golf Club were established in 1894, with sporadic club activities thereafter. In 1905, there was an effort to revive golf club activities through the organization of a general sports club. A new golf links and club were established with the efforts of Sir Meyrick Hewlett during 1913-1914 when he was Acting British Consul and members had inter-port matches during the late 1910s and 1920s.

However, due to the limited number of expatriates living in Newchwang, activities of the Golf Club never picked up in any significant scale. By the late 1930s after Newchwang became part of the Japanese Manchuria, the Newchwang Golf Club was listed in the *Golfer's Handbook* in the 1936, 1938, 1939 and 1947 editions. The Club was listed as "Newchwang Race Club (Golf Section), Manchuria, Membership, 24. 9 holes, Station–Yingkou (2 miles)" in the 1936 to 1939 editions of the *Handbook*.

/ 1936 Golfer's Handbook

/ 1939 Golfer's Handbook

Amoy Kulangsu Golf Club

Kulangsu (Gulangyu) is an island off Amoy (Xiamen) with an area of only 1.91 square kilometers. To protect the island's eco system and beautiful landscape, the island to this day does not allow automobiles. After the Opium War, Kulangsu became the most famous foreign settlement, after Shanghai. For over a century, the island was under the administration of the British colonialists.

Our research finds out that Kulangsu, as a major settlement of expatriates from the U.K. and other powers, may have been one of the earliest cities that boasted golf links. There were two golf courses in Amoy. One was a 9-hole golf links built on Kulangsu before 1897 and the other was a 9-hole golf course built in Amoy around 1910.

/ Today's Kulangsu

Kulangsu Golf Links

The English name of Kulangsu (also Koolangsu) was Wade-Giles spelling based on local pronunciation. One of the creators of Wade-Giles was Herbert Allen Giles, a British Sinologist in the late 19th century. Giles was a deputy consul and consul in Fuchow (Fuzhou), Shanghai, Tamsui (Danshui) and Ningp'o (Ningbo). In 1878 Giles published *A Short History of Koolangsu*, which gives a detailed description of the island and the expatriates living there.

Giles wrote in the book that by October 10, 1878, there were 251 expatriates living in Kulangsu and Amoy. Of these, 200 were residing in Kulangsu and 51 in Amoy. Of the total, 133 were British, 38 German, 21 American, 19 Portuguese, 16 Spanish, 8 Japanese, 7 Danish, 6 Italian and 3 French. A total of 2,835 Chinese were living on the island. The British obviously played a major role in the administration of the international settlement, with Sikhs working as policemen.

Giles wrote that shipping and trade were handled mainly by the British. "More than half of the entire trade is in British hands." In 1877, there were a total of 429 steamers at the Amoy port, of which 377 were British. Of the total of 243 sailing vessels, 103 were German, 93 British, 13 Danish and 10 Dutch.

The earliest western style building in Kulangsu was erected in 1859 and a Protestant church capable of accommodating 200 people was built. The Kulangsu Club, built in 1876, had a library, reading-room, billiard room, bowling-alley, bar and meeting room. Not far away was a Recreation Ground, which featured cricket, lawn

/ Amoy Race Course 1889 (John Oswald)

tennis and race course.

Kulangsu today boasts 931 buildings of different styles, both Chinese and Western. Together with well-planned streets, parks, natural beauties and scenery, the small island with 20,000 residents is a true "Garden on the Sea" and an "International Architectural Expo." On July 8, 2017, Kulangsu was successfully listed on the UNESCO's World Heritage List. The international settlement at Kulangsu was comparable in time and scale to Shanghai's international settlement.

The first golf links at Kulangsu appeared in 1897 or maybe even earlier. The proof of this historical fact can be found in an article published in the August 1897 issue of *The Badminton Magazine of Sports & Pastimes*.

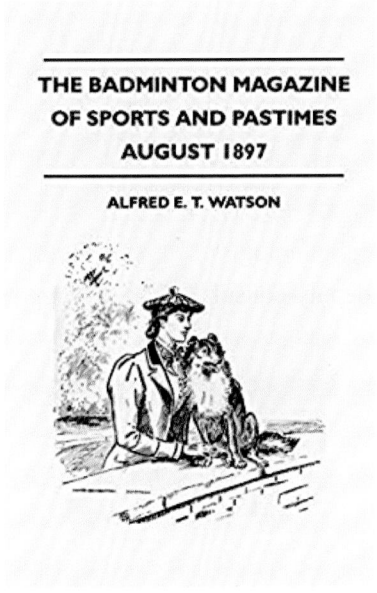

/ The Badminton Magazine of Sports & Pastimes, August 1897

The article, "A Foursome at Amoy," described the author's interesting foursome two-ball match with three friends at the Kulangsu Golf Links, with accompanying eight sketches.

The writer was T.T. Jeans, a Royal Navy Surgeon stationed in Hong Kong. During the horse race week in Hong Kong in the Spring of 1897, Jeans and his friend Reggy Pinhorn played a foursome at the Happy Valley links with friends Rusby and Calderson visiting from Amoy and won handsomely by three up. After the game, the four players sat at the golf club for a drink. Jeans and Pinhorn started to tease their friends about their loss. Already sore at his defeat and loss of two balls in the race course ditch, Calderson broke out from quietly puffing away at his pipe by saying "You fellows have beaten us on your own links, I bet two hundred dollars you won't on ours."

Golf links at Amoy? Neither Jeans nor Pinhorn ever heard of the Amoy Golf Links. But they accepted the challenge and agreed to play with them in two weeks on their way to visit the Foochow horse race.

In time Jeans and Pinhorn took a Jardine's steamer and arrived on the second evening at the Amoy harbor. As soon as they cleared customs, Rusby took them up on a sampan to Kulangsu. The foursome had a nice dinner after which Jeans and Pinhorn turned in for the night, ready for a fight on the Kulangsu Golf Links.

The next morning, they walked to the links, passing through a small village. As they were climbing a steep incline covered with stubbly grass and strewn with boulders, Calderson threw down his bag of clubs and looked around. "We've got there," he said, as he was kneeling down and scraping a little dry sand into a heap and trying to make a tee. Jeans looked around and "dotted in among huge boulders--planked down among innumerable concrete native graves--were several familiar red flags hanging limply in the morning calm."

Jeans and Pinhorn looked sadly at each other, and then at their drivers and brassies, realizing that they were practically useless there. The first green was on the near side of a wall which apparently separated two large graveyards, and was the only spot not covered with graves or stones. It was 80 yards away and both sides halved the hole by four shots.

/ They Had Lost Balls in the Ditch

From the next tee to the green on the shoulder of a hill was about 120 yards. Against Jeans' objections, Pinhorn decided to use his driver, and the ball flew over the green and disappeared in the ditch, nowhere to be found after spending a full 10 minutes searching for it.

The third green was on the edge of a cliff, the further edge overhanging the sea. Fortunately for Jeans and Pinhorn, Calderson "did not loft his stroke sufficiently, and the ball had so much pace on after touching the ground that it rolled over the cliff" into the ocean. Jeans and Pinhorn holed theirs in nine and score was back to even.

/ Nothing but Gravestones

"The fourth is the long hole—right out of sight over a sloping shoulder of rock, the hole itself being on the top of a mound surrounded by nearly vertical sand-bunkers." Pinhorn drove so carefully that his ball struck a large boulder which was a directing mark and rebounded and rolled into a mass of loose rocks. Jeans and Pinhorn lost the hole as well as the next short hole, which took them 16 strokes.

"At sixth hole, another short one, Rusby advised us not to go to the right, or we should lose our ball in a cow-yard about 300 feet below." He did exactly what he had advised against and Jeans and Pinhorn took one hole back.

The seventh tee was behind the rocks "on the turf-covered top of a big rock; the green on the side of a hill, the slope of which was covered with mandarins' graves. Between the two were three paddy fields, a ditch, a road—along which

/ Making Timid Little Shots

numerous coolies were tramping—another ditch, and a sandpit scooped out from the hill." Jeans' drive veered to the right and ended up in the ditch. For the eighth hole, Pinhorn drove the ball into the sand, ending up in 10 strokes, a total of three down.

Although Jeans and Pinhorn were able to win back the ninth hole, they lost two holes in the first nine.

The two sides had a heated fight in the second nine and squared even by the eighth hole. Rusby and Calderson won the final hole and got even with Jeans and Pinhorn at their own course.

The article published on pp. 154-162 of the August 1897 magazine was a vivid recount of a foursome match of British expatriates at the primitive Kulangsu Golf Links. It has established a historical fact that as early

/ Hit an Inoffensive Coolie

EARLY GOLF IN CHINA

/ Hit an Inoffensive Coolie

as in 1897, or maybe even earlier, there was a 9-hole golf links at Kulangsu. The golf links was rudimentary, built among rocks, boulders, graveyards, paddy fields and cow yard. The primitive nature of the golf links was already well-known among golfers in Hong Kong. As Jeans and Pinhorn were trying to find out about the Amoy Kulangsu Links from club members in Hong Kong, they were told that the bunkers over there were the "usual kind of bunkers" and the greens were the "usual kind of greens." A. Kan, the head-boy and steward at the Hong Kong Golf Club, only grinned and said that Amoy links were all the same, very good. There is therefore reason to believe that the Kulangsu Golf Links was built before 1897 and a golf club might have also been in existence.

One of the earliest reports about the Kulangsu Golf Links appeared in the September 19, 1902 issue of *Golf Illustrated*, official weekly of the Royal & Ancient Golf Club. On p. 225 of the issue was a photo story entitled "The Game in the Far East—Some Interesting Photos of Golf in China." The photos were taken by Lieutenant Craig, of the *HMS Ocean*. Craig wrote: "I enclose some photos which may be of interest to you, as illustrating, to a certain extent, the progress of the Royal and Ancient game in China. Two of the photos were taken on the golf course of the European Settlement Island Ku-Lung-Su, Amoy. This course is very sporting; in fact, too much so, as it consists chiefly of hazards, the principal ones being Chinese graves, with which the island is covered." The four other photos were taken at the links of Grass Island, Miro Bay.

/ The Rocky Terrain of Kulangsu (University of Birmingham)

The photo in the middle of the page has the following caption: "Playing out of an old grave to the sixteenth hole, Ku-Lung-Su Island." Further up across from the island should be Amoy on the mainland.

We suspect that the "sixteenth hole" might have been the seventh hole played in the second round. Given the limited open space at the Kulangsu Island, a 9-hole golf course was already in a tight space. This would be confirmed by reports of the Kulangsu Golf Club in the early 20th century.

/ The Game in the Far East

/ Playing out of an Old Grave

The second photo of Kulangsu was taken at the eighth green, with four golfers and three caddies on the putting green. Amoy was clearly visible on the other side of the ocean.

On October 11, 2023, the London-based Chiswick Auctions sold a silver trophy dated March 1904 during an Amoy Golf Club handicap competition. The winner was W.H. Wallace, Amoy manager of the Hongkong & Shanghai Banking Corp. and Chairman of the Amoy Municipal Council. This exquisite silver plate, made by Sui Chang in Chekiang and sold by Wang Hing of Canton, is 19 cm in diameter and 222 g in weight. On the plate are the words: "Amoy Golf Handicap March 1904 Won by W.H. Wallace."

/ March 1904 Amoy Golf Handicap Trophy

/ Kulangsu Eighth Green

According to the October 1, 1907 issue of *Overland China Mail*, a general meeting of the Amoy Golf Club was held at the Amoy Club on September 14. The report on p. 5 reads: "On the same afternoon a general meeting was held at the Amoy Club of the Amoy Golf Club, when Mr. H.F. Renkin, Esq.

> **THE AMOY AND KULANGSU GOLF CLUB**
> The annual meeting of this club was held on Friday evening, the 15th inst., at the Amoy Club, when the usual routine business was put through expeditiously.

/ *The Amoy and Kulangsu Golf Club Annual Meeting 1907*

was again chosen Hon. Secretary and Treasurer, and the accounts for the past year were passed." Apart from *The Badminton Magazine* story, this is the earliest record we have found that mentioned Amoy Golf Club.

The same newspaper printed another news story about the Amoy Golf Club on p. 8 of its November 30 issue in 1907. The report used "the Amoy and Kulangsu Golf Club" in reporting its annual meeting held on November 15.

The 1908 annual meeting of the Amoy Kulangsu Golf Club was reported in the supplement to the December 22, 1908 *Overland China Mail*. According to the report on p. 8, the annual meeting was held at the Amoy Club library on December 10 and attended by 15 members. The report reads: "It was decided after discussion to have the Amoy golf course put into working order as soon as possible. The cost of so doing was estimated at $150, and it was proposed to send round to the members for subscriptions towards the expense. $108 was promised during the meeting. The new Committee members elected were as follows: Messrs. Rankin, Weed, Fletcher, Milward and Thomas. Mr. Fletcher was elected Captain for the coming season."

A Montrose reporter stationed in Shanghai wrote an article about the Amoy Golf Course on p. 6 of the January 15, 1909 *Montrose, Arbroath and Brechin Review*. Titled "A Montrosian's Description of Amoy Golf Course," the article reads: "The foreign population of Amoy is, I understand, 112, and practically all of them reside on an island opposite to the city called Kulangsu. Here they have planted a golf course, and just before leaving I came across it. Had I not seen a couple of young Chinese boys acting as caddies and a lady and gentleman following, I should never have imagined that there was such a thing as a golf course there. In the whole island there is not a stretch sufficiently large and level to get a decent drive, and where they were playing the rocks were almost precipitous. It was a nine-hole course, and for the greater part was situated in a Chinese graveyard, being what you would describe as a very sporting course. A pull or slice would be attended with the most disastrous results. One player sliced the least bit, and his ball never stopped till it reached a path 100 feet below the tee, having in its descent bounded and rebounded off rocks and graves. There are nine holes, most of which could be reached with an iron or mashie. If you landed on the green, which as a rule had a radius of about six feet of grass from the hole, you could get it in two or three, but otherwise you might take twenty to each." The author lived in Shanghai and played at the Race Course 9-hole golf links. He said the course in Shanghai was "more like a bowling green" because "for miles round Shanghai the land is as flat as a pancake."

The 1910 annual meeting of the Amoy Golf Club was held on November 11, 1910, according to a report in the December 24 issue of *London and China Telegraph*. The meeting elected a new committee of the Club, which included: Hon. Sec.

A MONTROSIAN'S DESCRIPTION OF AMOY GOLF COURSE

A Montrosian, a journalist, stationed at Shanghai, writes that he was down at Amoy in connection with the visit of the American Fleet to that port:—"The foreign population of Amoy is, I understand, 112, and practically all of them reside on an island opposite to the city called Kulangsu. Here they have planted a golf course and just before leaving I came across it. Had I not seen a couple of young Chinese boys acting as caddies and a lady and gentleman following I should never have imagined that there was such a thing as a golf course there. In the whole island there is not a stretch sufficiently large and level to get a decent drive, and where they were playing the rocks were almost precipitous. It was a nine-hole course, and for the greater part was situated in a Chinese graveyard, being what you would describe as a very sporting course. A pull or slice would be attended with the most disastrous results. One player sliced the least bit, and his ball never stopped till it reached a path 100 feet below the tee, having in its descent bounded and rebounded off rocks and graves. There are nine holes, most of which could be reached with an iron or mashie. If you landed on the green, which as a rule had a radius of about six feet of grass from the hole, you could get in in two or three, but otherwise you might take twenty to each. In Shanghai we have a nine-hole course also, but very different. For miles round Shanghai the land is as flat as a pancake, and our course is more like a bowling green than anything else. Golf is going ahead in Shanghai, and attempts are being made to run a second course."

/ Amoy Golf Course

CHINA.

Amoy G. C., Koolan Soo.
Chiangkiang G. C., Chiangkiang.
Hankow G. C., Hankow.
Hong-Kong (Royal) G. C., Hong-Kong.
Pekin G. C., Pekin.
Shanghai G. C., Shanghai.
Wei Hai Wei Course, Wei Hai Wei.

/ 1912 Nisbet's Golf Guide & Yearbook

of past information.

In a bilingual book titled *Gulangyu* published in May 2020, Editor Su Xi wrote: "The British started building a simple golf course in 1897 on the slopes of the Swallowtail Mountain of Gulangyu to play golf." We believe her statement was based on the 1897 article, "A Foursome at Amoy."

The Amoy Golf Course

According to Li Shiwei, a local researcher, the earliest race course built in Kulangsu dated back to 1842, but it later moved to the mainland close to the former sports ground of the Xiamen University. Little had been reported about the Race Course after 1910. It was likely that the Amoy Golf Club moved to a new 9-hole links at the Race Course since 1911.

According to the 1912 edition of *The Directory & Chronicle of China, Japan, Corea, Indo-China, Straits Settlements, Malay States, Siam, Netherlands India, Borneo, the Philippines, &c.*, "A golf club has been formed and a course laid out on the Racecourse. The course is a sporting one, abounding in natural hazards, and is

Mr. Weed, Captain Mr. E. Stevens and members Messrs. Thomas, Denniston and Roberts."

It was interesting that the "meeting formally resolved to give up the Kulangsu links." The report shows that starting in 1911, the Amoy Golf Club built a new golf links at the Race Course newly opened in Amoy. The 1912 *Nisbet's Golf Guide & Yearbook* continued to list Amoy Golf Club to be at Kulangsu, most likely due to its use

The annual general meeting of the Amoy Golf Club took place on 11th ult., Mr. L. I. Thomas in the chair. The new committee elected were:—Hon. sec., Mr. Weed; captain, Mr. E. Stevens; and Messrs. Thomas, Denniston, and Roberts. The meeting formally resolved to give up the Kulangsu links.

/ Kulangsu Links Closed

/ Amoy Race Course

well patronized."

A report on p. 8 of the December 23, 1922 *Malaya Tribune* announced the establishment of the Eastern Golf Association. Amoy Golf Club was one of the clubs in China that joined the Association. Other Chinese golf clubs in the Association included Shanghai, Royal Hong Kong, Tungshan Recreation Club in Canton and Tientsin. The Honorary Secretary of the Royal Hong Kong Golf Club would act as Hon. Secretary of the Eastern Golf Association.

Both the 1926 and 1932 editions of the *Commercial Travelers' Guide to the Far East* published by the U.S. Commerce Department listed under Amoy the following information: "Clubs: Amoy Club; lawn tennis, cricket, and golf clubs. The race course owns extensive grounds."

By 1942 when Amoy and Kulangsu were occupied by the Japanese, golfing activities at the city gradually came to a stop.

Ichang Golf Course

Ichang (Yichang) was a small town on the banks of Yangtze River before it opened to trade in 1876 after the Chefoo Convention was signed between the Ch'ing Government and the United Kingdom. Ichang Maritime Customs was established on April 1, 1877, becoming the remotest customs office in western China. British steamers as well as steamers owned by the China Merchants Navigation Company sailed from Hankow to Ichang before moving up the Yangtze to Chongch'ing (Chongqing). Starting in 1877, consulate offices were set up in Ichang by Britain, the U.S., Germany, Japan, France,

/ Former British Consulate at Ichang Built in 1892

Belgium and Denmark. Other powers delegated their consuls in Hankow or Shashi to deal with affairs in Ichang.

The information about Ichang Golf Course was first brought up to the attention of the authors by David Hamilton, a noted Scottish golf historian and member of the Royal & Ancient Golf Club. In an email dated December 31, 2021, Hamilton sent us a copy of an engraving titled: "The Foreign Settlement of Ichang and the Graveyard Golf Links."

Further searching the web led us to an article on p. 3 of the September 16, 1899 issue of *St. Andrews Citizen* under "Golf Gossip". The

/ Former British Consulate at Ichang Built in 1892

author, named Cleekum, writes: "There is rather eerie note in the September *Century* that may have escaped the eye of some of your readers, but not without interest in this column. A great graveyard extends from the walls of Ichang city for a mile along the bank of the Yangtze River and half-a-mile inland; and in the midst of this gruesome suburb is the foreign settlement, with French, Scotch, Canadian, and American mission establishments, the consulates, customs buildings and a few Hongs, all solid brick buildings within high-walled compounds, which date from 1887. It is rather quaintly put: 'The foreigners even manage to play golf in this graveyard, a course of a thousand hunkers and hazards, with fine drives insured from teeing grounds fixed on certain superior mandarin mounds.'"

According to Hamilton, Cleekum was the penname of William H. Dalrymple, a frequent contributor to *St. Andrews Citizen*. The image was an insert to an article written by Eliza Ruhamah Scidmore, an American tourist writer. Her lengthy article, "Cruising Up the Yangtze," was originally published in the September 1899 issue of *The Century Illustrated Monthly Magazine*. Judging from the dress of the lady golfer in the picture, Hamilton stated, she was probably an American golfer.

The engraving of the Ichang graveyard golf links in Scidmore's article might be exaggerated, but it is proof that Ichang had a golf links as early as in 1899. It was built in a graveyard in the city's suburbs. Scidmore's original article reads: "A great graveyard extends from I-chang's city walls for a mile along the river-bank and a half-mile inland, and the foreign settlement is in the midst of this gruesome suburb. French, Scotch, Canadian, and American mission establishments, the consulates, customs buildings, and a few hongs, all solid brick-and-stone buildings in high-walled compounds, constitute the settlement, which dates from 1887, although conceded as an open port in the Chifu convention of 1876. The foreigners even manage to play golf in this graveyard, a course of a thousand bunkers and hazards, with fine drives insured from teeing-grounds fixed on certain superior mandarin mounds."

Rand Jerris, historian at the U.S. Golf Association, wrote to Hamilton on July 2, 2022 that the original engraving of the Ichang Golf Links is now in the collection of the World Golf Hall of Fame in Florida. The framed original, Jerris said, was originally with the PGA of America Hall of Fame at Pinehurst in North Carolina. But no further information is available about when and where they obtained the painting. In the picture, two gentlemen golfers are seen to the left of the lady golfer. One is putting, with a caddie looking on. The other is standing and looking at another green. Further away close to the mountains were foreign settlements.

Paul King, a life-long customs officer in China, published his memoir in 1924 titled *In the Chinese Customs Service: A Personal Record of Forty-Seven Years*. He visited Ichang in 1906, played golf along the banks of the Yangtze River and toured the Three Gorges. King writes: "The port itself consists of a short and badly finished, because irregular, Bund. Chinese dwellings and foreign houses jostle one another, but as the foreign settlement does not back, as is too often the case in the other riverine ports, on the native city, there is space behind for purposes of health and pleasure. The community owned quite a nice little athletic ground, and many were the good games of hockey and football played there when the Navy was in port."

While at Ichang, King had a novel experience playing golf in the bed of the Yangtze. "Our harbor master, Mr. E. Molloy—a fine

EARLY GOLF IN CHINA

/ *Yichang Graveyard Golf Links (World Golf Hall of Fame)*

specimen of an Australian—was an ardent golfer, and was reckoned as one of the longest drivers in the Far East. He naturally thirsted for something beyond the narrow confines of the recreation ground, so one day he and I scrambled down to the water's edge in the middle of the river—forty feet below the Bund level—and teed our balls for a down-river trip. It was the old original Scottish game, straight ahead for seven miles, with the bones of sunken junks and high stone boulders as 'hazards"—a unique and most exhilarating experience. Aided by a carrying wind, Molloy made some truly astonishing drives, while I plodded behind as best I could."

Molloy could have played at the graveyard golf links at Ichang.

Golf Courses and Clubs in Peking

Over the years Peking had five different golf courses. The first was built in 1900 at the Five Track Road (Wugudao), today's Maliandao North Street. The second was opened before 1910 outside of Antingmen (Anding Gate). The third was established in 1920 at Tien Shuen Shan (Tiancun Shan) in the western suburbs. The fourth was completed in 1924 at the P'aomach'ang (Race Course) in Papaoshan (Babaoshan). And the fifth was built in 1926 at Nanyuan.

British Legation Golf Links

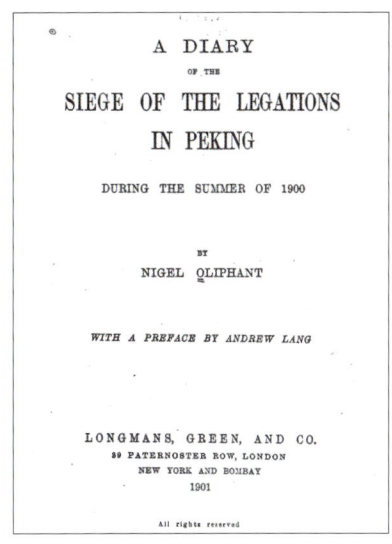
/ Nigel Oliphant Diary

In 1900, the British Legation in Peking built the city's earliest golf links outside of Hsipienmen (Xibianmen) and set up the British Legation Golf Club. The key person who was responsible in laying out the city's first golf links was Nigel Oliphant from St. Andrews. Oliphant was a student interpreter at the British Legation. Together with a marine captain and a Sikh division officer, they found an open space to the west of the city and laid out Peking's first golf links.

In his book, *A Diary of the Siege of the Legations in Peking during the Summer of 1900* published in 1901, Oliphant described how he went out to the west of the city finding a location and building a golf links in September 1900.

Oliphant came to Peking in 1899 at the invitation of Robert Hart, Inspector-General of China's Imperial Maritime Custom Service, to take up a position at the Chinese Postal Service. His diary was a first-hand record of the four months, from June 1 to September 30, when the Legation was under siege.

Oliphant's ancestor was David Olifard, who saved the life of David I, King of Scotland in 1141. Oliphant was born in the old house in St. Andrews, where Queen Mary used to stay when reportedly playing golf there.

/ Queen Mary Playing Golf

Oliphant's younger brother, David, came to Peking in 1897 and worked at the office of British Minister Sir Claude MacDonald. David was killed by the Boxers in July 1900. The Oliphant brothers from the home of golf were avid golfers. They laid out a putting ground on the lawn of the British Legation in June 1900. In September 1900, Nigel Oliphant and a few others from the Legation Sports Club went out to the west of the city and built Peking's first golf course. The process was recorded in detail by Nigel in his *Diary*.

On September 7, Oliphant writes: "There is a meeting to be held to-morrow of the Sports Club, to which the General has given the grounds of the Temple of Heaven as a racecourse, football ground, golf links, or anything they like to make it. I am going to try hard to get a golf course made, and I should like to give a cup in memory of David, for I am sure he would have done all he could to forward golfing interests. I fear it will not be easy to get men to start under the present difficulties, but there are a few keen players, and among the officers there may be more. We shall see to-morrow."

On the afternoon of September 9, Oliphant went to a Sports meeting at the Legation. A general committee was formed with two civilians and three Army men. Oliphant was on the golf committee with Captain J. and a yet unchosen officer of the 1st Sikhs. The golf committee decided to start working as soon as possible. Oliphant would "write to S. to inquire about the clubs that are coming out."

On September 11, Oliphant writes: "I saw J. at the auction, and he told me that he had spotted a good place for a links just outside the West City, so I am going with him on Thursday to see about it. I only hope we can manage to get it ready soon."

On September 13, Oliphant met Captain J. at 7:30 and rode ponies out to the West City and "prospect for a golf links." After half an hour, they arrived at the 1st Sikhs' mess and had breakfast. As "C., the third member of the committee was away on duty, J. and I rode alone to the Hole in the Wall, now called the British Gate, and found ourselves at our destination. The place in question is a fine stretch of ground, about one and a half miles long and from seventy to one hundred yards broad, with splendid grass and a few natural hazards, and we decided to make an eighteen-hole course eventually, though we may start with nine or twelve holes." They went back to the mess and found the Chifu palace, which was looted and out of repair. At the mess they met C. and made arrangements to get men to look after the green. The three agreed to go out again on Sunday morning and lay out the course.

On September 16, the three committee members went out early in the morning and had breakfast at the 1st Sikhs' mess. Oliphant writes, "Unfortunately, nothing has been done in the way of getting a green-keeper, so we only planned out the links, making an eighteen-hole course, and very fair it ought to be when we get the green made."

On September 17, Oliphant writes, "Up again at 5:30 and down to the golf course, where we got some holes cut and some tee boxes in position."

Oliphant left Peking in early October. On September 30, he writes, "I am leaving Peking in a few days, and am glad to say that I have got the golf course fairly started, and it is a very good one—for North China. I only hope it will prosper; if it does, I shall have the pleasing recollection of having introduced at least one branch of civilization into Peking."

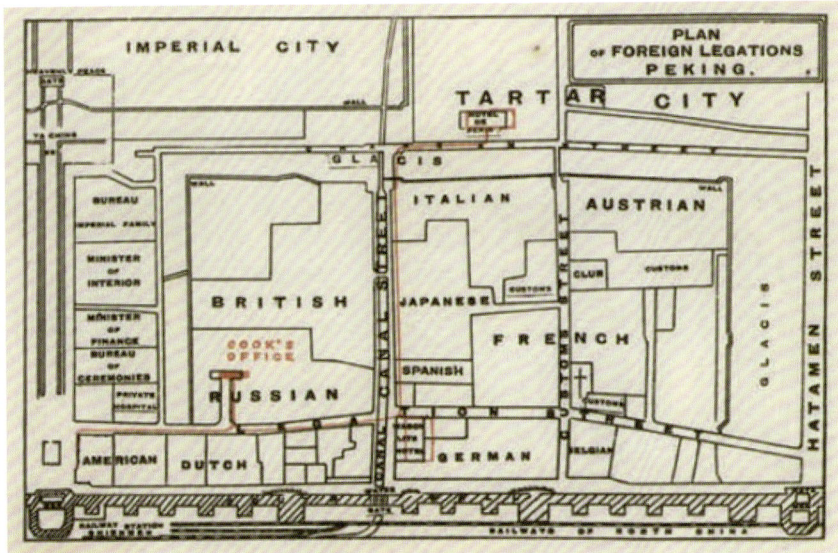

/ *Peking Legation Quarters*

Based on the descriptions in Oliphant's *Diary*, the first golf links in Peking was located in the "West City," reachable by at least half an hour on pony ride, not too far from the "Hole in the Wall" or "the British Gate." The "Chifu" palace may refer to the official residence of a magistrate. For reasons that will be discussed later in this chapter, we believe that the location of the rudimentary golf links was in the area of today's Maliandao North Street outside of Xibianmen. The British Legation Golf Club was formed soon after.

Golf Links outside of Antingmen

The second golf links of the British Legation Golf Club was built before 1910 on a piece of flat land outside of Antingmen to the north of the city. In the early 1860s, the place was once used as a race course organized by the student-interpreters at the British Legation and Imperial Customs. The site was not too far away from the European Settlements but was reachable by rickshaw or pony ride over long stretches of dusty roads. Bernard Darwin, the noted British golf writer vividly described the Antingmen Golf Links in his article, "Golf in the Far East," which was mentioned in the chapter on Tientsin. The article was published in the January 1910 issue of *C.B. Fry's Magazine*, with sketches by artist Tom Brown.

Unlike in Tientsin where the hazards were grave mounds, Darwin wrote: "They are however, of a less horrible character though possibly more

Peking golf links outside walls. Antung Men (gate) in distance.

/ *Golf Links Outside Antingmen*

difficult to play out of, since they consist not of graves, but of cabbage gardens, which the Chinaman plants at his own sweet will in the same rapid and light-hearted way." "You drive a raker straight on the hole; your partner takes the ingloriously safe line to the right and slices woefully into the bargain. You march towards the green with a dancing and triumphant step, only to find that a thick bed of rhododendrons has been dumped down in the night within five yards of the hole, and that your ball is hopelessly and impenetrably involved in them."

Darwin continues, "The difficulties of the situation are enhanced at Peking by the fact that the golfer is only allowed to play on condition that he does not disturb the cabbage patches. 'Golf is not agriculture'; so it has been written of those who tear vast and hideous divots from the shrinking turf. It is held to be true at Peking, and the native agriculturist will have the law of you if you interfere with the fruits of his industry. Cabbage patches are strictly out of bounds…. Other hazards of a less transitory character are camel roads which traverse the links from the mountains depicted in the distance. Along these roads there come, in addition to camels, great droves of ponies, which the Mongolians bring down to sell in Peking."

Darwin pointed out that another problem playing golf in Peking was the dust storm, "which is a terrible infliction. Dust-storms are perhaps best known to stay-at-home Englishmen from Mr. Rudyard Kipling's story 'False Dawn,' wherein a gentleman becomes so thoroughly bewildered with dust and darkness that he

/ Peking Legation Quarters

proposes to the wrong young lady. When a dust-storm arises—which it does with abominable suddenness—the game stops, and the players make for ditches and trenches, or cover behind mud walls. The stern rule which disqualifies those who shelter during a medal round is presumably suspended at Peking in regard to dust-storms."

In 1914, the former British Legation Golf Club was officially reconstituted as the Peking Golf Club, even though the name was already in use in the 1912 *Golfer's Handbook*. In 1920

/ Last Hole at Peking Golf Links

One of the mud greens. Entrance to club-house in distance.

/ A Mud Green, Clubhouse in Distance

/ Officers of Peking Golf Club

the name was again changed to Peking Golf and Country Club.

Peking Golf and Country Club

On December 9, 1919, *The North China Standard* published an article titled "Golf and Country Club for Peking Playing Rights Secured over Tien Shuen Shan (Tiancunshan) Plateau." The article reads: "An announcement which was more than local interest is herewith made. The Peking Golf Club, which has grown steadily in numbers despite the many disadvantages, has at length found a course more in accord with the old time associations of the Royal and Ancient game. The club has secured playing rights to run for several years over the plateau know as Tien Shuen Shan, situated about 6 miles west of the P'ingtszemen (Pingzemen)."

"The site," the article continues, "offers probably one of the most lovely views obtainable in the neighborhood of the Capital and the ground, which comprises roughly 500 *mou*, will be laid out in the best advantage to make a most sporting nine-hole course, with the possibility of lengthening it to 18 holes at a later date. Plans for a new Club House are being prepared, to which will be added plenty of garage and stabling accommodation. The building will be so designed as to allow for any possible extension that may be ultimately required. Arrangements will also be made to add Tennis Courts so that with advantageous surroundings for country riding there will be offered every facility for making a most successful Country Club, which will doubtless supply a long felt need in Peking. Across country it is only about 25 minutes ride from the Race Course at Pao-Ma-Chang, and it is anticipated that the Country Club will form a favorite rendezvous for the sporting community immediately after their ponies have been put through an early morning gallop. For the unfortunates, who are unable to run down to the sea-side for the week-ends during the summer, there will be offered at the Country Club the compensation of a clear bracing atmosphere in the vicinity of the Western Hills."

A similar report appeared on p. 682 of the December 13, 1919 *North-China Herald*, which announced that the Peking Golf Club was renamed the new Peking Golf and Country Club.

According to a report in *North China*

Standard dated October 17, 1920, the Tien Shuen Shan Golf Course, as well as the new clubhouse of the Peking Golf and Country Club, had formally opened. An inter-port game between Peking and Tientsin would be played, with eight members from each club in celebration of the opening.

According to a detailed report of the formal opening of Tien Shuen Shan Golf Course published in *North China Standard* on October 19, the new Peking Golf and Country Club was opened on Sunday. It reads: "Those who visited the place the first time must have been impressed with the wisdom of the selection of the site, with the extensive view of the beautiful countryside enriched by temples, trees, and historic associations, and many encomiums were passed upon the completed work of the committee as revealed in the well laid out links and the solid comfort of the Club House itself."

A match was arranged between eight members of the Tientsin Golf Club and eight local members. As neither had the advantage as the course was not known to any of the players, the Peking team won both the morning individual and the afternoon foursome matches. "A splendid tiffin was served at the Club House. Mr. A. C. Henning, the captain, welcomed the Tientsin players and the visitors. H.E. the Portuguese Minister replied on behalf of the visitors."

The newspaper also printed a Reuter's news on October 17 that said a total of 150 guests were at the luncheon. The delightful premises, it reads, "are probably the most picturesque in the Far East. Just about half an hour's journey by motor-car the course surrounds two hills on the highest points of which pavilions have been erected and a splendid view is obtained from there of the adjacent Western Hills and the surrounding country in all other directions. The links are said to be very fine but somewhat difficult for inexpert players owing to the undulating nature of the land."

The October 21 issue of the *North China Standard* published two photos of the opening ceremony.

/ *Tien Shuen Shan Clubhouse*

/ *The Opening of Tien Shuen Shan Golf Course*

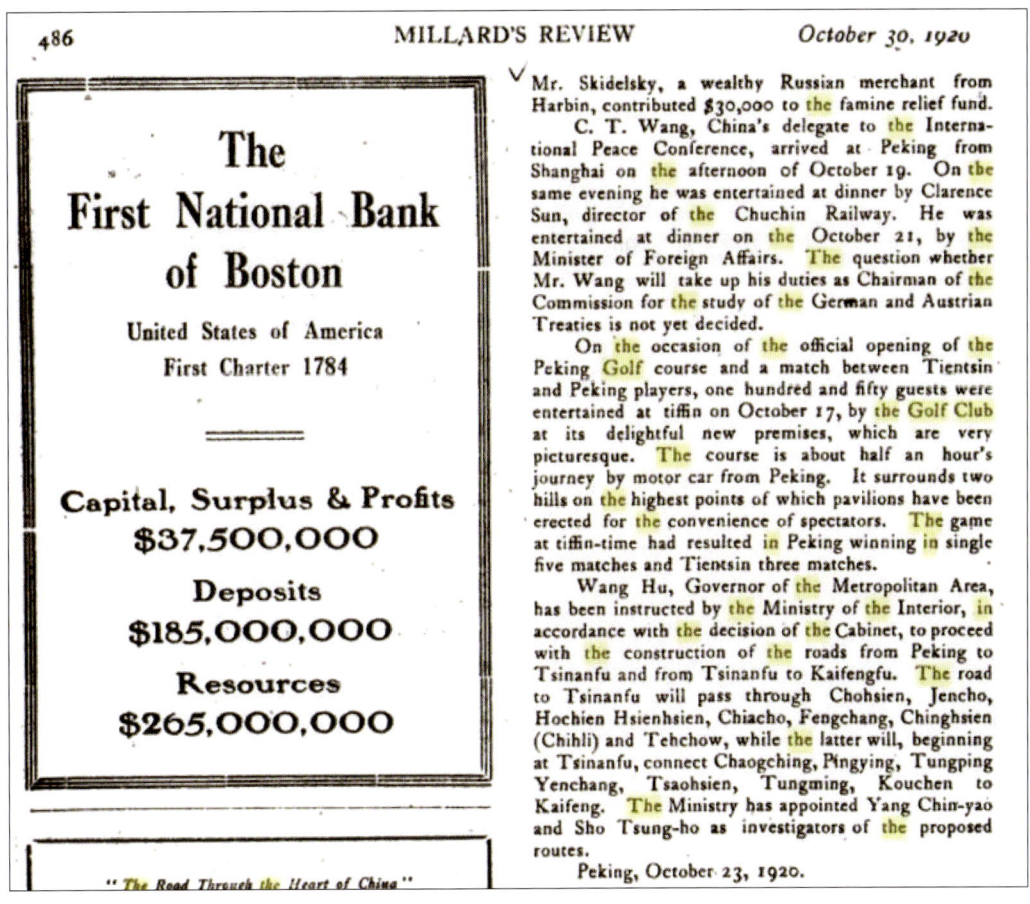

/ Millard's Review October 30, 1920

The *Millard's Review* dated October 1920 wrote about the opening of the new golf course and the Peking Golf and Country Club. It says on p. 486, "The course is about half an hour's journey by motor car from Peking. It surrounds two hills on the highest points of which pavilions have been erected for the convenience of spectators."

On the evening of October 25, 1920, Peking Golf and Country Club hosted a farewell dinner at the Peking Club for member A.H. Fergusson, according to a report in the October 27 *North China Standard*. The dinner was attended by 25 Club members and was presided by Captain A.H. Henning. Fergusson was the manager of Chartered Bank Peking and was transferred to Hong Kong. Henning proposed a toast to Fergusson at the end of the dinner and thanked him for the many years of contribution to the Peking Golf Club. Henning was quoted as saying that Fergusson had done more to advance golf in Peking than anyone else. Without Fergusson's constant work and attention, they would not have had their present excellent Golf and Country Club. Fergusson had arranged a 15-year lease of the new golf course and he was the guiding hand that had enabled them to lay out the excellent links they now had. Henning also spoke gratefully of the patience and zeal shown by Fergusson in teaching many of the members the finer points of the game of which he had become a master. Members all thanked Fergusson for all he had done for golf during his stay in Peking and hoped that he would have an opportunity of visiting Peking in the future and playing again on the links of the Peking Golf and Country Club for which he had worked so hard. Fergusson said he was pleased to have been able to work for the advancement of golf in the capital. If developed, he was sure the present course could be made the best in China.

Millard's Review also reported about the dinner on p. 550 of its November 6 issue. Fergusson had been captain of the Peking Golf Club in 1917-1918. Upon leaving, Fergusson kindly donated a Fergusson Cup for the new Club's annual competition. Starting in 1921, according to a report in the November 3, 1923 issue of *North-China Herald*, Peking Golf and Country Club had organized several Fergusson Cup competitions.

In 1921, Lord Alfred Harmsworth Northcliffe, British newspaper magnate and owner of *The Times* and *Daily Mail*, visited Peking during his travel around the world. In his book, *My Journey Round the World*, published in 1923, he describes on p. 135 his experience playing golf at the Tien Shuen Shan Golf Course:

"We went for a delicious motor drive below the Western Hills to the golf course, where we had a picnic lunch at the club house. The golf club is one of social centres of this very social Pekin(g). I shall not forget the golf. The greens are made of brown sand, and the tees are dark earth. The caddies carry little clay tees in tin boxes. Everybody has a Chinese caddy, of course; many with pigtails. I shall not forget that the caddy's fee was a penny-farthing for the round—nine holes. I halved the match with one of the best players of the club—entirely owing to my short game. The putting was most deadly; the 'browns' are very accurate."

On February 8, 1930, the *Illustrated Sporting and Dramatic News* published a photograph of participating members of the Peking and Tientsin Golf Clubs at a match at Tien Shuen Shan a few weeks earlier.

China Central Television aired a National Geographic program on January 14, 2003, which introduced Tien Shuen Shan Golf Course, one of two major golf courses in Peking. According to the broadcast, there is a small mountain eight kilometers west of Fuchengmen at Tiancun, or Tian Village, of the Evergreen Town. The height of the mountain, the closest one to the city, is less

/ 1930 Match Between Peking and Tientsin Golf Clubs

than 100 meters sitting on an area of a little under 10 square kilometers. The mountain stretches longer east-west but shorter north-south, with gradual slopes covered with opulent vegetation. The two mountain tops are lying east-west, with about 300-400 meters in between, looking like a camel sitting quietly from afar. In old days it was called the Camel Mountain. As it is located at the Tian Village, it has been called Tian Village Mountain or Tien Shuen Shan in the old days.

Li Tingfu, author of the broadcast script, writes: "Tiancun Shan is the closest high point scenic spot to the west of the Capital City. On a pleasant autumn day, visitors climb up the top of the mountain and enjoy a bird's-eye view of the Capital as well as the crowded market streets. Lying towards the northwest are mountain ranges and forests, with views of the Old Summer Palace, Summer Palace, Jade Spring Mountain and Fragrant Hills, dotted in between lakes and mountains. To the south is the expansive and endless farmland."

After the 1911 Revolution, descendants of Tien Shuen Shan sold the property, and it eventually was bought by Liang Shih-i, general manager of the Bank of Communications, who was known as "Liang the God of Wealth." Liang became co-investor of the "International Golf Course" in the 1920s. A clubhouse, referred to by locals as a "small western building," was built in the center of the golf course, with brick and mortar, western style windows and wooden floors. "Inside the courtyard of the club house were luxurious balconies and bars decorated with gripping vines. The building served Chinese and Western food, drinks and soda. It provided golf equipment and caddies for guests. The Golf Course was member-based and most of the members were foreigners such as diplomats, officials, officers, celebrities and businessmen. On weekends or holidays, the mountain became very crowded with golf players dressed in different costumes and speaking different languages. They would ride in all sorts of vehicles coming out of the Capital westward, passing the streets of Tian Village, out of its west gate to the south and parking at the foot of the mountain, before walking up about 100 meters to the golf course." The broadcast said that due to the increasing number of members and daily visit of scores of players, the 9-hole golf course was too crowded. The golf club acquired another 100 *mu* of land at Hejiafen Village to the south of the mountain for an expansion.

According to the CCTV report, there were close to 100 local people who were employed at the golf course. "Most of them were caddies who were called 'cane carrying' caddies. Unlike a modern golf course where golf carts are used to carry clubs, bags of clubs in those days were carried by hard-working young boys following golfers around the course. Golf club heads were angled on the sticks, like a walking cane, which was the reason why caddies were referred to as 'cane-carrying' caddies. Today some elderly people at Tian Village still have old golf canes, which testify to the golfing history of the village. Most of the young kids around Tian Village worked as caddies to help with family income. The golf course in those days was dirt instead of fairway lawns of today. After the day's play, employees used fine sand and dirt to spread on the green and then smoothed by a flat wooden rake before pressed firm down by a roller. There were people responsible to pick up stray balls on the outskirts of the course. Ordinarily, a golfer had two caddies, one carrying the bag and the other looking for where the ball landed. The golf clubs in a bag, around 10, were of different lengths and functions. Caddies were paid 40 coppers for a round of

9 holes and 60 for two rounds. Some skilled caddies knew what kind of clubs should be used and were able to timely pick them out for the golfer, who may reward them with a tip."

When the Young Marshall Chang Hsueh-liang was in Peking, he played golf frequently at the Tien Shuen Shan Golf Course. Noting the inconvenience of having to drive up the hill on a bad road to reach the golf club, he decided to rebuild it. This fact was mentioned in the November 1930 issue of the U.S. *Golf Illustrated* by Walter Buechler. On p. 52 of the magazine, Buechler writes: "Some of the better-class and more well-to-do Chinese have taken up golf and, further north, around Tientsin, Peking, and Mukden, one finds Chinese military officers passing the time in a game of golf. In fact, some time ago, a Chinese Militarist had road leading to the golf course properly repaired (something unusual in China!) simply because he had to pass over it every day to and from his way to the course, and the ride proved rather a strain on his good temper." We believe the "Chinese Militarist" referred to was Chang Hsueh-liang.

The CCTV broadcast described a story about Chang Hsueh-liang and a caddie in Peking. After a round of golf, Chang was giving out tips to the caddies. As he was handing a tip to a caddie named Gong Chengzhi from a village to the south of Tien Shuen Shan, the exhausted young lad dozed off sitting on the ground. Seeing that he did not respond, the Young Marshal said, jokingly: "You are not taking the money I am giving you. Do you want me to hand it into your hands? You seem to be more arrogant even than the little emperor Xuantong!" The caddie therefore was given a nickname "Little Emperor."

The report also said that after the Republican

/ *Chang Hsueh-liang Playing Golf at Tien Shuen Shang*

Government moved the capital to Nanking, the Ministry of Foreign Affairs decided to build a golf course at the Sun Yat-Sen Mausoleum to entertain foreign diplomats. They invited Tian Shao-wen from Tientsin, who was the general manager of Tien Shuen Shan International Golf Course, to Nanking to help build the golf course. A Pan Shou-shan took over his position at Tien Shuen Shan.

The Studienwerk Deutsches Leben in Ostasien e.V. in Munich has two photographs taken in 1936 of Peking Golf Club, now named Peip'ing Golf Club after the capital of the Republican Government was moved to Nanking. One shows two golfers with a caddie in front of the clubhouse and the other a golfer driving off the first tee.

/ Peip'ing Golf Club Golfers and Caddy

Based on the above sources from Chinese and overseas publications, we can conclude that the Tien Shuen Shan Golf Course was built in 1920. Until then Peking Golf Club had two golf courses. One had been laid out to the west of the city by Nigel Oliphant in 1900. The other was at a site outside Antingmen. The CCTV report mentioned that before the opening of Tien Shuen Shan, foreigners had been playing golf at an open space near Five Track Road outside of Xibianmen. The Five Track Road is today's Maliandao North Street, located at the southwest

/ Driving Off 1st Tee at Peip'ing Golf Club

corner of the Xuanwu District. According to an article by Chen Yin of the *Beijing Youth Daily*, Five Track Road covers an area from Lianhuachi East Road to the north and Guang'anmen Dajie to the south, bordering Haidian, Xuanwu and Fengtai Districts. The name of Five Track Road was given because Xibianmen Railway Station had five tracks, after the completion of the Peking-Hankow Railway in 1908. Thus the first and main golf course for the British Legation Golf Club and later the Peking Golf Club was therefore located at the Five Track Road. Unfortunately, due to limited membership, this golf course did not have much activity in the 20 years since it was laid out.

P'aomach'ang Golf Club

Horse racing started in Peking in 1861, thanks to the enthusiasm of the student-interpreters at the British Legation and the Imperial Maritime Customs Service. It was supported by Inspector General Sir Robert Hart and participated by the diplomatic missions. The race course moved to northern suburb outside Antingmen in 1863, attracting almost the entire foreign community. The following year it moved to a dried lake at White Cloud Temple at P'ingku (Pinggu), attracting 50,000 spectators, making it the largest racing event in the world.

In 1866, the Peking Race Course moved to Patach'uh (Badachu), six miles to the west of the city. The racecourse was located on a site surrounded by low hillocks or mounds for spectators in the thousands. It became a real Derby event in China with a larger race track of one mile. Due to a swamp in the middle, the race course moved in 1872 to a place to the east of the city but returned in 1882 to Pa Ta Ch'uh (Badachu), named P'aomach'ang. P'aomach'ang was run by the Peking Club and visitors would travel to the race events by carriages and sedan chairs or riding ponies or donkeys.

During the Boxer Uprising, the P'aomach'ang stand was burned down on June 12, 1900. With the Peking-Hankow Railway in service starting in 1908, a branch line was built to Tientsin with a station set at two miles from the P'aomach'ang. This made it easier for racing enthusiasts and visitors from Tientsin to participate at the Peking event. During each year's racing season, special passenger trains were added on Friday evenings and Saturday mornings for people to travel from the city to P'aomach'ang.

On October 24, 1923, *North China Standard* quoted a *Reuter's* report published the day before that a meeting had been held on Monday evening at the Hong Kong and Shanghai Banking office by subscribers of the P'aomach'ang Golf Course. The purpose of the meeting was to constitute themselves into a club. W.E. Southcott presided over the meeting and "it was agreed to form a club to be known as the P'aomach'ang Golf Club." Officers were elected, which included Captain G.A. Johnston, Hon. Secretary L.L. Davidson, Hon. Treasurer J. Boyd, committee members Dr. Cormack, Colonel Barnard, Cruickshank and Southcott.

The first of the monthly medal competition of the P'aomach'ang Golf Club took place on November 17 and 18, and the first monthly bogey competition took place on November 24 and 25, according to *North China Standard* quoting *Reuter's*. D.A. Johnston won the first medal competition and "receives the silver spoon and two points towards the aggregate cup, while Mr. E.C. Mierville, the runner-up, receives one point."

After the Republican Government moved to Nanking, Peking was renamed Peiping. So did the names of golf clubs. However, people by custom continued to use the word 'Peking.'

According to a report in the May 14, 1925 *London and China Express*, J.W. Stephenson, captain of the Peking Golf and Country Club, had presented a cup to be competed for between the two local clubs at Tien Shuen Shan and P'aomach'ang.

A short note from Peking published in the same newspaper on December 24, 1925 reads: "It is rather in the nature of poetic justice that it should have been Mr. D.A. Johnston, the principal originator of the P'aomach'ang Club, who was fined the first bottle of whisky under the new 'Birdie' rule for holing out in one at the 5th hole."

In the 30 years from 1920 to 1950, Tien Shuen Shan and P'aomach'ang became the two major golf links for the Peking Golf Club. According to a list

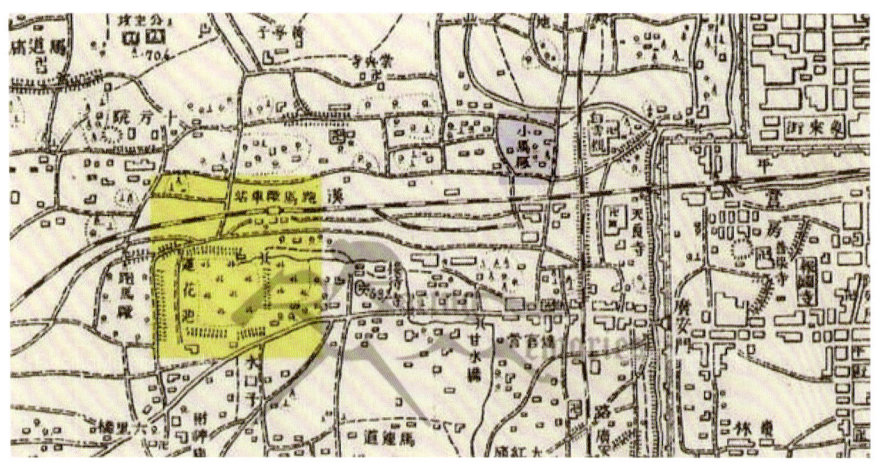
/ Driving Off 1st Tee at Peip'ing Golf Club

of captains and honorary secretaries of Peking Golf Club from 1914 to 1923, the original British Legation Golf Club reconstituted as Peking Golf Club in 1914 and again reconstituted as the Peking Golf and Country Club in 1920. The P'aomach'ang Golf Club was formed in 1924. But as mentioned earlier, P'aomach'ang GC had been formed in 1923.

PAST CAPTAINS AND HON. SECRETARIES		
1914	Former British Legation Golf Club Reconstituted as **PEKING GOLF CLUB**	
	CAPTAIN	HON. SEC.
1914	SIR JOHN JORDAN	K. W. TRIBE
1915	" "	" "
1916	" "	A. ARCHER
1917	A. H. FERGUSON	A. C. HENNING
1918	" "	D. R. MACKENZIE
1919	A. C. HENNING	" "
1920	**PEKING GOLF CLUB** reconstituted as **PEKING GOLF & COUNTRY CLUB**	
1920	A. C. HENNING	D. R. MACKENZIE
1921	MON. EVERTS	C. TONKIN
1922	" "	P. L. FOSTER
1923	" "	E. C. RICHARDSON
1924	PAO MA CHANG CLUB FORMED.	

/ Captains and Secretaries of Peking Golf Club 1914-1924

P'aomach'ang Golf Club created an annual championship silver trophy cup since its founding. It also started an annual inter-club competition with the Peking Golf and Country Club alternatively held at each other's courses. At an eclectic competition in March 1925, the Best Eclectic trophy was won by O. H. Hulme and the Worst Eclectic trophy was won by A.H. Barnard. Both trophies are now in the collection of the Golf Heritage Museum.

A Lady's Golf Club was formed inside the Peking Golf Club. On December 11, 1927 and a ladies' knockout singles was played at P'aomach'ang, according to a report in the *London and China Express* dated January 5, 1928. The winner was Mrs. D.R. Mackenzie, who defeated Lady Lampson 2 up and 1 to go. Lady Lampson had been elected as the Ladies' Captain for 1928. Mrs. Southcott would be the secretary. At a medal competition of the P'aomach'ang Ladies' Spring Tournament, a Mrs. Ching-fang Liu won with a net score of 72 for the two rounds, according to a report on April 12 in the same newspaper.

Another report in the same newspaper on May 12, 1928 said that P'aomach'ang beat the Peking Golf and Country Club in the Stephenson Challenge Cup competition by 2¾ points.

/ Best Eclectic Trophy

/ Worst Eclectic Trophy

A picture news story was published on p. 212 of the July 28, 1928 issue of the *Illustrated Sporting and Dramatic News*. The two photographs were taken at the P'aomach'ang Golf Course. One on the left shows the second green, where a golfer was putting and another golfer and two caddies were watching. The other on the right shows a golfer pausing to watch a wedding procession passing by. The caption under the photos reads:

"Our pictures were taken on the nine-hole P'aomach'ang course outside of the West Wall of Peking City. The 'greens' there are of hard mud rolled flat, with a dressing of finely sifted soil. They are very true and in every way satisfactory until the wind arises or a dust storm blows, but then -----! One of our illustrations shows a player pausing while a country wedding procession is passing by, the bride's sedan chair being seen just behind the decorated 'umbrellas.' In addition to such sights, soldiers at drill, strings of camels, herds of pigs and sheep, rickshaws and coolies are daily incidents on the course. In spite of this the Peking golfers, consisting of British, American, Chinese, Japanese, Italian, Danish and other players, get their game and enjoy it thoroughly."

In the Chapter on Hankow, we mentioned U.S. diplomat Lewis Clark and his 2012 memoir *Diplomacy as a Career: Hard Work, Hardship, and Happy Times*. Clark talked about his experience playing golf at both Peking Golf and Country Club at Tien Shuen Shan and P'aomach'ang Golf Club. In 1926, the 31-year-old Clark was sent to Peking as a secretary at the American Mission. After a short period of stay at Kalgan (Zhangjiakou) for consul affairs in Inner Mongolia, he came back to Peking in 1928 and assisted in the consul affairs of Tientsin while continuing with his study of Chinese and Chinese history.

Clark said in the memoir that he took up golf again that spring. "I played baseball and basketball and football in preparatory school, and, for two years I played basketball on the undefeated team of University of Virginia." As he was unable to participate in those games in Peking, he started to play golf and tennis. He said in those days everyone stopped work at 4:30 in the afternoon and played bridge, tennis, polo, golf, badminton or ice skating in winter.

Clark remembered: "We used to play golf on a hilly course near the Western Hills called Pa Pao Shan (Eight Precious Mountains) or at P'ao Ma Ch'ang (Race Course), located, as the name implies, near the race course. During my golfing career, I had two holes-in-one: one in Montgomery, Alabama, on a short hole, and one in Peking, at Pa Pao Shan on a long one of 316 yards. I wonder how many, if any, other 316-yard

/ The 2nd and 3rd Green at P'aomach'ang Golf Club

holes have been made in one! Four Japanese were putting on the 17th green when I made that hole-in-one. I ran into one of them years later in Paris. With the typical intake of breath and a smile, he recalled to me my exploit at Pa Pao Shan."

Clark continued: "I played on the Peking Golf Club team each year. We had two matches with the Tientsin Golf Club each year, one played in Peking and the other in Tientsin. They generally won in Tientsin and we in Peking. There was a lot in knowing your course. The greens were skinned greens; that is to say, they had no grass on them. They were baked clay with a thin layer of sand spread on top. When the wind blew, the sand was swept away, leaving the slick clay surface smooth as a tabletop. One day in Tientsin, I was playing a match in a strong wind. I had managed to chip my approach shot onto the green and the ball came to rest about four feet from the pin. When I putted, a gust of wind suddenly caught my ball and carried it back off the green into the fairway. It took four more shots to sink that putt. It was some golf, but it was fun."

Peking Golf Club after 1930

Page 49 of the 1930 *Guide to Peking* contains information about both the Peking P'aomach'ang Golf Club and Peking Golf and Country Club. The former's address was Hsipienmen Station, with C.C. Liang as Captain. The latter's address was Pa Pao Shan, with W.H.E. Thomas as Captain and Lieutenant M. McHugh as Hon. Secretary. The correct addresses for the two golf clubs, however, should be the other way around.

CLUBS

PEKING HUNT CLUB
Mr. Eric Teichman, Hunt Master.
Capt. C. T. Brooks, Hon. Sec. and Treas.
Address: Capt. C. T. Brooks, American Legation Guard.

PEKING POLO CLUB
Lieut. W. G. Wymans, Field Manager.
Capt. C. T. Brooks, Hon. Sec. and Treas.
Address: Capt. C. T. Brooks, American Legation Guard.

/ 1930 Guide to Peking

The *London and China Express* reported on p. 166 of the October 16, 1930 issue that the P'aomach'ang Golf Club had an annual general meeting. It was announced that a trophy cup had been presented by Mr. L.C. Arlington for international competition. The annual meeting elected the following officers of the Club for the coming season: Captain A.C. Henning, Hon. Secretary S.P. Chen, Hon. Treasurer W.J. Sutherland, committee members C.C. Liang, W. Park, K. Kanai, A. Carruthers and R.H. Hollis.

/ 1929 Match St. Andrews and St. George's Teams in Peking
(The Tatler 27 February 1929)

Walter Buechler's article, "Golf in China," published in the November 20, 1930 *Golf Illustrated* of the U.S. mentioned earlier, used one of the two photos of P'aomach'ang Golf Course that had appeared in the July 28, 1928 issue of the *Illustrated Sporting and Dramatic News*. The caption of the third green photo reads: "The so-called greens are flat, hard mud with a dressing of fine soil."

/ Peking P'aomach'ang in the 1930s (University of Bristol)

Golf Illustrated published a report on June 1, 1933 that said Peip'ing Golf Club had two 9-hole courses. One was at Patach'uh about five miles from the Legation Quarters, "a delightful place," and the other was at P'aomach'ang about 11 miles, built in 1924.

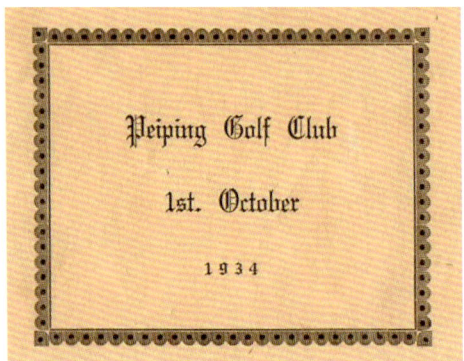
/ Peip'ing Golf Club October 1, 1934

During the winter of 1934-1935 when Lewis Clark returned to Peking from Hankow with wife Anne, the couple played a lot of golf. "Anne was particularly successful that winter," Clark said. "She won every one of the principal cups offered in the women's competitions. She also played in the Peip'ing lady's team in the inter-port competition with Tientsin. Most of Anne's trophies were won on the P'ao Ma Ch'ang golf course where, in addition to the normal traps, there were railway tracks, camels and other unusual hazards."

The Danish Golf Museum has a copy of member booklet of the Peiping Golf Club dated October 1, 1934.

A 1935 *Guide to Peip'ing* said Papaoshan or P'aomach'ang golf clubs could be contacted through Count Rene d'Anjou at 3 Rue de Lagrene.

On September 1, 1936, *Associated Press* reported that mounted Japanese soldiers invaded the Peip'ing golf links: "Players asserted the soldiers rode over the course, tearing up greens and fairways, then dismounted and executed setting up exercises. Witnesses said a number of them stripped naked and lolled on the turf. Chinese and foreigners expressed indignation. Numerous prominent Japanese are among the club's members."

The Straits Times of Singapore reported on p. 15 of its April 24, 1937 issue about the inter-port match between Peking Golf Club and Shanghai Golf Club at the Shanghai Kiangwan Golf Course. The report said that Shanghai gained a lead of six points to two in the four-ball matches on the first day, and again won the singles matches by six to two. "It is interesting to read though, that Dr. P.K.C. Tyau, the veteran Peking champion and former Consul in Singapore, and H.Y. Wu scored the only successes for the Northern city." The report quoted *North-China Herald* to say that H. Cheng of Shanghai was no match for Dr. Tyau, who "plays a very accurate game, his approaching and putting being very deadly. He won by six and five." Dr. Tyau had been five-time golf champion in Peip'ing. Bobbie Kan, the Shanghai Golf Club champion, overwhelmed C.H. Liang, one of the best Peiping players by seven and six, going round in 76 (two 38's).

According to a report in the July 13, 1937 *The Sydney Morning Herald*, fighting broke out all night near the golf course in Papaoshan. There was a curfew in Peip'ing. The Japanese troops reportedly intended to occupy the entire city.

A signed article published in the second issue of the 2019 *Beijing Culture and History Journal* (Beijing Wenbo Wencong) featured two photographs dated in the late 1930s during the Anti-Japanese War. The author, Liu Kang, was with the Culture and Tourism Bureau of the Shijingshan District. The two photos were taken near the golf course at Papaoshan not long after the Japanese invasion of Peip'ing on July 7, 1937. A division of the 29th Army was stationed at the golf course. One photo shows a solder on duty. To his right is a sign that reads "To 10 TEE," pointing to the direction of the 10th tee. The other photo shows soldiers crossing the golf course. Liu believes that the photos were taken in August when the troop withdrew from Papaoshan.

A map was also provided by the author, which marks P'aomach'ang, Papaoshan and the Golf Course close to the center. Tien Shuen is on top to the left. According to the above photo, the P'aomach'ang Golf Course at one point was expanded to 18 holes.

On August 18, 1937, *Illustrated Sporting and Dramatic News* published a story with two

/ To 10 TEE

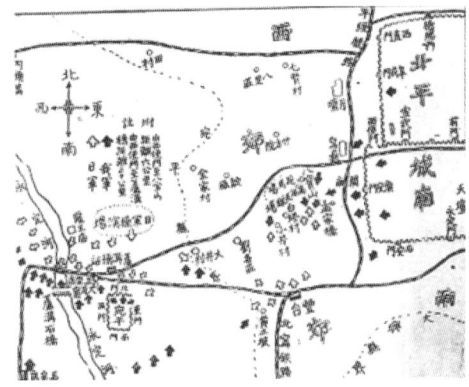
/ Golf Course near Papaoshan

photos showing the Paomachang Golf Course right after the Japanese invasion.

The Tien Shuen Shan and P'aomach'ang golf courses were clearly noted in the booklet *The Map and History of Peiping* published by the Peiyang Press Ltd. in 1936. The author of the booklet with a color map was Frank Dorn. Dorn was a graduate of West Point Military Academy

/ Papaoshan Course with Trenches
(The Sketch, August 18, 1937)

EARLY GOLF IN CHINA

/ *Two Golfers at Papaoshan Before the Military Occupation (The Sketch, August 18, 1937)*

after getting an art degree at the San Francisco Institute of Art. In the mid-1930s, Dorn worked at the U.S. military attaché office in Peking and later became an assistant to General Joseph W. Stilwell and rose to be Brigadier General.

The booklet contains a hand-painted map in English, 34 inches long and 29 inches wide, titled *The Map of Old Peking Folklore*. In March 2004, Beijing Xueyuan Publishing House reprinted the map.

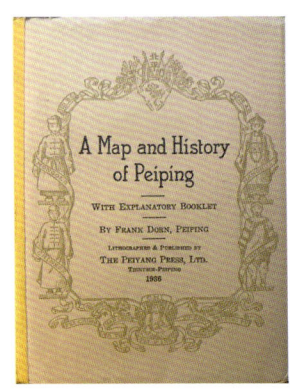

/ *A Map and History of Peiping*

/ *The Map of Old Peking Folklore (Golf Heritage Museum)*

/ *Tien Shuen Shan Golf Course at Patach'uh*

/ *P'aomach'ang Golf Course*

Although disproportionate, the *Map* clearly shows the two golf courses in Peking, Tien Shuen Shan and P'aomach'ang.

As a result of the Anti-Japanese War, membership of the Peiping Golf Club was reduced from 150 in 1936 to 100 in 1939. The 1939 *China Hong List* indicated on p. 650 that the Captain of the Club was C.H. Page and the Honorary Secretary was P.A. North.

Up until 1954, *Golfer's Handbook* listed the two golf courses under Peip'ing Golf Club: 9 holes at P'aomach'ang and 9 holes at Papaoshan. The Honorary Secretary was Dr. J. Cameron. Visitors pay $1 per day and $3 per week.

After the founding of the People's Republic in 1949, Peip'ing Golf Club was still operating until the late 1950s. The *Belfast Telegraph* published an article on p. 8 of its May 8, 1958 issue with the title "China Then and Now." The article writes: "When a caddy at the Peking

> Peiping G. C., Peiping. Membership, 100. Hon. Sec., Dr. J. Cameron. 9 holes at Paomachang and 9 holes at Paopashan. Visitors, 1 dol. per day; 3 dols. per week.

/ *1954 Golfer's Handbook*

EARLY GOLF IN CHINA

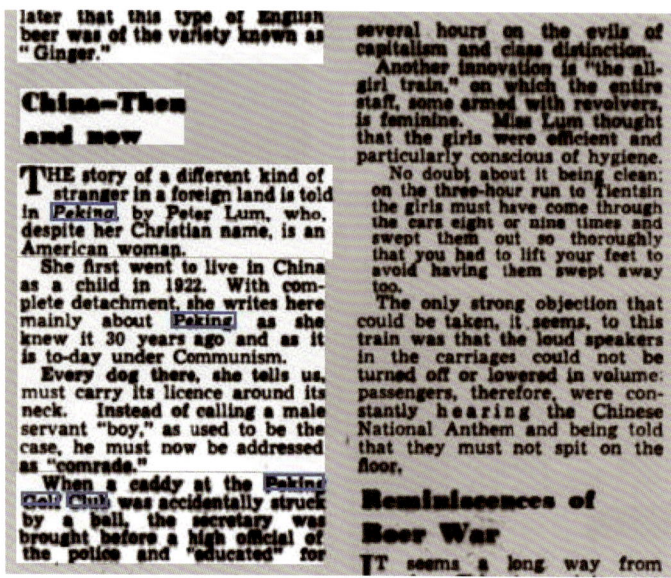

/ Belfast Telegraph May 8, 1958

Golf Club was accidentally struck by a ball the secretary was brought before a high official of the police and 'educated' for several hours on the evils of capitalism and class distinction."

Nanyuan Golf Course

On January 30, 1926, the *North-China Herald* published a news story on p. 187 saying that the Nanyuan Golf Course in Peking opened on January 17. This became Peking's third golf links. It had 9 holes and was in preparation to expand into 18.

The *London and China Express* reported on February 25, 1926 that the Nanyuan Golf Course in Peking opened on February (should be January) 17, making it the third links in Peking. "The course numbered nine holes but arrangements have been started to enlarge it to 18."

/ Nanyuan Golf Course Opened

Again, on March 4, the newspaper printed another story about Nanyuan in its supplement, which reads: "Members of the Peking Golf and Country Club were invited by the committee of the International Recreation and Race Club to attend the opening of the Nan Yuan Golf Course. The advent of this new course, the third in Peking, is indicative of the rising popularity of the game."

/ 南苑高尔夫球场

Golf Courses and Clubs in Weihaiwei

As Russia's lease of Port Arthur (Lvshun) and Dairen (Dalian) threatened Britain's interests in China, the British government forced the Ch'ing government to sign an agreement on July 1, 1898 to lease Weihaiwei (Weihai). According to the lease, "the territory leased shall comprise the Island of Liu-kung (Liugong) and all other islands in the Bay of Wei-Hai-Wei, and a belt of land 10 English miles wide along the entire coast line of the Bay." The term of the lease would be "for so long a period as Port Arthur shall remain in the occupation of Russia."

The historical fact of Great Britain forcing China to lease Weihaiwei was depicted by a British artist in one of his golf-related political cartoons. John Wallace (1841-1903) worked as an artist at Cope's Tobacco in Liverpool. The invention of gutter percha golf balls in the mid-19th century facilitated the popularization of golf in Scotland and England. Wallace, with the pen name of George Pipeshank, created golf-themed paintings to help the company market tobacco products among growing number of gentlemen golfers in the late 19th century.

One of the five golf-related political cartoons created by Wallace was titled "*The Open (Door) Championship*." In water color, it was about the lease of Weihaiwei in 1898. Following the American "Open Door" policy on China, world powers were dividing up their interests in China. The title of the cartoon obviously borrowed from "The Open Championship" of golf which started in Scotland in 1860. It is a vivid depiction of how Great Britain and other powers were dividing up China in a golf meet among leaders of world powers.

/ The Open (Door) Championship (University of Liverpool)

A chromolithograph print of this painting was purchased by the Golf Heritage Museum in 2019 through an auction. The print is 22.5 inches wide and 16 inches high. The references of Cope's Tobacco have been carefully painted over to blend in with the golfing scene. The original titles and descriptions were clipped out. But the title on top of the print, *The Open (Door) Championship*, is still recognizable. Fortunately, relevant information about this painting can be found on the back of the print. The title of the print was given a most appropriate new name: *Wei-Hai-Wei 1898*, with the subtitle *The Great International Foursome*. On the lower lefthand corner is the signature of George Pipeshank dated 1898.

/ *Wei-Hai-Wei 1898*

According to information on the back of the print, the figures depicted in the cartoon were as follows (from left to right): 1. South African President Paul Cruger; 2. The Kaiser; 3. The Czar; 4. French President Fèlix Faute; 5. Japanese Emperor Mikado; 6. U.S. President McKinley; 7. Li Hung-chang; 8. British politician Joseph Chamberlain; 9. British Prime Minister Lord Salisbury; 10. Speaker of British House of Commons A.J. Balfour; 11. ? Lord Wolmer; 12-14. Irish Members or T.U.C.; 15. British politician Harcourt; 16. British politician Asquith; 17. ? John Morley; 18. ? Lord Spencer.

The scene of the paining was set most likely at Weihaiwei, with three British warships docked out at sea. The caddie was Li Hung-chang, a top official and diplomat of the late Ch'ing Dynasty government. A bag of golf clubs in hand, Li was kneeling to tee up a golf ball for Balfour to drive. His partners Chamberlain, Salisbury and Wolmer looked on. The painting truthfully recreated the relationship between China and world powers in the late 19th century utilizing a golf course scene. The foursome in the center were decision-makers of the British Empire while Li, as caddie, represented the weak and humble Ch'ing government.

Weihaiwei was leased to Great Britain for 32 years from 1898 through 1930. As the Royal Navy base and summer resort, the Liukung Island remained under the British rule for an additional 10 years until 1940.

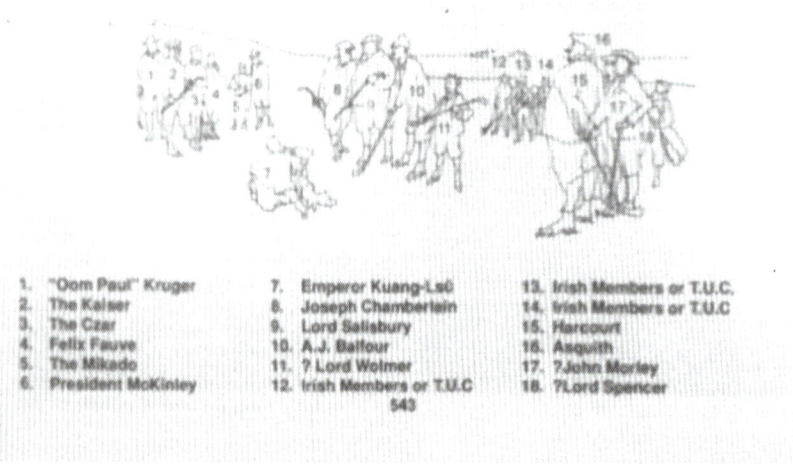

/ *Wei-Hai-Wai 1898 Politicians*

As if anticipated by John Wallace in 1898 through his artistic work, the Royal Navy built a 9-hole golf course on the Liukung Island in 1901 and formed the Weihaiwei Golf Club. Situated about 4 km off the coast to the east of Weihaiwei, Liukung Island is 4 km long and 1.5 km wide. The golf links was laid out on the east slope, stretching from the East Village in the west to the Tunghung (Donghong) Garrison in the east. The earliest mentioning of the Weihaiwei Golf Course in the press can be found in the 1902 edition of *The Golfing Annual*. Under "China" in the Index of the book, Weihaiwei Golf Course was listed behind Hankow, Royal Hong Kong and Shanghai. On p. 550, under "Wei-Hai-Wei (China)," are words: "A course has been laid out here."

According to a copy of the 1902 *Weihaiwei Golf Club List of Officials, Rules, Etc.* currently stored at the National Library of Scotland, the Club president was James Stewart Lockhart, Commissioner of Weihaiwei. Club Captain was Captain F.H. Henderson of the Royal Navy. And Honorary Secretary and Treasurer was Lieutenant G.S. Hobson. The Club had formal and honorary members. Officers of the army and navy may become members upon payment of a subscription. Others may "become members on being proposed and seconded by Service members duly balloted for."

/ Wei-Hai-Wai 1898 Politicians

The July 7, 1903 *Globe and Traveler* published an article by a navy officer about how the Royal and Ancient game was played in China. As a leased territory, the city was named Port Edward. British naval officers started playing golf on newly built links. According to the article, golf was not only played in Weihaiwei, it was played in almost every port in China. The greens on some of the Chinese links were excellent and even compared favorably with those at Hoylake and St. Andrews. But at putting greens in Weihaiwei,

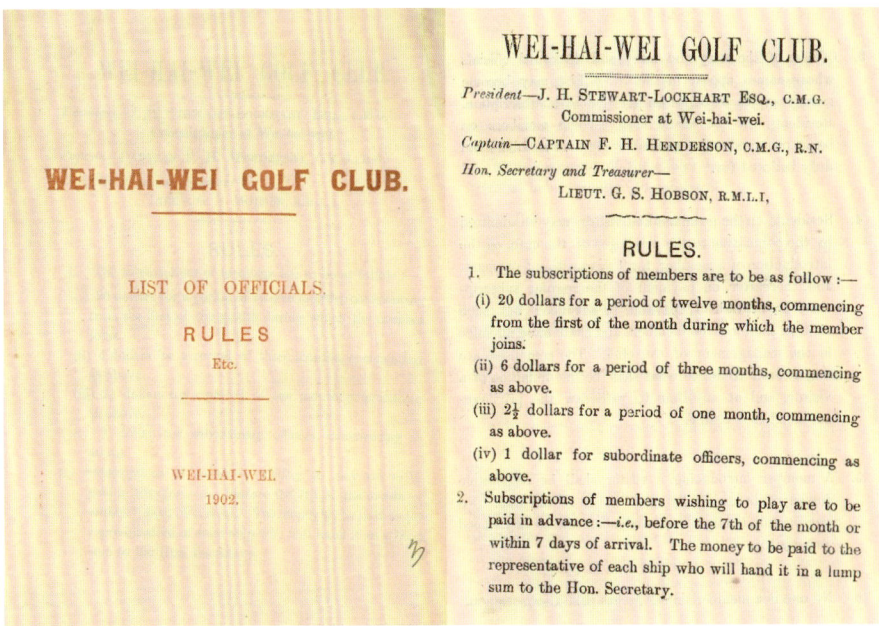
/ 1902 Wei-hai-wei Golf Club List of Officials and Rules

the holes were made in "hard rolled sandy gravel, and golfers are obliged by the rules to play only in India rubber-soled or rope-soled shoes, while on wet days play is forbidden altogether." The caddies were China "boys whose ages vary from about twelve to fifty; instead of one caddie to each player, two are necessary—one to carry the clubs, the other to go on in front to spot the balls." "One of the holes is at the top of precipice one hundred feet high, and the course is further hampered by rocks, walls, and even a rifle range. In spite of all this the naval officer plays golf in China with a fine relish, and is succeeding in making the game increasingly popular."

The original story appeared on the July 3 issue of *Golf Illustrated*, with three photographs of the golf course on Liukung Island. The "naval officer" writes: "Little did the combatants in the bombardment and torpedo attack on Wei-Hai-Wei imagine that in the short space of eight years the then impregnable port was to become a favourite putting green for numerous golfing British Naval serving their King and country in China."

The author goes on to describe his first photo as showing "how the Englishman has utilized the former drill ground."

The second photo shows a golfer driving on the Fifth Tee. The author writes: "Wei-hai-wei is a barren spot, and photo No. 2 gives a fairly good illustration of the kind of natural bunkers which one has to contend with. In this photo the crevasse directly in front of the person driving is about 20 feet deep and 30 yards wide, a stagnant pool being situated at the bottom, and woe betide the unfortunate golfer who cannot safely carry this obstacle, as all caddies will not 'retrieve' as well as the one I happened to see the other day,

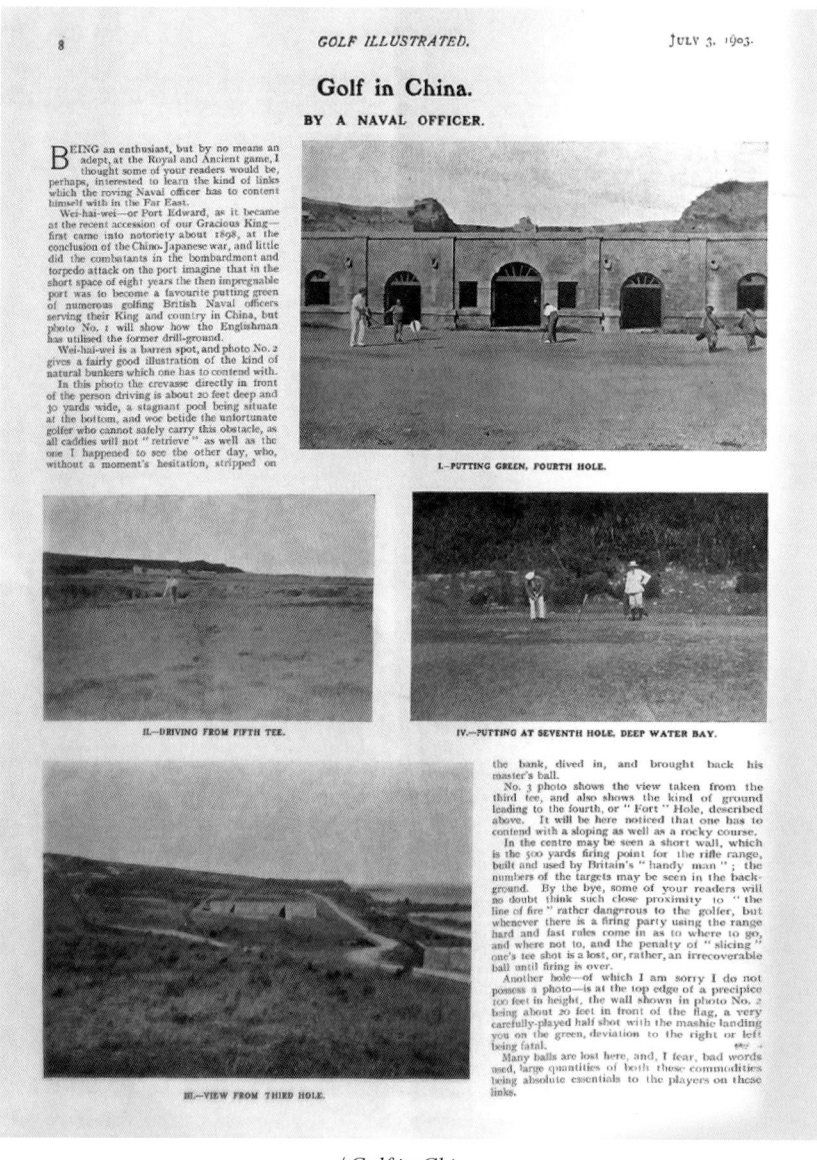

/ *Golf in China*

who, without a moment's hesitation, stripped on the bank, dived in, and brought back his master's ball."

"No. 3 photo shows the view taken from third tee," the author writes, "and also shows the kind of ground leading to the fourth, or 'Fort' Hole, described above. It will be here noticed that one has to contend with a sloping as well as a rocky course. In the centre may be seen a short wall, which is the 500 yards firing point for the rifle range, built and used by Britain's 'handy man'; the numbers of the targets may be seen in the background."

The Daily Mirror printed a photograph of a Chinese caddie at Weihaiwei on p. 9 of the May 28, 1905 issue with a short story about "Chinese Golf Caddie." It reads: "Turning from the horrors of present-day life in the Far East to its more humorous aspect, we have an amusing photograph of a Chinese caddie on page 9. The English officers at Wei-hai-wei which is not far from Port Arthur have laid out a golf course, and the fascination of the game have quite overcome the Chinese youngsters employed as caddies. In various places they are to be found, armed with imitation golf sticks they have fashioned for themselves, making attempts to drive and putt golf balls which players have mysteriously lost. The caddie who figures in this photograph was 'snapped' while practicing in the

/ *Putting Green, Fourth Hole*

/ *Driving from the Fifth Tee*

/ *View from the Third Hole*

streets of the town."

The photograph came from *The Sphere* dated March 25 of the same year. But the reprint of the photo in *The Daily Mirror* cut off the golf ball in the original photo, which led the editor to write the following photo caption: "The Chinese caddies in Wei-hai-wei, where the English officers have established a golf course, are enthusiasts. Here is one practicing with a stick and a 'lost' ball."

A postcard sent out from Weihaiwei in 1906 has this handwriting: "Feb. 8, 06 arrived safe. Golf links, Weihaiwei." On the postcard British Naval officers were drilling on the Golf Course.

The Weihaiwei Golf Club's 9-hole golf links had a total length of 3,310 yards (3,027 meters). The name of the Club was later changed to Royal Navy United Services Golf Club.

In 1907, the British administration at Weihaiwei built another 9-hole golf course on the mainland and formed the Port Edward Golf Club. This was described by Zhang Junyong of the Weihai Archives in the book *100 Years of Sports at Weihai* published in 2009 by the *Shandong Pictorial Publishing House*. Zhang writes in the first chapter, "The Modern Sport of Golf in

/ Weihaiwei Caddie

Liugong Island," that in the spring of 1907, "the Administration and British expatriates finished building a lawn golf course at the Parade Ground outside the Eastern Gate and organized the Port Edward Golf Club. Member categories included formal, associate, visitor and life-long. British expatriates were allowed to become formal members with a subscription. According to local residents, two other small golf links were also built at the western and southern suburbs, but no details about them could be found. Different from the Liugong Island Golf Club, the Port Edward Golf Club was mainly an investment project. In addition to serving the needs of local foreign

/ 1906 Postcard of Wei-hai-wei Golf Links

residents, its main goal was to attract travelers to Weihai. So, at the outset it was organized as an international club. Members were expatriates, especially foreign business people and families from Shanghai. The other difference from the Weihaiwei Golf Club on Liugong Island was its acceptance of women as members at half price." Inter-club competitions were organized between the two Clubs.

/ Port Edward Postcard

The 1908 edition of the *20th Century Impressions of Hong-Kong, Shanghai, and Other Treaty Ports of China* has the following description of golf clubs in Weihaiwei on p. 776: "Apart from the recreations in and on the water, the visitor may, for a small monthly subscription, indulge in the 'ancient and royal game' on the links of the Weihaiwei Golf Club at Liu-kung-tao or on those of the Port Edward Golf Club."

According to the 1908 edition of the *Weihaiwei Golf Club List of Officials and Rules*, Club president was still Commissioner Lockhart. The Captain was Royal Navy Colonel Seymour E. Erskine and the Honorary Secretary and Treasurer was Royal Navy Surgeon F.D. Lumley. Subscription fees were adjusted and 3-month subscription was replaced by 6-month. Wives or members and families of members under 18 years of age were allowed to play free of charge.

On May 6, 2018, Liu Weifeng of the Museum of Sino-Japanese War 1894-1895 on Liugong Island published an article titled "Liugong Island and the Sport of Golf". Quoting local senior residents on Liugong Island, Liu

/ Golfers and Caddies on the Liukung Island Golf Cours

writes: "Senior British officers who came to Liugong Island during summer played golf, mid-level officers played tennis and soldiers played football." As a game using sticks to hit a ball into a hole, Liu said that local Chinese called golf the game of "hole ball," "field ball" or "grass ball."

Weihai residents called golfing a game of "hitting eggs," and golf clubs were called "egg sticks." Liu met a 101-year-old Liu Yuanchang who witnessed the British playing golf. At the time a caddie would carry a small cloth bag with fine sand inside. When a golfer was ready to drive, the caddie would take out a handful of sand and place it on the grass into a small heap before putting a golf ball on top of it. A sand heap in the early days of golf served as the modern tee.

The Sketch weekly dated September 14, 1910 published two photographs from the *Illustrated London News* taken at the Weihaiwei Golf Club. The first one was at the eighth green with a bunker guarding it. A gofer was playing his ball out of the bunker. The second was "Quite a Celestial Spot: the Club House." The caption of the photographs reads: "The Way They Have it in Wei-Hai-Wei: The Local Golf Club. The greens of the Wei-Hai-Wei Golf club are all of mud, rolled flat, that form of green having been found best in view of the local climate."

The 1912 *Nisbet's Golf Yearbook* lists under "Wei-hai-wei (North China)" the following detailed information of the Weihaiwei Golf Club: "*Inst.* 1901. *Members*—568. *Nearest Large Town*—Dalny (*Dairen*), 80 miles. *Hon. Sec.*—Engineer-Commander H.W. Harris, R.N., Wei-Hai-Wei. *Entrance Fee*—2 dollars. *Subs.*—15 dollars. *Holes*—9 (on disintegrating granite soil). *Pro.*—A Chinaman. *Visitors*—3 dollars per month; there are Lady Members. Sunday play, with caddies."

According to Zhang Junyong, in the early days the golf links on Liukung Island was open only to officers of a certain level or civilians of similar ranks. Expatriates living in town were not allowed to become members. The same was true in the Navy and Army. Warrant officers, non-commissioned officers or British policemen on the Island were not allowed to become

/ 1910 Liukung Island Golf Links Eighth Green and Clubhouse

/ 1910 Lady Golfers Playing at Liukung Island Golf Links

> **WEI-HAI-WEI (NORTH CHINA).**
> **WEI-HAI-WEI GOLF CLUB.**
> *Inst.* **1901.** *Members*—**568.** *Nearest Large Town*—*Dalny*, **80** miles. *Hon. Sec.*—Engineer-Commander H. W. Harris, R.N., Wei-Hai-Wei. *Entrance Fee*—**2** dollars. *Subs.*—**15** dollars. *Holes*—**9** (on disintegrating granite soil). *Pro.*—A Chinaman. *Visitors*—**3** dollars per month ; there are Lady Members. Sunday play, with caddies.

/ *1912 Nisbet's Golf Yearbook*

members. Reginald Fleming Johnston, Assistant to Commissioner Lockhart, wrote in 1918 to the Commander House of the Royal British Navy at Liukung Island complaining about such stringent regulations.

In an article titled "The Links at Wei-Hai-Wei" published in the March 1, 2007 issue of *Through the Green*, British Golf Collectors Society's official journal, Miles Macnair wrote about his father's visits to Weihaiwei and experience of golfing there. Ian Macnair was a Royal Naval officer and visited Weihaiwei twice in the 1920s. The first visit was in 1920 when he was Third Officer on *HM Submarine L15*. He and his wife Ruth Macnair stayed at the Liukung Island Hotel. They enjoyed playing at the 9-hole golf links on the eastern end of the island. Ruth loved painting and photography and took a number of photos of the Liukung Island Golf Links.

/ *Liukung Island Golf Course in the 1920s*

According to Miles, his mother wrote about the golf links in a letter dated June 1920: "It is a very sporting little links--full of pitfalls--but most exciting. The tees are hard baked mud with a coconut door mat let in to drive off. The 'greens' are also hard mud with a little magic circle of sand round the hole--on a windy day it is almost impossible to remain on the 'green' at all!"

Ian and Ruth returned to Weihaiwei in 1927 when Ian was in command of *HM Submarine L27*. Miles said his father had spent the previous year supervising a major refit of the boat and had determined to take his motorcar, a Bleriot Whippet, out with him on his next voyage to the Far East. He was able to rebuild the ship with a torpedo-loading hatch considerably larger than all the other members of its class. Miles writes: "Reassembled on arrival, 'Bobjohn'

/ *1920 Weihaiwei Golf Clubhouse (Ruth Macnair)*

was the first car ever seen in Wei-Hai-Wei and I believe it must establish a record as the first (only?) car to have been 'smuggled' to an overseas posting on a Royal Navy Submarine." Ian was able to give rides to Reginal Johnston, who was then Commissioner of Weihaiwei, and had formerly been the English teacher of China's last emperor Pu Yi.

Jack Macnair, Miles' grandfather and Ian's father, was a noted golfer and twice won the championship of the Calcutta Golf Club in 1883 and 1885. He became Captain of the club in 1887 and was later honored as life Vice President of the second oldest golf club in the world after Scotland. Captain Edgar Dent, Miles' grandfather on his mother's side, was also a scratch golfer. He was for many years a member of the Pau Golf Club in France and in 1902 won the Shield of the Anstruther Golf Club.

According to a report from Shanghai in the January 10, 1924 *London and China Express*, Admiral Leveson of the *HMS. Hawkins* presented a trophy cup for competition to the Shanghai and Hungjao Golf Clubs on behalf

/ *Ian Macnair (Right) with Friends at Liukung Island Golf Links (Ruth Macnair)*

/ *East of the 9-Hole Liukung Island Golf Links (Ruth Macnair)*

of the United Service Golf Club (formerly the Weihaiwei Golf Club). The trophy was a tribute to the hospitality these clubs had accorded to naval officers during their service on the China Station. R.G. MacDonald, Captain of the Shanghai Golf Club, and R.J. Marshall, president of the Hungjao Golf Club, attended the ceremony aboard the *Hawkins* to receive it. The trophy cup was named "Weihaiwei Cup" and was competed for annually between the Shanghai Golf Club and Hungjao Golf Club.

/ *Colonel Macnair and Reginald Johnston (Ruth Macnair)*

According to Zhang Junyong, "after Weihaiwei was returned to China in 1930, Chinese Navy ships were often docked at Weihaiwei. The Royal Navy, which was permitted to stay at Liugong Island until 1940, started to communicate with the Chinese Navy in an effort to build a cordial relationship. The Weihaiwei Golf Club revised its rules on November 30, 1930 to accept Chinese officers, officials and navy officers of other foreign countries as honorary members. Shen Hung-lieh, Commander of China's Northeast Navy, and Hsü Tsu-shan, Commissioner of the Weihaiwei Special Administrative Region, were admitted as special foreign honorary members."

On September 27, 1930, *Illustrated London News*

/ *Liukung Island and Golf Course in the 1920s (Liu Weifeng)*

/ *Aerial View of Weihaiwei Golf Course in the 1930s*

published a photo news story on p. 538 about Liukung Island Golf Course. The caption of the photograph reads: "Showing the Golf Course: A View over the Island of Liu Kung-Tao, off Wei-Hai-Wei Which Will Serve as a Sanatorium and

Summer Resort for the British Navy for the Next Ten Years."

Zhang Junyong pointed out in his article that although Port Edward Golf Club had a popular golf links, due to its short 9 holes, it was not able to compete with golf clubs in Tsingtao and Dairen, which had large, 18-hole courses. For a time, it was reportedly trying to find a new site. After Weihaiwei was returned to China, the Port Edward Golf Course and the Liukung Island Golf Course were leased to British expatriates and the British Navy, respectively. According to the agreement between China and Britain with regard to the return of Weihaiwei, China was required to select appropriate land areas to function as public Parade Ground and golf course before they could redevelop the existing Parade Ground outside of the East Gate.

Port Edward Golf Course was located in the center of town and prevented the further development of the city. Hsü Tsu-shan was planning to rebuild the Parade Ground area using bricks of the old city wall and came to an understanding in November 1930 with the British Consulate and local expatriates to choose a new place for the golf course.

It was decided, at the suggestion of Ernst Clark, owner of Lavers & Clark Co., and Donald Clark, owner of the King's Hotel, to choose the

/ Liukung Island Golf Course in 1930

southwest side of Hech'ing Village as the new site for the golf course. Starting in October 1931, the Special Administration surveyed the area and planned to purchase 400 *mu* of the hill land for an 18-hole golf course. The British side was excited about the plan, believing that a new golf course, if completed, would surpass the Tsingtao Golf Course and become the best in North China. The plan failed due to opposition from the villagers and unexpected high cost for the purchase of the land.

According to the 1936, 1938 and 1939 editions of *Golfer's Handbook*, Weihaiwei Golf

/ 1930 Clubhouse of Weihaiwei Golf Course

Club was listed as he Royal Navy United Services Golf Club. The secretary was Royal Navy Surgeon A.C. Shaw in 1936. In 1938, the course was enlarged to 12 holes. The Secretary in 1939 was Royal Navy Surgeon A.A. Pomfret.

Liukung Island Golf Club was active after Weihaiwei was returned to China, according to Zhang Junyong. British naval officers and families flocked to Liukung Island during the summer and enjoyed golf. During the summer of 1933, total membership of the Liukung Island Golf Club reached 345, which prompted the British Consul to comment that Weihaiwei residents should be proud with the fact that the city boasted "one of only a few golf greens in China."

One of Liu Weifeng's collections is a photograph of sports trophies displayed on *HMS Kent* in 1933 during its visit at Liukung Island. British Navy warships organized all kinds of

/ *1937 Liukung Island Golf Course (Weihai Archives)*

/ *Weihaiwei Golf Course Caddies (Weihai Archives)*

/ *Liukung Island Golf Course in the 1930s*

sports activities during their stay in Weihaiwei, including but not limited to football, tennis, rifle shooting, races, sailing, canoeing, water polo, golf and bowling. The fourth trophy from the right of the third row has the words "Wei Hai Wei Cup" on it as well as a list of champions since 1911. The second on the same row is a golf trophy, sitting on three golf clubs attached to the bottom. Liu said that most of the silver sports trophies were made by local silversmiths.

Another photo in Liu's collection is *HMS Kent* taken in 1933 at the Weihai Bay. To the

/ Sports Trophies on Display at HMS Kent 1933 (Liu Weifeng)

/ Kent at Weihai Bay (Liu Weifeng)

/ Wei Hai Wei Cup

right of the bow of the ship was the "Four Eye Villa" built for the commander of the British Navy.

On October 1, 1940, the Japanese occupied Liukung Island and the British Navy withdrew on November 15. During the Pacific War, British expatriates were thrown into concentration camps. The one-time popular game of golf in Weihaiwei gradually declined.

In 2010, the Liugong Island Administration rebuilt the 9-hole golf course in an effort to

/ Weihaiwei Golf Club Postcard

/ Today's Liugong Island Golf Course

restore the historical sporting ground. On June 25, 2016, the China Golf Collectors' Society (now China Golf Heritage Society) was established and held its first annual meeting at the Liugong Island Golf Course. The meeting was attended by 13 founding members, including Michael Trostel, then Director of the USGA Golf Museum. A hickory golf tournament was held on the historical golf course.

For lack of approval from the central authorities, the golf course remains non-operational. The authors look forward to the future possible change in policy so that the Liugong Island Golf Course becomes a municipal public course open to local residents and visitors. If it happens, it would become China's earliest and existing golf course.

/ Hickory Meet of the China Golf Collectors' Society 2016

Foochow Golf Club

At the end of the Opium War, the late Ch'ing Government was forced to sign the Treaty of Nanking in 1842 and open five Chinese ports for trade, Foochow (Fuzhou) being one of them. In 1845, Great Britain set up a consulate office at Tsangshan (Cangshan) in Nant'ai (Nantai), Foochow and 17 other European countries and the U.S. followed suit. Foreign banks and businesses were established. Catholic and Protestant missionaries started to build churches, schools and hospitals.

Led by Great Britain, foreign consulates invested in building the Foochow Club in 1854. Alternatively referred to as the Billiard Room or International Club, the Foochow Club was completed in 1859.

Robert Nield pointed out in his book, *The China Coast: Trade and the First Treaty Ports*, that by the mid-1860s, the Foochow Club had "a billiards club, a fives courts, a bowling alley and a reading room."

In 1881, several British businesses applied to the government, via the British Consulate, to lease 161 *mu* of farmland at a cost of 1,400 taels of silver, to build a racecourse, which was approved. The area was located to the southern end of today's Park Road at Cangshan District. The School of Oriental and African Studies Archives at the University of Bristol has a photograph of the Foochow Race Course dated 1890. (https://www.hpcbristol.net/visual/os03-009)

We have found in historical documents the mention of "Foochow Recreation Club." This should be the alternative name for the Foochow Club after it added outdoor activities such as tennis, cricket and golf. According to a report from Foochow on p. 220 of the August 10, 1901 *Overland China Mail*, "Foochow Recreation

/ The Foochow Club (British Consulate on the Left)

/ 1890 Foochow Race Course (University of Bristol)

Club expects to receive $1,800 from the estate of the late Robert Lowe."

It was possible that the Foochow Recreation Club was formed in order to promote tennis, swimming, hunting and golf. As no specific information from overseas or domestic publications about the exact date the golf course was built in Foochow, we estimate that it should be around 1900 when the Foochow Recreation Club was formed.

According to the *London and China Telegraph* dating Monday March 6, 1905, "A scheme is afoot for the formation of golf links on the Foochow Recreation Ground. The links are to lie entirely within the creek which separates the Racecourse from the rest of the Recreation Ground. Arrangements are to be made that they do not interfere with cricket or lawn tennis, whilst no extra expense is involved, except possibly a small extra subscription from the votaries of the game."

One week later on March 13, 1905, the same newspaper confirmed that the subscribers to the recreation ground were almost unanimously in favor of golf links. "It will be a small course, but, with a creek all round and a good deal of ground that is very rough, the proposed seven holes will afford no little sport."

Ten years later, on February 1, 1915, *London and China Telegraph* quoted the *Foochow Echo* saying that golf once more came to the front at Foochow, "and quite a nice 8-hole links has been put in order. It is rumoured that Mr. Wilkinson has promised to present a cup for competition later on."

The earliest newspaper mention of Foochow Golf Club was found on p. 262 of the May 17, 1924 *North-China Herald* in a report about the Shanghai Golf Club. Titled "China Open Golf Championship," the report says: "It has been decided to establish an Open Amateur Golf Championship of China to be played for annually in Shanghai. The following clubs are asked to send in their entries before October 15, on which date the list of this year will be closed." The championship was planned for October 19 or 26. Foochow was among the 17 golf clubs invited in China, Japan and the Philippines.

CHINA OPEN GOLF CHAMPIONSHIP

An Annual Tournament to be Held at Shanghai in October: A Trophy Presented

It has been decided to establish an Open Amateur Golf Championship of China, to be played for annually at Shanghai. The following clubs are asked to send in their entries before October 15, on which date the list for this year will be closed:—

Hungjao Golf Club, Royal Hongkong Golf Club, Amoy Golf Club, Mukden Golf Club, Tientsin Golf Club, Weihaiwei Golf Club, Port Edward Golf Club (Weihaiwei), Hankow Golf Club, Nanking Golf Club, Peking Golf Club, Tsingtao Golf Club, Foochow Golf Club, Manila Golf Club, Tokio Golf Club, Yokohama Golf Club, Kobe Golf Club, Hodogaya Golf Club.

/ *China Open Amateur Golf Championship*

The Foochow Golf Course was built on a graveyard with only four holes in 1927, according to a letter by C.G.N. Graham, Lieutenant-Commander of the Royal Navy of Gillingham, Kent sent to the *Illustrated Sporting and Dramatic News* dated November 8, 1935. Titled "Golf in a Graveyard," Graham recounted his experience in 1927 playing golf at the Foochow Golf Club: "It was situated alongside the customs compound at Pagoda Anchorage, Foochow, whence started the famous tea clipper races of last century. This course was laid out entirely over a Chinese graveyard situated on the face of a hill, of gradient about one in five. There was a grave every few yards mostly with large stone fronts, lots of rocks, tufty grass, two joss houses, and a couple of cows;

in fact about three-quarters of an acre of golfing purgatory. The greens (or rather browns) were circular, about twelve feet in diameter, of packed sand, and surrounded by a three-inch wall fitted with a very necessary drain. The holes themselves were flowerpots. Flags were no longer supplied owing to the fondness of the nongolfing natives for acquiring them. The first hole, 120 yards long, was straight up the mountain side. The 100-yard second was straight down again, and the third was 100 yards across the face of the hill from right to left and required a neat cannon off a particularly large grave front to get on the brown. The fourth hole was back across the hill face 70 yards on to the second brown, thus four tees and three browns. Bogey was not published, but 50 strokes for four holes were quite good going. After 16 holes, a visit to the customs club, luckily not far away, was essential."

The fifth edition of the *Port Directory of the Principal Foreign Ports* in 1928 published by the U.S. Navy Department Office of Naval Intelligence listed Customs Club, Foochow Club, and Foochow Recreation Club under "Clubs." It reads: "The grounds of the Foochow Recreation Club may be obtained for baseball and other sports." Golf should have been one of the "other sports."

The revised edition of the 1932 *Commercial Travelers' Guide to the Far East* published by the Bureau of Foreign and Domestic Commerce, U.S. Department of Commerce listed clubs in Foochow as follows:

/ 1928 Port Directory of the Principal Foreign Ports

"Foochow Club (for Europeans); Japanese Club; Foochow Recreation Club (for tennis and golf)."

The 1936, 1938, 1939 and 1947 editions of the *Golfer's Handbook* all listed Foochow Golf Club under China. The address was Nant'ai, Foochow and the course had nine holes. It was indicated on p. 827 of the 1936 edition that

/ 1932 Commercial Travelers' Guide to the Far East

FOOCHOW

> 827
> **CHINA**
> Chiangkiang G. C., Chiangkiang.
> Chiaotso G. C., Chiaotso Honan, North China.
> Foochow G. C., Foochow. Membership, 40. Hon. Sec., D. G. Bruce, c/o Asiatic Petroleum Co., Ltd, Nantai, Foochow, China. 9 holes. Visitors' fees, 3 dols. per week.

/ 1932 Commercial Travelers' Guide to the Far East

> **CHINA**
> Chiaotso G. C., Chiaotso Honan, North China.
> Foochow G. C., Foochow. Membership, 40. Hon. Sec., J. Chubb, c/o Dodwell Co., Ltd., Nantai, Foochow, China. 9 holes. Visitors' fees, 3 dols. per week.

/ 1932 Commercial Travelers' Guide to the Far East

the club had 40 members with D.G. Bruce as Honorary Secretary and could be contacted at "c/o Asiatic Petroleum Co., Ltd., Nantai, Foochow, China." The Honorary Secretary of the Club was J. Chubb of Dodwell Co., Ltd. in 1939. Visitors' fees were 3 dollars per week.

Lin Liangmin, a resident of three generations at Tsangshan in Foochow, penned an article in March 2018 in the *HOMELAND* magazine titled "Create First-Rate Cangshan into a Unique Tourist Attraction in Southern China." He said in the article that after Foochow opened to foreign trade, Western culture started to be introduced into China. "Missionaries in Foochow realized that in order to integrate with local populace they must start with charity activities. Thus at Cangshan a number of educational institutions were established, including the Hwanan College, Union Theological Seminary, girls and boys middle schools, girls blind school, hospitals and churches. A number of foreign consulates were established and three cemeteries were built for British, American and French expatriates. Foochow Club, Rotary Club and Recreational Club were formed. Race course, golf course and tennis courts, etc. were also established." (http://www.xiujiangwang.com/newslist-3/39989418.htm)

Based on the above, our conclusion is that the Foochow Golf Course and Club were built around 1900 near the Foochow Maritime Customs at Tsangshan. It started with a few holes in a graveyard and later expanded to four and then nine holes. Due to the limited number of expatriates, the Foochow Golf Club had limited activities and it existed until the late 1940s.

Mukden Golf Courses and Clubs

Historically, Mukden (Shenyang) had three golf clubs and three golf links. The first one was the Mukden Cosmopolitan Golf Club with a "straight" 18-hole course built around 1904. The second was the Mukden Golf Club founded in 1911 with a 9-hole golf links at Peiling (Beiling or Northern Mausoleum). The third was the Mukden International Golf Club formed in 1935 and its 18-hole championship course was completed at Tungling (Dongling or Eastern Mausoleum) in 1938.

Mukden Cosmopolitan Golf Club

The mention of Mukden Cosmopolitan Golf Club was found on p. 6 of the January 1, 1905 issue of the London *Weekly Dispatch*. Reporter Charles E. Hands wrote a humorous story about the "Belated Knowledge Club" in Mukden, which reads: "We find plenty to do with our time. Mr. Frisk, the obliging polyglot manager of the Mukden branch of the Russo-Chinese Bank, has obtained a set of tennis things and given us the freedom of his asphalted court. So we have formed the Mukden Bouna Tennis Club, and are having silk clothes made by a Chinese tailor. The uniform is white with pink cummerbund and a red armlet with the letters 'B.K.' signifying 'Belated Knowledge,' in black."

He continues: "On Mr. Whigham's suggestion, the much-travelled correspondent of the '*Morning Post*,' who is a great golfer, we have also formed the Mukden Cosmopolitan Golf Club, and find the eagerness of the Chinese to serve as caddies very encouraging. The uniform is tweeds with a red band round the left arm bearing the black letters "B.K." signifying 'Beastly Knuisance.' We have an eighteen-hole straight course between the town and the railway station, but if you slice into the forbidden city you lose a stroke and do not get your ball back."

The "eighteen-hole straight course" was between the city and the railroad, next to Peiling (forbidden city). It should be a simple and straight course, 9-hole out and 9-hole in, built in 1904 or possibly even earlier.

Mukden Golf Club

In accordance with the 1903 and 1904 Renewed Treaty of Commerce and Navigation signed between the Ch'ing Government and Japan and the U.S., and related other agreements, Fengt'ien Prefecture (Fengtian Fu, or Shenyang) was open to foreign trade by order of the Ch'ing Government. As early as 1906, Charles Henry Oliver, the British Customs Commissioner, arrived in Mukden and opened the Fengt'ien Customs Office in February 1907.

The *London and China Telegraph* published a news story on February 24, 1908 about the establishment of an international club, the Mukden Club, with 33 founding members, which included eight Chinese, six Russians, five Japanese, five British, four Germans, three Americans, one Swiss and one Norwegian. Among the Chinese members were Tang Shao-yi and heads of various government departments.

The Mukden Club had a golf division founded in 1911 which later developed into the Mukden Golf Club. This historical fact was revealed in a report in the *Manchuria Daily News* on June 8, 1936. The report said that a ceremony of deed transfer was held on May 27 at the

Mukden Yamato Hotel between the newly formed Mukden International Golf Club and the former Mukden Golf Club. After the opening remarks by H.E. Parkinson, chairman of the Mukden Club, Y. Imagawa, Managing Director of the new club said: "In Mukden golf was initiated a quarter of a century ago by the people who established the Mukden Golf Club, which was the golfing section of the Mukden Club, and has been successfully developed to the present state of popularity."

The Mukden Golf Club was able to build a 9-hole golf course at Peiling in 1913-1914 after it was formed. A news story about the opening of the new golf pavilion of the Mukden Golf Club was published in the May 12, 1914 issue of the *Manchuria Daily News*. The report said the new Golf Pavilion was formally opened on Saturday the 9th in the presence of a large number of members. In an opening remark, T.D. Moorhead, Esq., President of the Mukden Club, paid "an eloquent tribute to the generosity and courtesy of the Chinese authorities in placing the Course on the historical Pei-Ling at the free disposal of the Club for a definite period." Moorhead thanked Mr. Witte in designing the "suitable and attractive" pavilion building. The pavilion was octagonal in design and situated near the first tee, commanding an uninterrupted view of the entire course. It had ample dressing room accommodation with lockers for both ladies and gentlemen. The central club room possessed a spacious covered verandah. After the ceremony, a match was played between the Golf Club Committee members and the rest, the former winning by half a point. The Golf Committee announced that it would entertain the members of the club to tiffin in the Pavilion on Saturday the 16th and the May Medal would be played.

There were reports in the June and July 1914 issues of *Manchuria Daily News* about the numerous competitions at the Mukden Golf Club, including five matches for the Newchwang (Niuzhuang) Cup and five matches for the Captain's Cup. At the semi-final competition for the Newchwang Cup in July, Cummings defeated C. Gunn 6 and 5 to play. Shaw defeated Fontanier 6 and 5 to play. In the final individual 36-hole match play, Shaw beat Cummings by 1 up.

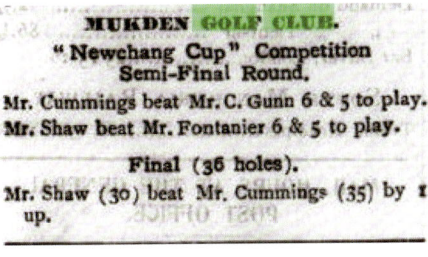

/ Newchwang Cup

The first round of Captain's Cup Competition was played among 24 members. After three rounds, the semi-final was played on October 22. F.W. Pickance beat E.A. Pritchard 2 up and B.B. Frost beat P.C. Colman 5 and 5 up. During the final competition of 36 holes held on October 24-25, Frost won the championship by beating Pickance 5 and 4 up. It was

/ Mukden Yamoto Hotel

one of the most successful match plays at the Mukden Golf Club, according to *Manchuria Daily News*. More than 30 members attended a dinner after the event and Captain Colman presented the Captain's Cup to the champion.

An inter-port competition was also held on October 24-25, 1914 between Mukden and Newchwang Golf Clubs, with six players coming from each side. Mukden defeated Newchwang by half a point in individual play. Mukden won the foursome matches by 3:0. A lady's competition was also played for the first time at Mukden, in which Mrs. E.S. Bolitho beat Mrs. H.H. Taylor 6 and 5 up. The Newchwang team was invited to dinner at the Mukden Golf Club after the competition.

/ *Mukden vs. Newchwang*

The Mukden Golf Links was located at the North Market outside of the Hsiao Hsi Men (Xiaoximen or Small West Gate) in Mukden, close to Peiling. It was built in a graveyard. According to Chinese language internet reports, the Young Marshall Chang Hsueh-liang organized a golf team under his name Han Ch'ing and built a special road leading to the golf club. As most members of the Mukden Golf Club were foreigners, it was referred to as the International Golf Club.

The July 10, 1920 issue of *North-China Herald* printed a piece of news from Mukden titled "Tennis in Full Swing." It reads on p. 91: "Golf has given place to tennis, although there are still a few enthusiasts who play every Sunday before breakfast in order to be in good form for the opening of next season."

The same newspaper published a letter dated July 22 from a T.S.S. in Shanghai on p. 395 of the August 5, 1922 issue, which reads:

"To the Editor of the *North-China Daily News*:

Sir, -- I have lately been in Mukden and was there also a guest at the local Golf Club.

Having been handed a copy of the 'Local By-Laws,' I was not a little astonished and amused to read the following unique paragraphs: --

3. Graves in course of construction and *open* coffins shall be regarded as ground under repair. Old grave pits are not covered by this 'By-Law.'

15. Graves and ditches surrounding graves are not bunkers. A ball may, etc.

The explanation is that the golf holes are located in the extensive cemetery of the city and curious to say its inhabitants and their spirits appear to have no objection at all."

The *Singapore Free Press and Mercantile Advertiser* of the same date reprinted the same letter from the *North-China Herald*.

Young Marshall Chang Hsueh-liang was an honorary member of the Mukden Club and the Golf Club and "an ardent supporter of it," according to a report on p. 446 of the September 20, 1924 *North-China Herald*. "He is often to be seen playing tennis with the few members who are equal to giving him a game. He is an excellent shot, a keen beginner at golf and fond of associating with foreigners by whom he is generally adjudged a sportsman and a gentleman."

Starting from October 1924, Shanghai Golf Club started to organize a China Open Amateur Golf Championship, according to a report in the May 17, 1925 *North-China Herald*. The Mukden Golf Club was among the dozen or so golf clubs being invited. The Open Amateur Golf Championship would be medal play of 72 holes, with a registration fee of $5.

Frank G. Carpenter, an American traveler published a book, *Carpenter's World Travels: China*, in 1925. The author wrote on p. 252 of

CHINA OPEN GOLF CHAMPIONSHIP

An Annual Tournament to be Held at Shanghai in October: A Trophy Presented

It has been decided to establish an Open Amateur Golf Championship of China, to be played for annually at Shanghai. The following clubs are asked to send in their entries before October 15, on which date the list for this year will be closed:—

Hungjao Golf Club, Royal Hongkong Golf Club, Amoy Golf Club, Mukden Golf Club, Tientsin Golf Club, Weihaiwei Golf Club, Port Edward Golf Club (Weihaiwei), Hankow Golf Club, Nanking Golf Club, Peking Golf Club, Tsingtao Golf Club, Foochow Golf Club, Manila Golf Club, Tokio Golf Club, Yokohama Golf Club, Kobe Golf Club, Hodogaya Golf Club.

/ *China Open Golf Championship*

his visit to Peiling and the Mukden Golf Links: "I drove out yesterday over the four miles to Peiling, as the North Mausoleum is known, passing in turn the mounds of an old Chinese cemetery and a golf course where the foreign residents of Mukden were driving their balls over the green turf. The East Mausoleum, or Tung-ling, is ten miles from the city, while the ashes of a third emperor lie buried in still another tomb, Yung-ling, almost a hundred miles distant."

On September 19, 1925, *North-China Herald* published two separate reports about a donkey riding event on September 5 near the clubhouse of the Mukden Golf Club. The story on p. 283 said, "a donkey gymkhana took place near the Golf Club with the maximum of fun and amusement." Participants had to ride without saddles, without whips and with but a single rein. "Needless to say, the donkeys did all that was expected from donkeys. Some did not start at all, others started and elected to take their riders back to where they came from." The story on p. 281 said that "in case there is no information to the Chinese government for the said race, the Chinese policemen of Mukden have consequently sent one officer to stop them. The Chairman (an Englishman of the Golf Club) did therefore stop the race immediately to show that they are obedient to the national articles for making good feelings to the Chinese to save some trouble."

The same report from Mukden on p. 283 said that despite rumors of war, Mukden on the surface was a prosperous city. The number of new foreign firms that had started in the city within the last six months was considerable. Building operations were being conducted on a large scale. A track for electric tram car service was laid out, a cinema planned and construction of several large hotels completed. The U.S. Steel Products Co. was competing with a European company for providing steel to build the Mukden-Heilung Railway.

The report confirmed that the Mukden Golf Links was located outside the Hsiao Hsi Men, also known as Wai Rang Men, to the northwest of the inner city. The place in the 1920s was the North Market, an area of 10 square km that was opened as a "free trade" zone after the 1894-1895 Sino-Japanese War. British and American tobacco companies were set up in the area, which became an important transportation hub for Mukden. To the west was the Japanese South Manchuria Railway and to the north the Chinese Peking-Fengt'ien Railway. Hsiao Hsi Men Station was the end of the Peking-Fengt'ien line. To the south was the horse rail line jointly operated by Japan and China, connecting Fengt'ien Railway Station with the inner city of Mukden.

On Sunday October 18, 1925, an inter-port golf match between Dairen and Mukden was held at the Mukden Golf Club, according to a report in *Manchuria Daily News* on October 20. The Dairen team of 12 golfers had arrived on Friday and played a practice rounds on Saturday. After a 6:6 tie in the singles event in the morning, the four-ball match had to be cancelled due to a blizzard.

Another report in the same newspaper dated March 27, 1926 was about the annual general meeting of the Mukden Golf Club held on the evening of March 23. Presided by F.F. Wilkinson, the Honorary Treasurer N.M. Fulton delivered the financial reports, which were approved. The new committee for 1926 were elected, which included V.L. Fairley, J.F. McMun, A.J. Carter, W.A. Hawkes and N.M. Fulton.

On April 29, 1926, the same newspaper reported that the Hoshigaura Golf Club in Dairen would visit Mukden on May 10 for an inter-port match. B. Yasuhiro, General Manager of South Manchuria Railway, would present a challenge cup for the competition. The fifth inter-port match between Dairen and Mukden was held at the Mukden Golf Club on October 17, 1927.

At the annual meeting of the Mukden Golf Club held on March 30, 1928, J.H. McMun was elected Captain, according to a report in *Manchuria Daily News* dated April 4, 1928. It was also reported that on October 15, in a match between American and British golfers at Mukden, the Americans beat the British 5:1 in individual event in the morning. The four-ball match in the afternoon was canceled due to a storm.

A photo news story was published on p. 259 of the July 30, 1927 issue of the *Illustrated Sporting and Dramatic News* in London with the

> **MUKDEN NOTES**
>
> (Mukden, Mar. 25)
> Mr. Tarrant, of the P.M. Railway, visited Mukden yesterday.
> The annual meeting of the Moukden Golf Club was held on Tuesday evening under the chairmanship of Mr. F. E. Wilkinson. The statement of accounts and balance sheet as presented by the Hon. Treasurer, Mr. N. M. Fulton, was approved. The Committee for 1926 was constituted as follows:
> Messrs. V. L. Fairley, J. F. McMun, A. J. Carter, W. A. Hawkes, and N. M. Fulton.
> While members of the foreign community regret the coming departure of Mr. Toshi Go, they join in congratulating him upon his well deserved promotion. Mr. Go, who has been appointed manager of the New York Office of the South Manchuria Raiway Company, leaves Mukden on March 31st.
> Mr. T. D. W. Bannister, of Shanghai is on a business visit to Mukden.

/ *1926 Mukden GC Committee*

caption "The Royal and Ancient in the Land of the Ancient Civilization: Marshall Chang Hsueh-liang with His Wife and Children." In the photo, Chang's wife Yu Feng-chih was ready to tee off with Chang standing on the left watching. Their two children and two caddies were watching below the raised teeing ground. The report says: "Marshall Chang Hsueh-Liang, who is twenty-six years of age, is the eldest son of General Chang Tso-Lin, the present dictator of North China. He graduated from the Mukden Military Academy. Though golf is his favourite recreation, he is also fond of tennis and bowls. Known as 'the Young General,' he has a charming wife, three sons and one daughter. His wife is here at a tee on a Chinese Course."

The Mukden Golf Course looked quite rudimentary in the photo.

The Sphere published a photo of Chang Hsueh-liang on a golf course with his secretary on p. 292 of the August 20, 1927 issue. The secretary should be Chen Ta-chang.

/ *Chang Hsueh-liang and His Secretary on the Golf Course*

/ *Chang Hsueh-liang and Wife Playing Golf in 1927*

In 1929, Wellington Ku, Foreign Minister of the Peiyang Government, stayed in Mukden as Chang Hsueh-liang's private advisor during the summer. In his memoir published in 1997, Ku said on p. 150 that he would play golf with the Young Marshall three or four times a week. Chang had to rest at a small house with veranda drinking fruit juice as his health was a problem due to drug addiction. The golf course was close to a railway line busy with trains passing by. One day Ku saw an entire train packed with soldiers going by. The Young Marshall told him that he was sending troops to the north trying to scare the Russians.

On July 8, 2016, the Chinese language *Daily Headlines* (meiri toutiao) published an article by Wenbohui which reads: "The Young Marshall's love of golf has become a hyping gimmick among Chinese golfers. As the No. 1 playboy of Republican China, Chang speaks English, drives a car, flies an airplane, and learns the popular European game of golf during the 1st World War in Europe." (https://kknews. cc/zh-my/history/ngqjb2. html)

The article went on: "After the Young Marshall took control of the Peiyang Government, he often went to the golf course at Peiling with Edith Chao. Golfers at Peiling were no ordinary people. They were close associates of the Young Marshall and foreign diplomats. The golf course was known as an International Golf Course. Chang played golf not only for exercise. He had two yellow office buildings to the west of the golf course and often arranged meetings with VIPs." The author said that the yellow office buildings are now next to today's Beiling Dajie and they

/ *Chang Hsueh-liang and Yu Feng-chih Playing Golf*

used to be the Northeast Office of the People's Liberation Army General Armament Department.

It was reported in the March 28, 1931 issue of *Manchuria Daily News* that at the annual meeting of the Mukden Golf Club held on March 20, "His

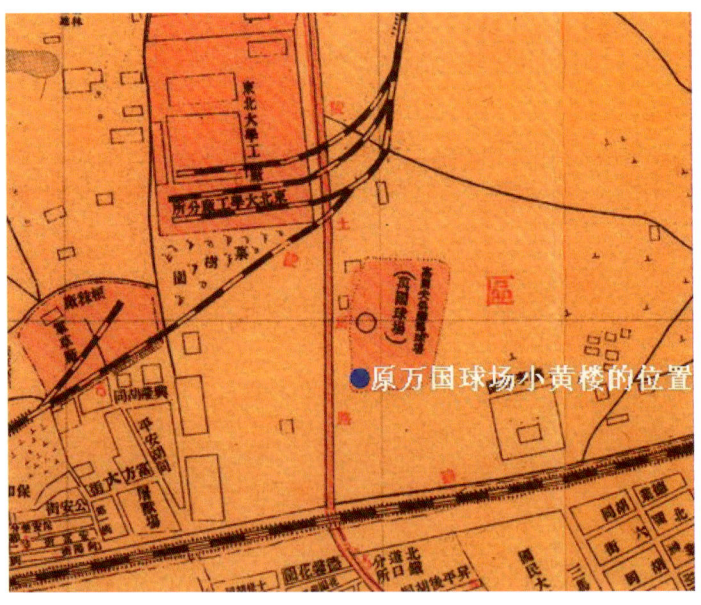

/ *International Golf Course 1931 and Yellow Building*

Excellency Marshall Chang Hsueh Liang was unanimously elected Hon. President of the Golf Club." The meeting also elected a new committee for 1931, which included F.N. Merritt, W. Donald, T.Y.C. Lee, L.C. Kampf and P. Monaghan. The Committee was endeavoring to make the course into first class conditions and work had been started on several minor changes which would be advantageous to all players. Kampf was manager of Andersen, Meyer & Co., Ltd. in Tientsin.

MUKDEN NOTES

(Mar. 26)

At the Annual General Meeting of the Moukden Golf Club, held last Friday, His Excellency Marshal Chang Hsueh Liang was unanimously elected Hon. President, of the Golf Club, and the following committee appointed for 1931, Messrs. F.N. Merritt, W. Donald, T. Y. C. Lee, L. C. Kampf and P. Monaghan. Much is in store for the Members this year as the committee is endeavoring to have the course in first class condition right from the start and work has already been started on several minor changes which will be advantageous to all players.

/ *International Golf Course 1931 and Yellow Building*

The same newspaper reported on June 18 the result of the Ladies China Cup golf competition at the Mukden Golf Club. Miss Anna Broad won the Cup. The golf medal for June was won by P. Monaghan.

Manchuria Daily News reported on February 1, 1933 that the Mukden Golf Club held an annual tea dance at the Mukden Club on January 29 and awarded the winners of the 1932 season competitions. These included Captain's Cup winner L. Kampf; Championship A winner L. Kampf; Championship B winner F.E.T. Marshall; International Cup (America) winners L.C. Jones, L. Kampf, E. Cummings, G.A. Booth, F.N. Merritt and M.S. Myers; Kiangwan Cup winners Shanghai Fours F.E.T. Marshall and E. Cummings; Spring Knockout winner A. Hobday; Mixed Foursomes Tombstone winners Mrs. Hobday and W. Mayger; Two Ball Mixed Foursome winners Mrs. E.H. Gordon and S.W.P. Perry; Captain Cup winner L.C. Jones; De's Cup winner Mrs. Hobday; China Cup winner Mrs. Gordon; Mike's Cup winner W. Mayger; Hong Two Ball Fours winners C. Christopherson and L.C. Venator; Papa Cup winner W. Mayger; Powhattan Cup winner G.M. Lister; Donald Cup winner: Mrs. Cummings; S.O.C.O.N.Y. Cup winner L.C. Jones; The Marshall's Cup winner G.A. Booth; Dodge Cup winners G.M. Lister and W.W.P. Perry; The Golfers Cups winners W. Storms and T. Ohno; Easter Bogey winner L. Kampf; April Bogey winner E. Cummings; April Medal winner L.C. Jones; May Medal winner A. Hobday; June Bogey winner W. Storms; June Medal winner G.C. Large; July Bogey winner L. Kampf; July Medal winner C. Christopherson; August Bogey winner A.O. Hyland; August Medal winner E. Cummings; September Bogey winner F.E.T. Marshall; September Medal winner A.O. Hyland; October Bogey winner L. Kampf; October Medal winner L.C. Venator. The list of extensive competition winners showed that 1932 was one of the busiest years for the Mukden Golf Club.

According to reports in *Manchuria Daily News* in September and October 1933, an interport competition between Mukden and Fushun Golf Clubs was held on September 10, 1933. Sixteen players from each team participated at the Fushun Golf Club. Mukden's Captain L. Kampf was unable to attend due to health reason. Fushun won both the individual play by 9:4 and the two-ball foursome by 5:3.

/ *1933 Players of Dairen Hoshigaura and Mukden GC*

/ *1934 Mukden and Fushun GC Inter-Port Match*

At an International Cup competition played on September 24, 1933 at the Mukden Golf Club, the British team beat the U.S. team by 20:18. The Japanese team came out 3rd. A lady's 18-hole medal play was held on October 14 and a 36-hole bogey competition was held on October 15.

On October 22, 1933, the first inter-port competition between Dairen and Mukden since 1930 took place at the Hoshigaura Golf Club in Dairen, with 12 players from each team. Dairen beat Mukden by a big margin. After lunch, players took a photograph at the golf course. The fourth from the left on the first row was J. Furusawa, Captain of the Hoshigaura Golf Club. Sitting behind him was L. Kampf, Captain of Mukden Golf Club.

On June 10, 1934, Mukden and Fushun had an inter-port competition participated by 20 members from each golf club, according to a report in *Manchuria Daily News*. Mukden beat Fushun 31:5, with individual play at 15:5 and foursome at 16:0. The players took a photo after the event at the Mukden Golf Club.

The Lafayette College library in the

U.S. owns two digital photographs of the Mukden Golf Club. The photographs were taken in April 1935 by Gerald Warner, U.S. Deputy Consul to Mukden. One photo shows the parking lot in front of the Golf Club, with a few cars. Written on the board to the right were the words: "Shenyang Golf Course, important site... not allowed." (https://ldr.lafayette.edu/concern/images/x633f215b)

The other is a photo of the clubhouse in front of which a golfer was practicing. An American car was parked to the left, with caddies standing.

According to the website of the U.S. Consulate General in Shenyang, "the U.S. Consulate in Shenyang was opened in 1904. It was originally housed in two abandoned Chinese temples, Yi Kung Ssu and Scwang Chen Ssu, located outside the Little West Commerce Gate. Sometime before 1924, the Consulate moved to No. 1 Wu Wei Lu, a building which used to house the Russian Consulate."

The website continues: "In the early part of the 20th century, northeast China underwent enormous economic development and population growth. Due primarily to the advent of the railroads developed by Japanese and Russian interests and the rapid in-migration of settlers from Shandong Province and the Korean Peninsula, Shenyang (known then as 'Mukden' to most Americans), Harbin, Dalian, Changchun, and other places grew from almost nothing into major cities. For the Americans who were stationed there in the 1930s and 40s, however, Shenyang increasingly resembled a frontier outpost marked by adventure and danger. Consulate staff dealt with rampant

/ *Mukden International Golf Course Parking Lot (Lafayette College)*

/ *Mukden Golf Clubhouse (Lafayette College)*

lawlessness, violence, and the complex conflict in Manchuria between an increasingly large Japanese presence in the region, continuing Chinese resistance, and lingering Russian influence." (https:// china. usembassy-china. org. cn/zh/embassy-consulates-zh/shenyang-zh/)

The website quoted a story published on p. 5 of the September 23, 1932 *New York Times* titled "American Golfers in Mukden Carry Guns to Resist Bandits." The story reads: "After bandits unsuccessfully attacked the American Consul General during a golf game, Americans began to carry guns whenever they went out to the golf course."

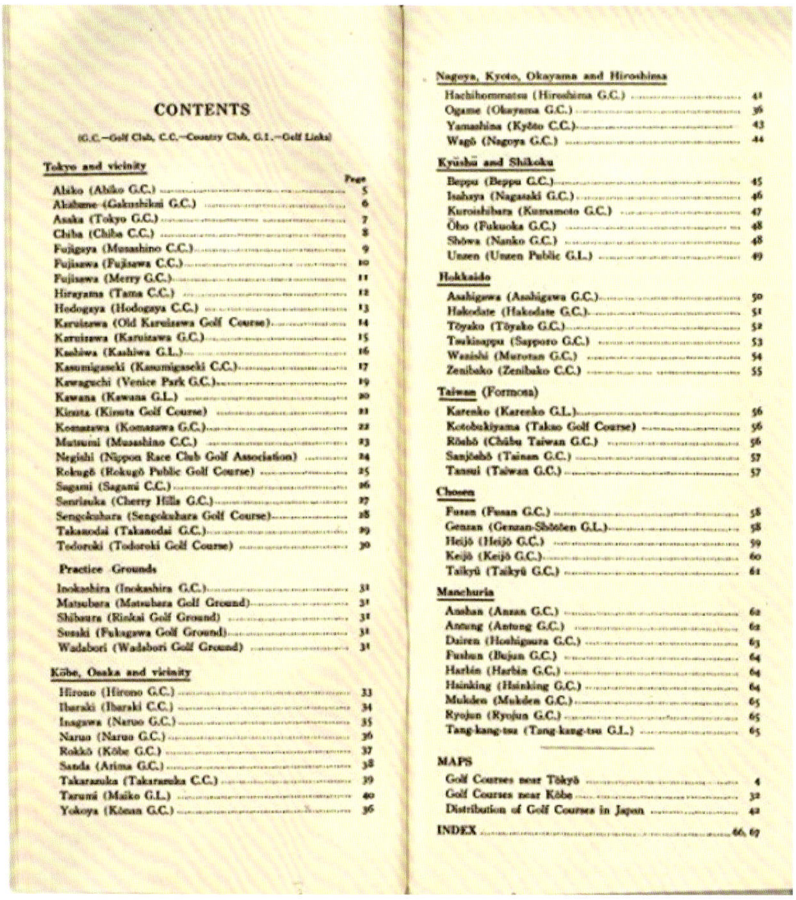

CONTENTS

(G.C.—Golf Club, C.C.—Country Club, G.L.—Golf Links)

/ *Golf in Japan*

In 1934, the Japan Government Railways Board of Tourist Industries published a pamphlet so-called *Golf in Japan*. It is a review of 30 years of development of golf in Japan since 1903 when an Englishman started a four-hole golf course in Kobe. In addition to the list of golf courses and clubs in Japan, the booklet also listed golf courses and clubs in Taiwan and Manchuria under Japanese control. Listed under Manchuria were golf clubs in Anshan, Antung (Dandong), Dairen, Fushun, Harbin, Hsinking (Changchun), Mukden (Shenyang), Ryojun (Lvshun) and Tang-kang-tzse (Tanggangzi).

The Mukden Golf Club listed in the so-called *Golf in Japan* has the following detailed information:

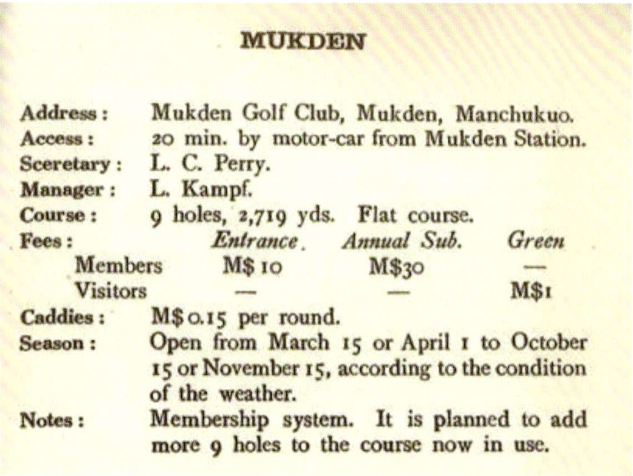

MUKDEN

Address: Mukden Golf Club, Mukden, Manchukuo.
Access: 20 min. by motor-car from Mukden Station.
Secretary: L. C. Perry.
Manager: L. Kampf.
Course: 9 holes, 2,719 yds. Flat course.
Fees:

	Entrance	*Annual Sub.*	*Green*
Members	M$ 10	M$30	—
Visitors	—	—	M$1

Caddies: M$0.15 per round.
Season: Open from March 15 or April 1 to October 15 or November 15, according to the condition of the weather.
Notes: Membership system. It is planned to add more 9 holes to the course now in use.

/ *Mukden Golf Club*

A Chinese web story claimed that the Mukden International Golf Club was built by Chang Hsueh-liang in 1927, which started with nine holes. This remains to be verified. During the time that Chang was the president of the Northeast University, he did plan to build a golf course as part of the project in the construction of the Peiling Sports Ground. But due to the Japanese invasion, the plan most likely did not materialize.

According to media reports during the period of the Republic of China, Chang Hsueh-liang established a T'ungtze (Tongze) Club in Mukden which included a 9-hole mini golf course. On November 14, 2015, http://golf.sina.cn reprinted a story published in the *Beijing Morning News* about the history of mini golf in Shenyang started by Chang Hsueh-liang in 1930. Titled "Chang Hsueh-liang Created 'Mini Golf' Course with 9 Sections and 9 Holes," Xiao Yifei reviewed a special report published in Volume 14 No. 673 of the *Peiyang Pictorial* in Tientsin on September 5, 1930. As the first of a special page dedicated to "Small Golf," the weekly newspaper featured an "Introduction to the T'ungtze Special Golf Course." According to the lead article, "Thoughts on the Founding of T'ungtze Mini Golf," the so-called "mini golf" referred to a golf course appropriately reduced in size to allow people enjoy the game of golf. The page also had an article about the scheme and methods of play titled "Structure of a Special Outdoor Golf Course."

The lead article reads: "The T'ungtze Club in Shenyang was created by Deputy Commander Chang (Chairman of the Board) of the Army, Navy and Air Force, with support from Mrs. Chang. After moving to the commercial district, the organizers made special efforts in developing the new area which has become a popular place in the city....The Club opened on the 23rd of last month which attracted large crowd of people as it was open free on the first day. Players pay only $0.40 per week, including entrance fee. The Club will organize a competition in a month and enthusiastic players are now practicing day and night in preparation."

The article continues: "This 'mini golf' course, the first of its kind in China, opened on August 23, 1930 in Shenyang, with free admission on the first day. Entrance fees are affordable. The unique structure of the golf course follows the geography of Peking-Tientsin-Hepei. The course is divided into 9 districts and 9 holes, with a standard Par of 50 strokes. The player starts driving out from the first district, 'Shenyang East Tower,' passing 'Shanghai Fort' into 'Tientsin' and then 'Peiping,' touring the 'Temple of Heaven,' 'Peihai Park,' 'Ming Tombs' and ending at the 'Summer Palace.' Playing at the mini golf course represents a tour from Shenyang to Peking." The page also features a picture of the Peking-Tientsin-Hepei layout. The T'ungtze Mini Golf Course was basically a putting golf course. (http://sports. sina. com. cn/golf/chinareport/2015-11-14/doc-ifxksqis4825645.shtml)

The *Illustrated London News* dated July 26, 1930, ran a special report about Chang Hsueh-liang on p. 154, with a photograph of Chang playing golf. The caption reads: "The Youngest Governor in China: Field-Marshall Chang Hsueh-liang Playing Golf." The report says: "His Excellency, who is a keen golfer, has given the Mukden community an excellent nine-hole course." We believe this refers to the T'ungtze Mini Golf Course.

The 1935 officers of the Mukden Golf Club were elected, according to a report in *Manchuria Daily News* dated April 16, 1935. These included Captain T. Ohno, Vice-Captain D.F.A. Wallace, Honorary Treasurer H.R. Malcolm, Honorary Secretary H.A. Rosemen, members L.C. Jones, J. Nittoh, J. Haag-Pedersen.

In a report dated July 1, 1935, the same

/ 1930 Chang Hsueh-liang Playing Golf

newspaper reported the result of the inter-port match between Mukden and Fushun Golf Clubs held on June 27. Mukden crashed Fushun with a score of 11:0. This was the third time that Mukden won the competition against Fushun, thereby winning outright the trophy cup presented by Kanji Usami. Mukden also took away Fushun's pennant. Players took a photo at the Mukden Golf Course after the event.

Mukden International Golf Club

According to an agreement reached between the boards of the newly formed Mukden International Golf Club and Mukden Golf Club, the former took over all of the latter's property assets and liabilities on May 5, 1935, as reported in *Manchuria Daily News* on May 6. Four members of the Mukden Golf Club—M.W. Wood, A. Boixo, E. Cummings and A. Hobday—took over seats on the board of directors of the new Club. Managing directors of the Mukden International Golf Club were Y. Imagawa, J. Nittoh and T. Ikeda.

/ Mukden International Golf Club

/ 1935 Mukden vs. Fushun

Mukden golfers decided to build a new golf course, according to a report in the May 21, 1936 *Manchuria Daily News*. The new Mukden International Golf Club founded a year ago and led by Chairman K. Usami and directors J. Nittoh, Y. Imagawa and T. Ikeda, would build a new 18-hole championship course in the environs of Tungling and the Hun River. The report said: "The site of the course, which will occupy 150 acres of land located from the General Direction of State Railway, will be just south of the Mukden-Kirin railway line, opposite Tungling Station. Mr. R. Akaboshi of Tokyo, a well-known Japanese golfer and golf-course architect, is planning the lay-out and is coming here to supervise the construction work, which will cost, including its club house, about 200,000 yen. The work will be completed in the second half of next year. It is expected that a new road will be built to the golf course and a regular bus service will be available. The course is also readily accessible by the local gasoline car service maintained by the General Direction of State Railways. The present nine-hole course located on the road to Peiling, will still be used until the new course is completed."

The report also said that the Mukden International Golf Club had been organized under Japanese laws by special permission from the Tokyo Foreign Office. The membership of the Club, which stood at 120, was expected to increase to 400.

The property transfer between the Mukden Golf Club and the new Mukden International Golf Club took place on May 27, 1936 at the Yamato Hotel, according to a report by the same newspaper dated June 8. After H.E. Parkinson, Chairman of the Mukden Club handed the Deed of Gift of the property at Peiling to the new Club, Y. Imagawa, Managing Director of the new Club said: "In Mukden golf was initiated a quarter of century ago by the people who established the Mukden Golf Club which was the golfing section of the Mukden Club, and has been successfully developed to its present state of popularity." Imagawa said that "the number of golfers has grown so much so that we now feel that the present golf course is too small. We therefore decided to plan the establishment of a new course occupying a larger area of land, and after some preparations we succeeded in organizing the Mukden International Golf Club. A fine course will be placed at your disposal in the near future at Tungling."

The first phase of the new course construction was completed by the end of November 1936. *Manchuria Daily News* reported on November 29 that Chairman K. Usami and the Club Committee inspected the new course, which covered an area of 250,000 tsubo (about 827,500 square meters). It was 20,000 tsubo larger than the Hirono Golf Course. The well-known Japanese golfer and golf course architect R. Akaboshi had been working here since May.

The *Fortnightly Supplement* of *Manchuria Daily News* on December 15, 1936 published a panoramic photo of the new course. The caption reads: "The new golf course of eighteen holes in the neighbourhood of the Hun River, occupying an area of 250,000 tsubo which has been lately completed for the Mukden International Golf Club. It is said to be the largest golf course in the Orient."

Manchuria Daily News on May 1, 1938 reported that the construction of the new 18-hole championship course of the Mukden International Golf Club was expected to be completed and open at the beginning of July. The new course, designed by noted Japanese course architect R. Akaboshi, had an area of 150 acres in the scenic

The new golf course of eighteen holes in the neighbourhood of the Hun River, occupying an area of 250,000 tsubo which has been lately completed for the Mukden International Golf Club. It is said to be the largest golf course in the Orient.

area next to Tungling and the Hun River. The course was located about 12 km from the Walled City. A regular bus service would be provided between the city and the golf course. It took about 25 minutes to reach the golf course from the Yamato District. As the course was situated just 1 km to the south of Tungling Station on the Mukden-Kirin line, it was readily accessible by local gasoline cars from the Station.

The new 18-hole championship golf course opened to the public in July 1938. A special summer train for afternoon trips to Tungling started operating daily from the Mukden Station. The train was scheduled to leave Mukden Station at 3:20 pm and return at 4:46 pm from Tungling.

A special golf tournament of 18-hole medal competition was held on May 14, 1939 to mark the opening of the new clubhouse of the Mukden International Golf Club, according to a report in *Manchuria Daily News* on May 21. The new clubhouse was built at a cost of 120,000 yen and was designed by local architect Kurolwa. Sitting on an area of 300 tsubo, the house "represents a beautiful building with a spacious veranda. It has a comfortable bar, a dining hall, a shower and lockers for golfers."

During the 2nd World War, the Mukden International Golf Course became a costume factory of the Japanese Kwantung Army, leading to its decline and closure.

Chinkiang Golf Club

The British Settlement in Chinkiang (Zhenjiang) was one of the seven settlements of the United Kingdom in modern China. The other six were Shanghai, Hankow, Tientsin, Kiukiang, Canton and Amoy. Chinkiang became the 3rd treaty port along the Yangtze River after the Treaty of Tientsin was signed between the U.K. and China in 1858. In early 1861, the Chinkiang Magistrate and a British Consul signed an agreement to lease an open area by the river about 2.5 km outside of the West Gate to the British, which included 150 *mu* of flat land and the Silver Mountain.

Thanks to its location at the intersection of the Yangtze River and the Grand Canal between Peking and Hangzhou, Chinkiang swiftly grew into a shipping and trade center during the 50 years from the late 19th to the early 20th centuries. Famous shipping and trading firms such as Jardine Matheson, Butterfield & Swire and the China Merchant Group built shipping docks and trading companies inside or near the British Settlement.

In an article, "Social Life and the Return of the British Settlement at Chinkiang" published on the Internet on September 11, 2020, Zhang Zhengrong writes: "With the growth of domestic and international trade and rapid economic growth, foreign expatriates and domestic immigrants flocked to Chinkiang. This led to growing ties between the settlement and the outside world. Different life styles and cultures interact inside the settlement, leading to a merger of new and old, Chinese and Western, creating a unique social and cultural life. There was a rise inside the settlement of Western entertainment and recreation activities such as parks, golf, dancing, night club, circus, horse racing, athletics, swimming, etc. The Sailor's Club at Chinkiang featured local opera, bowling, chess and a reading room. The settlement also organized a race course, tennis and sports ground at Taiku and Paoma Mountains."

Chinkiang Golf Club was founded in 1905, according to Volume 19 of the 1905-06 *Golfing Annual* published in London. On p. 221 was listed information of Chinkiang Golf Club as follows:

"Chinkiang Golf Club, INSTITUTED 1905. *Captain*--C.E. Holsworthy,

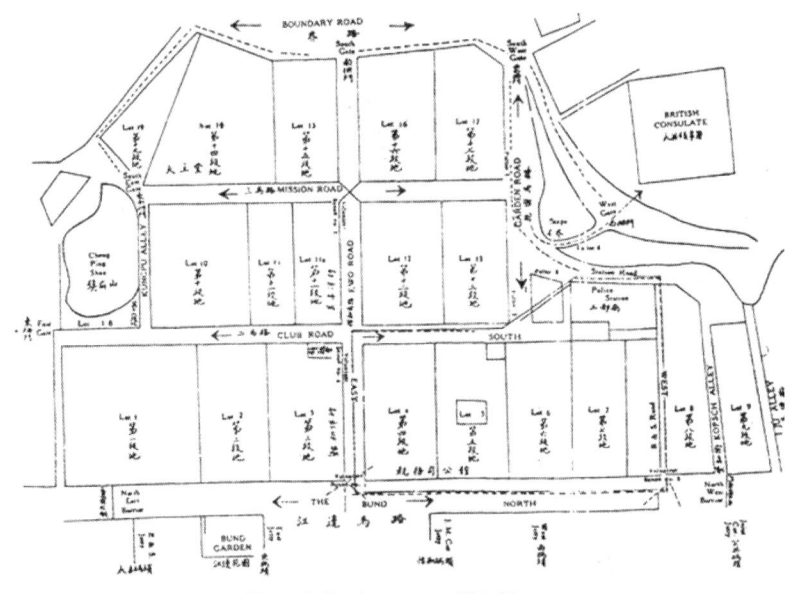

/ *British Settlement at Chinkiang*

EARLY GOLF IN CHINA

Hon. Secretary--B.G. Tours, British Consulate, Chinkiang. *Green Record*--41, by C.E. Holsworthy. The course is a hilly one, of nine holes, measuring one mile seven furlongs. Chinkiang is on the river Yangtze, almost 163 miles from Shanghai. Golfers are welcome."

Golf Illustrated, official weekly publication of the Royal and Ancient Golf Club, published a picture news story about Chinkiang Golf Club in the May 23, 1906 issue. Titled "Bunkers of Chinese Graves," the story reads: "The newest links in Asia have recently been inaugurated at Chinkiang, on the Yangtze River, in China. A fine sporting course of nine holes has been opened on the hilly downs overlooking the river. Playing members are as yet only half-a-dozen, but with the links an accomplished fact there are--as the missionaries say--plenty of 'enquirers' among the small band of foreign residents. The crater like excrescences seen in the photographs are Chinese graves, which are thick on certain hills, and make heart-breaking bunkers for the ball that doesn't fulfill the player's intentions."

/ *1905-06 Golfing Annual*

/ *Bunkers of Chinese Graves*

The descriptions of the four photos are as follows: "MR. C.E. HOLWORTHY (I.M. CUSTOMS) DRIVING FROM THE FIRST TEE." Note the spelling mistake here: Holworthy should be Holsworthy.

/ Holsworthy Driving from the First Tee

"MR. B.J. TOMS (H.M. CONSUL) ON THE NINTH GREEN." Note the spelling mistake: Toms should be Tours.

/ B.J. Tours on the Ninth Green

"LOOKING TOWARDS THE SIXTH HOLE--DOWN IN A VALLEY."

/ Looking Towards the Six Hole

"APPROACHING THE NINTH HOLE: VIEW LOOKING TOWARDS THE SECOND."

/ Approaching the Ninth Hole

Henry Leach's *The Spirit of the Links* published in 1907 mentioned that China had already established six golf clubs and Chinkiang had just built a new course. He writes: "And there is golf in China too, six clubs for it. We had no sooner come to the conclusion and officially announced some years ago that Wei-hai-wei was a very desirable resort, than the golf club was duly established there. In these days the building prospector first settles upon his golf course, and advertises it, and then he builds his houses round about; and in the same way it is realized that it is the proper thing when seeking to make a new centre of Europeans abroad to start with a golf course. I have been with men on shipboard who, having golfed on the queer course of Tangier, have then speculated unceasingly in the smoke-room as we sailed along the smooth waters of the West African coast about the kind of golf that would be vouchsafed to them on reaching the Canary Islands. Some time since I had a letter from a highly-placed British official at Chinkiang on the Yangtze River, and he told me how they had just begun to play the game out there on a new course which was covered with crater-like excrescences. These are Chinese graves, and they are said to make most excellent hazards. There are pig-tailed fellows for caddies, and it was carefully ascertained that no Chinese sentiment is injured in the matter."

Chinkiang Golf Club was listed in both the 1912 and 1936 *Golfer's Handbook*:

According to a report on p. 657 of the March 12, 1921 *North-China Herald*, the founder of Chinkiang Golf Club was a Scott named A.G. Elder. Elder was from Edinburgh and worked for 39 years at Shanghai, Kiukiang and Chinkiang Customs. He was the Chief Appraiser at Chinkiang Customs and was retiring from Chinkiang in 1921. The Customs staff had a farewell meeting for Elder at the Customs Club on March 6. F.J. Mayers, Commissioner of Customs said at the meeting that he had known Mr. Elder longer than anyone present. "He may perhaps remember a young 'subscript griffin' in Tamsui, North Formosa (Taiwan), some 30 years ago. Well, I was that griffin." So when Elder was appointed to Chinkiang, Mayers felt that it was an old friend, and no stranger. On behalf of the Customs, he wished the Elders the happiest of times at home and said: "The next time I visit Edinburgh I shall search all the golf courses for one of the founders of the Chinkiang Golf Club; and I think I shall find him!"

On March 24, 1927, the Northern Expedition troops took over Chinkiang. The Chinkiang Chamber of Commerce took over the Municipal Council and the Police Station of the settlement. British expatriates started to leave Chinkiang. On November 15, 1929, China formally took back the British Settlement. The Chinkiang Golf Club continued operation until around 1936 before it was closed.

CHINA.
Amoy G. C., Koolan Soo.
Chiangkiang G. C., Chiangkiang.
Hankow G. C., Hankow.
Hong-Kong (Royal) G. C., Hong-Kong.
Pekin G. C., Pekin.
Shanghai G. C., Shanghai.
Wei Hai Wei Course, Wei Hai Wei.

/ 1912 Golfer's Handbook

Tsingtao Golf Club

Founded in 1908, Tsingtao (Qingdao) Golf Club had two golf courses over the years. The first one was a 9-hole inside the Tsingtao Race Course at Huich'uan (Huiquan). The second was built in 1933 to the west of Chanshan (Zhanshan) Village, which was expanded into an 18-hole course in 1938.

Golf Links inside the Huich'uan Race Course

According to an article published by *Qingdao Daily* on October 10, 2014, Tsingtao Golf Club was formed in 1908 initiated by Reginald Eckford, General Manager of Cornabé & Eckford. The 9-hole golf links was built inside the Tsingtao Race Course at Huich'uan.

In an article titled "The Tumultuous 50 Years of the Qingdao Race Course" published on www.horsechinaone.com on October 4, 2013, Li Ming wrote about the history of horse racing in Tsingtao. The Germans built the Iltis military barracks in 1899 on the southern slope of T'aiping

/ *Tsingtao Race Course at Huich'uan*

(Iltis) Mountain after occupying Tsingtao. The open ground at the barracks first served as a temporary drilling ground. In 1903, it was developed into a horse racing ground that held sports competitions, entertainment and gaming. Visitor stands were built around an oval-shaped racing track divided into an inner and outer track. Outside the tracks were wooden fences about a meter high. "In 1908," the author wrote, "Englishman Eckford set up a golf club inside the race course, turning the site into a large scale outdoor sporting ground."

According to an article, "Ho Kee (He Ji) of

/ *Huich'uan Race Course*

Shandong," written by Professor Wei Chunyang of the Shandong College of Industry and Commerce, Reginald Eckford was the General Manager of Cornabé-Eckford in Tsingtao. The company was founded by his stepfather Andrew Eckford and W.A. Cornabé at Chefoo in 1864. Cornabé, Eckford and Co. (Ho Kee in Chinese) went into ocean shipping and transportation businesses in addition to trading yarn, handicrafts, peanuts, etc. and set up branches in Weihaiwei, Tsingtao and Dairen. After Andrew Eckford's retirement in 1901, Vivvy Eckford, his eldest stepson took over the Chefoo business and Vivvy's younger brother, Reginald, was in charge of the Tsingtao business. Reginald worked as British chargé d'affaires, deputy consul and consul in Tsingtao. His brother Vivvy built Chefoo's first golf course around 1890.

The Huich'uan Race Course was named after the Huich'uan (Huiquan) Village. "Huich'uan" in Chinese means "merging springs." Eckford was the first president of Tsingtao Golf Club. In 1927, he was also the president of the Tsingtao Rowing Club and the chairman of Tsingtao International Club.

The Race Course was right next to the Huich'uan Beach, a scenic spot of Tsingtao. Racing took place twice a year, in late April or early May for the Spring Race and in Late October or mid-November for the Fall Race. Each race was a four-day event. Occasionally racing was also organized during weekends. Li Ming writes in his article: "Similar to trading ports of Hankow, Shanghai, Hong Kong and Tientsin, etc., a golf links was built inside the Race Course which started the sport of golf in Tsingtao."

/ Tsingtao Race Course at Huich'uan

According to an article "Golf Courses of the Far East" published on pp. 24-26 of the February 1918 issue of *Golfers Magazine*, author James King Steele described the Tsingtao Golf Club as follows: "Tsingtau, China is said to be one of the finest seaside resorts in the world. Its bathing beach is magnificent and it has excellent accommodations for visitors. Just back of the bathing beach over the ground, which was formerly used as a race course, a nine-hole golf links has been laid out by the Tsingtau Golf Club. This course is 2,500 yards long, and its long hole of 530 yards presents a good drive for the most experienced; the short hole is only 125 yards and is an easy one. The course is only twenty minutes by rickshaw from the Tsingtau railway station and immediately adjoins the Strand Hotel where refreshments and accommodations can be obtained at all times. The Grand Hotel situated on the Tsingtau bund also affords excellent entertainment. Green fees for this course are $1.00 per day, $3.00 per week or $10.00 per month."

An article on *sohu.com* dated September 14, 2017 by "Southern City Archive" said that after the Chinese government took back the sovereignty of Tsingtao in December 1922, the Tsingtao International Recreation Club was organized by T. Adams, President of the American Chamber of Commerce, in association with other Chinese and Western personalities (https://kknews.cc/travel/g8vz8oy.html).

/ *International Recreation Club of Tsingtao*

Under the auspices of the International Recreation Club were football, tennis, mountaineering and golf clubs. Daily sports meets and competitions were organized inside the Race Course. Athletic equipment such as a horizontal bar, swing wood, monkey bars, etc. were installed.

According to a report in *North China Standard* dated April 21, 1923, Tsingtao Golf Club held an annual meeting at the Tsingtao International Club on April 10 presided over by T. Adams. The meeting approved the 1922 budget which showed a profit of $1,500. The newly elected General Committee included G.C.T. Russell, Collins, Adams, Yamamoto and Shimidzu. The Honorary Secretary and Treasurer was R.A. Russell, Acting Manager of Jardine, Matheson & Co. Handicap Committee members were W.A. Adams, Shimidzu, Yamamoto and Raeburn.

Shimidzu reported on the progress of building a new clubhouse. He said the new club house would be a great attraction to Tsingtao and ready for occupation before June. By then the alteration of the Golf Course with new holes would also be ready for play. To help with the cost of the new layout, it was decided that the monthly subscription would be raised to $3.00 from the first of May and visitor fees would be raised to $1 per day, $5 per week and $15 per month. Entrance fees would remain unchanged.

In March 1982, the *Bulletin*, official journal of the U.S. Golf Collectors Society (now Golf Heritage Society), published a letter about golf in Tsingtao. It was written on April 8, 1924 by Charles Sprague to his mother about a hilariously interesting golf match at Tsingtao golf course. Sprague was with the Tsingtao Branch of the New York Standard Oil Co. His niece, Helen Atwood, wife of GCS member Harlan Atwood, sent the letter to the GCS *Bulletin*.

The letter was a reprint of a story that Sprague wrote for his company publication, *Shield*, in Shanghai with the title: "Golf in Tsingtao, A New Version." Sprague and friends one day decided to have a foursome game in which only one club could be used by each player. So, the names of clubs were written on pieces of paper for the foursome to draw. With regard to rules, anything was allowed except stepping on the opponent's ball in soft ground. Sprague's opponents had a putter and a mashie-niblick. And Sprague and his partner got a driver and a mashie. The two sides fought all the way to the 17th hole and the result was still even. On the 18th green Sprague drove his ball 10 feet from the pin. While his opponents stood there, holding their laughs to see how he was able to put with a driver, Sprague lay down on the green and turned his driver around, using it as a billiard cue. "The ball ran straight as a die for the hole."

At an annual general meeting of the Tsingtao Golf Club held in July 1924, T. Adams was elected as president of the Club, according to a report on p. 180 of the July 10, 1924 *London and China Express*. A new committee was elected which included T. Shimidzu, G.C.F. Russell, T. Yamamoto, R.A. Russell (Hon. Treasurer), C.R. Rice (Hon. Secretary) and P. Jernigan. The report said: "A discussion took place as to the desirability of removing the embargo placed in 1920 on enemy subjects as regards joining the club—and it was unanimously resolved that Germans now be admitted."

Volume 1 of *Comacrib Directory of China* published in 1925 listed T. Adams as the president of Tsingtao Golf Club, C.R. Rice Honorary Secretary and R.A. Russell Honorary Treasurer.

Walter A. Adams, Tsingtao Golf Club Handicap Committee member, was the U.S. Consul to Tsingtao. He was a top-notch golfer at Tsingtao Golf Club and Club champion for 1925 when he was transferred to Chongqing that year, according to a report in *North-China Herald* dated May 2, 1925.

Jeff Wu, golf collector and secretary of the China Golf Heritage Society (formerly Golf Collectors Society), wrote an article for the Chinese edition of *Golf Magazine* about the golf clubs, trophies and photos of Tomokazu Hori, former Japanese consul in Tsingtao, in the 1930s.

According to Wu, Hori was Japanese Consult in Tsingtao during 1930-1933. He was

/ Huich'uan Square and Race Course

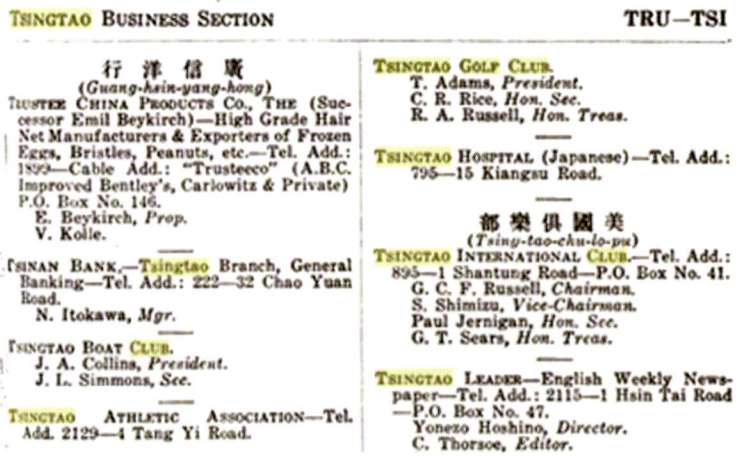
/ 1925 Comacrib Directory of China

a member of Tsingtao Golf Club and an excellent golfer, winning numerous trophies during the four years there.

Hori won a total of five silver trophy cups, two silver boxes and a set of silver spoons, which were given to Jeff Wu by Hori's descendants.

Jeff Wu also received a set of eight hickory clubs used by Hori. Made by Spalding, the set includes irons from 2 to 7, a 19 niblick and a putter. The clubs were typical of the late 1920s, with stainless steel heads and hickory shafts. Hori should have used these clubs playing at the 9-hole golf links inside the Huich'uan Race Course.

Chanshan Golf Course

In an article "Reminiscence of Yan'an 3rd Road in Qingdao" published online on April 23, 2018, Dai Xinge wrote: "During the German occupation of Qingdao, two small golf practice sites were built at Guanhai Shan (Ocean View

/ *Golfers and Caddies at Tsingtao GC in the Early 1930s (Jeff Wu)*

/ *Hori Playing Golf at Tsingtao GC (Jeff Wu)*

/ *Tsingtao GC Trophies Won by Hori (Jeff Wu)*

Mountain) and Huiquan Square. During the 1930s, under the administration of Republican Mayor Shen Hung-lie, a golf course was built to the east of the southern end of Taizhan Road (now near the Retirement Home at Yancheng Road). It was later expanded and a golf club was organized. The clubhouse of the 17-hole (should be 18-hole) golf course had locker rooms and a coffee bar. It was one of the best golf courses in China then." The author published a photograph of the golf course at Chanshan (https://www.sohu.com/a/229046655_727163).

The *Qingdao Daily* website published an article on January 20, 2016, titled "The Golf Club Led Expatriate Organizations in Qingdao before the 1950s." The article listed major recreation clubs in Qingdao before liberation. Under "Golf Club" it was written: "The golf club was first organized in 1908 by Englishman Eckford inside the Huich'uan Race Course. It was moved to the west of Chanshan Village. Eckford was president of the club and members were primarily foreigners. In 1935, membership reached about 200."

/ *Hori's Spalding Hickory Iron Set (Jeff Wu)*

/ *Chanshan Golf Course*

According to http://qdsq.qingdao.gov.cn/, Tsingtao government decided to build a tennis court inside the Race Course in 1931 and with approval of Mayor Shen Hung-lie, a golf course was built to the west of Chanshan Village. An area of 34.45 acres of land was leased to the club for 20 years, from November 1933 to October 1953. The terms of the lease were changed in June 1946 to 10 years, until the end of May 1956, with an annual rent of $10,000.

TSINGDAO

According to the lease, the Chanshan Golf Course was completed in 1933, first with only nine holes. The Tsingtao Golf Club was moved to Chanshan (today's Yan'an 3rd Road) in the same year."

North-China Herald reported on October 24, 1934 that the Tsingtao Golf Club "recently opened its new course which has been laid out on the hills where the Germans and Japanese fought in 1914. It is a beautiful site overlooking the sea. A new club-house in the functional type of architecture has been built."

According to the 1936 edition of *Golfer's Handbook*, Chanshan was still a 9-hle course. L.A. Scotchmer of the Texas Co. was the Honorary Secretary. The course was 1.25 miles from the Tsingtao Station. The Club had a membership of 120. Visitors' fees were $1 per day to play.

By 1937, Tsingtao Golf Club decided to issue debentures in order to further expand the golf course into 18 holes, according to a report in *North-China Herald* on April 7, 1937. At an annual meeting of the Club in April 1937, it was decided that "all members should be obliged to take up at least one $300--debenture at 3 percent (and transferable) in order to raise $16,000--to make up a deficit, which was required to complete the course which is perhaps the finest in China." The Club committee made the decision at a meeting held on March 16. But it was unclear whether those who could not or would not take up these debentures would have to resign. In a follow-up report by the newspaper on May 19, 1937, there were not many members participating at the opening of the new season on the new golf course. As members were required to take up at least one debenture of $300 to make up for the deficit, "some of the members have either resigned or transferred to the non-playing list."

Tsingtao Golf Club's Chanshan Links was expanded into 18 holes by 1938, according to the year's *Golfer's Handbook*. The golf course was 3 miles from the Railway Station. Membership was 250. Honorary Secretary was W. Stoy Elliot. The address was Tsingtao Golf Club, P.O. Box No. 281, Tsingtao, North China. Visitors' fees were $2 per day and $3 Saturdays and Sundays.

The address of Tsingtao Golf Club in 1939 was P.O. Box 281, with a telephone number of 5620, according to the 1939 issue of *China Hong List*. Club President and Honorary Secretary was W. Stoy Elliott, Captain E.H. Gordon, Honorary Treasurer G.A. Bell, and committee members M. Takahashi, H. Lowe and F. Funatsu.

The address of Tsingtao Golf Club in 1941 was changed to P.O. Box 231, according to the 1941 edition of *Tsingtao-Hong-List*. The President of the Club was M. Takahashi, Captain was H. Lowe, Honorary Treasurer was S.V. Svensen and Honorary Secretary was J.V. Webb.

An article published on September 27,

Tsingtao G. C., Tsingtao, North China. Membership, 120. Hon Sec., L. A. Scotchmer, c/o The Texas Co., Tsingtao. 9 holes. Station—Tsingtao (1¼ miles). Visitors' fees, 1 dol. per day.

/ *1936 Golfer's Handbook*

Tsingtao G. C., P.O. Box No. 281, Tsingtao, North China. Membership, 250. Hon Sec., W. Stoy Elliott. 18 holes. Station — Tsingtao (3 miles). Visitors' fees, 2 dols. per day; 3 dols. Saturdays and Sundays.

/ *1938 Golfer's Handbook*

Tsingtao Golf Club

Tel 5620 PO Box 281
Elliott, W. Stoy, pres. and actg. sec.
Gordon, E. H., captain
Bell, G. A. hon. treas.
Takahashi, M.
Lowe, H.
Funatsu, F.

France

5 Chi Hsia-rd
Tel 3378   TA Tatarinoff
Tatarinoff, A. A., consular agent
Yourieff, W. G., sec.
Yourieff, A. G., "
Gao, L., sec.

Germany

1 Tsingtao-rd   Tel 4384
TA Consugerma

/ 1939 China Hong List

2019 on www.thatsqingdao.com discussed about activities of the U.S. Marines in Tsingtao in 1945-1949. The article said that Tsingtao was a home port for the U.S. Navy Asiatic Fleet in the 1930s. Tsingtao also served as the headquarters of the Western Pacific Fleet of the U.S. Navy from 1945-1949. There was an American School in Tsingtao. "The Tsingtao golf course was on the east side of Iltis Hook overlooking Iltis Bay." Iltis was the German name for Pacific. The golf course mentioned in the article should be the Chanshan Golf Links.

Two U.S. Marines, David Rapp and Russell Menelly, wrote about their life in Tsingtao after the Japanese surrendered in 1945. The recollections were published on pp. 44-55 of Volume 18, 2016 of the *Virginia Review of Asian Studies*. Rapp remembered he played golf at the Tsingtao Golf Club with a few friends. He writes: "Some friends and I tried out the golf course one time. It seemed to be well laid out on interesting terrain, but we soon found out that it was impossible to play because a large group of ragamuffins moved on with us. They retrieved our balls after each stroke and obliged us to buy them back. That proved to be such a deterrent to our golf ambitions that we never took the opportunity to play there again."

On June 25, 1950, the Chanshan Golf Course was taken over by the Tsingtao People's Government, leading to its closure. An article titled "The Case of Taking Back the Golf Course" was published on http://qdsq.qingdao.gov.cn/ that detailed what happened:

"After Qingdao was liberated, the golf course was ordered to stop operation due to concerns of national defense. On June 21, 1950, the Qingdao Garrison Command sent a notice to the Foreign Expatriates Office of the Qingdao

RUSSIAN ORTHODOX CHURCH
34 1st Kinkow Rd.
Rev. Archpriest
  Valentine Sinuysky
Klitor, Geo. Semenovsky
Churchman, E. Chjao
Chapel-Master, G. Veberoff
Church Keeper, N. Beketoff

青島天主堂
Tsing-tao-tien-chu-tang
ST. MICHAEL CATHOLIC CATHEDRAL
Tel. 4204—1 Chufu Road, corner Chekiang
Road—P. O. Box 278
Cable Add: "Catholic Mission"
Exc. Magr. Dr. Weig, Georg, Vicar Apostolic
Rev. Fath. Dr. Weig, John, Parish Priest
Rev. Fath. Dahlnkamp, John, Pro-Vicar
Rev. Fath. Vos, John, Rector
Rev. Fath. Seidel, Max, Procurator
Rev. Fath. Heming, Gerard
Rev. Fath. Chang, Peter
Rev. Fath. Tabellion, Nicholas
Rev. Fath. Rygula, Adolf
Rev. Bro Gorgonius, Boos
Rev. Bro. Domificus Wirgowski

J. A. F. I. CLUB
  (Hunting & Fishing)
Headquarters c/o Hirsch Co.
48 Shantung Road, Tel. 4653
Carl Geschke-President
A. Hirsch-Secretary

ROTARY CLUB OF TSINGTAO
A. R. Hogg O.B.E., Pres.
H. Lowe, Vice Pre.
A. E. Drew, Hon. Sec.
F. C. Bruns, Hon. Treas.
H. J. Zimmerman, Serg. at Arms
G. H. Chan, Director
J. G. Schuette, Director

TSINGTAO GOLF CLUB
Tel. 5620—P. O. Box 231
M. Takahashi, Pres.
H. Lowe, Capt.
S. V. Svensen, Hon. Treas.
J. V. Webb, Hon. Sec.
G. A. Bell
F. Funatsu
T. Ikeda

TSINGTAO INTERNATIONAL CLUB
Tels. 2895, 4724—P.O. Box 226
1 Shantung Road

/ 1941 Tsingtao-Hong-List

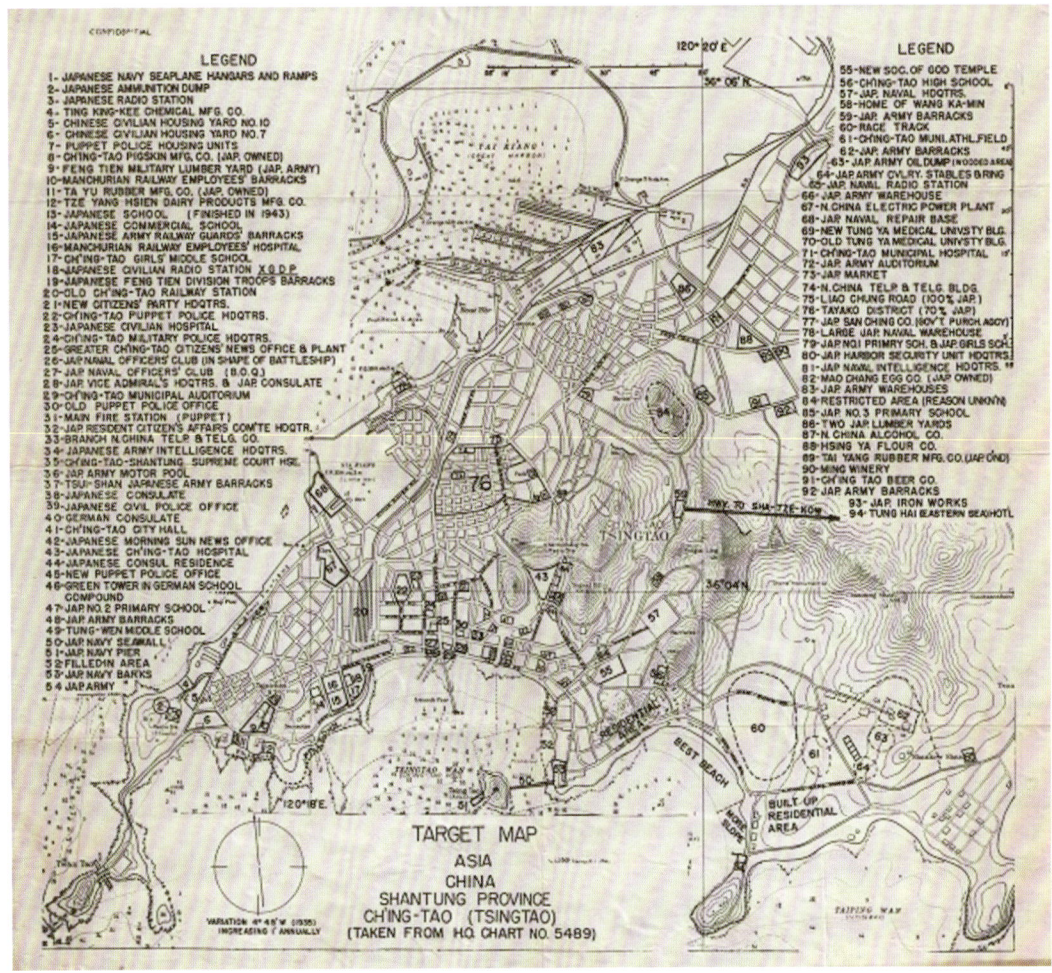

/ Map of Tsingtao Around 1940, Race Course #60

People's Government that the area of the golf course would be included in the area subject to martial law as of June 22. The Golf Club must stop operation and vacate the course within deadline.

"While agreeing to move out of the golf course, Club President Pullman raised the issue of property inside the golf course. The government responded, stating that the property should be demolished by the Club in accordance with the lease. The government would assist by purchasing the property at a lower price.

"On August 4, the Golf Club wrote a letter to the government, saying: 'The Golf Club wishes that the government would consider reopen the golf course in the future. If so, the Club would like to make two requests: 1) The Club will not sell the property to the government, but is willing to lend it to the government free of charge; and 2) decisions on continuing with this agreement or making any changes will be made on March 1-15, 1951. The Club requested a written response to the proposals for the record.' The government replied, 'Although the property inside the golf course should be demolished by the Golf Club based on terms of the lease, the request to wait until March 1-15, 1951 for a final decision seems reasonable. We hereby approve to wait until then to resolve the issue based on the lease.' Thus, the case about the Tsingtao Golf Course came to an end."

Tungshan Golf Club, Canton

Students of golf history in China have been wondering if there ever was a golf course and club in Canton (Guangzhou). As China's only trading port for many years during the Ch'ing Dynasty, foreign trade was controlled by the Thirteen Hongs, or trading houses both Chinese and foreign, along the banks of the Pearl River since 1757. Canton was at one time China's largest trading port even shortly after the Opium War, attracting British and other foreign expatriates working and living in the city. Golfing should have been a possible activity in the city.

Through our preliminary research, we have discovered the existence of a 9-hole golf course as well as a club named Tungshan (Dongshan) Golf Club in Canton. The course was located near Dongyuan (East Garden) in the former Tungshan District (today part of Yuexiu District) and was built after the Canton-Kowloon Railway was completed. The Tungshan Golf Club was organized around 1910 and operated until around 1929.

In his 1913 book, *China Revolutionized*, John Stuart Thomson wrote on p. 377 in the chapter "Foreign Cities in China:" "Not only has Hongkong two very fine golf courses, but Canton, Macao, Hankau, Shanghai, Peking, Tientsin, and other treaty ports have excellent courses famous for their novel bunkers of tombstones, etc., and club-house."

The Tungshan area became the center for foreign missionary activities after 1901, according to an online presentation on December 24, 2020 by Zeng Haiyan, a librarian at the Canton Library. The American Southern Baptist Convention established the Pooi To (Peidao) Middle School for girls at Tungshan in 1903. Other Protestant missions in Canton flocked to Tungshan building churches, schools, orphanages, kindergartens, nursing homes, etc. (*http://www.gzlib.org.cn*) The Tungshan Baptist Church was built in 1909 and later expanded in 1927, becoming the largest protestant church in Canton, accommodating up to 1,000 people.

The flourishing of church schools at Tungshan attracted both expatriates and returned overseas Chinese to live and work in the area, giving rise to more than 1,000 Western-style buildings in Tungshan.

The Canton-Kowloon Railway started construction in 1907, adding a station called Tungshan Mouth (Dongshankou) leading to Tungshan. The opening of railroad travel to Tungshan made the area more attractive to both businesses and residents. Professor Peng Changyin of the South China University of Science and Technology's Department of Architecture attributed the rise of Tungshan to the railway construction as well as the building

/ *Tungshan Protestant Church*

/ A Bird's Eye View of Tungshan

of other public facilities. Peng was quoted in an article by the *Guangzhou Daily* dated October 30, 2018 as saying: "At the start of the construction of the Canton-Kowloon line in 1907, the railway company first built 10 buildings at Dongyuan as engineer housing designed by Purnell & Paget. In 1909, the Dashatou Station was completed, becoming a landmark construction in Canton. To meet the recreation needs of British engineers, an open ground nearby was developed into a golf course."

Pu Songzhu, author of the article, said that Purnell & Paget was the most famous architectural partnership of Australian architect Arthur Purnell and American engineer Charles Souders Paget in Canton in the early 20th century. They designed many of the famous buildings in Canton including the Postal Office, Canton Customs, the Cement Factory, Customs Club, Canton Christian College, Martin Hall, Dashatou Railway Station, Pooi To Middle School, etc.

Athletic meets were organized at Tungshan, according to Cheng Jun in his article "That City" published in www.163.com on November 23, 2020. The 2nd Provincial Athletic Meet was held in 1907 and the 4th was held in 1910.

Tungshan Golf Club was mentioned in a number of publications in the U.K. and the U.S. The earliest mention we have found was the January 29, 1915 issue of the *Overland China Mail*. On p. 17 was a report of the result of the monthly Excelsior Cup competition at Tungshan Golf Club in Canton. The Cup was presented by H. Bent Esq. in January 1914.

/ 1915 Excelsior Cup Competition

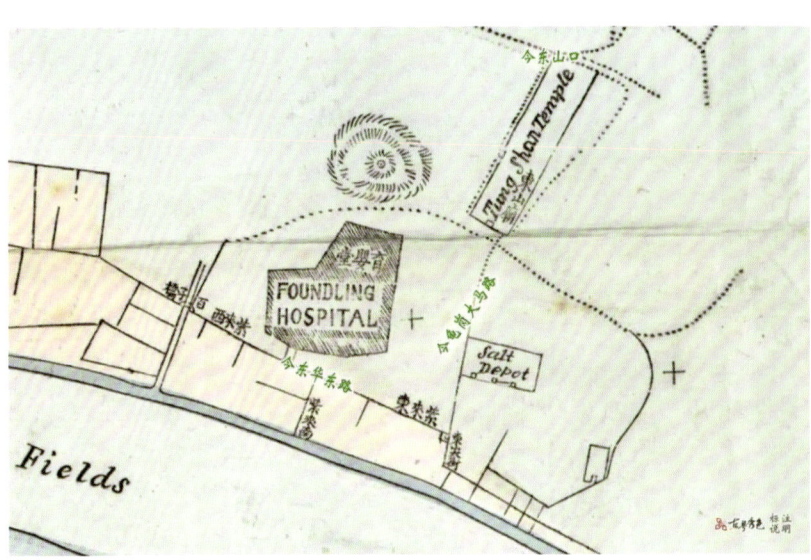

/ Tungshan in Late 19th Century

The supplement to *The London Gazette* dated December 11, 1916 listed "Tungshan Golf Club, Canton":

The same newspaper on February 16, 1917 once again listed Tungshan Golf Club (https://www.thegazette.co.uk/London/issue/29948/supplement/1717/data.pdf). The *Ceylon Government Gazette* also featured the Club on p. 665 of its July 13, 1917 issue:

Tungshan Golf Club appeared on p. 2140 of Canada's 1917 edition of *Orders in Council and Documents Relating to the European War*:

The *Official Gazette of the East Africa Protectorate* published in Nairobi on November 7, 1917 and in Kenya on February 27, 1918 both listed the Tungshan Golf Club:

```
2140         Department of the Secretary of State, Canada.

      Ton Ying & Co.
      Tong Cheong & Co., Amoy.
      Tong Seng & Co., Amoy.
      Tonglin & Co., Canton.
      Toshado Shiten, Shanghai.
      Towa & Co., Newchwang.
      Travers Smith & Sons.
      Truman, R. N.
      Tschurin, I. I., & Co., Harbin.
      Tshun Tak Disp., Swatow.
      Tsui, Y. Y., Dr., Tientsin.
      Tsung Tsoon Sing, Amoy.
      Tsurutani.
      Tung Chi Dispensary, Shanghai.
      Tung Ho & Co., Newchwang.
      T'ung Hsing Sino-Foreign Coal-mining Company, Ltd.,
   Tientsin (Dovey & Co., Managers).
      Tung Shen Te, Tientsin.
      Tung Tai & Co.
      Tung Teh Heng, Chefoo.
      Tung Yu Brothers, Shanghai.
      Tungshan Golf Club, Canton.
      Tunkadoo Dock, Shanghai.
      Tunkadoo Wharves.
      Turner, E. W.
      Twigg, P. O'Brien, Shanghai.
      Twyford, J., & Co.
```

/ *1917 Orders in Council and Documents Relating to the European War*

```
SUPPLEMENT to the LONDON GAZETTE, 11 DECEMBER, 1916.  12083

Talow Dispensary.                              Tungshan Golf Club, Canton.
Tan Seong Chee & Co., Amoy.                    Tunkadoo Dock, Shanghai.
Tannerie franco-chinoise.                      Tunkadoo Wharves.
Tata, Sons, & Co., Shanghai.                   Turner, E. W.
Taylor, Albert.                                Twigg, P. O'Brien, Shanghai.
Taylor & Co.                                   Twyford, J., & Co.
Technische Export Maatschappÿ Azie, Shang-     Tze Hop Shing, G., & Co., Tientsin.
```

/ *1916 London Gazette*

```
Tung Chi Dispensary, Shanghai.    Wells Fargo & Co.                        Yue Chong Tai.
Tung, Ho. & Co., Newchwang.       Wen Hua Printing Press, Hankow.          Yue Loong Hing Kee, Canton.
T'ung Hsing Sino-Foreign Coal-mining   Western Electric Co.                Yuen Cheong and Co., Shanghai.
  Company, Ltd., Tientsin (Dovey &  Westinghouse Electric Export Co.,      Yuen Sui Chang Dispensary, Swatow.
  Co., Managers).                     Shanghai.                            Yuen Tah & Co., Shanghai.
Tungshan Golf Club, Canton.       Westminster Tobacco Company.             Yu Feng Kung Ssu, Chefoo.
Tung Shen Te, Tientsin.           West of Scotland Insurance Office,       Yui Tai & Co., Tientsin.
Tung, Tai, & Co.                     Limited, Shanghai.                    Yung Fong Photo Supply Co., Peking.
Tung Teh Heng, Chefoo.            Westphal, King, & Ramsay, Limited.       Yung Hing Printing Co., Shanghai.
Tung Yu Brothers, Shanghai.       Wheelock & Co.                           Yu Tai.
Tunkadoo Dock, Shanghai.          Wheen, Edward, & Sons.                   Yuwusei Yoko, Tieh Ling.
Tunkadoo Wharves.                 Whitall & Co., Limited.
Turner, E. W.                     Whiteaway, Laidlaw & Co.                 Za Chong Shun, Shanghai.
```

/ *1917 Ceylon Government Gazette*

CANTON

```
November 7, 1917.          THE OFFICIAL GAZETTE                    1117

Tien Zung & Co., Shanghai.              United Netherlands Lloyds.
Tientsin Bicycle Company.               United States Steel Products Company.
Tientsin Club.                          Urbaine Fire Insurance Co. of Paris.
Tientsin Dispensary.
Tientsin Dispensary.                    Vacuum Oil Company.
Tientsin Gas and Electric Light Company. Vaid, K. Edulji, Canton.
Tientsin Ironworks Limited.             Van Ess, A., & Co.
Tientsin Lighter Co., Ltd.              Vanderloo & Co., Shanghai.
Tientsin Native City Waterworks Limited. Vanderstegen, L. & Co., Hankow.
Tientsin Press Limited.                 Vania, A. D., Canton.
Tientsin Soap Manufacturing Company.    Varalda & Co., Shanghai.
Tientsin Tobacco Company.               Varenne, Th., & Compagnie, Canton.
Tientsin Waterworks Company Limited.    Vasunia, J. P., Canton.
Tilley & Limby.                         Venturi, F., Shanghai.
Times Dharwar & Co.                     Veroudart.
Tin Fah Hong (China Trading Co.),       Vicajee, F., & Co.
  Shanghai.                             Viccajee, H., & Co.
Tin See Tong Dispensary, Amoy.          Vickers, Limited.
Tiram Estates Limited.                  Vicula Morosov, Newchwang.
Tiriolo, C., & Co., Antung.             Villa, A. P., & Brothers, Canton.
Tisdall, B. D., Amoy.                   Viloudaki & Co., Shanghai.
Toa & Co., Ltd., Tientsin.              Vogue, Shanghai.
Toa Koshi, Shanghai.                    Volkart, Adolf, Shanghai.
Toa Tobacco Company, Newchwang and      Vrard & Co.
  Shanghai.
Tobacco Products Corporation.           Wadman, H. P., Shanghai.
Toeg & Read, Shanghai.                  Wa Sun, Canton.
Toh Tiong Hok, Amoy.                    Wah Chang Mining and Smelting Co.,
Tom, H., Tientsin.                        Changsha.
Tom, S., Chefoo.                        Wah Loong, Canton.
Ton Ying & Co.                          Wah Mei Dispensary, Canton.
Tong Chee Drug Co., Amoy.               Wah Ming Optical Company.
Tong Cheong & Co., Amoy.                Wah On Company, Canton.
Tong Seng & Co., Amoy.                  Wai Chi, Tientsin.
Tonglin & Co., Canton.                  Walker, Livingstone.
Torin & Co., Canton.                    Wallem & Co., Shanghai.
Toshado Shiten, Shanghai.               Wang Hung Kee, Shanghai.
Towa & Co., Newchwang.                  Wang, Y. N., Dr., Tientsin and Peking.
Travers Smith & Sons.                   Waunieck, L., Peking.
Trumann, R. N. & Co.                    Warren, C. E., & Co., Canton.
Tschurin, I. I., & Co., Harbin.         Wassiamull Assomull & Co., Canton.
Tshun Tak Disp., Swatow.                Waste Silk Boiling Company.
Tsui, Y. Y., Dr., Tientsin.             Watson, A. S., & Co., Limited.
Tsung Tsoon Sing, Amoy.                 Watt, W. T., Dr. (Imperial Medical
Tsurutani.                                College).
Tung Chi Dispensary, Shanghai.          Wattie, J. A. & Co. Limited.
Tung Ho & Co., Newchwang.               Watts & Co.
T'ung Hsing Sino-Foreign Coal-mining    Wee Hock Siang & Co., Amoy.
  Company, Ltd., Tientsin (Doney & Co., Weeks & Co. Limited.
  Managers).                            Wegelin, L.
Tung Shen Te, Tientsin.                 Weihaiwei Land and Building Company.
Tung Tai & Co.                          Weippert, W. H. C., Amoy.
Tung Teh Heng, Chefoo.                  Wells Fargo & Co.
Tung Yu Brothers, Shanghai.             Wen Hua Printing Press, Hankow.
Tungshan Golf Club, Canton.             West of Scotland Insurance Office Limited,
Tunkadoo Dock, Shanghai.                  Shanghai.
```

/ 1917 Orders in Council and Documents Relating to the European Warte

The *Commonwealth of Australia Gazette* dated February 5, 1919 listed Tungshan Golf Club on p. 150 as follows:

The *Malaya Tribune* on December 23, 1922 carried a news report titled "The Eastern Association" on p. 8, which reads: "The following Clubs have joined the above Association: --Madras Gymkhana Club, Karachi Golf Club, Singapore Golf Club, Pioh Golf Club, Penang Golf Club, Selangor Golf Club, Shanghai Golf Club, Royal Hongkong Golf Club, Amoy Golf Club, Tungshan Recreation Club, Canton, and Tientsin Golf Club." It said that as of October 1, 1922, the Honorary Secretary of the Royal Hongkong Golf Club would act as Honorary Secretary of the Eastern Golf Association.

On p. 28 of the 1922 edition of *China Who's Who* was listed a Russian named A.A. Archangelsky who was assistant district inspector of Salt Gabell Service in Amoy. He was also Acting District Inspector for Canton from June 1911 to June 1921. During his time in Canton, he was a member of Tungshan Recreation Club (Golf) and the Canton Rowing Club.

U.S. Navy's 1928 edition of *Port Directory of Principle Foreign Ports* told travelers to consult the consul general when they arrived in Canton. It reads on p. 723: "Facilities are very

150　　　　　　　　　　THE OFFICIAL GAZETTE　　　　　　　February 27, 1918

Tabaqueria Filipina	Toa Koshi, Shanghai
Tackey, W M , & Co	Toa Tobacco Company, Newchwang and Shanghai
Tai, E , Tientsin	Tobacco Products Corporation
Tai Feng Kung Sen, Shanghai	Teog & Read, Shanghai
Tai Fu Lim, Dr Newchwang	Toh Tiong Hok, Amoy
Tai King & Co , Canton	Tom, H , Tientsin
Tai On & Co (The Canton Medical Hall), Canton	Tom, S , Chefoo
Tai Wah Dispensary, Swatow	Ton Ying & Co
Taikoo Sugar Refining Co Limited	Tong Chee Drug Co , Amoy
Taiping Rubber Estates	Tong Cheong & Co , Amoy
Taiseng & Co , Foochow	Tong Seng & Co , Amoy
Taiseng Printing Office, Hankow	Tonglin & Co , Canton
Tait & Co	Torin & Co , Canton
Takaiwa, K , & Co	Toshado Shiten, Shanghai
Takata & Co , Shanghai	Towa & Co , Newchwang
Takkee & Co , Foochow	Travers Smith & Sons
Taku Tug and Lighter Company Limited	Trumann, R N & Co
Talati Brothers, Peking and Tientsin	Tschurin, I I , & Co , Harbin
Talati & Co , Tientsin	Tshun Tak Disp , Swatow
Tan Seong Chee & Co , Amoy	Tsui Y Y , Dr , Tientsin
Tannerie Franco Chinoise	Tsung Tsoon Sing, Amoy
Tata, Sons, & Co , Shanghai	Tsurutani
Tay Choon Keng, Amoy	Tung Chi Dispensary, Shanghai
Tay Tjhiang Hong (Handel Maatschappij N V), Shanghai	Tung Ho & Co , Newchwang
Taylor, Albert	T'ung Hsing Sino-Foreign Coal-mining Company, Ltd , Tientsin (Doney & Co , Managers)
Taylor & Co	Tung Shen Te Tientsin
Technische Export Maatschappij Azie, Shanghai	Tung Tai & Co
Teerathdas, N , Shanghai	Tung Teh Heng, Chefoo
Teesdale & Godfrey	Tung Yu Brothers, Shanghai
Teh Kee Dispensary, Hankow	Tungshen Golf Club, Canton
Tehun Tet Dispensary, Swatow	Tunkadoo Dock, Shanghai
Tek Hau Dispensary, Swatow	Tunkadoo Wharves
Tek Shun Hing, Chefoo	Turner, E W

/ 1918 Official Gazette of the East Africa Protectorate

No. 16.—5th February, 1919　　　　　150　　　　　　　　　Commonwealth Gazette

T'am Lai t'ing, Canton.
Tabaqueria Filipina, Shanghai.
Tackey, M. M., & Co., Shanghai.
Tai, E., Tientsin.
Tai Feng Kung Sen, Shanghai.
Tai Fu Lim, Dr., Newchwang.
Tai King & Co., Canton.
Tai On & Co. (The Canton Medical Hall), Canton.
Tai Sang & Co., Swatow.
Tai Wah Dispensary, Swatow.
Taikoo Sugar Refining Co. Limited.
Taiping Rubber Estates Limited.
Taiseng & Co., Foochow.
Taiseng Printing Office, Hankow.
Tait & Co., Amoy.
Takaiwa, K., & Co., Shanghai.
Takata & Co., Shanghai.
Takkee & Co., Foochow.
Taku Tug and Lighter Co., Ltd., Tientsin.
Talati Brothers, Peking and Tientsin.
Talati & Co., Tientsin.
Tanah Merah Estates (1916) Limited.
Tan Seong Chee & Co., Amoy.
Tannerie Franco-Chinoise, Tientsin.
Tata, Sons, & Co., Shanghai.
Tay Choon Keng, Amoy.
Tay Tjhiang Hong (Handel Maatschappij N.V.), Shanghai.
Taylor, Albert, Shanghai.

Touliatos, Gérassimo, Manchuria Station, C.E.R.
Towa & Co., Nawchwang.
Trans-Pacific Corporation, Shanghai.
Travers Smith & Sons, Tientsin.
Trumann, R. N. & Co.
Tschurin, I. I., & Co., Harbin.
Tshun Tak Dispensary, Swatow.
Tsui, Dr. Y. Y., Tientsin.
Tsuji & Co., Shanghai.
Tsung Tsoon Sing, Amoy.
Tsurutani Yoko, Shanghai.
Tuck, Chas. H., Harbin.
Tuckwo Egg Factory, Yin Cheng.
Tung Chi Dispensary, Shanghai.
Tung Ho & Co., Newchang.
T'ung Hsing Sino-Foreign Coal-mining Co., Ltd., Tientsin (Doney & Co., Managers).
Tung Shen Te, Tientsin.
Tung Tai & Co., Shanghai.
Tung Yu Brothers, Shanghai.
Tungshan Golf Club, Canton.
Tunkadoo Dock, Shanghai.
Tunkadoo Wharves, Shanghai.
Turner, E. W., Shanghai.
Turner James (Eastern Engineering Works), Tientsin.
Twigg, P. O'Brien, Shanghai.
Twyford, J., & Co., Tientsin.
Tze Hop Shing, G., & Co., Tientsin.

/ 1919 Commonwealth of Australia Gazette

poor. Officers may be put up at the Canton Club on Shameen, at the Tung Shan Recreation Club, at the Shameen Lawn Tennis Club, and, in summer time, at the Swimming Bath Club."

A news story about U.S. Vice Consul in Canton published in the March 1929 issue of *The American Foreign Service Journal* said that "Vice Consul Bonbright is the first American to uphold the national golf tradition in these ports for some time. He has just won the golf championship of Canton at Tungshan Golf Club, defeating the former champion by 10 up and 9 to play, after doing the first 9 holes in 33."

The November 4, 1930 *North-China Herald* published a report about a recent competition at Hungjao Golf Club. The report said that K.M. Cumming won his fifth champion at the Hungjao Championship. "He has previously been credited twice with the championship of the Royal Hongkong Golf Club, once with that of the Canton Golf Club."

Archangelsky A. A.
(Swatow), assistant district inspector, Salt Gabell Service: *b.* March 21, 1881 at Sredne-Achtubinskoya, Astrakan district, Russia: *f.* Alipily Archangelsky: *m.* Rost: *educ.* Oriental Institute, Vladivostock, Russia: *mar.* Maria Sirneff, August 28, 1911: one son, Alexis, one daughter Olga: *arr. C.* August 25, 1914: Was with Russian-Chinese Institute, Peking, 1914: Salt Gabelle 1915; Acting District Inspector, Canton from June 1911 to June 1921: *clubs,* Canton, Tungshan Recreation (golf), Rowing (Canton), Swatow, Kialat, Customs, (Swatow): *add.* Swatow Salt

establish the "Central China Post". *n.* British.

Argent, W. A.
(Shanghai), *o.* Commercial, Managing Director, Mackenzie & Co., Ltd.: *r. add.* Yuyuen Road: *o. add.* 7a Canton Road *n.* British.

Arlington, Lewis Charles,
(Peking), formerly in Chinese Navy, Customs, and now in Posts: Postal Commissioner, functioning as Chinese Secretary at the Directorate General of Posts, Peking: *b.* 1860 at San Francisco: *f.* Charles Henry Arlington: *m.* Isabel Burney: *educ.* Normal School, San Jose, Cal.: *arr. C.* 1879:

/ *1922 China Who's Who*

Boat landings.—At the British jetty, Shameen, and customhouse landing, the bund. Other landing steps on Shameen are available at high tide. The British jetty is lighted at night and good at all tides.
Shore boats.—Shore boats are plentiful. No official tariff in force; usual fare is 10 cents silver.
Shore leave.—Consult the consul general. Facilities are very poor. Officers may be put up at the Canton Club on Shameen, at the Tung Shan Recreation Club, at the Shameen Lawn Tennis Club, and, in summer time, at the Swimming Bath Club. Petty officers and the men are usually welcome at the British Sailors' Canteen on Shameen.
Patrols.—Arrangements for patrols should be made with the municipal authorities through the American consul general.
Swimming, bathing, and athletics.—Swimming should not be allowed in the river because of the filthy condition of the water. A swimming pool on Shameen may be used at specified times during the summer for reasonable fees. There is a baseball field at Lingnan University; permission for its use would have to be obtained from the authorities

Please report all corrections, changes, and additions to Office of Naval Intelligence, Washington, D. C.

/ *1928 Port Directory of Principle Foreign Ports*

mountains of Shantung, because early in December he passed through Hong Kong en route to Tsinan to resume his former post.

Vice Consul Bonbright is the first American to uphold the national golf tradition in these parts for some time. He has just won the golf championship of Canton at the Tungshan Club, defeating the former champion by 10 up and 9 to play, after doing the first 9 holes in 33. We hear that the only reason he didn't win the Shameen tennis competition was that he felt sorry for the local boys and didn't enter. However, he came down to Hong Kong last summer and helped the American baseball nine, led by Consul John Muccio, climb out of its cellar position in the local league.

Jan. 21: Major General Wm. Lassiter, newly appointed commander of 8th Corps Area, headquarters at San Antonio while visiting Laredo, Tex., on an inspection trip called at the Consulate, accompanied by Major Charles Williams, Commanding Officer, Fort McIntosh, Laredo, Tex., and by his aides.

Feb. 2: Ambassador Dwight M. Morrow passed through Laredo and Nuevo Laredo en route to Mexico City on his return from leave in the United States. He was accompanied by Mr. George Rubblee.

Feb. 3: Consul Richard F. Boyce went to Ciudad Victoria, which is the capital of the State of Tamaulipas, to attend the inauguration of the new Governor of that State, Lic. Francisco Cas-

/ 1929 The American Foreign Service Journal

K. M. CUMMING'S FIFTH CHAMPIONSHIP

Mr. K. M. Cumming is working up a sort of Bobby Jones record in China golfing circles. He has previously been credited twice with the championship of the Royal Hongkong   once with that of the Canton   and now he has won the championship of the Hungjao   for the fifth time, having defeated Mr. F. G. Harrison in the final of this year's championship, over 36 holes, by 4 and 3. The winner completed the first round in 72 and was 3 up. For the 15 holes of the second round he was two over fours.

/ K.M. Cumming's Fifth Championship

The Tungshan Golf Club in Canton operated for about 20 years, but never was able to develop into a well-known golf club during the Republican Period due to limited membership. This was because Canton gradually lost its top trading port position after China opened major port cities such as Hankow, Shanghai, Tientsin, etc. The rise of Hong Kong as a free port soon overshadowed Canton. Starting from the late Ch'ing Dynasty, Canton also became the focal point for the anti-Ch'ing, anti-imperialist, Nationalist Revolution and New Democratic Revolution. Social turmoil in Canton led to the departure of foreign expatriates and greatly affected golfing activities.

Gyantse Golf Course, Tibet

According to some historical records, early golf activities in Tibet (Xizang) were started by a Scotsman and an Austrian. Hugh Edwards Richardson (1905-2000) was born in St. Andrews. After passing civil examination, Richardson became an Indian Civil Service officer in 1930 and was posted to Bengal in 1932. He became a British trade representative at Gyantse in July 1936 and visited Lhasa, Tibet as a member of the British mission. He then stayed in Tibet from 1936 to 1940 and again in from 1947 to 1950.

According to a biography of Richardson, "His hobbies were ornithology, botany and gardening and he was also an enthusiastic photographer. Another of Richardson's passions was golf, which he introduced to Tibet, although he noted that the ball tended to travel 'rather too far in the thin air'." In 1951, Richardson spent a short time in Malaya before retiring to St Andrews and "continued to play golf as one of the longest serving members of the Royal and Ancient Golf Club." (http://tibet.prm.ox.ac.uk/tibet_Hugh_Richardson.html)

The Austrian, Heinrich Harrer (1912-2006), lived in Tibet in 1943-1950. Harrer was a mountaineer and skier. He was a member of the Austrian National Team to compete in the downhill and grand slalom in the 1936 Winter Olympics. He was captured by the Allied Forces in 1939 when he was trying to climb the Himalaya Mountain and thrown into concentration camp. In 1943 he escaped into Tibet and began studying the Tibetan language and history. A friend of Richardson, Harrer later became private tutor to the 14th Dalai Lama.

After returning to Austria in 1951, Harrer restarted golf in his country and became the Austrian National Champion in 1958. From 1964 onwards he was the President of Austrian Golf Association until his death in 2006.

/ Hugh Richardson

/ Heinrich Harrer

While it was probable that Richardson and Harrer might have created rudimentary golf courses in Tibet and helped start golfing there, there were other pioneers of golf in Tibet before them. According to an article published in the March 15, 1912 issue of *Golf Illustrated*, the earliest golf course in Tibet appeared in Gyantse before 1912. Gyantse was the 3rd largest city after Lhasa and Shigatse and a historical trading hub for Tibet with Bhutan, Sikkim, Nepal and India.

In December 1903, British Indian forces led by Francis Younghusband invaded Tibet, trying to establish a diplomatic mission in order to resolve the border disputes between Tibet and Sikkim and prevent Russian from expanding into Central Asia. Younghusband's military expedition first

/ Golf in Tibet

took over Gyantse and then marched into Lhasa. The 13th Dalai Lama fled to Mongolia and the Lhasa Government was forced to sign the Treaty of Lhasa in August 1904. Younghusband and his army returned to Sikkim in September.

According to the Treaty of Lhasa, Britain was allowed to set up trading agents in Yatung, Gyantse and Gartok. Tibet was forced to pay a large sum of indemnity. British forces took over Chumbi Valley before the indemnity was paid up in February 1908. Britain set up a trading office in Gyantse in 1904 as well as a representative office in Lhasa in 1937.

According "The Establishment of the British Trade Agencies in Tibet: A Survey," published in the November 1992 issue of the *Journal of the*

Royal Asia Society, the trade agencies at Yatung, Gyantse and Gartok since 1904 originated from Indian Political Service, which had about 150 people, mostly selected from the Indian Civil Service or officers of the British Army through exams. Most of the trade agents sent to Tibet were bachelors and the majority were Scottish or Irish.

For trade agents stationed in Chumbi Valley, living conditions were harsh and monotonous. So, these bachelors would engage in sports and entertainment such as hunting, polo, hockey, football and wrestling. It was likely that Scottish agents built simple golf links and started to play the Royal and Ancient game.

The article in *Golf Illustrated* was written by an anonymous writer and featured three photographs. It was titled: "Golf in Tibet: The Highest Golf Course in the World." The full text of the article reads as follows:

"The chief claim to fame that Gyantse possesses is the part it played in the Tibetan Mission of 1904; in time, perhaps, this fame may be eclipsed by the fact that it boasts the highest golf course in the world. The next highest is the course at Gulmarg in the Himalayas, which is only 8,500 feet above sea level, but Gyantse, standing at a height of 13,100 feet, easily bears off the palm for golf at a high altitude. Gyantse does not, to the casual observer, suggest golf, nor does it even appear to be able to furnish room for golf course; but where Scotchmen congregate, though their total number be only three, a course had to be made, and it has been.

"Provided the caddies are willing, golf is possible all the year round, the most unsuitable months being January, February, and March, these being the months of the famous, or rather infamous, dust storms. The course is one of nine holes situated on the right bank of the Niang Chu River; the average length of the holes is 280 yards, the longest being over 500 yards and the shortest 120 yards. There is no grass on the course, the whole surface being a hard baked clay, over which, especially in winter, a film of sand is blown; where this sand drifts a 'bunker' is formed. The chief hazards are collections of stones, pits, withered trees, wild irises, and sand. One of the two last named not even a Braid could play, and it is here that the advantage of the local rules is seen. Some of these may be of interest: --

/ The 2nd Hole

"(1) No ball can be lost in Gyantse; if not found within a reasonable time another is put down where the first one is thought to have been lost, without penalty.

"(2) The lie of a ball in sand can be improved by scraping round it with hand or club (even then the difficulty of the shot has to be experienced to be appreciated).

"(3) All thorns may be removed from the ball.

"Besides the usual caddies (one of whom, by the way, is a Tibetan girl) a forecaddie is an essential here. His studies are not limited to watching where the balls go; he has other tasks to perform, the most important of these being to remove all the flagstaffs from the various holes and carry them to a place of safety after the round is completed. The reason of this is that firewood is very scarce in Gyantse, and even such a slender piece of wood as a flagstaff would be too tempting a bait for a Tibetan. The hole tins are also, to judge by their rapid disappearance, not unpopular, though no one can definitely say to what use they are put.

/ The 9th Hole

/ Gyantse Golf Course (Gyantse Jung in Background)

"A Chinese sentry and a few Tibetans watch the Sahibs drive off; the expression on their faces seems to be one of astonishment that anyone could be foolish enough to waste so much energy chasing a ball. Why not sit at home and drink 'Chang' (tea)? they seem to say. They little know the attractions of golf, however, and not even the obstacles which nature has put in its way prevent Gyantse golf from flourishing.

"Tibetans already play one Scotch game, curling; perhaps in a few years they may take up golf and a future champion may hail from the land of the Lamas."

Judging from the date of publication of this interesting recount of the Gyantse Golf Links, we may conclude that the earliest golf course in Tibet was built in 1911 or even earlier.

Dairen and Ryojun Golf Clubs

There were two golf clubs and golf links in Dairen (Dalian) built by the Japanese South Manchuria Railway Co., Ltd. One was the Hoshigaura (Star Beach) Golf Club at Star Beach established in 1913 with 9 holes and expanded to 18 in 1927. The other was the Ryojun (Lvshun) Golf Club that had a six-hole course built in the early 1930s.

Hoshigaura Golf Club

During the Russo-Japanese War of 1904-1905, the victorious Japanese took over Dairen and then Ryojun, starting a 40-year reign. In 1909, South Manchuria Railway built the Hoshigaura Park at Star Beach and then the Yamato Hotel in the following year.

On www.oldtokyo.com there are two photographs, one of Yamato Hotel in the 1920s and the other a bird's eye view of Star Beach. (https://www.oldtokyo.com/yamato-hotel-hoshigaura-star-beach-dairen-manchuria-c-1910/)

Hoshigaura Park was situated to the southwest of Shahekou (Sand River Mouth) or to the west of today's Star Beach Square. Local people referred to the rock protruding from the gulf waters as "Star Rock," hence the name Star Beach. Star Park covered a total area of 15 acres and was Dairen's largest beach park by the ocean.

Hu Pixiu, a blogger at blog.sina.com.cn published a chronology of Dairen compiled by the Dairen Society in 2009. It was an unofficial list of major events between 1904 and 1947 in Dairen.

According to the chronology, Japan occupied Dairen on May 30, 1904 and took control of Ryojun on January 13, 1905. South Manchuria Railway (SMR) moved its headquarters to Dairen on April 1, 1907. In April 1909, SMR purchased the land at Hoshigaura and invested heavily to develop the area. The Yamato Hotel opened for business in September 1910. In November 1915, an upscale restaurant opened for business at Hoshigaura.

Dairen Golf Club started as the Dairen Tennis & Golf Club. SMR Vice-President S. Kunisawa was Club Chairman. A report in the *Manchuria Daily News* dated December 29, 1913 said that the retiring S. Kunisawa "has resigned the Chairmanship of the Dairen Tennis & Golf

/ 1920 Yamato Hotel, Star Beach

Club owing to his prospective departure from Dairen."

CHAIRMAN OF DAIREN TENNIS & GOLF CLUB.

Mr. S. Kunisawa (retiring Vice-President of the S. M. R. Co.) has resigned the Chairmanship of the Dairen Tennis & Golf Club owing to his prospective departure from Dairen.

/ *Dairen Tennis & Golf Club Chairman*

On April 21, 1914, the same newspaper reported that the Dairen Tennis & Golf Club would open on April 25 and a Club annual general meeting would be held at 6:00 pm on the evening of April 27th. Members were requested to contact J.E. Owen, Honorary Secretary and Treasurer for participation.

Manchuria Daily News reported on May 22, 1916 that in order to promote an interest in the game of golf among the residents, both Japanese and foreign, a few enthusiasts of the game had been discussing arrangements as to how to improve the current course at Hoshigaura by permanently hiring an experienced and competent golfer to supervise the course work. As 25-30 laborers would be needed, the report said the Club would "hold a meeting tomorrow at 5 p.m. in a room at the Yamato Hotel to discuss the matter of raising the necessary funds, and, when the parties interested see their way clear to obtain sufficient fund, a Golf Club will be formed and an executive committee be duly elected to look after its interests."

The new Hoshigaura Golf Club was officially formed on June 28, 1916 at a general meeting held at 5:00 pm, according to a report in the June 27 issue of *Manchuria Daily News*.

The newspaper reported again on June 28 that the Hoshigaura Golf Links would be designed and built by SMR. It reads: "The golf links laid out by the S.M.R. Co. on the hillside above Yamato Hotel, Hoshigaura, the popular Summer Resort at 45 minutes' tram car ride from Dairen, are splendidly located. The trees and greens are disposed over gorges, ravines, and knolls, which combined make up a complement of picturesque scenery together with the favorite summering place facing the turquoise sea dotted with green islets lifting their heads above the water." The report said there were a few finishing touches to be put on the golf links in order to make them an almost ideally perfect ground. But a drawback was there had not been "enough enthusiasts to keep the links well patronized."

The report listed seven Japanese and foreign enthusiasts who had undertaken to organize the new golf club, with support of SMR. The general meeting held at Yamato Hotel discussed the rules of the Club and elected members of the general committee. The president of the Club would be assumed by an SMR representative.

The following rules were approved at the meeting: membership fees were to be determined; monthly subscription fee G¥2; the General Committee would select a Green Committee of four and a Handicapping Committee of three from among themselves; a Balloting Committee of five would be elected in addition to the General Committee.

Members may introduce their friends to play with them, subject to payment of the green fee at the following rates: G¥0.90 one day per person, G¥2.50 per week, G¥7.50 per month and G¥15 per three months.

Hoshigaura Golf Links was owned by SMR and members had the privilege of playing on the links. The rules of the game would be those of the Royal and Ancient Golf Club of St. Andrews for the time being, with such additions or modifications the Committee may consider necessary to make them applicable to the Club. In the absence of a clubhouse, players could use the Yamato Hotel.

According to further reports in *Manchuria Daily News* on June 29 and 30, J. Furusawa was elected Honorary Treasurer and Secretary. The General Committee members elected were T. Adachi, Chadwick, S. Dogura, Inomata, Kabayama, L.E.Q. Mitchelmore and Ross. Balloting Committee members included Ebara, Hori, Kubo, Mitchelmore and Soper.

/ *A Bird's-Eye View of Star Beach in the 1920s*

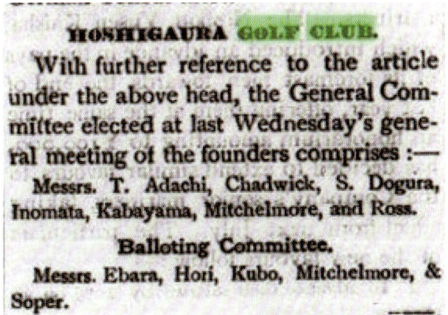
/ *1916 Hoshigaura GC Committee*

The following postcard from the authors' collection shows a section of the Hoshigaura Golf Links.

Hoshigaura Golf Links only had nine holes at the beginning. In an article "Golf Course of the Far East" published on pp. 24-26 of the February 1918 issue of *Golfers Magazine* in Chicago, James King Steele wrote that one of the most attractive hotels built by the South Manchuria Railway was the Yamato Hotel at Hoshigaura. "In order to further increase its attraction to tourists the railway company has also laid out a very excellent course of nine holes at Hoshigaura, a noted bathing resort 45 minutes by electric train from the City of Dairen. This course has nine holes and is well provided with natural hazards, the fairways being guarded with pine woods and cut up with deep ravines and gullies; it is 2,737 yards long and the bogey is 44. Guests of club members are permitted, on introduction, to play over the course on payment of green fees of 25c per day, $1.25 per week, $3.75 per month or $7.50 for three months."

A report about SMR's hotel development in Manchuria was published in the May 1918 issue of *The Hotel Monthly*. The report said that

/ *Postcard of Yamato Hotel Hoshigaura*

Hoshigaura was "one of the finest seaside health and holiday resorts in the Far East, 15 minutes' drive by automobile from Dairen." The report printed a photo of Star Beach, showing a general view of the hotel and its golf course and bungalows. There were twenty bungalows and villas in European and Japanese styles. Tennis, golf, boating, and other sports attracted visitors. The golf course was laid out over the hills at the back of the hotel.

/ The Rolling Hoshigaura Golf Links

In order to attract American tourists, SMR advertised destinations in Manchuria in U.S. publications during the early 1920s. The advertisement, titled "Manchuria's Health Resorts Attract World Travelers," was found on p. 748 of the September 1922 issue of *Asia, American Magazine on the Orient* and on p. 31 of the October 1922 issue of *Vanity Fair*. It described tourist attractions in Dairen, Port Arthur, Mukden, Tangkangtze (Tanggangzi), Antung, etc. For Hoshigaura the ad reads: "Hoshigaura or Star Beech--A seaside resort twenty minutes by motor from Dairen. Modern summer hotel; picturesque bungalows, bathing, tennis and golf." Included in the ad was a photograph of a golfer driving off at Hoshigaura Golf Links, with two young caddies attending.

On October 18, 1925, an inter-port golf match was held between the Dairen and Mukden Golf Clubs, according to a report of *Manchuria Daily News* dated October 20. The Dairen team arrived in Mukden on Friday evening and practiced on Saturday at the Mukden Golf Links. Twelve members from each team participated in the competition. The result of the morning individual meet came out even at 6:6. The afternoon foursome match was

/ Driving Off on Hoshigaura Golf Links

unfinished due to a storm.

The *Manchuria Daily News* reported on April 29, 1926 that members of the Hoshigaura Golf Club would visit Mukden Golf Club on May 10 for a match. B. Yasuhiro, SMR's General Manager, would present a Challenge Cup for the competition.

At an inter-port competition between Hoshigaura and Mukden Golf Clubs at the former's links on October 24, 1926, Hoshigaura won by a big margin at 9½:2½, according to a report in *Manchuria Daily News* on October 25.

/ 1926 Dairen-Mukden Inter-port Match

The *Commercial Travelers' Guide to the Far East* published by the U.S. Department of Commerce in 1926 listed Hoshigaura Golf Club on p. 74. In the same year, SMR published a pamphlet, *Manchuria: Land of Opportunity*, which included the same photograph of a golfer driving off at Hoshigaura used in its earlier advertisements.

"Hoshigaura Golf Club 18 Holes Course Laying-Out Celebrated," reads a news report published on June 13, 1927 in *Manchuria Daily News*. The report says: "It was shortly after 1:30 p.m. that Baron Okra on the S.M.R. Co. Directorate drove the first ball on the newly laid-out 18 holes course just completed, followed by the players who started at five minutes' intervals, in celebration of the construction of the new enlarged course of the Hoshigaura Golf Club yesterday." Refreshments were served at the Golf Club prior to the opening tournament. Club Vice Chairman Furusawa reviewed a brief history of the Club. Besides Japanese members and guests, American Consul Leo D. Sturgeon, Acting British Consul Mr. and Mrs. W.L. Carney and their guest Mrs. Brawn, Mr. & Mrs. Cartlidge and Mr. Wilken were present at the ceremony.

Oswald White, British Consul in Dairen from 1925-1927, reports in his memoirs that life was very pleasant during those years. "There was a good golf course in Hoshigaura (Star Beach) to which the foreigners belonged. It was run on somewhat autocratic lines by an inner clique of Japanese with one or two foreigners, who, however, were heavily outnumbered." According to the author: "There was one hole at Hoshigaura with a bunker designed to catch a drive with a short carry. This bunker shifted backwards and forwards more than once and it was popularly supposed that it varied accordingly as the Captain and President was 'on' or 'off' his drive. Here, as elsewhere, the keenness of the Japanese put the foreigner to shame. Whenever they had time to spare, the Japanese were out practicing and, after a long Sunday of three rounds or so, many of them would be found going over again and again the shots they had been missing during the day. If application counts, the Japanese should make the best golfers in the world."

On April 18, 1931, *Manchuria Daily News* published a news story about the founding of miniature golf links in Dairen. The report said that "Tomorrow, on the 19th, at 10 a.m., the new miniature golf links laid out within the enclosure in Central Circle at the west of the Chamber of Commerce & Industry, Dairen, will be opened by the promoters of the Dairen Baby Golf Club, Mr. H. Mine being manager, with his office in the basement of the Dairen Chamber." The miniature links would be temporary until the founding of an indoor golf links for winter. Currently there was no monthly fee and anyone could play by purchasing a ticket for 24 rounds at a cost of G¥5. Anyone invited by a member may join a competition for 25 *sen*. Each member was allowed to participate in the monthly competition. The first winner of a periodical competition would be awarded a champion cup. Three directors would be selected from among the members to guide and oversee Club management.

The SMR Co. published in 1933 a pamphlet in English titled *Tales of Three Cities in Manchuria*, about Dairen, Mukden and Hsinking (Changchun). On p. 10, the pamphlet writes about Star Beach: "There is irresistible temptation for loafers, professional and otherwise, in this bit of rock-studded water with its stretch of golden strand which makes up the Port of the Stars. Not even the 18-hole golf course covering some 550,000 square meters on the other side of the highway is able to destroy the magic of the place."

Josaku Furusawa, Captain of Hoshigaura Golf Club, was elected the new President of the Dairen Rotary Club on July 6, according to a report of the July 10, 1933 *Manchuria Daily News*.

On October 22, 1933, the first inter-port competition between Dairen and Mukden was held at Hoshigaura Golf Links, with Dairen coming out to be the winner. The players took a photograph at the links after lunch. The fourth from left in the front row was Hoshigaura Captain J. Furusawa. Mukden Captain Kampf was sitting right behind him.

The 1934 pamphlet *Golf in Japan* had a

/ *1933 Dairen-Mukden Inter-Port Match Players*

detailed description of Hoshigaura Golf Club. The introduction reads: "The place known as 'Star Beach' is noted as the foremost beauty spot in Manchuria." Visitors could dine at the Yamato Hotel or the Club House. It took 15 minutes by motor car from the center of Dairen to the golf course. The course was hilly and total length of the 18th holes was 6,077 yards:

The information of Hoshigaura Golf Club in *Golf in Japan* comes with two photographs. One shows golfers dining at the Club House. The other shows four golfers on the sandy putting green, dressed in the popular plus-fours, with two caddies were attending.

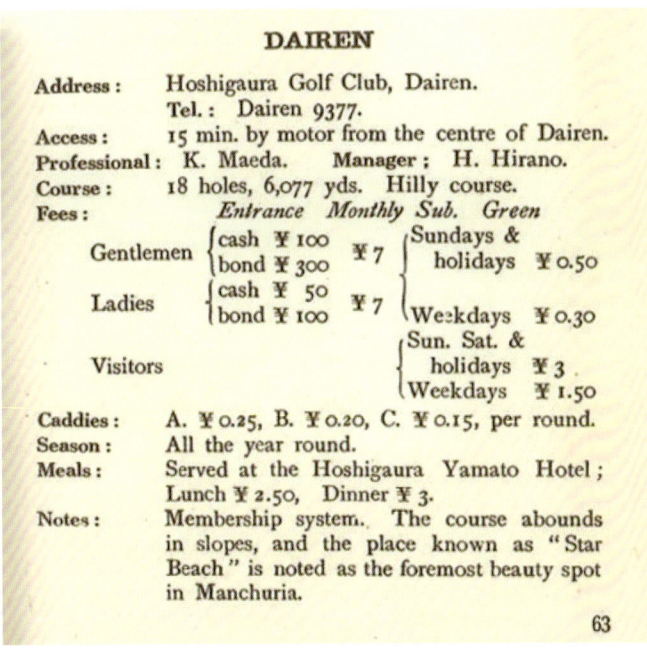

/ Hoshigaura Golf Club

To attract Western players to the links, the Hoshigaura Golf Club published an English edition of Club Rules in June 1935, which included 60 articles. It was translated and printed by the *Manchuria Daily News*. By 1935, the Club had 30 foreign members.

An Australian traveler wrote about his visit to Dairen in an article published on p. 8 of the December 2, 1935 *Sydney Morning Herald*. He writes: "The Hoshigaura hotel is situated in the middle of a spacious park on the seashore. It is surrounded by bungalows, which are let furnished at moderate rentals. And its own tariff is extremely reasonable. One can obtain a single room for from *yen* 5 per day (or *yen* 10 with meals) upwards, and a double room with bath for *yen* 10 (*yen* 15 including meals) upwards. Meals are also served à la carte in the hotel dining-room, and one can get quite a substantial breakfast for 80 *sen*, and a good lunch for *yen* 1. The best rooms at the Hoshigaura hotel overlook the sea, and one can bathe on the shore immediately in front, though the beach is better a little distance to the west. Immediately behind the hotel is the Hoshigaura golf course, which is open to visitors at moderate fees (which are increased during the weekends, owing to the number of Japanese resident members who play)."

Hoshigaura Golf Links would close soon, according to a report in *Manchuria Daily News* dated May 4, 1937. The Hoshigaura Golf Club had been notified by the SMR three years before that the present site of the golf links was urgently wanted for children's playground, camps and homestead plots. After three years of work, the Club management had decided to choose a new site at Yingchengtzu (Yingchengzi) on the Dairen-Port Arthur Branch Line. Construction would start in the summer. The report said: "It is really an excellent location, and will be developed, according to the same officials, into the finest golf course in the Far East." The new course could be reached by car or bus in 30-40

/ Sandy Putting Green at Hoshigaura Golf Links

minutes or by the Dairen-Port Arthur railway in about 50 minutes. "Yingchengtzu is destined to become an elite summer resort with the transfer of the Dairen Golf Club from Hoshigaura there in next few years."

The same newspaper reported on May 5 that Rokuro Akabochi, famous Japanese golf course architect, had visited the site and was to start designing the new course. However, due to the outbreak of the 2nd World War and China's Anti-Japanese War, the Yingchengtzu Golf Links never materialized.

In 2015, the Shandong Pictorial Publishing House released a 25-volume *Illustrated History of Japanese Invasion of China* edited by Zhang Xianwen. The voluminous book used a large number of photo images taken during the Japanese invasion to illustrate the history. Volume IV was titled "Forty Years of Occupation of Dalian (1905-1945)" edited by Guo Tiechun, Guan Wei, etc. Of the various photographs of athletic facilities created in Dalian and sports competitions organized, there were two photos of Hoshigaura Golf Links (https://kknews.cc/history/22mxbqz.html).

The 1939 *China Hong List* listed Hoshigaura Golf Club, Dairen on p. 735. The Honorary Secretary was T. Ogura and Secretary was C. Shimomura.

According to the *History of Dairen, Continued* compiled by the Japanese Dairen Society in 2009, the Hoshigaura Golf Links became an aviation training ground on March 24, 1941.

/ *Hoshigaura Golf Links (Top Left)*

/ *Golfers and Caddies at Hoshigaura Golf Club*

/ *1939 China Hong List*

/ *1941 Hoshigaura Golf Links*

DAIREN

RYOJUN (PORT ARTHUR)

Address :	Ryojun Golf Club, Port Arthur.
Access :	20 min. by carriage from Ryojun Station.
Manager :	R. Takata.
Course :	6 holes, 1,141 yds. Hilly course (sand green).
Fees :	¥ 2 per month.
Season :	All the year round.
Notes :	Membership system. The links located on a hill, just above the Kwantung Government Office, with many "ups and downs," command an extensive view of the harbour, hills and all parts of New Town.

/ Ryojun Golf Club

Ryojun Golf Club

In addition to the Hoshigaura Golf Links, Dairen had a six-hole golf links in Ryojun and the Ryojun Golf Club was formed. The Club was also listed in the 1934 *Golf in Japan*. The golf links was built on the slope of a mountain, and the greens were sand greens. The actual location of the links was on top of the Kwantung Government Office. The hilly course was 1,142 yards in length and commanded an extensive view of the harbor, hills and all parts of the New Town. The course was reachable by car in 20 minutes from the Ryojun Railway Station. Manager of the Club was R. Takata. The course was open year-round.

/ Ryojun

/ Former Kwantung Government Office in Ryojun (Mike Gu)

Nanning Golf Club

The history of Nanning Golf Links and Golf Club was recorded by Reginald Follett Codrington Hedgeland, an Englishman who worked in China for more than 30 years.

According to https://www.hpcbristol.net/, Hedgeland was born on December 18, 1874 in Exeter, Devon. He was educated at St Paul's School in London and graduated from Pembroke College, Oxford in 1897. He joined the Chinese Maritime Customs Service in May 1898. He was first posted in Hoihow (Haikou), Hainan Island. Later posts included Nanking, Tientsin, Macau, Kowloon, Nanning, Swatow (Shantou), and Canton. He became Deputy Commissioner at Nanning in 1917 and Commissioner in 1921. After a vacation back to England in 1923, Hedgeland returned to be in charge of Aigun (Aihui) on the Amur River in Manchuria. He was later in Swatow and Canton. After working in Hankow for about half a year in 1929, Hedgeland retired in April 1930.

As an amateur photographer and a collector of photographs, Hedgeland recorded his 30 years of life and work in China with a camera. His three albums of close to 600 black-and-white photographs are now housed in the Special Collection of Historical Photographs of China at the School

/ 1898 Hedgeland in Hoihow with Servants

of Oriental and African Studies (SOAS) of the University of London.

Hedgeland loved tennis and golf and often participated in competitions held in the cities where he worked. One of his photos titled "Courtyard Golf" shows Hedgeland playing golf in a courtyard. Based on the buildings in the

/ 1918 Hedgeland at Nanning Customs

picture as well as the serial number of the photo in his collection, it is likely to have been taken when he was working in Nanking Customs in the early 1900s.

Hedgeland took a number of photographs of himself playing golf with friends in Nanning. The SOAS Library said in an article published on June 7, 2018 that Hedgeland's "photographs of the club house and golf course in Nanning show the somewhat improvised nature of the entertainment available there." Judging from the photographs, the

/ Hedgeland Playing Golf in Courtyard

Nanning Golf Links was located on the west bank of the Yong River in Nanning. The Nanning Customs building was on the east bank of the river, so players had to cross the river by boat.

Hedgeland may have been the founder of the Nanning Golf Links, although this needs to be confirmed through further research. But the photographs show that the golf links was very rudimental and built on uneven and coarse ground. Golfers had to ride ponies to play golf there.

/ Hedgeland and Friends on Boat to Golf Links

/ The Course by the River

/ Riding Ponies at the Course

EARLY GOLF IN CHINA

/ Hedgeland on Horseback in 1920

The "Club House" of Nanning Golf Club was a simple mat shed under which golfers were able to rest and enjoy a simple lunch. Hedgeland's golfing partners were B.B. Anthony from the Standard Oil Co. of New York, Customs Inspector A.W. Barney and Customs Officer H.L. Andersen.

Judging from the dates the photographs

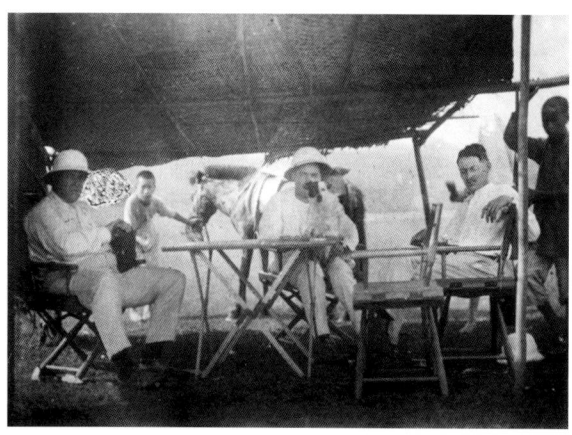

/ Hedgeland, Anthony and Barney in 1920

/ Hedgeland, Anthony and Andersen in 1920

/ Hedgeland and Friends at the Mat Shed in 1919

/ Hedgeland and Caddies

/ Caddies on the Nanning Golf Links

were taken, it seems that Hedgeland and friends started playing golf at the Nanning Golf Links as early as 1919. Given the many caddies shown in the photographs, there should have been a golf club, even though unofficially. The existence of a formally organized Nanning Golf Club can only be ascertained through further research.

/ A Break at Mat Clubhouse

Tongshan Golf Club

Tongshan (Tangshan) Golf Course and Club were closely related to horse racing in the city. The rise of this modern industrial city was driven by the construction and development of Kailan (Kailuan) coal mines.

During the late 19th century Westernization Movement led by Li Hung-chang, a prominent Ch'ing Dynasty senior official, the China Merchants Steam Navigation Company was established, which later evolved into the China Merchant Group. The Group established the Kaiping Mines in 1878 after rich coal deposits were discovered. Production started in 1881 and within 20 years, coal output reached 730,000 tons. To improve logistics, the Kaiping Railway Co. was formed and cargo ships operated between the ports of T'angku (Tanggu), Tientsin, Shanghai and Newchwang to transport coal.

In 1900, British merchants acquired a controlling stake in the Kaiping Mines after the company ran into financial difficulties. They later took ownership of the Kailan Mines, setting up the Kailan Mining Administration in 1912.

Lao Tao published an article in 2003 titled "Horse Race and Porcelain Plate of Tangshan Race Course." According to the article, Kaiping Mines built villas for senior foreign engineers and administrative staff to the west of the Tangshan Mine. A cement road from the housing area to Xishan Road inside the mine was also built. After the Kailan Mining Administration was formed in 1912, Tongshan grew into an economic and industrial hub in North China by the 1930s. Mining gave rise to other industries such as cement, porcelain and steel, attracting a large number of foreign engineers, financiers and businessmen. During the 70 years before 1950, Kailan employed more than 500 foreigners from 18 countries. Large numbers of domestic engineers and administrative talents also came to work and live in Tongshan. Chinese and Western cultures mingled in this modern industrial city and helped change the political, economic, cultural and social landscape, as well as ordinary life and entertainment.

With the growing expansion of Kailan's industrial operations and increasing number of employees, the Kailan Administration started to build cultural and athletic facilities to enrich the lives of employees. The first was a race course, which was referred to by locals as the Horse Race Ground.

/ Horse Race Ground at Fenghuang Shan (Phoenix Hill)

According to a detailed report about the Kaiping Mines published on pp. 392-394 of the August 17, 1906 *North-China Herald*, "Between forty and fifty Europeans are employed at Tongshan. There is a Club and a race course, as well as other indications of advancing civilization and progress."

/ 1936 Race Track at Kailan (Lao Tao)

Major Edward Nathan of the Royal Engineers was the first executive general manager of Kailan Mining Administration. With his experience in horse racing in Tientsin, he reportedly started racing in Tongshan.

According to Lao Tao, the Horse Racing Ground was situated to the east of today's Shuangfeng Shan (Fenghuang Shan). It occupied an area of 150 *mu* of land between today's Southern Gate of Tangshan Workers' Cultural Palace and the People's Air Defense Office to the north. Local people as well as people from Tientsin would participate in horse races on the weekends at Tongshan as the city was located in between Tientsin and Peitaiho (Beidaihe). Lottery tickets, named "Tongshan Small Champaign," were sold to visitors at $1 each, with chances of winning $100. The race track was about 1,500 meters long with fences around. Horse racing stopped in 1927. After liberation, the People's Government reconstructed the racing ground into the Workers' Palace in May 1951. It is now the site of the Tangshan Museum.

Lao Tao owned a color porcelain plate made in Tongshan in the 1920s. The oval-shaped plate is about 28 cm long, in fairly good condition. Inside the plate is a horse and a lady rider, with Shuangfeng Shan in the background. Underneath is written "Made by Tongshan Race Course." The dark-red horse and modern lady rider reflect the style of Chinese imperial painting influenced by Western art. The decorative edge in green was made using Japanese spray technology.

/ Tongshan Horse Race Porcelain Plate

Inside the spacious racing ground, senior executives of the Kailan Mines started the game of golf, shooting and other sports activities. In the late 1920s, Kailan Administration expanded athletic facilities across Tongshan, the East Mining District and Chinwangtao. These included skating rinks, pool tables, a bridge room, basketball and football courts. A golf links and club were also set up at Linsi (Linxi) Mines.

Linsi Mines were located to the east of Kaiping. Its rich and much larger coal deposits soon led to a speedy development of the area, with large living quarters for foreign engineers and executives.

In an article published on February 28, 2021 on the Internet, Qiu Tong wrote an article about his school titled "My Linxi, My School." The article said that Linsi was an old town dating back to the Warring States period in Chinese history. He writes: "Our main school was built over a green landscape on the eastern slope of Liangshan. The rostrum at the southern end of the playground was a British structure with a high ceiling and an orchestra pit. To the south of the school was a golf course, named by the British. We used to congregate here…."

The *Pan Bohai News Network* published an article on August 10, 2018 by Wang Shili titled "The Opening of Tangshan and Formation of a Modern City." The author wrote that a modern culture flourished in Tongshan in the early 20th century along with the growth of the city's industry, commerce, transportation and communications. The Kaiping Mines built a racing course at the foot of the Fenghuang Mountain. In the late 1920s, a Kailuan Senior Staff Club was established with facilities such as a golf course, tennis and badminton courts, a skating rink, a swimming pool and entertainment such as pool tables, a bridge room, a ball, a cinema and a bar. A theater troupe and basketball team were also organized.

Editor Zhao Lian said on p. 433 of his 2015 book, *History of Linxi Mine in Kailuan*, that after the founding of the 2nd Club of Linxi, a golf course was built to the north of the mine. It was converted into an employee athletic ground after the founding of the People's Republic of China.

Pan Pei wrote on www.sport.sina.cn an article on September 24, 2010 titled: "The Picturesque Golf Course Complemented an Ecological City." The article said that in Tongshan, golf appeared about 80-90 years ago. The early golf course appeared in Linsi, near today's Linxi Mine. During the last century when the British were building an industrial facility here, they brought with them entertainment and sports of an industrialized nation. Ma Xinji, retired deputy director of Tangshan Sport Commission who was in his eighties, and 90-year-old Ma Guoxun, former teacher at Kailuan No. 2 Middle School, were quoted as saying that they remembered seeing golfing activities at Tongshan when they were young.

A September 7, 2019 article titled "Sports in Old Kailuan" published on www.toutiao.com said that before the founding of New China, there had been modern sports facilities at Kailan Mines. Golf courses were built in both Tangshan and Linxi. Snooker and ping-pong tables were available at the Kailuan Hotel (formerly a Club for senior Kailan executives) and Linsi Guest House. Swimming pools were available at the Kailuan Hotel and foreign residence at the Zhaogezhuang Mine.

The November 1933 issue of *The Journal of the Royal United Service Institution* published a speech by Admiral Sir Howard Keely, Royal

/ Tongshan Golf Club Silver Trophy

Navy's Commander-in-Chief in China, delivered on October 4. The speech, titled "British Interests in China," said that Tongshan was building an 18-hole golf course. This should be referring to the golf course in Linsi.

A silver "Viewers' Trophy" of the Tongshan Golf Club dated June 20, 1942 was auctioned on September 11, 2018 at Cordy's auction house in Auckland, New Zealand. This unique trophy is in the shape of a coal cart sitting on four wheels. On the body of the trophy are the words: "TONGSHAN GOLF CLUB, VIEWER'S TROPHY, 20-6-42." The trophy weighs 435 grams and has dimensions of 10.2x7.4x10 cm.

Chinwangtao Golf Club

Historically there were two golf courses in Chinwangtao (Qinhuangdao). One was a 9-hole course in the Port District built around 1920. The other was a smaller 9-hole golf course built later in the Peitaiho (Beidaihe) District.

Chinwangtao Golf Club

Chinwangtao, or the Island of Emperor Ch'in (Qin), was a small island and so named after the first emperor of China's Ch'in Dynasty, who built a palace on the island during his journey to the east searching longevity. With the development of the Kailuan Mines in the late 19th century, Chinwangtao as a non-freezing port in North China offered an ideal outlet for coal. After liberation, the City of Qinhuangdao was established with three districts: the Port, Beidaihe and Shanhaiguan.

In an article, "Qinhuangdao: From Marsh to Port City" published in the November 3, 2016 *Hebei Daily*, Liu Jian wrote that after the completion of the Tianjin-Shanhaiguan Railway in March 1891, Li Hung-chang, leader of the Ch'ing Dynasty's Westernization Movement sent T'ang T'ing-shu, supervisor of the Kaiping Mines to Chinwangtao to explore possibilities of expanding the railway. T'ang discovered that the harbor was superior than Taku (Dagu) in Tientsin. The gulf of Chinwangtao was sandy and calm, with no silt for lack of major rivers running into the sea. Due to mild weather as well as high content of salt in the ocean, the harbor rarely freezes during winter.

In order to promote commerce, the Ch'ing Government approved on March 26, 1898 the opening of Chinwangtao as a trading port. It also designated an area of 1.5 km from Chinwangtao to Jinshazui on the east of Beidaihe as a summer resort for foreigners and Chinese. This led to the establishment of an open port owned by the Chinese along with a special tourist attraction open to foreigners.

Between 1904 and 1906, a Labor Recruitment Station was set up in Chinwangtao to send Chinese laborers to work in gold mines in South Africa. A total of 43,000 workers were dispatched from Chinwangtao in 30 groups to South Africa. In 1905, Chinwangtao built its first cement road named Harbor Road. It was renamed Kailan Road in 1912 after the merger of Kaiping and Lanchow Mines. In 1919, the Kailan Mining Administration built the Nanshan Club for senior executives working in Chinwangtao. Together with the rise and development of the Chinwangtao port, a number of modern industries were established in the city, which included the Shanhaiguan Bridge Factory and the Yaohua Glass Works. Up to 1924, the total population at Chinwangtao increased to 71,300.

According to Wang Qingpu, a senior

/ 1915 Bird's-Eye View of Chinwangtao Harbor (Liu Zhao)

researcher of local port history and staff of the Office of History at the Qinhuangdao Port Group Corp., the city saw the establishment of the first hospital of Western medicine known as the port hospital, the first postal office, telegraph office, milk house, golf course, tennis court, bar, cinema and other related facilities one after another."

There have been few reports in local media about a golf course and club in Chinwangtao other than the information above. Questions still remain as to when and where and by whom a golf course and a club were built in Chinwangtao.

We have identified, however, through extensive research of overseas historical records, the time and location of the Chinwangtao golf course and club. The 7th edition of the *Pacific Ports Journal* published in 1921 in Los Angeles stated on p. 188 under "Chinwangtao" that "The climate here is very healthful, and the port is sought as a summer resort by those desiring to avoid the extreme heat prevailing elsewhere in North China. There are good golf links, tennis courts, two staff clubs, and excellent bathing facilities."

We did not find information about Chinwangtao Golf Links in the 1919 edition of the magazine and are unable to locate the 1920 edition. But it is safe to conclude that a golf club must have been established in 1921 or earlier and the golf links were open to the public.

Mrs. Pamela Masters from the U.K. was an inmate at the Weihsien (Weixian) Concentration Camp in Shandong set up by the Japanese during the 2nd World War. She wrote about her life in China in a memoir published in 1998 titled *The Mushroom Years: A Story of Survival*. Born as Pamela Simmons in Weihaiwei in 1927, she came to Chinwangtao in the early 1930s when her father, George Simmons, was appointed Chief Accountant at Kailan Mines' Port of Chinwangtao. On p. 18, Pamela writes:

"The exclusive island-aspect of the port was emphasized by the three points that attached it to the mainland: the railroad tracks to the south, that ran from the station in the native city out to the docks; the high earthen levee to the west, that held in a large pond where we skated in winter; and a picturesque little white bridge to the north where a highly decorated kiosk, which doubled as a guard-house protected the road to the golf course and barred anyone coming down the Shanhaikuan beach road from entering the port."

The "picturesque little white bridge" mentioned by Mrs. Masters is believed to be the one in the following photograph:

/ 1921 Pacific Ports Journal

/ Little White Bridge Leading to Chinwangtao Golf Course

On June 17, 1935, *Manchuria Daily News* carried a report sent from Chinwangtao dated June 9 about a "Red Letter Day." The report said: "Yesterday was somewhat of a red letter day in the history of the port of Chinwangtao. In the afternoon the Chinwangtao golf club played the officers of the 2nd battalion of the Worcestershire Regiment, which resulted in a win for the club. Messrs. Chilton and Robinson defeated Lt.-Colonels Pelly and Stokes-Roberts by 3 and 1. Messrs. Faulkner and Ashby won their match with Major Ford and Captain Hargreaves by 4 and 3. At 7 p.m., the Chairman (Mr. W.B. Chilton) and the members of the new Chinwangtao club entertained their friends at a cocktail party."

Where were the Chinwangtao Golf Links

/ Chinwangtao Golf Course

> (June 9)
> RED LETTER DAY—Yesterday was somewhat of a red letter day in the history of the port of Chinwangtao.
> In the afternoon the Chinwangtao golf club played the officers of the 2nd battalion The Worcestershire regiment which resulted in a win for the club. Messrs. Chilton and Robinson defeated Lt.-Colonels Pelly and Stokes-Roberts by 3 and 1. Messrs. Faulkner and Ashby won their match with Major Ford and Captain Hargreaves by 4 and 3.
> At 7 p.m. the Chairman (Mr. W. B. Chilton) and the members of the new Chinwangtao club entertained their friends at a cocktail party. Among their numerous guests were:—
> Maj. G. A. Herbert, M. C., of HBM consulate-general, Tientsin, Lt.-Colonel J H. Pelly, commanding, 2nd battalion the worcestershire regiment, Lt.-Colonel and Mrs. Stokes-Roberts, Captain and Mrs. Hargreaves, 2nd battalion the worcestershire regiment, Mr. Hsia Shao-kong, Manchoukuo commissioner for foreign affairs stationed in Shanhaikwan, Mr. Haynes H. Reed, chief accountant, Kailan Mining administration Tientsin, Lt. J. Lion McNerney and Mrs. McNerney, Miss Frede Marsh, Mr. N. Wolfe of the APC., Tientsin and Mr. R. N. McLeod Coppin, M C., of the General Direction, Manchoukuo State railways.

/ New Chinwangtao Golf Club

and the Club? We can find their trace in Foreign Relations of the United States 1948, Volume VII, The Far East: China published in 1948 by the U.S. Department of State. Document #39 in the book was a telegraph sent by the U.S. Consul General Smyth in Tientsin to the Secretary of State at 1:00 pm on October 2, 1948. The telegram said that the national defense in Chinwangtao "have 'folded up,' although not in actual contact with Communists." "Twenty-sixth Division from Shanhaikuan said fallen back on Nanlichwang (Nanlizhuang), village near Chinwangtao golf course."

Nanlichwang, or South Li Village, is located in the northeast of the Port District, close to the railway and therefore considered to be within the center of the city.

As was discussed earlier, Chinwangtao developed into the major port for the transportation of Kailan coal and large numbers of British and other foreign personnel were employed in Chinwangtao by the Kailan Mines and other foreign businesses. The Kailan Mining Administration built a club at Nanshan for senior company staff. The golf course at Nanlichwang was built by Kailan Mines around 1920 for senior staff of the company as well as tourists at the Peitaiho resort.

893.00/10–248: Telegram

The Consul General at Tientsin (Smyth) to the Secretary of State

TIENTSIN, October 2, 1948—1 p. m.
[Received October 2—3:12 a. m.]

274. Re my 492, September 28.[53] According to KMA[54] report yesterday p. m. from Chinwangtao, Nationalist defenses in that general area have "folded up" although not in actual contact with Communists. Troops being pulled in from surrounding region. Twenty-sixth Division from Shanhaikuan said fallen back on Nanlichwang, village near Chinwangtao golf course. Fighting reported 3 miles east of Shanhaikuan. Railway transferring rolling stock from Shanhaikuan to Chinwangtao. KMA reports low morale of Fan Han-chieh troops that area.

Local press today reports Changli evacuated by Government troops but not confirmed. Railway says line open east of Anshang today.

KMA here reports several vessels commandeered yesterday at Tangku to transport troops and supplies to Hulutao, including two fuel control ships used for coal shipments to Shanghai.

Sent Nanking 500, repeated Department 274, Shanghai 479, Peiping and Mukden.

/ 1948 Telegram to Department of State

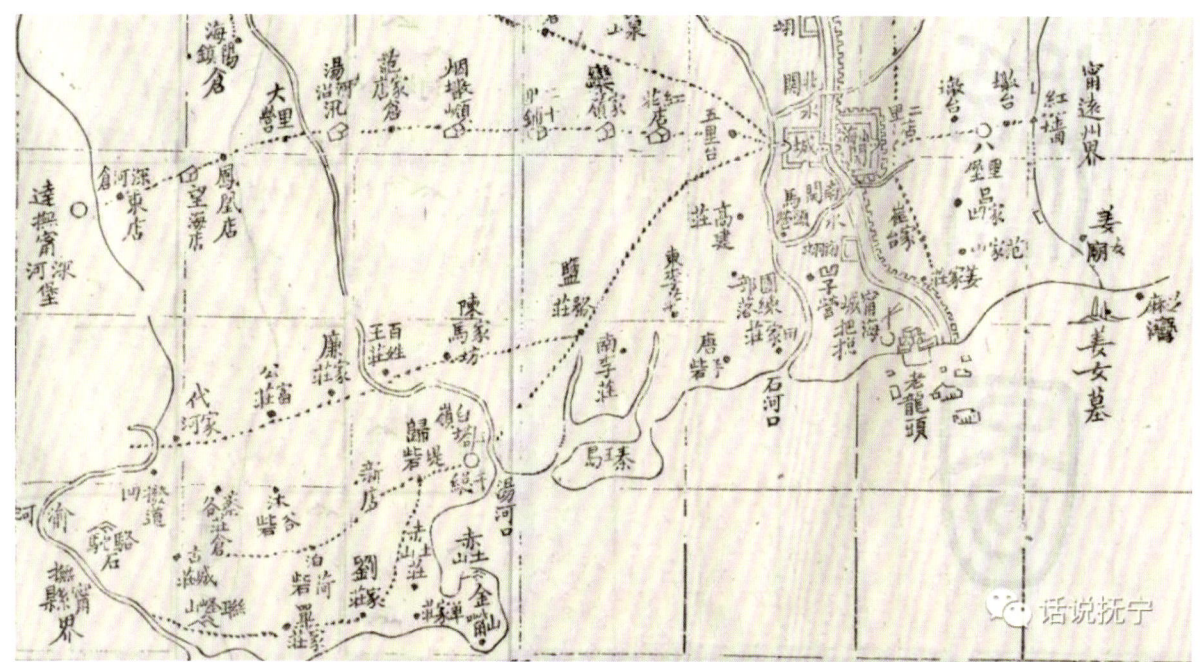

/ 19th Century Chinwangtao and Nanlichwang (http://www.qhdlkx.com/view_435.html)

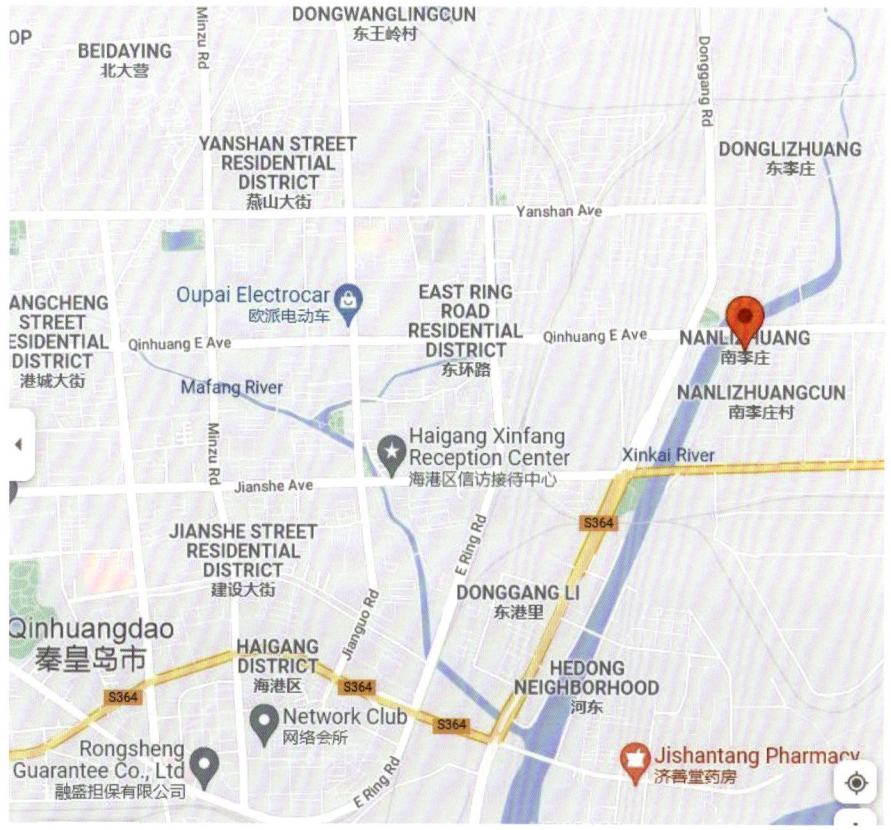

/ Today's Nanlizhuang

Two silver trophy plates obtained by the Golf Heritage Museum testify that the Chinwangtao Golf Club was operating in the 1930s and 1940s. Both plates have a silver dollar in the center. The round trophy plate was presented to the winner of a mixed foursome competition held in 1936, with J.S. Jones being probably one of the winners. The square one was the trophy for a bogey competition held in 1941.

/ Chinwangtao Golf Club Silver Trophy Plates

Peitaiho Golf Course

Information about an early golf course in Peitaiho (Beidaihe) can be found on the website of the Beidaihe Pine Rock Golf Club. According to the website, Chu Ch'i-ch'ien, transportation minister of the Peiyang Government found out during a visit to Peitaiho that all kinds of societies and associations were formed by expatriates there, which could interfere with domestic politics. He led a group of 16 people to file a request on June 16, 1919 for the approval of setting up a "Peitaiho Public Welfare Society." The government replied on July 21, approving the society and praised the sponsors for their donations in building roads, setting up health clinics and running charity operations.

Under Chu's leadership in the following 10 years, the Public Welfare Society helped

/ Peitaiho in 1910

with the development of Peitaiho, soliciting member donations for the funding of building roads and bridges, setting up a hospital and an elementary school, fixing buildings of historic interest and building the Lianhuashi (Lotus Flower Stone) Park. It also built a small scale golf course in 1929 for Chang Hsueh-liang. Unfortunately, the golf course closed after the July 7th, 1937 incident when the Japanese invaded Peking. (https://xw.qq.com/cmsid/20200508A0PA3A00?f=newdc)

Whether the claim of the Pine Rock Golf Club is true or not, it remains to be proven with further research.

Antung Golf Club

The city of Dandong was originally known as Antung. The first mention of Antung Golf Course was in a letter of Antung Maritime Customs in 1930. On August 18, 1930, F.L. Bissell of the Antung Customs wrote to a Mr. Lawford, a colleague at the Shanghai Customs who might be transferred to Antung, about life in the city, including "local food supply, the house boy, cook and other coolies." In the letter Bissell writes: "My predecessor, Fukumoto, had a car. I have contented myself with hiring one whenever necessary. There are motor repair shops here. The only use a car to you would really be for the golf course (9-holes)."

The letter was mentioned on October 16, 2020 by a blogger named Tiebi Shanfang in his blog on www.sohu.com: "History: What Did Foreigners Do Daily in Antung?" The letter is now with the archives of the Antung Customs. (https://www.sohu.com/a/425226017_693584)

/ Bissell's Letter to Lawford (Tiebi Shanfang)

In the meantime, the blogger also published a photo of a golfer driving off at the Antung Golf Course dated May 11, 1930.

According to a report in *Manchuria Daily News* dated April 15, 1933, Antung Golf Club would hold a preliminary competition for the Yonezawa Cup on April 16. Final competition would be held on April 23. There would be 38 Club members participating, two of whom were foreigners. Mr. Wang, the prefect of Antung, was the only Manchurian member of the Club. The rest of the participants were Japanese.

/ *Golfer at Antung May 11, 1930 (Tiebi Shanfang)*

/ *Antung Golf Tourney*

According to the 1934 *Golf in Japan*, the Antung Golf Club was situated at Mount Chinko (Zhenjiang Shan). The City of Antung, neighboring Korea, was a major station along the Chosen-Mukden Line of the South Manchuria Railway. The details of the Club are as follows:

According to an article published in the Chinese *Golf Weekly* on January 20, 2006, Antung Golf Course was located on the western slope of Mount Chinko. The area of the entire mountain and flat space facing today's Central Party Committee School used to be the site of the golf course, horse racing and dog racing courts. It is now Antung's old residential district. (http://sports.sina.com.cn/golf/2006-01-20/10202004257.shtml)

Tiebi Shanfang also published a tourist map of Antung in the 1930s in his blog, in which the Antung Golf Course is marked in Japanese on the top left.

/ *Antung Golf Club*

Zhang Jinshuo, a *Dandong Daily* reporter, published an article on November 4, 2019 titled "Golf Course on the Northern Slope of Mount Jinjiang 100 Year Ago." Mount Chinko was also named Mount Jinjiang. The article had a picture showing the location of the golf course in the 1920s and 1930s.

Zhang wrote about a week-long research conducted by Yuan Huaying of China

/ *Golfer at Antung May 11, 1930 (Tiebi Shanfang)*

/ *Antung Tourist Map (Tiebi Shanfang)*

that it was a standard and even first-rate golf course in China. It was one of the earliest golf courses in Northern China. (https://article.xuexi.cn/html/14215695260312973387.html)

The article failed to give any supporting documents about the year the course was built. Antung Maritime Customs was first established in 1906 and an Englishman was the Commissioner. A number of other Englishmen became commissioners

Forestry University as partial fulfillment of his Master's degree. Yuan was on the staff of the Course Management Committee of the China Golf Association. Yuan concluded in his research that the Antung Golf Course was built around 1916 based on available historical records. Based on his survey, the site of the golf course was determined. Yuan said that Antung Golf Course had 9 holes, a clubhouse and other related facilities, showing

/ *Golf Course on the Northern Slope of Mount Jinjiang (Zhang Jinshuo)*

thereafter. But we do not yet have enough information to conclude that Antung Golf Course was first built around 1916.

A sohu.com blogger, Pen Ma, wrote an article on December 8, 2018 titled "Photographs of Antung Mount Zhenjiang (Now Mount Jinjiang) Old and New." The blogger wrote that Mount Jinjiang was an unknown bare mountain full of ravines and gullies facing the Yalu River. It was named Mount Zhenjiang by a Japanese monk who named it Mount Chinko (Zhenjiang) in 1904 to bury the dead Japanese soldiers during the Russo-Japanese War. In 1912, the South Manchuria Railway started to build a park for Japanese residents and completed it in 1926. In 1918, the park was selected to be one of the eight scenic sites in Northeast China. (https://www.sohu.com/a/ 280444937_120031672)

Based on the fact that Antung was under the Japanese control through the South Manchuria Railway since 1905, we believe that Antung Golf Club was most likely founded by the Japanese around 1920.

The Chinese language *Golf Weekly* published article on golf.sina.com.cn dated January 20, 2006. Titled "The Mystery of the Antung Golf Course," the article reads: "On June 13, 2004, a reporter from the *Yalu River News* in Dandong told me that the president of Alp Alpine Co, Ltd. spoke about Dandong Golf Course in a recent visit to Dandong. He said that as early as in 1940, there was a golf course to the west of Mount Jinjiang, one of the earliest in China. The place was good for rest and entertainment. The golf course had nine holes and golfers were often seen playing at the course. There was a building on top of the hill where the river was in view." *Golf Weekly* reporter immediately decided to make a research trip to Dandong.

The focus of the *Golf Weekly* research was meeting with elderly people in Antung who worked as caddies at the golf course. One of the people interviewed was 80-year-old Zhang Chengshu. His family moved to Antung near the golf course after he was born in 1925. His neighbor, surnamed Li, was an interpreter for the Japanese, and through him, Zhang started to work as a caddie for three years when he was 12. At the time, the course area was covered by green grass, occupying an area of 500-600 *mu*, according to Zhang. The course had nine holes and downhill on the flat area was a racing course for horses, donkeys and dogs.

Zhang was quoted as saying: "Most of the players were Japanese, Koreans and some VIPs of Manchuria. More people played on weekends, up to two dozen. There were fewer people during the week. They were dressed in Western suits and sports

/ *Zhang Chengshu Imitating Golf Swing*

pants. The golf bag had 7-8 sticks, 1-2 were woods and 6-7 were irons. They would team in a group of three or four and start playing downhill. They used a round-headed wood stick to play the first strike, for the longest distance. Then they would use iron sticks. When they started, they would place a ball on a 2-inch-long thin stick in the grass, aim at the ball, and turn the body to hit the ball with eyes on the ball. They competed and whoever had the least number of hits to finish the hole would be the winner." (http://sports.sina.com.cn/golf/2006-01-20/10202004257.shtml)

Zhang said: "They would play the ball into a hole surrounded by sand. Once the ball was on the sand, they would change a stick and gently tap the ball into the hole. The marks of balls on the sand were smoothed by a flat board before the next player." This shows that the greens at Antung in those days were hardened mud covered by fine sand.

"There was a two-storied building (clubhouse) on top of the mountain with office, dining room, tables and chairs. Players would bring food and eat there.

/ *The Former Club House*

The dining room provided green bean soup. The building also had a bathroom and showering facilities. It still stands on top of the mountain today."

Zhang said: "I made 40-50 cents a day carrying bags for golfers, sometimes a little over one *yuan*. Thanks to my good relationship with neighbor Li, I was often first introduced to the Japanese golfers. If I picked up a lost ball, I could sell it to the golfer for 20 or even 40 cents. The 20-cent ball had round dots on it. But the 40-cent ball had square dots, considered to be a better ball. After the Japanese left in 1945, the golf course went out of business. Chinese workers were hired to maintain the golf course. They used grass-cutting machines that could automatically propel forward. Those people also left after the course was closed. The area was divided among the local villagers as farm land during the Land Reform Movement in the 1950s. But people often found sand underneath. Later the land became a nursery as well as a residential area."

Another elderly person interviewed by *Golf Weekly* was 77-year-old Cai Jizhen, who had also been a caddie. Cai said he became a caddie for fun and at the same time to make some pocket money. "I was 11 or 12 in 1940 and a 2nd grader at the Furong Elementary School right beside the golf course. Every Sunday or holiday, I would go to the golf course together with some of my friends to carry golf bags and pick up golf balls for players. We could make 20-50 cents a day, enough to buy a pair of new shoes.

"Most of the players were Japanese. They wore big-rim hats covering the entire face and long socks passing the knee, quite an expensive outfit. We would follow the player up the mountain with a bag of clubs, about 4-5 of them in a bag, not heavy. Once they hit a ball from the mountain, we would run down to find the ball. After 1944, the horse and dog racing ground and the golf course at Mount Jinjiang went out of business. The golf course has become today's nursery."

Other people interviewed by *Golf Weekly* all confirmed that the Antung Golf Course was located to the west of Mount Jinjiang during the 1930s and 1940s, which is today's garden nursery on the slope of the mountain.

Harbin Golf Club

According to the 1934 *Golf in Japan*, Harbin Golf Club was just a 10-minute car ride from the Railway Station. It featured a 9-hole flat course of 2,791 yards. The secretary was H. Haag and the professional was V. Smirnoff.

HARBIN

Address: Harbin Golf Club, Harbin, Manchukuo.
Access: 10 min. by motor-car from Harbin Station.
Secretary: H. Haag.
Professional: V. Smirnoff.
Course: 9 holes, 2,791 yds. Flat course.
Fees: *Entrance   Annual Sub.   Green*
  Members   ¥40   ¥70   —
  Visitors   —   —   ¥1 per day
Caddies: A $.60, B $.40 per round.
Season: April to October.
Notes: Membership system.

/ Harbin Golf Club

After the 1917 October Revolution, many Belarusians fled to Harbin, the largest city in Northeast China. During the 1920s there were between 100,000 and 200,000 Belarusians living in Harbin, so it is not much of a surprise that a Russian named V. Smirnoff, was the local golf professional. Harbin came under Japanese control starting in 1932.

H. Haag was Howard Lee Haag, an American born in 1893 in Michigan. Haag graduated in 1917 with a bachelor's degree in Psychology and taught English at a middle school. He went back to the U.S. and became a YMCA secretary at Grand Rapids in charge of membership, and then executive secretary in 1919. He went to Cleveland, Ohio to study Russian in 1920 and took up the position of general secretary of the Harbin YMCA in 1921 and was in charge of Russian refugee affairs. In the 15 years from 1921 to 1935, he worked with the YMCA to set up elementary and middle schools as well as universities in Harbin. He worked at YMCAs in the Philippines, Japan and Korea after 1935 before returning to work at the Bridgeport YMCA in Connecticut after the War until his retirement.

With the few available historical resources, we estimate that Harbin Golf Club could have been established in the early 1920s.

The *Manchuria Daily News* published a number of reports about Harbin Golf Club in the 1930s. A report on September 20, 1932, for example, said that in bright daylight on a Sunday afternoon, a group of golfers at Harbin Golf Club were attacked by brigands trying to kidnap two bankers. The report reads: "Swinging and whacking with golf sticks at Mauser-armed brigands is rather a new stunt, 'put over' recently by Manager Melhuish and Ass't-Manager Hansell of the Hongkong and Shanghai Banking Corporation (Harbin Branch) at the Harbin Golf Club grounds. They swung the slim clubs so heartily that the bandit leader had his nose broken, and the whole pack skidooed with their customary alacrity, having heard before of fighting bankers…. Mr. Hansel was hit by a Mauser pistol bullet, and hurriedly taken to the

Sanitas Hospital. A bone of his arm was fractured. But Mr. Melhuish suffered only slight injuries to his face and head."

The report continues: "The kidnap attempt happened on a golf course with a number of male and female golfers over the spacious greenswards. The brigands had carefully selected their intended preys, thinking the bank officials were the wealthiest persons on the club grounds." As a result, the Bank had to advertise in a Harbin Russian daily newspaper that it would never pay any ransom for any of its officials or employees kidnapped by bandits.

A report about the annual general meeting of Harbin Golf Club was published in the paper's June 8, 1939 issue. It said a new executive committee of the Club was selected during the meeting, which included: Chairman E.J. Mahon, manager of National City Bank of New York; Honorary Treasurer W. Hoplak of Hongkong & Shanghai Bank; Honorary Secretary H.W.G. Nicholis of I.I. Tchruin & Co., Ltd.; J.M. Allan, manager of Chartered Bank of India, Australia & China; J.M.R. d'Almeida; G.R. Turral, British Consul; and G.E.B. Tyler, of Hongkong & Shanghai Bank.

The report also said that the monthly medal competition was held on Sunday. The Bankers' Cup would be played on June 11 for over 16-hole medal play. The report mentioned that "golfers here are somewhat alarmed over the shortage of balls."

The paper reported on June 18 that Harbin Golf Club organized the Bankers' Cup competition on Sunday the 11$^{th.}$ The Cup was won by Mr. Sonnehara with a net score of 46+41=87-12=75. The runner-up was H.W.G. Nicholis, with a net score of 45-43=88-11=77.

The same report said that Harbin Golf Club was sending a team of eight golfers to take part in the golf tournament at Mukden on Sunday, June 18. Most of the team members going were Japanese.

The paper's July 7, 1939 issue published a report about two recent competitions at the Club. At the Mitsui Cup competition held on June 25, R. Izumi won the 36-hole competition, with a score of 92+106=198, a net of 172. Due to bad weather, only 10 players participated. At the Shimada Cup competition held on July 2, D. Takai won the 18-hole playoff, with a total score of 91 and a net score of 68. The runner-up was H.W.G. Nicholis with a total of 88 and a net of 77. The report said an 18-hole competition would be held on July 9 for the Kawasaki Cup.

Due to the Anti-Japanese War and the intervention of the Soviet Union in the 1940s, the operation of Harbin Golf Club was affected and by 1945 the Club eventually closed when the Japanese surrendered.

Nanking Golf Courses and Clubs

There were two golf clubs in Nanking (Nanjing) before 1950. One was the Nanking Golf Club founded in the early 1920s. The other was the Nanking Golf and Country Club instituted in 1934, the first and only golf club in history invested by the Chinese Republican Government.

Nanking Golf Club

The two earliest reports on the Nanking Golf Club were found in British publications of the 1920s. The first report appeared in the *Bucks Herald* dated April 26, 1924. Quoting a story from the *Nanking Bulletin of Church and Community* about a funeral of a Miss Burnham, the report reads: "The entire community of Nanking was very deeply grieved last Friday morning (29th February), when it became known that Miss Grace Evelyn Burnham had passed away at the Foreign Hospital, succumbing to heart failure and blood poisoning following an operation for appendicitis.... As a mark of respect to the deceased the flags of many of the business houses were half-masted and sporting fixtures at the Nanking Golf Club of which the deceased was a member, were postponed on the day of the funeral."

The second report was a photographic news story published on p. 236 of the April 23, 1927 *Illustrated Sporting and Dramatic News*. The photo, taken at the Nanking Golf Club as the troops of the National Government had reached Nanking in its Northern Expedition, titled "Where the Greens Were Blown Up by Cantonese Soldiers: A Lunch Time Scene at the Nanking Golf Club." The caption underneath the photograph reads: "In view of the recent fighting at Nanking during which it is reported that the Cantonese soldiers blew up the golf greens, the picture is of interest. Watching their patrons, the native caddies can be seen in their white coats with numbered sashes." The picture was attributed to Graphic Photo Union.

/ Lunch at Nanking Golf Club

Based on the photograph, the course of the Nanking Golf Club was rather rudimentary and the clubhouse was a simple shed. Judging from the two dozen or so players and the many onlooking caddies, the Club and course seemed to be quite active, especially during the time of domestic war. The Nanking Golf Links and Club were most likely founded by British expatriates since the city was opened to foreign trade as early as the late 19th century. The course and club might have been founded earlier than the 1920s, but this remains to be determined by further research.

unch at Nanking Golf Club to the caddies can be seen in thier is of interest. anking Golf Club."sporting fixtures at the Nank

A report from Nanking in the January 29, 1927 issue of the *North-China Herald* said that officers of the three Royal warships from Shanghai visited Nanking and held a golf competition with members of the Nanking Golf Club.

Nanking Golf and Country Club

In 1927, China's National Government decided to move the country's capital to Nanking. According to reports by the *Central Daily News*, due to a lack of appropriate entertainment activities among the growing number of diplomats, Minister of Foreign Affairs Dr. C.T. Wang and Minister of Education Chiang Monlin worked with foreign consuls and established an International Club. C.T. Wang was the president and British Consul Meyrick Hewlett was the vice president. The Club had 15 directors and was registered with the Executive Yuan.

According to Zhou Anqing's article on https://kknews.cc/history/ja38rje.html, the International Club was formally established with an opening ceremony on July 1, 1929. The event featured music, dance, luncheon, speeches, photography, film and fireworks. The site of the Club was the former German Consulate to the north of the city. The building was renovated with government funding and excellently furnished.

Sir Meyrick Hewlett, a veteran British diplomat to China and Consul in Nanking, was a good friend of C.T. Wang and participated in the organization of the International Club. In addition, he personally helped choose a site in the Sun Yat-sen Mausoleum for the building of a golf course. Hewlett remembered the founding of the International Club and the golf links in his 1943 autobiography, *Forty Years in China*. He writes: "With the help of Dr. Wang the International Club was inaugurated. The building was given and furnished by the Foreign Ministry and Dr. Wang was the first president, myself being vice-president."

Hewlett said that in the winter of 1929, he and Willys R. Peck, American Consul General, "spent an afternoon looking for a golf course and found a lovely site in the beautiful park country outside of Nanking. A huge stadium was built and

/ Nanking Golf Clubhouse (Shitou Shiji)

a lovely bathing-pool; ground, too, was reserved for a race-course."

The July 22, 1934 *New York Times* published a report sent in on June 18 by its special correspondent in Nanking. The report, "Golf on Purple Mountain – First Club of Its

Kind Opened in Chinese Capital," reads: "The highest officials of the National Government were among those who took part a few days ago in the formal opening of the capital's first golf and country club, on the slopes of Purple Mountain."

The report continues: "Sponsored and financed by the Ministry of Foreign Affairs in the belief that recreational advantages should be available for government officials, and in the hope that foreign legation staffs eventually will move from the old to the new capital, the club already provides nine holes of as sporty golf as can be had in China, and in the not distant future nine more holes are to be added. Caddies may be hired for approximately 3 cents a golf round or 10 cents for a day's work." The present president of the Nanking Golf and Country Club was Mr. Lo Wen-kan, formerly Minister of Foreign Affairs, while the vice president was Willys R. Peck, U.S. Consul General and counselor of the American Legation.

According to an article by Yu Feng published in *Jinling Evening News* on August 22, 2006, the site of the golf links was located at Dongwazi Village on the southern slope of Purple Mountain. The Foreign Ministry leased about 1,200 *mu* of hilly land close to the village at an annual rent of 1,800 gold *yuan* and built a 9-hole golf links and a clubhouse. The clubhouse was a two-story building complete with an entrance hall, a bar, offices on the ground floor and meeting rooms, bedrooms and shower facilities on the second floor.

The article said that local people called the Nanking Golf and Country Club "Foreign Ministry Field Golf Course" or "Suburban Golf Course." The purpose of building the course was to expand the relations of the Nanking Government with the international community in Nanking, mostly

GOLF ON PURPLE MOUNTAIN

First Club of Its Kind Opened in Chinese Capital.

Special Correspondence, THE NEW YORK TIMES.

NANKING, June 18.—The highest officials of the National Government were among those who took part a few days ago in the formal opening of the capital's first golf and country club, on the slopes of Purple Mountain.

Sponsored and financed by the Ministry of Foreign Affairs in the belief that recreational advantages should be available for government officials, and in the hope that foreign legation staffs eventually will move from the old to the new capital, the club already provides nine holes of as sporty golf as can be had in China, and in the not distant future nine more holes are to be added.

Caddies may be hired for approximately 3 cents gold a round or 10 cents for a day's work.

The present president of the Nanking Golf and Country Club is Mr. Lo Wen-kan, formerly Minister for Foreign Affairs, while the vice president is Willys R. Peck, United States Consul General and counselor of the American Legation.

The New York Times
Published: July 22, 1934
Copyright © The New York Times

/ *New York Times July 22, 1934*

diplomats, their families and business people. It provided them, especially those moving in from Peking, with opportunities to enjoy outdoor golfing popular in the West. The Foreign Ministry later organized a Suburban Golf Society.

Yu stated that the Suburban Golf Society was headed by Foreign Minister Hsu Mo with Ho Ying-ch'in serving as vice president. There were six categories of membership: honorary, full, alternate, life, non-resident and non-playing. Subscription fees ranged from $15 to $500 depending on the membership level, with monthly dues of $2-$7.

North-China Herald published a signed article on May 14, 1935 with the title "Boxer Indemnity Students, Twenty-Six Young Chinese Going to Britain to Complete Studies." The article said Dr. Irvin, the British Consul, and some other British officers organized a tea party a few days ago "at the beautiful golf club some miles from Nanking." The students were on their way to study at British universities under the Boxer Indemnity Funds. The article reads: the tea party "was set in the handsome club house with the beautiful golf links spreading out in the distance. It would be difficult to imagine a more charming place: a delightful wide veranda, shady rooms, and all the modern conveniences of a first-class golf club. Nanking and golf: what a magnificent idea."

Most members of the Suburban Golf Society were foreigners. Chinese members were

/ *Nanking Golf and Country Club (Yu Feng)*

mostly high-ranking government officials. The Golf Course became a platform for important diplomatic events and meeting place for foreign and Chinese politicians. The four-day 2nd Annual Meeting of the Chinese Association of Political Science was held at the clubhouse on July 3, 1936, with 46 participants, including former Foreign Minister Wang Shih-chieh.

/ *Madame Soong Mei-ling at Nanking Golf and Country Club*

Julius A. Barr, personal pilot for both the Young Marshall Chang Hsueh-liang and Chiang Kai-shek, had an album of 339 black-and-white photographs taken during his time in China from 1934 to 1937. One of them was a photo of a vehicle parked on the road near the Nanking Golf and Country Club dated 1937. It was on page 112 of the album with an inscription of "The Nanking Golf Club."

In the photo, the two-storied clubhouse is visible from a distance and the car was a 1931 Studebaker President. It was a popular sedan in China during the 1930s, according to Tom Lieb, a U.S. collector of antique cars. Barr's album is now kept at the Museum of Flight Archives in Seattle.

On January 12, 1937, the *New York Times* published a news release by *Associated Press* in Nanking with the headline "Chang Golfs under Guard of 8 Submachine Guns." Chang Hsueh-liang was playing golf at the Nanking Golf and Country Club. The report reads: "Nanking, China, Jan. 11.— General Chang Hsueh-liang, under technical detention as a result of his coup at Sian Dec. 12, when he abducted Generalissimo Chiang Kai-shek, played golf at the Nanking Country Club today under the muzzles of eight sub-machine guns. Whether the eight guards, each lugging a weapon as they accompanied him over the course, were there to protect the 'young marshal' or were detailed to prevent a possible escape went unexplained. After the round, the guards gathered up the golf clubs and, still carrying the submachine

/ *1937 Nanking Golf and Country Club (Museum of Flight Archives)*

guns, clambered into automobiles to return to the residence of T.V. Soong, brother-in-law of Chiang Kai-shek, where Chang Hsueh-liang is a 'prisoner.'"

Time Magazine published the same story on January 18, which states: "Recently-kidnapped Premier Chiang rested in quiet retirement this week and his recent kidnapper, Young Marshal Chang Hsueh-liang, although pardoned by the Nanking Government, was still under such extremely heavy guard last week that it was difficult to say whether or not he was in custody. He was once more the 'guest' of Banker T.V. Soong and last week played around the Nanking Country Club golf course accompanied by soldiers carrying eight submachine guns."

Before Nanking fell to the Japanese, diplomatic missions moved further inland in December 1937 following the National Government. The Nanking Golf Links was soon deserted. Neither did the Japanese try to utilize the golf course. According to an article by Wang Guodong published in *Jinling Evening News* on April 15, 2017, the National Government returned to Nanking after the surrender of the Japanese forces in August 1948 and tried to revive the golf links. Diplomatic missions made similar requests. U.S. Major General Robert B. McClure of Chinese Combat Command wrote a letter to Mayor Ma Chun-ch'ao requesting refurbishing the golf links, and the letter was transferred to the Mausoleum Administration. In November 1946, the Ministry of Foreign Affairs wrote to the Mausoleum Administration to renew the lease of the golf course. After the lease agreement with new terms was signed, the

Chang Golfs Under Guard Of 8 Submachine Guns

By The Associated Press.

NANKING, China, Jan. 11.—General Chang Hsueh-liang, under technical detention as a result of his coup at Sian Dec. 12, when he abducted Generalissimo Chiang Kai-shek, played golf at the Nanking Country Club today under the muzzles of eight submachine guns.

Whether the eight guards, each lugging a weapon as they accompanied him over the course, were there to protect the "young marshal" or were detailed to prevent a possible escape went unexplained.

After the round the guards gathered up the golf clubs and, still carrying the submachine guns, clambered into automobiles to return to the residence of T. V. Soong, brother-in-law of Chiang Kai-shek, where Chang Hsueh-liang is a "prisoner."

/ *New York Times January 12, 1937*

Foreign Ministry again delegated the operation of the golf course to the International Club. With funding from foreign diplomatic missions, the golf course was rebuilt and reopened. Until Nanjing was liberated on April 23, 1949, most of the players at the course were American military officers and diplomats.

Since liberation, the Nanking Golf Course and Club ceased operations. Fruit trees were planted inside the course and local residents started to call the area "New Orchard." Today the old course serves as nursery of the Mausoleum of Dr. Sun Yat-sen.

Wuchow Golf Club

According to *The Special Article Appended to the Burma Convention* signed between China and Britain on February 4, 1897, cities along the West River including Wuchow (Wuzhou) were opened to foreign trade. On June 4, a Maritime Customs office was set up in the city followed by the office of the British Consul. British firms Jardine Matheson, Butterfield & Swire and Hong Kong, Canton & Macao Steamboat Company began to set up shipping offices. Wuchow quickly developed into a central trading hub on the West River, linking Hong Kong, Canton, Kwanghsi (Guangxi), Yunnan and Sichuan, becoming the largest trading port in Southern China, second only to Canton.

/ A 20th Century Bird's-Eye View of Wuchow

Wuchow Club was organized in 1901 when expatriates attended the opening ceremony on March 2, according to a report in the March 11 issue of *Overland China Mail*. The opening was presided by Mrs. Schweigner and participated by Mrs. Macdonald, Captain Thomas, Mr. Campkin, Mr. Harris and Mr. Howard.

The clubhouse was a newly erected wooden building. It added a few greenhouses close to the side of the mountain in the following two years and built a tennis and cricket court in front. A shooting range was also built at the foot of the mountain. As the city is located in a mountainous area, every flat space was utilized to its full. In July 1903, the British Consul opened for services. By 1922, the Maritime Customs had completed construction of seven more buildings as business steadily expanded.

J.G. Farrell's 1978 novel, *The Singapore Grip*, was recreated into a TV series. The book featured an interesting dialogue about Wuchow

/ 1915 Wuchow

Golf Club in Chapter 4. One of the characters in the book said: "I think it was the morning after we left Canton and we were steaming up a river into Wuchow in Kwangsi Province. Anyway, someone pointed out a golf club on the left-hand bank and said it was definitely the most exclusive one in the world and when I asked why? he said it only had four members, the manager and assistant-manager of Standard Oil Company and the same of the Asiatic Petroleum Company, but that's ridiculous, isn't it? A golf club with only four members. He was only joking, wasn't he? Really! Good heavens! How d'you mean? 'Chinese don't play golf?' Now you're making fun of me."

The above description of Wuchow Golf Club might not have been fictional. Oil and kerosene companies were among the first foreign businesses that set up shops in Wuchow after it was opened to trade. Asiatic Petroleum Co. started operating in July 1905 and Standard Oil built its oil tankers in September 1915. Texaco followed in 1926. Wuchow Golf Links and a Club were most likely set up by managers of the British and American oil companies before 1920. For lack of flat land, the golf links was likely built along the banks of the West River, with no more than 9 holes.

/ View of Wuchow from the British Consulate (Beloit College)

A news story filed from Wuchow on May 12, 1923 said that "The Wuchow course has been put out of use for the time through the flooding of it," according to a report in *North-China Herald* on June 2.

John Rigg, a British expatriate and member of the Shanghai Golf Club, was the first person to document Wuchow Golf Club's existence. In his article, "Pre-War Golf in China" published in the September 2004 issue of *Through the Green*,

/ 1923 Wuchow Golf Course Closed Due to Flood

Rigg said that in comparison with the greens at Hungjao Golf Course in Shanghai, "Wuchow relied on browns," indicating that the greens in Wuchow were made of hardened mud. Rigg sent Jeff Wu in Shanghai an early photograph of Wuchow, captioned "A Brown at Wuchow."

Wuchow Golf Club operated until the late 1930s, according to an article dated March 4, 1937 written by A.B.C.–G, a British Naval Officer. Published in the April 1976 issue of *Naval Review*, the author recalled his boat trip from Kwangtung (Guangdong) to Kweilin (Guilin) via Wuchow. The author writes: during the stay at Wuchow, "I had four rounds of golf, so did well for exercise. The golf course is now most spring like with very green grass, wild roses, white violets and a great deal of a pretty dark blue wild larkspur."

/ *A Brown at Wuchow (John Rigg)*

Fushun Golf Club

Fushun golf Club was founded in the mid-1920s, starting with a 9-hole golf course. By the early 1930s, the Club added a new 9-hole golf course.

Fushun was one of China's coal cities. Japan took over the southern part (Changchun to Dairen) of the Chinese Eastern Railway from Russia after winning the Russo-Japanese War of 1904-1905 and obtained the special privilege of operating the Fushun Mines. The Japanese set up the Southern Manchuria Railway Co., Ltd. in Dairen in 1906, with a total investment of 200 million *yen*, half of which was contributed by the Japanese government and the other half by the Japanese Royal Family, aristocrats and officials. The SMR officially opened for business in April 1907.

From the early 20th century to the late 1930s, the Japanese administration initiated a number of municipal development plans in Fushun, including the Qianjinzhai (Thousand Gold Fortress) New Streets, Fushun New Streets and Fushun Metropolitan Development, according to Fu Bo and Li Xiang in an article published on www.fs7000.com. In May 1908, SMR purchased land to the north of Qiantaishan and west of Qianjinzhai to build a "new street" for Japanese residents. The new street was centered to the north of the Qianjinzhai Railway Station, with the east side designated for the residence of SMR engineers and employees and the west designated for ordinary local residents.

With the growth in mining and related businesses, Qianjinzhai became densely populated. The local administration decided to convert 21.5 acres of farm land to the north into a new residential area for the local Chinese. In order to further expand on developing the rich mines underneath Qianjinzhai, SMR once again decided in 1918 to build open mines in the area. As a result, it was decided to move both the old Qianjinzhai area and the new area of Chinese residents to the Fushun New Streets.

The Fushun New Streets were located in front of the Fushun Railway Station at Yung'an Tai. The high ground in between Yung'an Tai and East Village Mine was allocated for the residence of Japanese and employees of the mine. In March 1919, SMR finalized the plan for the move of the residential areas at the same time when it decided on the operation of the open mines. Moving preparations were completed in April. In the fall of 1921, engineering was conducted on site and design of the new residential area was completed in February 1922 and approved in April.

The New Streets area was divided into three parts: residential, commercial and industrial. The new Fushun Railway Station became the center of the area, with the eastern hilly area as residence of Japanese and mine employees and western flat area as New Streets.

It took two years to complete the building of the new railway station in July 1924. Japanese residents at Qianjinzhai started moving in 1924 to the New Streets at Yung'an Tai and the move was completed in 1928. Three parks were built in the New Streets: East, West and South Parks. East Park is today's Labor Park. West Park is today's Children's Park and South Park, which is located in Nanyang, had a racecourse and golf links.

After the September 18 Incident in 1931,

SMR transferred the administrative authority of its territory to the puppet Manchukuo. Starting from 1938, SMR operated in railway, coal mine and other businesses. Up until Japan's surrender in 1945, the total assets of SMR reached 4.2 billion *yen* and its employees grew from 110,000 to 398,000.

According to an article published in kknews.cc on August 13, 2018, the author "sxhx139," provided a photograph of an outdoor golf practice range inside the East Park. (https://kknews.cc/travel/5orlall.html)

Fushun Golf Club was listed in the 1934 *Golf in Japan*, which indicated that it had two 9-hole golf links, old and new. Details are as follows:

/ East Park Golf Practice Range (sxhx139)

FUSHUN

Address:	Fushun Golf Club, Fushun, Manchukuo. Tel.: Fushun 2213.
Access:	2 hours by train from Mukden.
President:	T. Kubo.
Secretaries:	K. Sumita & T. Hirata.
Course:	(A) Old course (9 holes), 3162 yards. (B) New course (9 holes), 2480 yards.
Green Fees:	Weekdays (A) ¥1 (B) ¥0.50 Sundays & holidays (A) ¥2 (B) ¥1
Caddies:	¥0.10 (9 holes) per round.
Season:	April to November.
Meals:	Japanese & European meals served at the Club House.
Notes:	Membership system.

/ Fushun Golf Club

We estimate that the Fushun Golf Course inside the South Park should have been the original 9-hole golf course built between 1924 and 1928. The new course should have been built between 1932 and 1933.

Fushun Golf Club was quite active in the early 1930s and often sent teams to Mukden for inter-port competitions. The *Manchuria Daily News* reported on September 14, 1933 that Fushun and Mukden had a competition with 16 players from each team. Fushun won with a score of 9:4 in individual matches and 5:3 in foursome two-ball matches. Mukden's Captain Kampf was absent due to health.

At an interport match between the two on June 10, 1934, Mukden crashed Fushun by 31:5, with individual matches at 15:5 and foursome at 16:0. Twenty members from each team participated and took a photograph at Mukden Golf Club after the event.

/ 1934 Fushun and Mukden Inter-Port Match

On June 17, 1935, Fushun and Mukden Golf Clubs faced off again in Mukden and Fushun suffered another loss, with a score at 0:11. Mukden was able to keep the Kanji Usami Cup and also took away Fushun's club pennant. Players took a photo at the Mukden Golf Course.

/ 1935 Fushun and Mukden Inter-port Match

But on September 24, 1935, Fushun beat the old opponent in a match play at Fushun Golf Links by 22:14. In the twosomes matches Fushun won by 13:5, and in the foursomes, the two sides broke even with 9:9.

/ September 1935 Fushun and Mukden Match Play

Chiaotso Golf Club

Angelo Luzzatti, an Italian engineer who toured China in 1896, discovered that China's Henan, Shanxi and Shaanxi were rich in coal mines. After returning to Europe, he founded the Peking Syndicate Limited in London and through negotiations with the Ch'ing Government, the Syndicate obtained the right to mine at Chiaotso (Jiaozuo).

/ 1902 Peking Syndicate Railroad

On August 20, 2008, blogger Hai Langyong wrote an article on sina.com.cn titled "Modern Sports Activities in Jiaozuo." The article said that British residents in Chiaotso built a racecourse in 1902 near today's Hexi Area of the People's Park. The first elementary school set up in 1906 at Xiwangfeng Village made "physical exercise" a mandatory lesson. After the Chiaotso Mine started business, the Peking Syndicate established a Mining and Railway School on March 1, 1909. It became China's first institution of higher learning on mining. The Town of Chiaotso was formed in 1910 by the Ch'ing Government centering on the western part of today's Jiaozuo. In 1924, the Mining and Railway School grew into the Syndicate Mining University. The city's first sports ground, named Exercise Ground, was built on the west side of the campus. Basketball, volleyball, football, tennis and track-and-field teams were soon organized at the University. The first middle school, Syndicate Middle School, was founded in January 1925, which had courses in track-and-field and ball games. "In the same year," the article stated, "a Chiaotso course was built to the north of the school." The "Chiaotso course" mentioned here could likely be the site of the Henan Golf Course in Chiaotso. (http://blog.sina.com.cn/s/blog_4ca49d9f0100ai7q.html)

The 1936 edition of the *Golfer's Handbook* has a listing for the Chiaotso Golf Club under China.

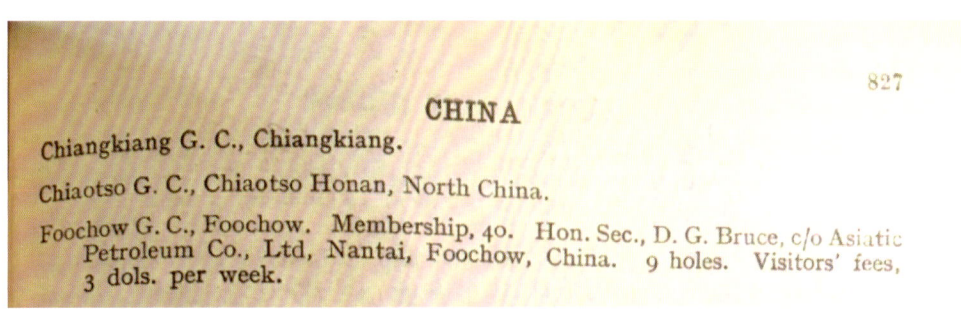

/ 1936 Golfer's Handbook

The 1939 edition of the *China Hong List* under Tsiaotso (Chiaotso) also had a listing for Honan (Henan) Golf Club. The Club's Honorary Secretary was G. Rogers.

The Chiaotso Golf Club was last mentioned in the 1947 *Golfer's Handbook*.

TSIAOTSO, Hon., 1939

華商業銀公司
Hua-ying-shang-yeh-kin-kung-sze
Anglo-Chinese Finance & Trade Corp., Ld.
(Incorp. in England)
TA Sindacato Tsiaotso
Bell, A. J., A.C.A., repr. in China

中福兩公司合辦事處
Chung-fu-lien-ho-pan-ssu-chu
Chung Fu Joint Mining Administration

CHUNG FU JOINT MINING ADMIN.—*cont.*
Secretariat—
Hsieh, H. L.
Strangman, T. G. A.
Lee, T. C.
Yao, T. K.
Tien, T. W.
Ivanoff, Mrs N. T.
Li-Ho Colliery—
Chang, H. F., colliery mgr.
Yen, T. T., engr.
Wang Feng Colliery—
Tang, C. P., colliery mgr.
Tseng, G. C., engr.
Brusienko, N. P.

中原股份有限公司
Chung-yuan-ku-fen-yu-

Honan Golf Club
Rogers, G., hon. sec.

中福公司清算委員會
Fu Chung Corporation
(In liquidation)
Liquidation Committee—
Tou, F. T.
Hu, S. C.
Chow, S. S.
Bell, A. J.
Bisseker, F. D.
Milligan, J. R., sec.
Chien Yung,
Wang, Y. M., legal adviser

/ *1939 China Hong List*

709

CHINA

Chiaotso G. C., Chiaotso Honan, North China.

Foochow G. C., Foochow. Membership, 40. Hon. Sec., J. Chubb, c/o Dodwell Co., Ltd., Nantai, Foochow, China. 9 holes. Visitors' fees, 3 dols. per week.

/ *1947 Golfer's Handbook*

Anshan & Tangkangtzu Golf Club

There were two golf courses and clubs in Anshan. One was the Anshan Golf Club and the other was the Tangkangtzu (Tanggangzi) Golf Club. Both were built by the Japanese and each had a 9-hole golf course.

Anshan Golf Club

The *Golf in Japan* published in 1934 listed Anshan Golf Club as being only "a few minutes' walk from Anshan Station. The course had 9 holes of 2,965 yards, hilly and rough. Golf season was from May to October. Club Secretary was Y. Tominaga and Manager was I. Satō. Details are as follows:

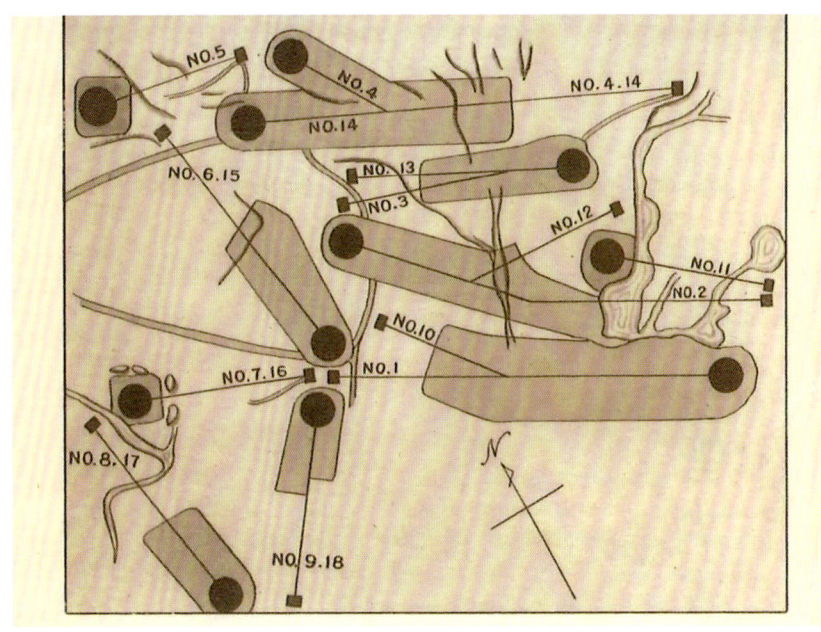

/ 11 Greens of 9-Hole Golf Course

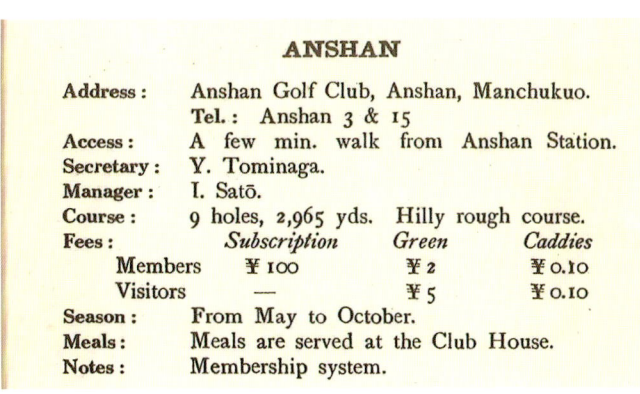

/ Anshan Golf Club

According to a course map in the booklet, Anshan Golf Club's 9-hole course uniquely had 11 greens, offering changing distances and directions and generating interest in playing a round of 18 holes.

The course map indicates that when playing the course for a round of 18 holes, holes 1 and 10, 3 and 13 both had different tee grounds but shared the same greens. Holes 2, 11 and 5 each had their specific tee grounds and greens. Hole 12 had a special tee ground but used the 2nd green. Holes 4 and 14 used the same tee ground but heading to two different greens. The rest of the holes, namely 6 and 15, 7 and 16, 8 and 17 and 9 and 18, used the same tee ground and greens.

In an inter-port competition between Anshan and Mukden Golf Clubs on July 25, 1937, Anshan beat Mukden with a score of 10.5:7.5, according to a report in *Manchuria Daily News*. The match took place at the Matsumigaoka Golf Course in Anshan, with 14 members from each team participating in twosome and foursome matches.

/ Former Health School (Anshan Bureau of Education)

/ 1937 Anshan-Mukden Competition

According to Zheng Jiyu, author of *100-Year History of Steel Capital Anshan* and other web-based writings, the location of Anshan Golf Club was at the area of the former Anshan Health School (today's Anshan Bureau of Education) and the swimming lake inside the Eryijiu (February 19) Park.

The Eryijiu Park was the former Asahi Park close to the former Taiding area of Japanese villas, or today's Dongfeng Street, Yingbin Street and 12th Street at the Tiedong District. Taiding occupied a total area of 200,000 square meters on the slope of East Mountain and the villas were built for the senior employees of South Manchuria Railway (SMR).

According to the *Anshan Local Chronicles*, the city became SMR's territory after the Russo-Japanese War. SMR set up the Anshan Iron Works in 1916 and took over Lishan, Ch'ianshan

/ Taiding

AUSHAN

/ Golfer at Anshan Golf Club (Zheng Jiyu)

and Tangkangtzu from Russia. Zheng Jiyu in his book published a photograph of a golfer driving at Anshan Golf Club.

season. The course was planning to extend to 18 holes. Details of the Club are as follows:

Tangkangtzu Golf Club

In addition to the Anshan Golf Club, there was another golf course built at Tangkangtzu to the southwest of the Anshan. Tangkangtzu Golf Club was listed in the 1934 *Golf in Japan*. It was a 9-hole golf course owned and operated by the Tangkangtzu Hot Spring Company. Located only a few minutes' walk from the Tangkangtzu Station the 9-hole flat course was 2,520 yards in length. It was open all year round except during the snow

TANG-KANG-TZU

Address: Tang-kang-tzu Golf Club, Tang-kang-tzu Hot Spring, Manchukuo.
Access: A few min. walk from Tang-kang-tzu Station.
Manager: C. Saitō.
Course: 9 holes, 2,520 yds. Flat course.
Caddies: ¥ 0.05 per round, ¥ 0.10 for one hour.
Season: Open all the year, except snow season.
Lodging and Meals: Lodging and meals may be obtained at the near-by Japanese hotel which is well equipped.
Notes: The course is owned and maintained by the Tang-kang-tzu Hot Spring Company for the comfort of the guests staying at the hotel of the company. Extension to 18 holes is now being planned.

65

/ Golfer at Anshan Golf Club (Zheng Jiyu)

Tangkangtzu Hot Spring was one of China's four most famous hot spring resorts. It is located 14 km to the southwest of Anshan. After the Russo-Japanese War, SMR took over the resort and built a number of facilities such as Jade Spring Hall, Double Emerald Pavilion, Pure Forest Hall, etc. Northeast warlord Chang Tso-lin built the Dragon Spring Villa in 1921. Pu Yi, puppet Emperor of Manchukuo, rebuilt the Double Emerald Pavilion in 1931 and moved in the following year.

Blogger Xu Ming of the Tanggangzi Hospital wrote on July 5, 2010 at blog.sina.com.cn that he had contacted an elderly resident named Zhang Hengjiu, who kept a pamphlet in Japanese about the Hot Spring printed during the Japanese occupation. With the help of Sun Guitian, it was translated into Chinese. The pamphlet mentioned Tangkangtzu golf course. (http://blog.sina.com.cn/s/blog_68ce34ab0100kcxd.html)

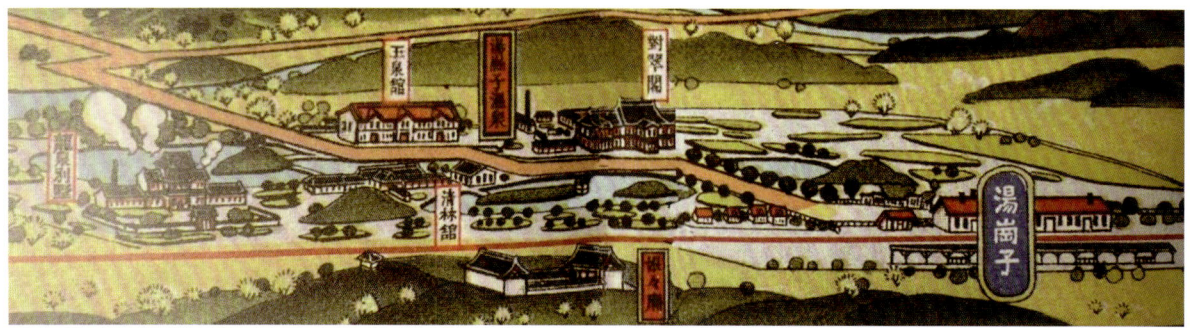

/ *A Bird's-Eye View of Tangkangtzu Hot Spring (Zheng Jiyu)*

Hsinking Golf Club

The Hsinking (Changchun) Golf Club was founded in 1933 with a 9-hole golf course, which was expanded to 18 holes in 1934, taking up an area of 330,000 square meters.

On March 9, 1932, the puppet regime of Manchukuo (Manzhouguo) was founded by the Japanese in Northeast China and Changchun was renamed Hsinking or New Capital. According to Wang Guofan of the Changchun Local Chronicles, the South Manchuria Railway started to map out the construction plan of Hsinking. A "Capital Construction Bureau" was set up to plan and execute the construction.

The Capital Construction Bureau completed the "Greater Hsinking Metropolitan Plan" in November 1932, which was secretly approved by the Japanese Northeast Military Command. According to Pan, Hsinking would encompass an area of 200 square kilometers, including 100 square kilometers of suburban area and another 100 square kilometers of city proper. The city proper included the original 21 square kilometers of the city. Another 20 square kilometers would be built in five years with a planned population of 500,000.

Zhang Xianda wrote about the "Greater Hsinking Metropolitan Plan" in an article published on January 6, 2013 in the *Changchun Evening News*. The article said the Plan was drafted by Japanese municipal construction experts, taking into consideration of the 19th century rebuilding of Paris, the British idea of a "garden city," American metropolitan plans of the 1920s and Chinese traditional municipal planning. The design style was similar to Canberra, capital of Australia. The layout of Hsinking was centered around Tat'ung (Datong) Square, now People's Square, vertically expanding along Tat'ung Avenue (today's People's Avenue) and horizontally expanding along Hsingren (Xingren) Boulevard (today's Liberation Boulevard).

The Hsinking Administration Center was located in the area from Anmin Square (today's Xinmin Square) to Shunt'ian (Shuntian) Avenue (today's Xinmin Avenue), where the "Imperial Palace, Imperial Courts, the State Council" and departments of government were located. According to Wikipedia, parks, fish ponds, swimming pools, anti-air raid tunnels, tennis courts and a small golf course were built for

/ Pu Yi Playing Golf

Pu Yi. (https://en.wikipedia.org/wiki/Museum_of_the_Imperial_Palace_of_Manchukuo)

Zhang Xianda said in his article that the center of Hsinking was at the Tat'ung Square where the Central Bank, Electricity Corp., Capital Construction Bureau and Capital Police Station were located. In the cultural and educational district at Nanling and Union Square, the largest zoo and botanical garden, as well as a general sports center, were planned. A social center was planned at the Mukden Boulevard (today's Nanhu Boulevard) and Heping Boulevard. The Japanese entertainment area was set at K'aiyun Avenue, with luxury hotels, bars, casinos, high class brothel, golf course and race course. Chinese entertainment area was located at Hsint'ianti (Xintiandi, today's Taoyuan Road). The Hsinking Station (today's Changchun Station) and South Hsinking Station were designed as large-scale international transfer stations. Up till the collapse of Manchukuo on August 15, 1945, 79 square kilometers of Hsinking had been developed with a population of more than 850,000.

The 1934 *Golf in Japan* listed detailed information of Hsinking Golf Club. The 9-hole flat golf course of 3,140 yards should have been built before 1934 as part of the new capital construction plan. The course was open year-round and an expansion was already planned. Details of the Golf Club are as follows:

Captain Malcolm Duncan Kennedy studied Japanese in Japan in 1910 before becoming a freelance journalist and writer. In his memoir, *The Diaries of Captain Malcolm Duncan Kennedy 1917-1946*, he wrote about Japan's gigantic plan to build the new Hsinking. Kennedy visited the Foreign Office in Tokyo on April 28, 1934. He writes in the memoir: "While visiting Kawasaki Torao of the Foreign Office, I was taken up to the roof of the new Justice Ministry, which is at present shared by Foreign Office, and had the new city of Hsinking construction plans explained by one of Kawasaki's Manchurian assistants, one William Wu by name. They are certainly showing extraordinary vigour and enterprise, laying out magnificent wide asphalted roads and boulevards, parks, and even a golf course, and fine big buildings going up apace. Two consecutive 5-year plans are to be carried out and a really fine city should be the outcome."

On June 25, 1934, the Hsinking Golf Club held an inaugural tournament to celebrate the opening of the new clubhouse, according to a photo story in *Manchuria Daily News* on June 26. By this time, the golf course had been expanded to 18 holes. It was located on the west side of the railway tracks. The caption of the photos reads: "The links are set out in a treed and rolling country and in a few years should develop into one of the best in the country. Pending the cultivation of grass greens, temporary winter greens of sanded clay are used." The top picture gave a view of the clubhouse and the 18th green.

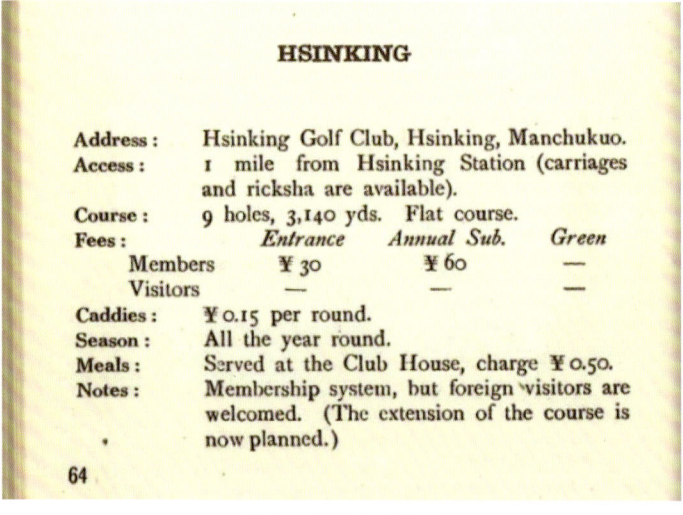

/ Hsinking Golf Club

/ New Clubhouse of Hsinking Golf Club

The lower picture provided a full view of the golf course.

Yunze Xuezhang wrote in https://kknews.cc/ on October 29, 2019 that the Hsinking Race Course was completed in September 1935. He also said that the Hsinking Golf Club was built in December 1936, although the date was questionable. But the author did publish three photographs of the Hsinking Golf Course. The first one was the same as the lower photo published by the *Manchuria Daily News* above, allowing us to conclude that the 18-hole golf course at Hsinking was completed in June 1934. The second picture showed two golfers and two caddies carrying bags of clubs. And the third picture was an expansive view of the course.

/ Hsinking Golf Course (Yunze Xuezhang)

/ *Golfers and Caddies at Hsinking Golf Course (Yunze Xuezhang)*

/ *Extensive View of Hsinking Golf Course (Yunze Xuezhang)*

/ *1939 Golf and Race Course at Hsinking (Yunze Xuezhang)*

Yunze Xuezhang pointed out that the northern part of the course was later taken over by the Headquarters of the Manchuria Air Command. The actual site of the golf course was located to the south of today's Xi'an Boulevard, to the north of today's Haoyue Boulevard and to the east of Zhengyang Avenue. The area to the east of today's Zhengyang Street was the golf course while to the west was the racing ground.

According to the *Maps of Changchun Streets* edited by Fang Youliang, the Japanese had already built golf courses in Harbin, Dairen and Mukden before the founding of Manchukuo. It would have been inappropriate if the new capital did not have a golf course. According to the "Capital Construction Plan," the Hsinking Golf Course would be a standard 18-hole course, with tee grounds, rivers, ravines, deep grass area, ponds, fairways, greens, pins and flags. A clubhouse for members, visitors, offices and administration and logistics were also planned.

William Shaw Sewell wrote his Ph.D. thesis titled *Japanese Imperialism and Civic Construction in Manchuria: Changchun 1905-1945* in January 2000 at the University of British Columbia. In Chapter 6, "Planning Manchukuo's Capital," Sewell writes: "Small parks,

/ Hsinking GC Clubhouse and No. 10 Hole

a golf course (330,000 square meters), a horse track (also 330,000 square meters), nurseries, cemeteries, and small tracts among residential neighborhoods completed Shinkyo's (Hsinking) green space, although the zoo and sports complex awaited the second five year plan."

Kenneth J. Ruoff in his 2010 book, *Imperial Japan at Its Zenith*, quoted on p. 138 a Japanese visitor to Hsinking in 1940 as saying that a visitor could play at the city's 18-hole golf course for 2 *yen* ($0.50) a round during the week and 4 *yen* a round on the weekends.

On May 11, 2018, a writer pen-named "Drizzling Life" posted on https://kknews.cc/ a photograph taken in front of the clubhouse of Hsinking Golf Course. It showed a sign pointing to the 10th Hole, a Par 4 of 360 yards, which indicates that the golf course had 18 holes.

APPENDIX
TIMELINE OF EARLY GOLF IN CHINA

1870

James Ferrier from Carnoustie, Angus, built China's first golf links together with Scottish friends in Hankow (Hankou), China. Ferrier arrived in China in 1869 as a marine engineer employed by the China Merchants Steam Navigation Company. He was a scratch amateur golfer and an ambassador in China of the Scottish modern game of golf. Lauded as the "Tom Morris of the Far East," Ferrier was one generation earlier than the first Carnoustie group of club-makers and professionals who emigrated to the outside world in the late 19th century.

1871

James Ferrier and friends built a golf course of only a few holes in the center of the Shanghai Race Course.

1878

Hankow Golf Club was instituted, with James Ferrier as one of the founders.

1883

September
The Hankow golf course grew into 9 holes, which were named: Starter, Stand, Stone, Straight, Pond to the Mountain, Consulate, Gully, Grog and Gate. Ferrier was the champion at the September competition, with a score of 38 in the front 9 and 37 in the back 9, a total of 75.

1889

May 10
Thirteen golf enthusiasts met at the Hong Kong Club to form the Hong Kong Golf Club. Royal Navy Captain Robert Murray Rumsey was the first captain of the Club. The Club was designated Royal in 1897 and was again renamed Hong Kong Golf Club after Hong Kong was returned to China in 1996.

1890

The first golf links in Chefoo (Yantai) was built near the ocean by Vivvy Eckford, manager of Cornabé-Eckford and was playable only at low tide.

1891

September
Two members of the Hong Kong Cricket Society played a match with golfers in Shanghai inside the Shanghai Race Course.

1893

December
The Golf Links at the Shanghai Race Course was expanded to 6 holes.

1894

Newchwang (Yingkou) Golf Club was formed, with a simple course built on the mud

APPENDIX

bank at the mouth of Liao River. During the 1910s, Newchwang and Mukden (Shenyang) golf clubs had numerous inter-city matches. Mukden Golf Club had an annual Newchwang Cub competition. Golfing activities at Newchwang continued until the 1940s.

January 10

Eighteen enthusiasts met at the Shanghai Club and decided to form the Shanghai Golf Club and obtain the 6-hole golf links at the Shanghai Race Course. Presided by Brodie Augustus Clarke, a Scotch and chairman of the Shanghai Horse Bazaar, the meeting elected a preparatory committee comprised of Messrs. B.A. Clarke, James Ferrier, E.F. Alford, Wade Gard'ner, E.A. Arbuthrot, A.G. Rowand (Hon. Treasurer) and R. Carr (Hon. Secretary).

March 15

The first general meeting of the Shanghai Golf Club was held and club rules were established. B.A. Clarke was elected chairman and the number of members was set at 75. Before receipt of golf clubs made in Scotland, members were able to use clubs rented from the Hankow Golf Club.

October 1

The Shanghai Race Course Golf Links was expanded into 9 holes and formally opened to members. The longest hole was 283 yard, the shortest 163 yard. Iron clubs must be used in three holes in order to cross ditches and highland.

December

The Shanghai Golf Club organized its first mixed competition participated by 19 couples.

December 26

The first handicap completion was held at the Shanghai Golf Club participated by 29 golfers. James Ferrier set the first course record of 86 for an 18-hole play.

1895

Tientsin (Tianjin) Golf Club was established with 20 members. The Club built a 9-hole golf course inside a graveyard at the southeast corner of the Russian concession. The founder of Tientsin Golf Club was Scotsman Duncan Houston Mackintosh who was then manager of the Hong Kong and Shanghai Banking Corp. in Tientsin.

1896

January 2

Shanghai Golf Club organized the first Hankow Challenge Cup competition. The Cup was presented by the Hankow Golf Club. The semi-annual competition of the Challenge Cup was played a total of 30 times by 1910. James Ferrier became the Captain of Shanghai Golf Club.

1897

The Amoy Kulangsu (Gulangyu) Golf Club was founded. Its primitive 9-hole golf course was built among rocks, graves, rice field and cow-yard by the ocean.

James Ferrier brought back a silver Ferrier Cup from Scotland, named after his father, for competition at the Shanghai Golf Club.

Shanghai Golf Club made a silver trophy for Hankow Golf Club in return for its earlier present, the Hankow Challenge Cup. Named the Shanghai

Challenge Cup, the exquisite jug-shaped trophy stands 20 inches high and was made by Shanghai silversmith Luen Wo. On the jug are inscribed the words: "Challenge Cup Presented by the Shanghai Golf Cub to the Hankow Golf Club 1897."

The St. Andrews Cup competition was held at the Hankow Golf Club. The 26.5cm tall and 642g silver trophy was made by the Shanghai silversmith Hung Chong. Two dragons were etched on the trophy cup, which stands on the base with three bamboo sticks. On the front of the cup are the words: "Hankow Golf Club." Underneath are two crossed golf clubs followed by the words "St. Andrew's Cup." On the back of the cup are the words, "Won by J. Shearer, 1879." Together with the Shanghai Challenge Cup, the two silver trophies are the earliest golf trophies found existing. The trophy is now in the collection of the Golf Heritage Museum in Shenzhen, China.

1898

From 1898 to 1913, the Hankow Golf Club organized a total of 24 competitions for the Shanghai Challenge Cup, twice every year. The names of the champions were etched on the trophy and silver plates on the base. Hankow Golf Club's Vice-Captain Walter Hughes Corsane won the Shanghai Challenge Cup for the third time in 1913, after previously winning twice in 1907 and 1912. The Cup became his property and it is now owned by his grandson, Gerard Corsane in the U.K.

November 19

Shanghai Golf Club's new pavilion clubhouse formally opened. James Ferrier, the Club president, presided over the opening ceremony. Club members reached 150.

1899

Ichang (Yichang) Golf Club was formed and its golf links was built among "a thousand graves" on the suburb of the city along the middle reaches of the Yangtze River.

1900

The Foochow (Fuzhou) Golf Club was formed with a course of only 4 holes laid out over a graveyard on Tsangshan (Cangshan) Hill. The course was later expanded to 9 holes by the 1920s. Club members reached 40 in 1936 and the Honorary Secretary was D. G. Bruce of the Asiatic Petroleum Co., Ltd.

September

The British Legation Golf Club was formed in Peking (Beijing) and a rudimentary golf links was laid out by Nigel Oliphant from St. Andrews, a student interpreter, together with a marine captain and a Sikh officer. The British Legation Golf Club was later renamed Peking Golf Club.

1901

The Weihaiwei Golf Club was formed by the British Royal Navy on the Liukung (Liugong) Island, its training base off of Weihaiwei (Weihai). The Club had a 9-hole golf course built on the eastern slope of the Island, with a total length of 3,029 meters. Club president was James Stewart Lockhart from Edinburgh, Commissioner of Weihaiwei.

May 5

A.J. Wicks won the open championship of the Shanghai Golf Club and received a gold shield. This is the earliest gold medal found so far and it is owned by Jeff Wu of Shanghai.

1902

Women members of the Shanghai Golf Club applied to form a Ladies Golf Club section and the application was approved.

June

Shanghai Golf Club organized the first of a caddie competition and 16 caddies participated. They played one round of the ladies' course using only irons in the presence of a foreign umpire. The champion was Lali Sung, who scored 53 and won 4 silver dollars. The runner-up and 3rd place scored 60 and 61 and received 2 and 1 silver dollars, respectively. Two caddies tied for fourth place, each given 50 cents.

1903

Shanghai Ladies Golf Club held its first annual championship competition. The competition continued uninterrupted annually until 1921.

February 2

The Captain's Cup competition was played at the Shanghai Golf Club between J.H.T. McMurtrie, ex-champion of Hong Kong and J.A. McGill, ex-champion of Singapore. McMurtrie, a scratch player, conceded strokes for three holes and beat McGill by 3 up and 1 to play. The silver cup was presented by H.G. Gardner and it was made by the famous Shanghai silversmith Luen Wo. The Chinese style silver cup is 17.5 cm high and weighs 963g, with three dragons as handles. On the cup are inscribed the words: "SHANGHAI GOLF CLUB 1903 CAPTAIN'S CUP PRESENTED BY H.G. GARDNER WON BY J.H.T. MCMURTRIE." The silver trophy is now in the collection of the Golf Heritage Museum in Shenzhen, China.

April 5

James Ferrier, the "Tom Morris of the Far East," passed away during sleep due to several weeks of influenza. Ferrier sailed back home with family from Shanghai in April 1901 and lived in a Retreat Cottage in Carnoustie and continued playing golf at his home course. He was 56 years of age. The Carnoustie *Evening Post* published his obituary on April 6, which reads: "The deceased was a well-known golfer in his early days and had been connected with the Carnoustie Golf Club for over forty years. In many ways he manifested his interest in that club, and it was only ten days before his death that he was presented with a handsome medal by the members as a token of the honorary life membership conferred upon him. In China he was the foremost golfer in all matches and tournaments."

1904

A simple golf course was built at Chefoo in 1904, with greens of 12 inches in diameter made of hardened earth. It was difficult to put on the greens full of cracks.

March

Amoy Golf Club had a handicap competition and the winner was W.H. Wallace, manager of the Hongkong & Shanghai Banking Corp. and Chairman of the Amoy Municipal Council. Wallace was presented with an exquisite silver trophy plate, 19 cm in diameter and 222g in weight. On the plate are the words: "Amoy Golf Handicap March 1904 Won by W.H. Wallace."

The silver plate is now in the collection of the Golf Heritage Museum in Shenzhen, China.

The Mukden Cosmopolitan Golf Club was formed and a simple and straight golf course was built between downtown and the railway station, out by 9 holes and in by 9 holes.

The Tientsin Golf Club purchased a movable military barrack from German troops and erected it on the site of a lumber yard as clubhouse. The Club expanded its course into 18 holes, and 5 of them were built near the demolished old mud wall.

1905

The Chinkiang (Zhenjiang) Golf Club was established and a 9-hole golf links was built on a hilly graveyard with a total length of 3,300 yard. The Club was founded by A.G. Elder from Edinburgh, then Chief Appraiser at Chinkiang Customs. The captain was C. E. Holsworthy of Chinkiang Customs who held a course record of 41. The Honorary Secretary was B.G. Tours of the Chinkiang Consulate.

November 2
The Shanghai Ladies Golf Club held its first general meeting participated by 19 founding members. An Executive Committee was elected to include: Captain Mrs. Winston, Vice-Captain Mrs. E.O. Cumming, Hon. Treasurer Miss Ivy, Hon. Secretary Miss Hunt, Mrs. Pemberton, Miss Buyer and Miss Mann. A bogey competition was held later in the month.

1906

Hankow Golf Club organized a St. Andrews Cup competition and a silver trophy was presented to the winner. The trophy was made by Luen Wo and weighs over 500g. Two reliefs of flying dragons are made on the cup, with two dragon handles. Etched on the bottom of the trophy are the words: "Hankow Golf Club St. Andrews Cup 1906 Won by Walter Hughs Corsane." The trophy is now in the collection of the Golf Heritage Museum in Shenzhen, China.

1907

The Port Edward Golf Club in Weihaiwei was formed and a new 9-hole lawn golf course was built at the Parade Ground outside the Eastern Gate.

1908

The Tsingtao (Qingdao) Golf Club was founded by Reginald Eckford, General Manager of Cornabé & Eckford. The 9-hole golf links was built inside the Huich'uan Race Course, with a total length of 2,500 yard. The longest hole was 530 yard and the shortest 125.

1909

April 14
British enthusiasts at Hongkew (Hongkou) district in Shanghai met and elected a provisional committee of six people to arrange the formation of the Shanghai Junior Golf Club. At a general meeting on April 23, it was resolved to build a clubhouse inside the Hongkew Park. Earlier, a 9-hole golf course was built with the approval of Scotsman MacGregor, who was head of municipal parks under the Municipal Council.

1910

Amoy Golf Club members started to play

on a new 9-hole course built on the mainland.

The Gyantse (Jiangzi) Golf Club in Tibet was formed, with a 9-hole golf course built on the east bank of the Niang Chu River. Standing at a height of 13,100 feet, the average length of the holes was 280 yard. The whole surface was hard baked clay. The longest hole was over 500 yard and the shortest 120.

The Tungshan (Dongshan) Golf Club in Canton (Guangzhou) was formed and a 9-hole golf course was built near today's East Garden after the completion of the Canton-Kowloon Railway.

The Hankow Golf Club built a short 9-hole golf links inside the Race Course to the northwest suburbs, near today's Race Course Corner.

The 2nd golf course of the Peking Golf Club was laid out near a cabbage field outside of Anting (Anding) Gate. The greens were packed dirt and golfers were often hit by sand storms during play.

1911

The golf division of the Mukden Club was formed, which was later named Mukden Golf Club. It built a 9-hole golf course at a graveyard in Peiling (Beiling). Total length of the course was 2,719 yard.

August 10

It was decided at a general meeting of the Shanghai GC to lease land at the Kiangwan (Jiangwan) Race Course from the International Recreation Club to build an 18-hole champion golf course.

1912

October 8

Scottish professional golfer Richard Graham arrived in Shanghai at the invitation of the Shanghai Golf Club to be China's first resident professional. A skilled golfer, Graham scored 33 at the Race Course's nine holes, 78 at Kiangwan and set a course record at Hongkew links with a score of 33 and 35. Unfortunately on the night of November 12, just a little over a month in Shanghai, Graham suddenly died of a heart attack during sleep.

November 30

China's first 18-hole golf links formally opened at the Kiangwan Race Course. The Kiangwan Golf Course was designed by two members of the Shanghai Golf Club. It had a total length of 5,135 yard, with the outgoing 9 at 1,991 yard and the incoming 9 at 2,144 yard. By now, Shanghai Golf Club had a total membership of 736, with 100 women members.

1913

The Hoshigaura Golf Club, then known as the Dairen Tennis & Golf Club, in Dairen (Dalian) was formed by the South Manchuria Railway. A 9-hole golf links was built at the Star Beach, with a total length of 2,737 yard. It was expanded to 18 holes of 6,077 yard in 1927.

March 17

Samuel Green, the 2nd professional golfer from the U.K. at the Shanghai Golf Club arrived in Shanghai. The 24-year-old Green had a handicap of 3 and was a course architect. Green, as well as Graham before him, was able to order quite a number of golf clubs from Scotland for golfers in

Shanghai. The iron club heads bore the names of the professionals as well as Shanghai. Green died of pneumonia in Shanghai on March 21, 1919 at the age of 30 after only six years of service.

October 11

The new North China Golf Club was formed in Tientsin and merged into the Tientsin Golf Club. Club president Duncan Houston Mackintosh presided the opening ceremony. The Club had a total membership of more than 200. Between 1905 and 1924, Tientsin Golf Club organized a total of 21 Club Open Championships.

1914

June

China Golf Society was formed in Turnberry, Ayrshire and has been in existence for over 100 years. First named China Golf Association, it was formed by 14 Scots who had worked in China. It later developed into a society where British citizens who had worked in China and the Far East could meet and associate on the golf links. With 300 members today, the Society has a Hong Kong branch.

1915

October

Sixteen British investors formed a consortium to purchase the land formerly owned by the Dallas Horse Repository and formed the Hungjao (Hongqiao) Golf Club.

1916

Antung (Dandong) Golf Club was formed and a 9-hole golf course was laid out at Mt. Chinko (Jinjiang) with a total length of 2,494 yard.

October 21

The Hungjao Golf Club's 9-hole golf course and a clubhouse formally opened and a Foursome Competition was played. Located at the corner of the Hungjao and Rubicon (today's Hami) Roads, the private club had a limited membership of 100. The Hungjao Golf Links was expanded to 12 holes in 1917.

1919

The Nanning Golf Club was founded by Reginald Follett Codrington Hedgeland, Commissioner of Nanning Customs and his friends. The golf links was built on the west bank of the Yong River, a primitive mud place. Golfers had to take a boat to reach the course and often they would ride on ponies during play. The clubhouse was a simple mat shed.

The Wuchow (Wuzhou) Golf Club was formed, with a 9-hole golf course built along the bank of West River. The "greens" were referred to as "browns" since they were made with hardened mud. The course was forced to close in 1923 during a major flood in the city.

1920

An 18-hole golf course was built near the Hankow Race Course. By the 1930s, the course employed as many as 120 caddies.

The Chinwangtao (Qinhuangdao) Golf Club was founded and its 9-hole golf course was built near Nanlichwang (Nanlizhuang) at today's Port District.

The Harbin Golf Club was formed with a 9-hole golf course of 2,791 yard.

The Nanking (Nanjing) Golf Club was founded and a primitive golf course built, with a mat shed as clubhouse. The Club boasted quite a number of local caddies.

The Shanghai Japanese Golf Club was formed and members played golf and organized Club Championships at the Hongkew Golf Course before the Club built its own course at Kiangwan.

October 17
The Peking Golf Club opened its Tien Shuen Shan (Tiancun Shan) Course and a new clubhouse in the western suburbs of the city. The course started with 9 holes and later expanded into 18, becoming a major golf course for the Peking Golf Club, which was renamed Peking Golf and Country Club. On the opening day of the course and clubhouse, eight golfers from Tientsin GC competed with a team of Peking Golf and Country Club. Peking won the morning individual match as well as the afternoon four ball completion.

1922

Shanghai Ladies Golf Club added 37 new members in the year, bringing the total number of memberships to 300.

December
Amoy Golf Club joined the Eastern Golf Association. Other golf clubs that joined the Association included Shanghai, Hong Kong, Tungshan Recreation Club in Canton and Tientsin.

1923

A course record was set during a competition played at the Wuhu Golf Club, according to a silver cigarette plate now in the collection of the Golf Heritage Museum.

The Hungjao Golf Course was expanded into 18 holes, with the front 9 at 2,585 yard and back 9 2,915 yard, a total of 5,500 yard. The names of the 18 holes were: Bamboos, Second, Hole Across, Mrs. Liddels, Dead Man's Pool, Punch Bowel, Creek, Village, Ginger Beer Hole, Tenth, Red Joss House, Graves, Pond, Death or Glory, Road, Corner, Second Last and Home.

April 16
A VIP dinner was held at the Shanghai Union Club hosted by Fu Siao-en, director and general manager of the Commercial Bank of China. Fu said that the Shanghai Golf Club had started to accept local Chinese as members. General Ho Feng-ling, Defense Commissioner of Shanghai and Sungk'iang, was already an honorary member.

July
The St. Paul High School in Anch'ing (Anqing), Anhui Province, built a 5-hole golf course for students due to the closure of the tennis courts during the flooding rainy season.

October
Investors of the Peking Paomachang Golf Course met at the Hong Kong and Shanghai Banking Corp. and decided to form the Paomachang Golf Club. The following were elected members of the committee: Captain G.A. Johnston, Honorary Secretary L.L. Davidson, Honorary Treasurer J. Boyd, members Dr. Cormack, Colonel Barnard, Cruickshank and Southcott.

November 30
The first Shanghai Ladies Golf Championship

was held. Mrs. Burton and Mrs. Enticknap squared off in the final competition. Mrs. Burton finished the morning round of 18 holes with a score of 76 and defeated Mrs. Enticknap in the afternoon by 15 up and 13 to play. Mrs. Burton's morning round of 76 "would cause the leading men players in Shanghai to look to their laurels":

Out: 4, 5, 5, 4, 5, 3, 4, 4, 3: 37
In: 4, 3, 4, 6, 6, 3, 4, 3, 6; 39

1924

The Tientsin Golf Club organized a Championship of North China "open to all amateur members of any recognized golf club in the world." J.M. Dickinson, President of Tientsin Chamber of Commerce, donated a Dickinson Challenge Cup for play. The Ladies Section of the Tientsin Golf Club was renamed Tientsin Ladies Golf Club, with P.C. Young as Captain.

January 10

Admiral Leveson of the *H.M.S. Hawkins* presented a trophy cup for competition to the Shanghai and Hungjao golf clubs on behalf of the United Service Golf Club (formerly Weihaiwei Golf Club). The trophy was a tribute to the hospitality these clubs had accorded to naval officers during their service on the China Station. R.G. MacDonald, Captain of the Shanghai Golf Club, and R.J. Marshall, president of the Hungjao Golf Club, attended the ceremony aboard the *Hawkins* to receive the "Weihaiwei Cup," which was played annually between the Shanghai Golf Club and Hungjao Golf Club.

October 19-26

The Shanghai Golf Club organized the first China Open Amateur Golf Championship at the Hungjao Golf Course. Participating golfers came from golf clubs in Hong Kong, Amoy, Mukden, Tientsin, Weihaiwei, Port Edward, Hankow, Nanking, Peking, Tsingtao, Fuchow, Manila, Tokyo, Yokohama, Kobe and Hodogaya. The China Open Amateur Golf Championship was held 17 times from 1924 to 1948, with the exceptions in the years 1937, 1941-1947.

1925

The Fushun Golf Club was formed and a 9-hole golf course was built at the South Park. In the early 1930s, a new 9-hole course was added. The old course was 3,162 yard and the new one 2,480 yard. A practice link was also built at the East Park. During the 1930s, inter-city golf competitions were held between the Fushun and Mukden golf clubs.

The Chiaotso (Jiaozuo) Golf Club was formed, which was also called Honan (Henan) Golf Club. Honorary secretary of the Club in 1939 was G. Rogers.

March

At an eclectic competition held at the Peking Paomachang Golf Club, the Best Eclectic silver trophy was won by O.H. Hulme and the Worst Eclectic silver trophy was won by A.H. Barnard. Both trophies are in the collection of the Golf Heritage Museum.

1926

January 17

The Peking Nanyuan Golf Course formally opened. The 9-hole course was built by the Peking International Recreation and Race Club. It was Peking's 3rd golf links. Plans were made to expand into 18 holes.

March 27

The 18-hole Seekingjao (Sijingqiao) Golf Course formally opened and became the 3rd golf links of the Shanghai Golf Club. The front 9 of the Course was 3,179 yard and the back 9 2,965 yard, totaling 6,144 yard. A large number of people attended the opening, which included Shanghai GC President R.G. MacDonald, British Consul-General Sidney Barton, U.S. Consul-General Edwin S. Cunningham, Shanghai GC Vice-President J.B. Ferrier, Captain C.W. Porter, Hon. Secretary R. Haves, Fu Siao-en, Hsu Yuan, etc.

October 2

The Kiangwan Country Club built by the Shanghai Japanese Golf Club formally opened with the completion of a 9-hole golf links. The 9-hole Kiangwan Country Club course was 2,260 yard long, with four par-4s, two par-3s and three par-5s.

1927

December 11

A Ladies Golf Club was formed inside the Peking Golf Club and organized a ladies' knockout singles at Paomachang Course. The winner was Mrs. D.R. Mackenzie, who defeated Lady Lampson 2 up and 1 to go. Lady Lampson had been elected as the Ladies' Captain for 1928. Mrs. Southcott would be the secretary. At a medal competition of the Paomachang Ladies' Spring Tournament, a Mrs. Ching-fang Liu won with a net score of 72 for the two rounds.

1928

March

The Standard Oil Co. of New York in Putung (Pudong) built a 6-hole golf course for its staff and foreign expatriates. The course was later expanded to 9 holes.

1929

The Peitaiho (Beidaihe) small 9-hole golf course was built at the Lotus Flower Stone Park by the Public Welfare Society.

May

Local sporting circles in Shanghai were contemplating forming a Chinese golf club and inviting Charlie Chung, a professional in Los Angeles, to teach golf. Chung, a Chinese-American who had won the Honolulu Golf Championship, was the first Chinese to become a professional. Although supported by several scores of enthusiasts, the effort never materialized.

1930

The Ryojun (Lvshun) Golf Club was founded, with a 6-hole golf course of 1,141 yard.

The size of the Hungjao Golf Course expanded to 277,000 square meters. The Hungjao Golf Club was open only to foreign expatriates, but hired 30 local Chinese, including 10 caddies. Membership was increased to 175.

November 30

The Weihaiwei Golf Club revised its rules to accept Chinese officers. Shen Hung-lieh, Commander of China's Northeast Navy and Hsü Tsu-shan, Commissioner of the Weihaiwei Special Administrative Region, were admitted as special honorary members.

1931

March 20

At the annual meeting of the Mukden Golf Club, "His Excellency Marshall Chang Hsueh Liang was unanimously elected Hon. President of the Golf Club." The meeting also elected a new committee for 1931, which included F.N. Merritt, W. Donald, T.Y.C. Lee、L.C. Kampf and P. Monaghan.

1932

March

As the Japanese invaders expanded military operation in China, the Kiangwan golf course became a battlefield. The clubhouse was damaged by bombs and much of the members' golf equipment was destroyed.

1933

Tsingtao Golf Club built a 9-hole golf course to the west of Chanshan (Zhanshan) Village. An area of 34.45 acres of land was leased to the Club for 20 years. The Club moved to the new course which was open in October 1934. It was expanded to 18 holes in 1938 and located 3 miles from the Railway Station. Membership increased to 250 and the secretary was W. Stoy Elliot.

Tongshan (Tangshan) Golf Club was formed and started building an 18-hole golf course at Linsi (Linxi).

Hsinking (Changchun) Golf Club was founded with a 9-hole 3,140-yard golf course open year-round. The course was expanded to 18 holes in 1934 and a new clubhouse was built.

Anshan Golf Club was formed and a 9-hole, 2,965-yard course was built. The course had 11 greens that offer variations of both distance and direction when playing an 18-hole game.

Tang-Kang-Tzu (Tanggangzi) Golf Club in Anshan was founded, with a 9-hole, 2,520-yard course open year-round. It was located near the Railway Station.

1934

June

The Nanking Golf and Country Club was founded by the Ministry of Foreign Affairs of the Republican Government. The course started with 9-holes near the Sun Yat-sen's Mausoleum at the Purple Mountains. It was later expanded into 18 holes.

November 1

Marshal Chang Hsueh-Liang won a handicap competition held at the Hankow Golf Club. Sir Meyrick Hewlett, the British Consul General, presented him a trophy. Chang beat Commander Harland of *H.M.S. Aphis* by five and four.

1935

May 5

The Mukden International Golf Club was founded and took over the property assets and liabilities of Mukden Golf Club.

June 8

The new Chinwangtao Golf Club was formed with Chilton as president. Members of the new Club played officers of the 2nd Battalion of the Worcestershire regiment. Chilton and Robinson defeated Lt.-Colonels Pelly and

Stokes-Roberts by 3 and 1. Faulkner and Ashby won their match with Major Ford and Captain Hargreaves by 4 and 3.

1936

Members of the Tientsin Golf Club reached 350. The Course was 3 miles to the east of the Tientsin Railway Station.

September 1

Mounted Japanese soldiers invaded the Peip'ing golf links. Witnesses said the soldiers rode over the course, tearing up greens and fairways, then dismounted and executed setting up exercises. A number of them stripped naked and lolled on the turf. Chinese and foreigners expressed indignation.

1937

April

An inter-port match between the Peiping Golf Club and Shanghai Golf Club was played at the Shanghai Kiangwan Golf Course. Shanghai led 6:2 in the four-ball matches on the first day, and again won the singles matches by 6:2 on the second day. Dr. P.K.C. Tyau, the veteran Peiping champion and H.Y. Wu scored the only successes for the northern city. Tyau was former Consul to Singapore and he "plays a very accurate game, his approaching and putting being very deadly." Dr. Tyau had been five times golf champion in Peiping. Bobbie Kan, the Shanghai Golf Club champion, beat C.H. Liang, one of the best Peiping players by 7 and 6.

1938

July

The new 18-hole championship golf course of the Mukden International Golf Club formally opened to the public. The course was located about 12 km from the Walled City. A regular bus service would be provided between the city and the golf course. It took about 25 minutes to reach the golf course from the Yamato District. A special summer train for afternoon trips to Tungling started operating daily from the Mukden Station. The train left the Mukden Station at 3:20 pm and returned at 4:46 from Tungling (Dongling).

April 14

During their world tours, noted U.S. professional golfer Walter Hagen and Australian-American professional golfer Joe Kirkwood were invited to visit the Hungjao Golf Club and played a 9-hole exhibition match. Hungjao Golf Club was then occupied by the Japanese troops with 600 fully armed soldiers stationed there.

1939

May 14

A special golf tournament of 18-hole medal competition was held to mark the opening of the new clubhouse of the Mukden International Golf Club. The new clubhouse was built at a cost of 120,000 yen and was designed by local architect Kurolwa. Sitting on an area of 300 tsubo, the clubhouse had a spacious veranda, bar, dining hall, shower and lockers for golfers. During the 2nd World War, the Mukden International Golf Course became a costume factory of the Japanese Kwantung Army, leading to its decline and closure.

1940

November 25

The final round of the China Ladies Open Amateur Championship was played at the Hungjao Golf Club, in which Mrs. Reynell beat Mrs. Piercy at the 37th hole.

1946

Shareholders of the Hungjao Golf Club set up the Hungjao Golf Club Ltd. in Hong Kong in an effort to save and transfer the Club assets. But the Hong Kong entity was dissolved in 1953.

1948

October 24

The last China Open Amateur Golf Championship (the 17th) was held at the Hungjao Golf Club. Tony Rickets consecutively won the fifth time.

1949

May 21

At its annual dinner, 32 members of the China Golf Society decided to donate £50 to the Hungjao Golf Club in support of its continued operation. The fund was transferred via Hong Kong. After Shanghai's liberation, the Club was taken over by the Shanghai People's Municipal Government. In 1954, it was converted into the Western Suburban Park.

June

The Hungjao Golf Club reopened 9-holes after it was closed in 1949 during fighting and became busy with growing activities. The Club had been in preparation, though unsuccessful, for the China Amateur Open Championship.

1950

June 25

The Tsingtao Golf Course at Chanshan was taken over by the city's People's Government and stopped operation.

1958

May

When a caddy at the Peking Golf Club was accidentally struck by a ball, the secretary was brought before a police officer and educated for several hours on the evils of capitalism and class distinction.